The Neuroscience of Creativ‹

What happens in our brains when we compose a melody, write a poem, paint a picture, or choreograph a dance sequence? How is this different from what occurs in the brain when we generate a new theory or a scientific hypothesis?

In this book, Anna Abraham reveals how the tools of neuroscience can be employed to uncover the answers to these and other vital questions. She explores the intricate workings of our creative minds to explain what happens in our brains when we operate in a creative mode versus an uncreative mode.

The vast and complex field that is the neuroscience of creativity is disentangled and described in an accessible manner, balancing what is known so far with critical issues that are as yet unresolved. Clear guidelines are also provided for researchers who pursue the big questions in their bid to discover the creative mind.

Anna Abraham is a Professor of Psychology at the School of Social Sciences in Leeds Beckett University, UK. She is a Fellow of the Royal Society of the Arts, the Salzburg Global Seminar, and the Higher Education Academy. She is also a Member of the International Society for Fiction and Fictionality Studies, the Association for Psychological Science, the Cognitive Neuroscience Society, and the American Psychological Association's Division 10: Society for the Psychology of Aesthetics, Creativity and the Arts. She edited the 2015 book *Madness and Creativity: Yes, No or Maybe?* and has authored numerous publications on the human imagination.

Cambridge Fundamentals of Neuroscience in Psychology

Developed in response to a growing need to make neuroscience accessible to students and other non-specialist readers, the *Cambridge Fundamentals of Neuroscience in Psychology* series provides brief introductions to key areas of neuroscience research across major domains of psychology. Written by experts in cognitive, social, affective, developmental, clinical, and applied neuroscience, these books will serve as ideal primers for students and other readers seeking an entry point to the challenging world of neuroscience.

Books in the Series:

The Neuroscience of Expertise by Merim Bilalić
The Neuroscience of Intelligence by Richard J. Haier
Cognitive Neuroscience of Memory by Scott D. Slotnick
The Neuroscience of Adolescence by Adriana Galván
The Neuroscience of Suicidal Behavior by Kees van Heeringen
The Neuroscience of Creativity by Anna Abraham
Cognitive and Social Neuroscience of Aging by Angela Gutchess

The Neuroscience of Creativity

Anna Abraham
Leeds Beckett University, UK

CAMBRIDGE
UNIVERSITY PRESS

University Printing House, Cambridge CB2 8BS, United Kingdom

One Liberty Plaza, 20th Floor, New York, NY 10006, USA

477 Williamstown Road, Port Melbourne, VIC 3207, Australia

314–321, 3rd Floor, Plot 3, Splendor Forum, Jasola District Centre, New Delhi – 110025, India

79 Anson Road, #06-04/06, Singapore 079906

Cambridge University Press is part of the University of Cambridge.

It furthers the University's mission by disseminating knowledge in the pursuit of education, learning, and research at the highest international levels of excellence.

www.cambridge.org
Information on this title: www.cambridge.org/9781107176461
DOI: 10.1017/9781316816981

First published 2018

A catalogue record for this publication is available from the British Library.

Library of Congress Cataloging-in-Publication Data
Names: Abraham, Anna, 1977– author.
Title: The neuroscience of creativity / Anna Abraham.
Description: Cambridge, United Kingdom; New York, NY: Cambridge University Press, 2019. | Series: Cambridge fundamentals of neuroscience in psychology | Includes bibliographical references and index.
Identifiers: LCCN 2018029876 | ISBN 9781107176461 (hardback) | ISBN 9781316629611 (paperback)
Subjects: LCSH: Creative ability. | Cognitive neuroscience.
Classification: LCC BF408.A235 2019 | DDC 153.3/5–dc23
LC record available at https://lccn.loc.gov/2018029876

ISBN 978-1-107-17646-1 Hardback
ISBN 978-1-316-62961-1 Paperback

For my parents,

Shaino Abraham, the reigning world champion of steadfast optimism, and

George (Lalu) Abraham, the coolest cat to have walked the planet.

Contents

The color plate section can be found between pp. 204 and 205.

Figures

Boxes

Preface

Our capacity to be creative is a true marvel of nature. We experience it in our daily lives in myriad forms, and we reap the joys and benefits of its fruition not only as agents but also as recipients. Creativity is often heralded as representing the epitome of uniquely developed human abilities. It is one that we lay a great deal of premium on in our daily lives across all walks of life, and it is essential to human development and progress at every level, from the individual to societal. However, the inherently abstract and intricate nature of creative thinking renders a certain mystery and ineffability to its workings.

Although relatively new to the enterprise of scientific enquiry, neuroscience as a formal discipline is one that has been witness to exponential growth in terms of research output and knowledge that benefits all domains of human perception, cognition, and behavior. Creativity is no exception to this revolutionary trend. But it is unique in that the many complexities involved in investigating this astonishingly complex human ability render the explosion of published work in relation to it extremely challenging to understand with sufficient depth.

The objective of this book is to provide a systematic overview of the neuroscience of creativity where the many disparate strands of academic theory and research in the field are integrated and summarized in an accessible manner. In other words, it is aimed to help anyone equipped with nothing but a deep interest in understanding the creative mind find their bearings. It is, in fact, the book I wish I'd had on hand when I began to investigate creativity. A Baedeker Guide to Creativity and the Brain, so to speak.

May this resource be a useful guide in your exploration of the creative mind.

Acknowledgments

Writing this book has been a whirlwind adventure in my mind that began at a snail's pace and ended at lightning speed. I hope the book reflects both qualities: the gentle ease of a loafer and the zeal of a hyperfocused meditator, unified in the mission of making sense of the creative mind.

I have been obsessed with creativity for as long as I can remember. Many of my earliest memories are of being privy to dazzling moments on the screen, on the page, and in the air; through film, sports, music, and books. Precious moments that triggered me to action. I memorized and recited whole movies to entertain friends. Masterful sequences played back in my mind. And no one could stop me from singing. I am grateful to countless creators, artists, and performers the world over for all the magic. To be bestowed the chance to study the creative mind has been an extraordinary privilege for me, and I am indebted to an incalculable number of people who have aided me in my pursuits over the years.

I thank everyone at Cambridge University Press and affiliated organizations involved in the process of making this book take form, from start to finish. In particular, I thank Matthew Bennett for approaching the skeptical me with the idea for this book and putting his trust in my ability to write it. I thank David Repetto, Stephen Accera, Bethany Johnson, and Helen Flitton for their support and advice. Special thanks to Kate O'Leary for her meticulous diligence in copy-editing, and Emily Watton for her prompt, patient, and warm guidance.

I thank Sarah Asquith and Halima Ahmed, my fabulous doctoral students, for reading through the first couple of chapters and providing their valuable feedback. I thank Greig Abraham for rushing to my aid and providing beautiful sketches in a matter of days.

I thank the many wonderfully talented and hardworking people I have had the great honor to work with and alongside – colleagues, collaborators, students, and assistants – in my formal quest since 2001 to better understand the creative mind. A big shout out to Barbara Rutter, Sören Kroger, Susan Beudt, Zohra Karimi, Till Schneider, and Sabine Windmann.

I thank Onur Güntürkün for taking a chance on me so early on, for giving me the complete freedom to pursue my naïve and zany ideas for my PhD project, and for leading by example in showing how important it is in science to have the right attitude (open, constructive, and resolute) and to be unafraid to question.

I thank D. Yves von Cramon for the incredible opportunity of working with him and for allowing me free rein in testing a range of unconventional ideas. The devil's advocate style project inception meetings and the intensive wonder-filled data discussions were possibly the most challenging and fulfilling scientific exchanges I have ever had. I am truly fortunate to have trained with someone whose absolute passion was the pursuit of deep knowledge, and who had zero patience for BS.

I thank the rare souls who make academic events worthwhile with their giddy enthusiasm and quirky questions, those serendipitous encounters that spark great ideas and memorable moments. In particular, I thank the engaged collective of the Neuroscience of Art Salzburg Global Seminar. I am grateful beyond measure to have been a part of that event, and I particularly cherish the curious, crazy, and comforting conversations that continued after.

I thank my friends, my family, and my friends who are family – all the wonderful souls who have supported me in numerous ways, big and small, over the many years. Too many to name but you know who you are. Thank you.

I thank Sukriti Issar, Andreja Bubić, and Uta Wolfensteller – North, South, and East – for keeping the raft afloat.

I thank my brother, Greig, the first person I recognized as a creative soul in my life, for being so much fun to grow up with, and for the unfailing ability to make me giggle uncontrollably with a mere look, no matter what the mood.

I thank my son, Marius, for the boundless love, affection, and creativity.

Above all, I thank my parents, Amma and Appa, without whose unparalleled love, absolute conviction, and enormous personal sacrifice, nothing would have been possible for me. I was blessed to bear witness to the lives of such exceptional beings whose limitless generosity, warmth, and good nature touched all who knew and know them.

CHAPTER ONE

What Is Creativity?

"Creativity is the defeat of habit by originality."

(Arthur Koestler)

Learning Objectives

- Recognizing the parallels between creative outputs across different contexts
- Pinpointing the defining components of creativity
- Grasping the challenges of defining creativity comprehensively
- Understanding the difficulties faced when evaluating creativity
- Identifying different types of creativity
- Distinguishing creativity from related concepts

1.1 Recognizing Creativity

This is a book about our incredible creative minds and their extraordinary workings. It is one that will serve as a reliable and enthusiastic guide in helping you explore what we know about our creative minds, and how we can study it – from inside out and outside in – through the confluence of behavioral and brain-based perspectives. To begin the journey of discovering the mechanisms and maneuverings of the creative mind, we must begin with a clear and unanimous picture of the phenomenon we are attempting to understand. We will be best placed before setting off if we are steered by some fundamental questions at the starting line. How do we know when something is creative? What are the indicators that enable us to recognize an instance of creativity? Let us begin with a few examples of creative achievements across different fields of human enterprise to help us envisage this better.

1.1.1 Scientific Domains

An event that showcased iconic displays of inventiveness in the engineering domain was the *Apollo 13* mission to the moon in April 1970.

A three-person crew together with a team of flight controllers and support personnel at NASA's mission control in Houston successfully solved a series of problems that transpired over three days under conditions of extreme pressure. The most famous instantiation of creative problem solving during this event was the making of an improvised device called the "mailbox" (see Figure 1.1) using the limited material available on the spaceship. The excess carbon dioxide in the air could be drawn out using this device, enabling the crew to stay alive long enough to get back to Earth. Throughout the entire event the team generated novel and workable solutions to problems they had neither encountered nor imagined before (King, 1997).

The creative mind does not only come into play under conditions of time pressure when quick and spontaneous engagement is necessary. It is just as vital in the case of deliberate innovation. *Design that Matters* is a non-profit company that engineers products with the potential to have a positive social impact by feasibly improving the standard of healthcare for the poor in developing countries. One great example of such a product is its design for an incubator made entirely of car spare parts, the NeoNurture (see Figure 1.1). The promise of this product lay in the fact that the team, led by Timothy Prestero, Founder and CEO, identified that one of the reasons that pre-term infants in Africa have an extremely poor prognosis is not so much the paucity of aid but the lack of sustainability in maintaining the technology that has been made available through aid. Incubators break down over time and the general lack of spare parts as well as repair services meant that, when an incubator broke, it remained in a state of disrepair and could not be used any further. The novelty of the NeoNurture therefore lay in how this logistical problem was circumvented by designing a product using car parts that were readily available in that regional context – owing to the abundance of motorized vehicles – which would allow for quick and cost-effective repairs locally.

The previous examples demonstrate the brilliance of creative minds during problem solving in applied domains of science and technology. The end products to evaluate are concrete and exist in physical space. But often, the end products of creative minds are not concrete things that we can all consciously perceive using our senses of touch, sight, sound, taste, or smell. I am referring here to ideas that are more conceptual in nature, but no less powerful than physical objects.

Within the scientific domain there are countless examples of groundbreaking ideas, theories, and discoveries, which come about through observation, experimentation, and introspection. Marie Curie, the only

Figure 1.1 Exemplars of scientific creativity

(a) Interior view of the *Apollo 13* lunar module and the "mailbox."
Courtesy: NASA/JPL-Caltech. (b) Sketch of the NeoNurture device.
© Greig Abraham. (c) Portrait of Marie Curie [1867–1934],
Polish chemist, wife of Pierre Curie. Credit: Wellcome Collection. CC BY.
(d) Charles Robert Darwin. Wood engraving by [FW].
Credit: Wellcome Collection.

person to date to have won the Nobel Prize twice, in different sciences, was recognized for her pivotal contributions in radioactivity research with the 1903 Nobel Prize in Physics as well as with the 1911 Nobel Prize in Chemistry on account of her discovery of the elements, radium and polonium. Although the work of Charles Darwin was not of the kind that would have enabled him to receive this most prestigious of all scientific awards, in formulating his seminal theory of evolution he has had a colossal impact, not only on the field of biology but far beyond (Ridley, 2015), making him among the most influential figures in the history of mankind.

1.1.2 Artistic Domains

The artistic domains of human enterprise, which indeed are most dominantly associated with the concept of creativity (see Box 1.1), also boast an abundance of examples of the creative spirit in action across a range of different fields (Figure 1.2). Let's take four examples from the fields of painting, music, fashion, and literature.

Box 1.1 Types of Creativity

Within psychological research, the most common division in terms of types of creativity is that of scientific versus artistic creativity, particularly in personality-based studies on creativity (Barron & Harrington, 1981; Feist, 1998). Across the domains of science and art, highly creative people show greater openness to novel experiences, are attracted to complexity, and display heightened aesthetic sensibilities. Some recent work has shown, though, that "openness to experience" is predictive of creative achievement in the arts whereas "intellect" is predictive of the same in the sciences (Kaufman et al., 2016).

This simplistic division does not, however, adequately represent the breadth and complexity of creativity in human enterprise (Gardner, 2011). For instance, domains like architecture and creative design represent a combination of artistic and scientific creativity. In fact, Donald MacKinnon studied architects for this very reason because they "as a group reveal that which is most characteristic of the creative person" given that "if an architect's designs are to give delight, the architect must be an artist; if they are to be technologically sound and efficiently planned he must also be something of a scientist" (1965, 274). Other theorists have distinguished between art, science and humor (Koestler, 1969), spontaneous and deliberate creativity (Dietrich, 2004b), as well as problem solving and expression (Abraham, 2013). And some have taken the opposite approach by seeking to identify what is common to both, such as the drive to get closer to "truth" and "beauty" given that "for what the artist creates must be 'true to itself,' just as the broad scientific theory must be 'true to itself'" (Bohm, 2004, 40). So the jury is still out with regard to the types of creativity and how best to conceive of their commonalities and distinctions within a single viable framework. From the neuroscientific perspective, theoretical frameworks that posit brain-based differences in artistic versus scientific creativity are rare (Andreasen, 2012).

Figure 1.2 Exemplars of artistic creativity

(a) *Seated Peasant* by Paul Cézanne (ca. 1892–1896). Courtesy: Metropolitan Museum of Art: Walter H. and Leonore Annenberg Collection. **(b)** Sketch of Miles Davis playing the trumpet. © Greig Abraham. **(c)** Coco Chanel, 1931. © Bettman via Getty. **(d)** Commemorative stamp celebrating 125 years since the birth of Franz Kafka (1883–1924). Courtesy: Deutsche Post AG; designed by Jens Müller and Karen Weiland.

Paul Cézanne is credited as being the father of modern art, both visually and conceptually, on account of the fact that his extraordinary work represented the nexus between Impressionism and the later art forms, such as Cubism and Fauvism. Pablo Picasso is said to have remarked, "Cézanne! He was like the father of us all." Henri Matisse went even further in his praise: "Cézanne, you see, is a sort of God of painting." His approach has been described as "groping for a conciliation of the methods of Impressionism and the need for order" with the need "to convey the feeling of solidity and depth" (Gombrich, 2011, 544). Cézanne once stated, "I want to make them [Nature and Art] the same. Art is a personal apperception, which I embody in sensations and which I ask the understanding to organize into a painting." To Merleau-Ponty (1993, 65, 70), this meant that Cézanne aimed "to make *visible* how the world *touches us*" as "distinctions between touch and sight are unknown in primordial perception."

While Cézanne's work is a testament to the mastery that derives from a profound and focused raison d'être, other eminent artists are known for the evolution in their visionary output over time. Described as "probably one of the finest conceptualists of music in American history," the jazz trumpeter Miles Davis is considered "a great innovator" as his creative contributions were central to several different stylistic developments in jazz; so much so as to be considered as one who had "several distinct creative periods like Picasso" (Early, 2001, 3, 15). He was a prolific musician and composer and found great success throughout his career. In fact, his album "Kind of Blue" is still the top-selling jazz album of all time, and set the benchmark for the then-emerging modal jazz style. He was renowned for his unconventional approaches, such as minimalism in composition, focus in listening, and the quite astonishing ability to have "always played the most unexpected note, and the one that is the perfect note," in the words of the producer, Quincy Jones (Tingen, 2001).

Still others make their mark by achieving critical success and acclaim across several domains. Coco Chanel exemplified such creative innovation in the world of fashion by setting wildly popular trends across a range of products such as clothing, perfume, and accessories. She is credited with fundamentally changing how women dressed in Western Europe through the influence of her designs of elegant yet comfortable clothes and by upturning centuries of clothing etiquette by establishing the outfit that could be worn on any occasion – *la petite robe noire* or the little black dress. Her innovative use of jersey fabric in the 1920s, for instance, has been attributed to the success of her designs as other more expensive materials were scarce at the time of war and the sheer practicality of the fabric meant that women could move with ease and were no longer dependent on others to dress them (Wallach, 1998).

However, recognition within one's lifetime, acclaim in the form of accolades, or exceptional financial success are not prerequisites for creative eminence. The case of Franz Kafka, who died at the age of 40, illustrates this point well as he was relatively unknown within his lifetime having published only a few collections of short stories. His reputation slowly grew and was fortified following the publication of his three incomplete novels after his death. In his singular style of writing, he juxtaposed surreal and ambiguous contexts that provoke feelings of discomfort with the very real existential experience of anxieties that emerge within contexts of powerlessness in the face of unrelenting authority that emanate from power structures at home, at work, and in society. So groundbreaking was the perspective accorded by his prose that it necessitated the addition of a new word "Kafkaesque" to the English language to accommodate this conceptual leap. Kafka was both widely admired by and hugely influential for several eminent writers and philosophers (Sandbank, 1989). Nabokov went so far as to dub Kafka "the greatest German writer of our time" and continued, "[s]uch poets as Rilke or such novelists as Thomas Mann are dwarfs or plastic saints in comparison with him" (Nabokov & Bowers, 1980, 255).

1.2 Defining Creativity

Now that we have a few exemplars of exceptional creative achievement across different domains in science and art, let us broach the important issue of the definition of creativity. Our preliminary aim in this context will be to make cross-domain generalizations. If we try to identify what aspects of the solutions or ideas expressed in the examples above are common to all of them, at least two factors should readily stand out. Can you identify these?

The first commonality that you were probably able to glean from those examples of creativity was that each of them involved generating an idea that was new in some way. This is, in fact, the primary defining attribute of creativity (Runco & Jaeger, 2012). For an idea to be considered creative it must be original or novel. Originality is what renders an idea to be unique or unusual compared to other ideas that are afloat at any given time. We experience an idea as being new, original, or novel when we have not encountered it in quite that distinctive manner before. In quantitative terms, an original idea is one that is statistically rare or infrequent.

While originality is the central factor in determining the degree of creativity associated with an idea, it is not the only necessary factor. A second component needs to be added to the mix to arrive at a reasonably close characterization of creativity, and the component in question is that of appropriateness, relevance, or fit. In the examples expounded earlier (Section 1.1), this is reflected in the fact that each of the generated

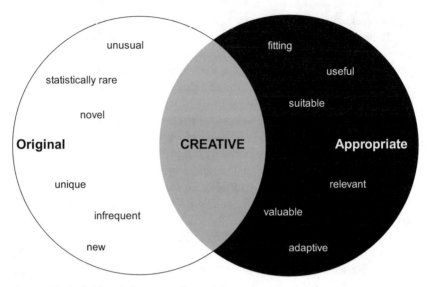

Figure 1.3 Definitional elements of creativity

solutions or expressions was useful, workable, effective, satisfying, or adaptive. So appropriateness refers to the value or fit of the response in terms of how meaningful or suitable it is in a given context.

With this, we have the two central defining elements of creativity (Figure 1.3), namely, that a creative idea is one that is deemed to be both *original* and *appropriate* within a particular context (Runco & Jaeger, 2012; Stein, 1953).

So how are these elements determined? Let us peruse selected quotations from some of the early pioneers in the field of creativity research who grappled with these issues. Originality or "the extent to which a work is novel depends on the extent to which it deviates from the traditional or the status quo" (Stein, 1953, 311). However, an idea that is only original cannot be considered creative because "uncommon responses which are merely random, or which proceed from ignorance or delusion" are not "adaptive to reality" (Barron, 1955, 479). So a product or idea is considered to be creative if it "is a novel work that is accepted as tenable or useful or satisfying by a group in some point in time" (Stein, 1953, 312). This means that, "it must serve to solve a problem, fit the needs of a given situation, accomplish some recognizable goal. And this is as true for the expressive arts as for scientific and technological enterprises; in painting, the artist's problem is to find a more appropriate expression of his own experience; in dancing, to convey more adequately a particular mood or theme, etc." (MacKinnon, 1978, 50).

While several researchers have attempted to define creativity accurately and comprehensively across the decades (Dacey & Madaus, 1969), there is presently broad agreement regarding originality and appropriateness as being the two defining factors of creativity across domains of human enterprise. However, the buck does not stop there. There is less unanimity about whether these two components are sufficient to capture the full extent of creativity. In fact, influential theorists have argued for the importance of other factors, such as "surprise" and optimal "realization" (Boden, 2004; MacKinnon, 1978), which are discussed in the next section.

1.2.1 Comprehensiveness in Defining Creativity

Surprise is certainly a key factor in determining creativity in specific contexts, such as in the case of the US patent office where an invention or process can only be patented if it evidences a nonobvious (i.e., surprising) step (Simonton, 2012b). That this quality of "the unexpected" is a defining attribute of creativity has been most strongly advocated by Margaret Boden (2004), who defined a creative idea as one that is novel, surprising, and valuable. She distinguished between two forms of originality or novelty in creativity – psychological (P-creativity) and historical (H-creativity). P-creativity occurs when an idea is experienced as being new and valuable to the person generating it regardless of how many others have generated that idea before. The scope of experience in the case of H-creativity fits at the other end of the continuum in that it reflects an idea that is so entirely novel that no one else, as far as is known, has generated it before.

These ideas parallel those of Mihaly Csikszentmihalyi's (1997) little-c versus Big-C magnitudes of creativity (see Section 1.2.2) and MacKinnon's (1978) concept of "frame of reference" or "range of experiences" in determining whether a given idea or product is original. Frames of reference can be at the level of (a) an individual, which is akin to P-creativity, (b) a group, or (c) mankind, which is akin to H-creativity. So the "creativeness" of an idea when evaluated in terms of "statistical infrequence is always relative to a given population of products. Those that are most creative are the ones that are novel or original in the experience of an entire civilization or of all mankind" (ibid., 50).

Alongside the dual typology of P versus H novelty, Boden (2004) also advocated three instantiations of *surprise*. An idea may be "statistically surprising," which is what comes to pass when two or more relatively unfamiliar concepts are brought together in unusual ways (e.g., use of metaphor in poetry, double entendre in advertisements). This idea-form comes about through combinatorial idea generation. The second type is when an idea is experienced as unexpectedly surprising so as to evoke a "shock of recognition," which occurs because it fits with a style of thought that is present in one's repertoire (e.g., development of new forms of artistic style such as "performance poetry" – an evolving art form that stems from the crossroads of theater, literature, and music). Exploratory idea generation often results in this idea-form. The final type is that of "impossible surprise" and one experiences it that way because it is astonishing that such an idea even occurred to oneself or anyone else (e.g., Schoenberg's twelve-tone technique, Freud's theory of the unconscious mind, and Cajal's discovery of the structural relationship between nerve cells). These revolutionary forms of idea creation are a result of transformational idea generation. Although these three qualitatively distinct instantiations of surprise map on to three principles by which new idea-forms are generated, these abstract principles of combination, exploration, and transformation are not mutually exclusive and can therefore be used in conjunction with one another.

The importance of "surprise" as a defining component of creativity is gaining traction, although it has not been systematically investigated or discussed within the empirical realms of psychology or neuroscience. What is rarely acknowledged, though, is that dissociating between novelty and surprise can be quite difficult. This is because, more often than not, something that is novel is also surprising. Indeed, as surprise is a conative or emotional state, its association with creativity potentially reflects the phenomenological experience that accompanies the eliciting or generation of an original and appropriate idea. An alternative concept is that of "freshness" of an idea, which can be said to be a combination of novelty and surprise. This is because something that is fresh "means more than just 'new' or 'novel' because 'refreshing' may involve making strange things familiar as well as familiar things strange" (Pope, 2005, xvi). Within this conceptualization, creativity is described as "the capacity to make, do or become something fresh and valuable with respect to others as well as to ourselves" (ibid.).

Mackinnon (1965), on the other hand, emphasized another alternative factor as being one of the "absolute criteria" in the definition of a creative product, namely, the optimal implementation or *realization of the idea*. He averred that, "true creativeness involves a sustaining of the original insight, an evaluation and elaboration of it, a developing of it to the full" (160). In the absence of the actual instantiation of the idea, the full worth of the idea cannot be fathomed, appreciated, or evaluated, and hence it cannot be considered to be significantly creative. For instance, only when an original and appropriate idea for a concept or plot of a screenplay is fleshed out in its entirety as a detailed story with dialogue, can we really gauge and consider the degree of creativity associated with that substantive piece of work. From this perspective, then, as creative potential is only achieved upon optimal realization, one can only speak of true creativity upon the actual instantiation of the idea. A fully creative product is one in which the "insightful organization that underlies it [is] sustained, evaluated, elaborated, developed and communicated to others – in other words, the creative product must be produced" (MacKinnon, 1978, 48).

1.2.2 Critical Factors to Keep in Mind When Defining Creativity

Although most creativity theorists are not likely to subscribe to MacKinnon's view in the extreme, virtually none would deny the need to distinguish between *creative potential* and *creative achievement* (Helson & Pals, 2000; Hennessey & Amabile, 2010; Runco, 2004; Sternberg, Grigorenko, & Singer, 2004) (also see Box 2.1). The ability to create is often seen as a capacity given that, "it is a 'potentiality' or 'possibility' and may or may not be realized in fact, as an act or an achieved state (though preferably it is)" (Pope, 2005). Guilford (1950), for instance, differentiated between creative potential and production and made a case for personality and motivation in the latter: "Whether or not the individual who has the requisite abilities will actually produce results of a creative nature will depend upon his motivational and temperamental traits" (444).

What should be apparent at this juncture is that the addition of these two supplementary factors ("surprise" and "realization") to the definition of creativity beyond the two elemental factors ("originality/novelty" and "appropriateness/fit") leads, somewhat counterintuitively, to a widening of the concept rather than a narrowing of the same. This is because they necessitate the consideration of broader individual, disciplinary, and sociocultural factors in terms of their impact on the quality and quantity of the creative output (Amabile, 1983; Csikszentmihalyi & Sawyer, 1995; Harrington, 1990).

We need to, for instance, take into consideration the *magnitude of creativity* associated with the idea/product in question as this can take 4 different forms: mini-c, little-c, Pro-c, Big-C (Kaufman & Beghetto, 2009). At the most basic level, mini-c creativity reflects "personally meaningful interpretations of experiences, actions and events" as well as the "developmental nature of creativity" (Beghetto & Kaufman, 2007, 73). In discovering a new and personally meaningful way to use papier-mâché, a 7 year old exhibits early signs of creative expression. However, one cannot legitimately compare this kind of mini-c display, which showcases the genesis of creative ability, with that of genius, eminent or Big-C creativity, like Picasso's *Les Demoiselles d'Avignon*, which represents creativity on a monumental and lasting scale. For that matter, one cannot equalize mini-c creativity even with its more immediate counterparts: little-c creativity, which reflects creative engagement beyond the merely intrapersonal realm (e.g., winning a primary school poetry competition), or Pro-C creativity, which is at the level of professional expertise where significant creative accomplishments are evidenced.

One way to overcome these difficulties in the definition of creativity when applied to creativity research is (a) to clearly identify which magnitude of creativity will be the focus of any given investigation ranging from creative eminence (Big-C) (Gardner, 2011) to different forms of everyday creativity (little-c, mini-c) (Amabile, 2014), and (b) to be circumscribed in one's approach so as to limit generalizations concerning the implications of those findings within that particular magnitude level. Following the guidelines of the scientific method, such as controlling for potential intervening variables (Wilson, 1991), the output of creative cogitation, regardless of whether it takes the form of ideas, responses, or products, can then be identified by the presence or degree of the two definitional elements of originality and appropriateness (Figure 1.3).

1.3 Understanding "Appropriateness" Appropriately

The issue of estimating appropriateness is thornier than one might expect, for several reasons. For one, the connotation of value differs across types of creativity:

The nature of value depends on the domain of creativity. For example, a painting is judged by its aesthetic value; a scientific discovery, by its theoretical value; a business venture, by its commercial value; and so forth. To cover value of all kinds, we speak simply of effectiveness as a criterion for creativity. To be effective, in this sense, is to be of value. (Averill, Chon, & Hahn, 2001, 171–172)

An idea or response is held to be appropriate insofar as it is valuable, useful, fitting, relevant, suitable, adaptive, satisfying, and so on, within a specific context (Figure 1.3). But the manifold terms used in this context are not entirely interchangeable. Margaret Boden (2004), who was cited in Section 1.2.1 in defining a creative response as being new, surprising, and valuable, also stated the following:

I said earlier that 'new' has two meanings, and that 'surprising' has three. I didn't say how many meanings 'valuable' has – and nobody could. Our aesthetic values are difficult to recognize, more difficult to put into words, and even more difficult to state really clearly. (2012, 39)

There are potentially unlimited ways in which we could construe value or appropriateness as this differs as a function of context and time. For instance, cultural differences abound in our conceptions of value. Let's take the case of clothing as a simple example. The usefulness of animal hide to make fur coats is limited to geographical regions of the world that experience long periods of very cold weather. In comparison, a fur coat is likely to be a useless and therefore inappropriate product in warmer, tropical areas of the globe.

Things get more complicated when we take other factors into consideration, such as the fact that our sense of value or appropriateness can change over time even within cultures, and the grounds for this change can be virtually anything, ranging from necessity to ideology. Let's stick with the example of clothing. Mink coats were items of fur clothing that women in many parts of the western hemisphere aspired to possess until just a few decades ago. Now, however, with the rise of animal rights awareness and activism, the fur coat industry is exceedingly unpopular and openly derided. So a product that was seen to be unanimously appropriate a few decades ago is no longer regarded in the same way.

There are also problems in relation to the semantics of some of the terms (see Box 1.2). The word "valuable" has a positive connotation, as do allied terms like "adaptive" and "useful," which also refer to appropriateness. However, creative ideas, products, and responses need not be positive, life-affirming, or for the good of mankind. Indeed, creative solutions or ideas can have terrible consequences. Examples of creativity in the service of underhand motives abound across different domains of human life, with particularly noteworthy cases stemming from the worlds of crime, law, and finance where the need for creative problem solving emerges from finding and exploiting loopholes in the system. A prime example of this is the case of Bernie Madoff who pulled off the biggest case of financial fraud in US history. His "success" over decades was attributed to the creative rebooting of an old accounting trick – a Ponzi scheme – through which he defrauded thousands of clients of varying sums of money that accrued to the order of billions of dollars.

This problem of semantics with regard to the issue of value occurs because we conflate the "value" of an idea with the eventual "value" of the outcome that leads from the idea, which can be monetary, social, or environmental. While the former refers to fit or suitability to a particular end goal (e.g., a new handgun model whose value lies in the fact that it weighs less than others in the market and is therefore easier to handle and carry), the latter is about the consequences that result from realization of the idea (e.g., positive – higher profits for the gun manufacturer;

Box 1.2 Connotations of the Terms "Creativity" and "Creative"

Terminology is an issue of note, as the word "creative" in itself has many connotations. When you ask someone if she considers herself to be creative, and she says yes, her answer is usually based on her belief that she is creative because she engages in pursuits that are considered *ipso facto* to be creative (e.g., painting, writing, playing a musical instrument). Such activities are seen as being creative because the responses are open-ended and one is attempting to "create" something (e.g., a drawing, a poem, a tune). What is important to note, though, is that this connotation of the terms "creative" or "creativity" is *not* the same as that expounded in Section 1.2 on the definition of creativity. In penning a poem, I may be "creating" a poem. But, from the standpoint of scientific inquiry, it would not be considered a "creative" poem if it lacked originality.

Several terms are also often used interchangeably with creativity, although they have quite different connotations. These include divergent thinking (open-ended idea generation), innovation (applied creativity; successful execution of ideas), imagination (representation of conceptual content in the absence of sensory input), genius (achievement to the level of eminence), inspiration (to be driven to do or feel something as a consequence of being mentally stimulated), and play (engaging in intrinsically driven activities associated with recreational pleasure). None of these are synonymous with the concept of creativity, as outlined in this chapter, as the phenomena in question (divergent thinking, genius, imagination, inspiration, play) do not always necessitate or result in originality. Moreover, creative pursuits are neither always enjoyable (unlike play) nor do they necessarily lead to profits or benefits in terms of the lesser or greater good (innovation).

negative – a rise in gun-related injury). Moreover, what is considered a valuable consequence in one context (e.g., free trade increases global prosperity) is not necessarily so in another context (e.g., the erosion of middle-class prosperity as a consequence of free trade).

One final issue to discuss in the context of appropriateness is its relation to originality. While these two factors have been discussed independently of each other thus far, it should be noted that they are not orthogonal to one another. A simple thought trial illustrates this point. An idea can be original and appropriate (creative), original and inappropriate (nonsensical), as well as unoriginal and appropriate (commonplace). However, it is not viable to conceive of an idea that is both inappropriate and unoriginal.

This is because something that is inappropriate or unfitting in a particular context is necessarily also odd or unusual (and therefore original) within that context (Kröger et al., 2012; Rutter, Kröger, Stark, et al., 2012). The nature of the relation between the factors of originality and appropriateness in creativity are rarely discussed in psychological or neuroscientific literature. However, the non-orthogonal association between these factors was alluded to in Hans Eysenck's conceptualization of "overinclusive thinking," which is a cognitive style that is characterized by a wider conception of appropriateness or relevance than is conventional. Eysenck (1995) highlighted the need to consider overinclusive thinking as a critical factor that leads to individual differences in creative ability given that if one's conception of what is relevant in a given situation is broader than usual, one would have a larger realm of conceptual associations to draw from and, as a consequence, be more likely to generate unusual or original responses.

1.4 Challenges in Recognizing or Evaluating Creativity

Now that we have a reasonably good handle on how to define creativity, we can approach the next stumbling block head on – the problem of recognizing creativity when faced with instances of it in any form. In the examples cited at the outset of this chapter (Section 1.1), it was relatively simple to identify what was creative about those ideas or solutions because there is broad consensus in terms of whether they showcase creativity. This is partially reflected in the fact that all are well-known and prominent cases of documented creativity in each of those domains. However, such prototypical examples notwithstanding, it is quite challenging to recognize creativity in most situations. There are two reasons for this: (a) the ability of the individual to recognize or estimate creativity, and (b) the correspondence or consensus within a group in their evaluations of creativity. Both these challenges can be better understood when contrasting the outputs of creativity with that of memory, another widely studied cognitive ability, which is also both complex and heterogeneous.

1.4.1 How Do We "Recognize" Creativity?

Let us imagine for a moment that you have a friend who brags about her fantastic memory. Her memory for faces, in particular. She never forgets a face, apparently. And let's say that you wanted to verify the truth of this claim. If you wanted to determine whether your friend truly has a terrific memory for faces, how would you assess this? There are several objective and relatively simple ways to do so. One option would be to show her a series of 50 photographs of faces of different strangers that she can look at for a brief period of time. You could then test her memory for the faces after a delay by selecting half the photographs she has seen and mixing them with 25 new photographs of other strangers that she has not yet seen. Her task would be to indicate when she recognizes a familiar face from this second series of photographs. The greater the number of photographs that are correctly recognized, the better her memory. So if your friend's memory was very good, we would expect a higher than average level of accuracy on her part in correctly picking out the pictures she had previously seen.

It is reasonable to presume this simple experiment would not be met with much disagreement from onlookers with regard to whether memory for faces is being tested, and whether the performance index (accuracy) is appropriate or sensible with regard to the recognition of memory skills. Recognizing creativity, though, is a decidedly more complex affair when it comes to both accuracy in judgment and unanimity of judgment. For one, it involves recognizing that something is new and fitting. Therein lies the problem – how can we recognize originality given that the information is unknown or new?

When something is unknown, we are likely to ignore or not process that piece of information keenly, particularly if it has no salience for ourselves. So a simple one-to-one matching in terms of accuracy or familiarity ("yes" when correct/known; "no" when incorrect/unknown) does not apply in the case of creativity. The word "recognize" is therefore misleading in this context as it suggests that the process involves matching to a known association in memory. Checking whether your name has been misspelt in a document involves recognition or matching what is present with what you know to be a fact. This is not comparable to the recognition of creativity within a new type of dance move or a novel scientific hypothesis as there is no match between what we perceive and the information stored within our memories.

A more accurate way to think about estimating the creativity associated with a particular idea is in terms of decision-making processes. Deciding whether to eat eggs or pancakes for breakfast involves estimating your choices and their potential outcomes. This is a valuation that takes place in the known space. Determining whether something is creative, however, means making a valuation in a knowledge space that is as yet still unraveling. Unlike a jeweler who has the physical tools of a loupe or an assay balance to estimate the quality of precious stones or metals, the mental tools in estimating the value in a new idea or product are necessarily subjective and vary across contexts.

⚹

· need not be a difficulty re: c.v.

At lower levels of magnitude (mini-c, little-c), such as in everyday acts of creativity, such judgments do not require extensive domain knowledge because the person's own background experience is the chief relevant gauge. I might deem the poem I penned last night as reflecting more originality than the one I wrote two months ago, for example. At higher levels of magnitude (Pro-c, Big-C), though, evaluation necessitates *domain expertise*. For instance, in order to estimate the level of creativity associated with a novel psychological paradigm that has been developed to assess consciousness, one needs to have prior knowledge about the existing empirical paradigms within that field of research. Regardless of the differences in magnitude, though, what is common to all instances is that these evaluations result in the expansion of the evaluator's own conceptualizations of the possibility space. This is because what is being evaluated as creative is new, fitting, and surprising to you – the evaluator/judge/recipient – as well.

So what is going on in our minds when we are evaluating an idea, response, or outcome with regard to its instantiation of creativity? This is as yet unclear. What we can say is that it is not directly comparable to the mental operations that take place during other forms of complex cognition. Some evidence has shown that it is as though the initial non-matching owing to unfamiliarity (novel-originality) rapidly gives way – prior to the decision point – to a subsequent matching owing to the detection of possibility (fit-appropriateness) (Kröger et al., 2013; Rutter, Kröger, Hill, et al., 2012). It is as though something that was obscure suddenly clicks, fits, or feels right. This is akin to the experience of an insight, which is a sudden awareness of a new understanding. Perhaps this is whether the phenomenology of "surprise" enters the equation. In this sense, then, the parameters that are in play when recognizing an act, response, idea, or product to be creative are complex in that they involve a kind of estimation that can be best described as a "no, but yes" or *volte-face*. There is, however, no guarantee that such an estimation will result in the "acceptance" of a creative idea. In the words of Eysenck, "there is nothing more painful than the pain of a new idea" as "creativity is a threat to the great uncreative majority" (1994, 234). So it is worth bearing in mind that complex factors can prevent the acceptance and propagation of new ideas.

1.4.2 To What Extent Can We Agree about Creativity?

The second difficulty in recognizing creativity is that of *consensus*. Let's go back to the hypothetical memory test for faces that we conducted on your friend. Let's imagine that your friend correctly recognized 90% of the previously shown faces. Most people, regardless of whether they are experts or non-experts, would agree that 90% accuracy in recall on a memory task is an indicator of good memory performance. In the case of creativity, though, people are unlikely to be as unanimous in their estimations. The reason for this has been alluded to within the definitions quoted in Section 1.2. Some point out that, "creativity is a phenomenon that is constructed through an interaction between producers and audience. Creativity is not the product of single individuals but of social systems making judgments about individuals' products" (Csikszentmihalyi, 1999, 314). Social judgment therefore enters into the equation right away as recognizing and accepting that a work is creative requires some degree of consensus within a particular group. This is the reason why some theorists have advocated that any given product or idea can only be legitimately evaluated by experts within that particular domain to estimate the presence and degree of associated creativity (Csikszentmihalyi, 1988; Hennessey & Amabile, 1988).

The *degree of subjectivity that is intrinsic to a field* is also a factor to consider in this regard as this would differ considerably between different domains of human enterprise. For instance, consensus about whether a particular idea is creative or not would be higher in a relatively objective discipline like mathematics compared to that of literature. Agreement among artists on the degree of originality associated even within singular works of art (e.g., Wagner's *Tristan and Isolde*, Duchamp's *Fountain*) would be less than among scientists on the degree of originality associated with paradigm-shifting advances in science (e.g., Einstein's theory of relativity, Darwin's theory of evolution). These differences are inevitable. After all, the former involves estimations of expression that are, in themselves, relatively subjective whereas the latter concerns estimations of truth that are (or at least ought to be), in themselves, objective. There are infinite ways to depict a falling apple, but limited ways to accurately explain why the apple falls in a downward direction.

What's more, the degree of intrinsic subjectivity in a field is also necessarily influenced by additional factors like the accessibility of the field as well as the levels of expertise of the group passing the judgment. For instance, an amateur art appreciator or avid reader may be less likely to appreciate the value of the works from some of the contenders of the Turner prize or the Booker prize than art experts or book critics. This is because, unlike in the sciences, the relatively high accessibility of fine art and literature means that one needs little domain knowledge to begin to engage with such works meaningfully and form opinions on the same. This is one of the reasons why it is more difficult to reach a consensus about both the originality and relevance of products and ideas in the arts than the sciences.

Now that we are drawing toward the end of this rather guarded section, it is perhaps important to inject an optimistic note. At this point it might seem to the reader that the challenges faced in studying the phenomenon of creativity are substantial. While this is not untrue, one need not be unduly daunted by the prospect. Just because it is not a simple matter to recognize or agree on whether an outcome, event, idea, or object is creative, it doesn't mean that it is useless or unproductive to tackle this topic. Quite the contrary. It only means that the phenomenon escapes easy evaluation. It might help to bear in mind that other immensely complex topics, such as movement, language, and consciousness, also have to undertake similar challenges and have all nonetheless been subject to scientific enquiry through the lens of neuroscience. So creativity is not the only field of research that faces an uphill task.

As there is at least broad agreement or consensus concerning originality and appropriateness as the defining components of creativity, researchers in experimental psychology and neuroscience zone in toward these two components as the critical ones to investigate.

1.4.3 Consciousness and Creativity

One final point to mull over in terms of the challenges associated with recognizing and evaluating creativity is that of consciousness in terms of self-recognition of creativity. Is an idea a creative one if the entity generating it is not aware of its own creativity? You might be wondering why we are contemplating this question at all. Some theorists have stated that, "by definition, creative insights occur in consciousness" (Dietrich, 2004b, 1011); that "[t]he 'a-ha' moment is exactly that, the moment the idea makes its way into conscious awareness" (Runco, 2007b, 108); and that "a product is creative if it is novel and if it was produced intentionally" (Weisberg, 2015, 111).

The assumption that creativity is marked by one's own recognition of one's leap of originality during idea generation is a sensible one to make. It is particularly obvious when one reads diaries and logbooks maintained by people who have achieved creative eminence. Extensive notes made by Charles Darwin, for instance, reveal that all the ingredients for his pioneering theory were present in his mind long before he reached his creative insights and formally formulated his views (Ridley, 2015).

It is worth bearing in mind, though, that it is not always possible to determine or prove that subjects are aware of or consciously recognize their own output as creative. Situations where this might be particularly tricky are in the case of populations with communication difficulties owing to as yet immature brain development (e.g., early childhood) or brain insufficiencies as in neurological and psychiatric disorders (e.g., aphasia, autism). The question of self-awareness and creativity gets even more interesting (and complicated) when taking into consideration that several species of non-human animals display creative problem solving (see Box 1.3).

Box 1.3 Animal Creativity

Wolfgang Köhler published the first empirical evidence of creativity in animals with his work on chimpanzees (Köhler, 1926). In his landmark studies within the domains of learning and problem solving, he demonstrated that learning could take place by means of insight, as opposed to trial-and-error learning and reward-based learning. Following this, skills such as problem solving, social learning, and the use or modification of tools in chimpanzees has also been shown in other species, both primates (e.g., orangutans, gorillas) and non-primates (e.g., octopuses, dolphins, elephants) (Kaufman & Kaufman, 2004). So far, though, robust evidence of creative problem solving, as evidenced by novel, deliberate, and spontaneous solutions, is only clear in New Caledonian crows (Weir & Kacelnik, 2006).

Adopting a perspective beyond learning and problem solving across the wider repertoire of animal behavior reveals exceedingly interesting manifestations of other patterns that are also suggestive of originality or novelty (Kaufman & Kaufman, 2015; Ramsey, Bastian, & van Schaik, 2007). Examples include aesthetic sensibilities in bower birds as revealed in the buildings of their bowers (Diamond, 1982; Endler, 2012), as well as flexibility and complexity in the generation of songs in songbirds (Oller & Griebel, 2008). An example of unconventional behavior can be seen in the documentary film *Chimpanzee* (Disneynature, 2012) in which an infant chimp whose mother died is adopted by the unrelated alpha male of the group. Given that such behavioral patterns are relatively unknown to this species and demonstrate "the emergence of creative behavior in spite of the high cost" (Wiggins, Tyack, Scharff, & Rohrmeier, 2015), such a response would certainly qualify as novel, valuable, and surprising.

1.5 The Purpose of Creativity

As we inch closer to the end of this introductory chapter, we have yet to grapple with a central question that will enable us to come to terms with what is generally meant or understood by creativity. And the question concerns the purpose of creativity. Why do we have a creative mind? What is it for? What function(s) does such a mind serve?

On the basis of archeological records, we know that the evolution of our creative mind, the mind of *Homo sapiens sapiens*, a species that emerged 100,000 years ago, displayed early signs of creative innovation some 90,000 years ago in the form of problem solving and development of technology. This was followed by a "creative explosion" that appeared independently across the globe beginning about 40,000 years ago in the form of creative expression via the development of art and body ornaments (Carruthers, 2002; Mithen, 2014). In fact, it has been suggested that the enormous increase in brain size in our species alongside the increased differentiation and complexity of our neocortex, which is the most recently evolved part of the mammalian brain, set the stage for the unparalleled growth and manifestation of complex cognitive skills, such as creativity (Defelipe, 2011). There is little doubt that creativity and innovation are central to cultural transformation and evolution (Fogarty, Creanza, & Feldman, 2015).

A key factor to consider when inferring the potential general functions of the ability to be creative is that it is one that applies across all types of human activity. My creative mind is at work regardless of whether I come up with a new recipe, poem, theory, scheme, strategy, formula, gadget, or widget. So the essential function of the creative mind must be generalizable across different contexts. As the creative mind is the enormously fertile foundation that enables *the birth of ideas*, it can be essentially characterized as an idea generator. And it is this central function of the creative mind that makes it the basis of creation, invention, discovery, innovation, and revolution across all spheres of human life. It affects every domain of human enterprise, be it the arts and crafts, science and technology, or businesses and services, as it is integral to the very foundation of change, progress, and development.

1.5.1 A Road Map for Using this Book

What you are holding in your hands or viewing on your screen is a well-informed and up-to-date book where theory and research that are relevant to grasping what we know so far about the neuroscience of creativity are presented in an accessible manner. The book is divided into 12 chapters, each of which will be self-contained thereby enabling the reader to gain all the necessary information pertaining to the topic covered within that chapter without necessarily having to refer forwards or backwards within the book.

This introduction to the concept of creativity is followed by an exposition of the approaches and methods from the field of psychology to measure our creative faculties (Chapter 2). Theoretical frameworks from cognitive psychology that have been put forward to understand our creative minds will then be outlined (Chapter 3). Competing hypotheses on the neural underpinnings of creativity will be explored in terms of global explanations (Chapter 4) and local explanations (Chapter 5). Brain-based methods that have been employed to investigate the brain basis of creativity will then be outlined (Chapter 6) followed by a discussion of critical issues that need to be kept in mind when adopting such approaches (Chapter 7).

In a 1993 interview with the *Paris Review*, Fran Lebowitz remarked that, "There are only four kinds of artists: choreographers, writers, composers and painters. What they do is to make whole inventions." Even if one does not fully endorse this view, this intuitive classification is a useful one that helps to distinguish between categories of artistic creativity. Overviews of different domains of creativity that will be discussed include musical creativity (Chapter 8), literary creativity (Chapter 9), visual artistic creativity (Chapter 10), and kinesthetic creativity (Chapter 11) alongside scientific creativity (Chapter 12). The book ends with a brief Afterword reflecting on the creative mind and how to continue studying it.

My objective in writing this book is to provide you, the reader, with a systematic and detailed overview of the neuroscience of creativity field that will be a vital aid in helping you navigate this fascinating domain of knowledge. My big hope is that it will be a source of illumination to help you fathom concepts that can be quite obscure as well as a dependable reference resource that points you toward useful literature that will enable you to deepen your knowledge further. The greatest achievement will be if it motivates you, the reader, to join in this ambitious quest – to explore your creative mind more than you already do. From inside out and outside in.

Chapter Summary

- A creative idea is one that is "original" as well as "appropriate" in a given context.
- Other factors that need to be considered when evaluating the degree of creativity in an idea are "surprise" and optimal "realization."
- There are several conceptualizations regarding types of creativity beyond generic notions of artistic and scientific creativity.

- Variables to keep in mind when evaluating creativity are the magnitude of creativity with regard to creative potential versus creative achievement.
- The mental processes by which we are able to recognize creativity are best characterized as *volte-face* estimations.
- Challenges in evaluating creativity stem from factors such as domain expertise, subjectivity, and consensus.
- The purpose of the creative mind is novel idea generation, a purpose that applies across all contexts of human endeavor.

Review Questions

1. What are the key factors to consider when defining creativity?
2. How is appropriateness in creativity construed? Is it always associated with positive outcomes?
3. Identify the unique challenges encountered when evaluating creativity compared to other aspects of complex cognition.
4. On what basis can we differentiate between types of creativity?
5. Why do we have creative minds?

Further Reading

- Boden, M. (2004). *The creative mind: Myths and mechanisms* (2nd edn.). London: Routledge.
- MacKinnon, D. W. (1978). *In search of human effectiveness*. Buffalo, NY: Creative Education Foundation.
- Pope, R. (2005). *Creativity: Theory, history, practice.* New York: Routledge.
- Runco, M. A., & Jaeger, G. J. (2012). The standard definition of creativity. *Creativity Research Journal, 24*(1), 92–96.
- Sternberg R. J. (1999). *Handbook of creativity*. Cambridge: Cambridge University Press.

CHAPTER TWO

How Can Creativity Be Assessed?

"Write it. Shoot it. Publish it. Crochet it, sauté it, whatever. MAKE."

(Joss Whedon)

Learning Objectives

- Identifying the different approaches used to investigate creativity
- Learning how creativity is assessed in relation to the four approaches
- Understanding how the approaches apply in the neuroscience of creativity
- Distinguishing between divergent and convergent thinking in creativity
- Differentiating between process-general and process-specific measures
- Advantages and disadvantages of different measures of creativity

2.1 Approaches to Investigating Creativity

Your friend from Chapter 1 (Section 1.4.1), the champion face memorizer, has followed you to this chapter. And this time she is telling you another fact about herself over coffee. She says that she is very creative. More creative than most people, apparently. She wants to prove this but the trouble is that she doesn't quite know how to do so. It doesn't seem to be as simple as proving that she has a good memory for faces. "How do you measure creativity?" she asks. Another friend joins in this conversation. He has been quiet the whole time but his interest is now piqued. He wonders whether creativity can be quantified at all because, if it is possible, he'd like to know how as well. He is a primary school teacher, you see, and he'd like to have a measure of some sort that will indicate the level of creativity among the children in his class. More importantly, he wants to know whether their creativity changes with time, and what factors influence such changes. Both your friends are looking to empiricists for clear answers. Let's see if we can help them.

In order to do so, we need to keep in mind some of the lessons from Chapter 1. The ability to be creative was defined as the capacity to generate ideas or responses that are both original (novel/unusual/unique)

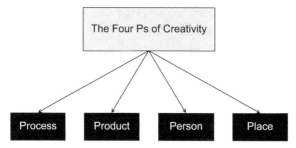

Figure 2.1 Rhodes's (1961) Four Ps of creativity

and appropriate (fitting/meaningful/adaptive) (Runco & Jaeger, 2012). James Melvin Rhodes provided the earliest formulation of different "strands" of conceptualization within the definition of creativity:

The word "creativity" is a noun naming the phenomenon in which a person communicates a new concept (which is the product). Mental activity (or mental process) is implicit in the definition, and of course no one could conceive of a person living or operating in a vacuum, so the term *press* is also implicit. (1961, 305, emphasis in original)

This widely influential formulation is commonly referred to as the "four Ps of creativity," which reflect the approaches one can adopt in investigations of creativity in terms of the person, product, process, and press/place (Figure 2.1). Each of these will be outlined in more detail in the sections that follow.

2.1.1 Person

This approach involves the study of creativity with reference to the person generating the creative ideas or acts. In doing so, it "covers information about personality, intellect, temperament, physique, traits, habits, attitudes, self-concept, value systems, defense mechanisms, and behaviour" (Rhodes, 1961, 307). An implicit assumption of this approach is that it is possible to differentiate between people who are highly creative from those who are less so, and the grounds for these differences are apparent from factors that are individual (within the person). Let us look at a few examples of studies that have used a person-based approach.

Identifying the constellation of stable personality traits of people who are deemed highly creative has been the focus of abundant research in the field of creativity. MacKinnon (1978) coined the phrase "briefcase syndrome of creativity" to reflect the fact that the generic image of the creative person as an "emotionally unstable, sloppy, loose-jointed Bohemian" is actually more befitting of uncreative people. This is especially so when considering that traits such as "deliberate, reserved, industrious and thorough" have been used to describe creative people (18). MacKinnon goes on to state,

> A truly creative individual has an image of himself as a responsible person and a sense of destiny about himself as a human being. This includes a degree of resoluteness and almost inevitably a measure of egotism ... there is a belief in the foregone. (18)

Across domains of science and art, highly creative people have been found to show greater openness to novel experiences, are attracted to complexity, display heightened aesthetic sensibilities, are unconventional as well as intrinsically motivated, and are characterized by a heightened sense of confidence, independence, and ambition (Barron & Harrington, 1981; Feist, 1998). Some recent work has gone further in showing that "openness to experience" or "cognitive engagement with perception, fantasy, aesthetics, and emotions" is predictive of creative achievement in the arts whereas "intellect" or "cognitive engagement with abstract and semantic information, primarily through reasoning" is predictive of the same in the sciences (Kaufman et al., 2016, 248).

Intelligence is another variable within the person-based approach, which is perhaps the most extensively and consistently studied variable in relation to creative thinking throughout the history of empirical investigations into creativity (Barron & Harrington, 1981; Batey & Furnham, 2006; Kaufman & Plucker, 2010; Simonton, 2000; Sternberg & O'Hara, 1999). The ambitious longitudinal study by Lewis Terman is a striking example of the pioneering work in this field. He identified gifted schoolchildren (1,528 from an initial sample of 250,000) and followed them into adulthood with the express aim of identifying how many made eminent creative contributions (not a single person, as it turned out). These findings highlighted that intelligence was important in relation to creativity but only up to a certain threshold beyond which there was no noteworthy correlation between intelligence and creative achievement. "The data reviewed indicate that above the IQ level of 140, adult success is largely determined by such factors as social adjustment, emotional stability, and drive to accomplish" (Terman & Oden, 1940, 83–84).

As it currently stands, the threshold hypothesis of intelligence and creativity reflects the notion that there is a positive linear correlation between creativity and IQ up to a threshold of 120 IQ points, such that low IQ is associated with low levels of creativity, and vice versa. Beyond an IQ threshold of 120, though, the same relation does not apply (Batey & Furnham, 2006). This hypothesis has been widely investigated and the field largely remains divided on this issue (Fuchs-Beauchamp, Karnes, & Johnson, 1993; Runco & Albert, 1986). Some recent evidence showcases a novel and more nuanced approach in postulating that different IQ thresholds impact different aspects of creativity (Jauk, Benedek, Dunst, & Neubauer, 2013). An IQ threshold of 100 fitted a liberal criterion of ideational originality (generation of two original ideas), whereas a threshold of 120 met the more stringent criterion (many original ideas). Ideational fluency or the number of ideas generated (regardless of the associated originality of the ideas) was linked to an IQ threshold of 85.

Within the neuroscientific realm, applying a person-based approach takes the form of looking for structural brain markers in relation to creativity. So one is looking for evidence of differences in structure or activity within the brains of highly creative and less creative individuals. There is evidence, for instance, of neuroanatomical differences within brain regions that are known to orchestrate motor and auditory processing as a function of musical training (Barrett, Ashley, Strait, & Kraus, 2013; Schlaug, 2001). These are interpreted as neuroanatomical markers in relation to domain-specific creative performance (musical creativity in the above example).

Other neuroscientific investigations have focused instead on domain-general creative thinking abilities through the use of laboratory-based tasks (e.g., divergent thinking, creative achievement) (see Section 2.3), and individual differences on such measures of creativity have been evaluated with respect to corresponding differences in terms of brain structure or connectivity. Rex Jung, for instance, reported higher cortical thickness in medial regions of the parietal lobe in relation to better creative performance on divergent thinking measures, whereas greater creative achievement was associated with higher cortical thickness in lateral regions of the parietal lobe (Jung et al., 2010). There is also evidence for the effects of short-term training in divergent creative thinking on neuroanatomical features (Sun et al., 2016). Increasingly, researchers are investigating creativity-relevant personality traits (openness to experience and intelligence) in relation to brain function (Jauk, Neubauer, Dunst, Fink, & Benedek, 2015; Li et al., 2015; Taki et al., 2013).

One issue that should be noted about person-based approaches to the neuroscience of creativity is that they are relatively rare in comparison to the sheer number of investigations of the same within the psychology of individual difference. So it is, as yet, not possible to glean a consistent picture from the manifold single findings of correlations between the different ways in which to examine creativity and the many brain structures that are differentially implicated in the same. Existing studies have also largely focused on normative creativity (high versus low creative groups as determined by performance on a creativity task or comparing individuals from purportedly creative versus uncreative professions) as opposed to exceptional creativity (genius or eminence) (see Box 2.1). So there are several avenues that remain to be explored using the person approach within the neuroscience of creativity.

Box 2.1 Magnitude: Everyday Creativity versus Creative Genius

One of the critical issues in the context of assessing creativity is to adequately consider the magnitude of creativity that we are attempting to study. This can take on four different forms: mini-c, little-c, Pro-c, Big-C (Kaufman & Beghetto, 2009). At the least mature level of mastery, mini-c creativity reflects "personally meaningful interpretations of experiences, actions and events" as well as the "developmental nature of creativity" (Beghetto & Kaufman, 2007, 73). So a 5 year old making up his own words to a tune is revealing early signs of creative expression. The next level of mastery is little-c creativity, which refers to creative engagement beyond the intrapersonal space (e.g., winning a school photography competition). Pro-C creativity is at a substantially higher level in terms of professional expertise, where significant creative accomplishments are evidenced (e.g., exhibiting work at a professional gallery). At the end of the continuum lies eminent or Big-C creativity (e.g., Frank Gehry's design of the Guggenheim Museum in Bilbao), which represents creativity on a monumental and lasting scale.

Big-C creativity can only be assessed using domain-specific measures (e.g., in Feist's (1993) domain-specific publications, citations and awards of recognition in scientific eminence). Empirical investigations of creativity using the tasks outlined in this chapter (following the process, product, and person approaches) are all assessments of little-c creativity and they are domain-general for most part (Simonton, 2012a).

2.1.2 Product

This approach involves the study of creativity through the output that comes from creative engagement, and the output in question can be an idea, a response, or an artifact. As Rhodes (1961, 309) stated: "The word idea refers to a thought which has been communicated to other people in the form of words, paint, clay, metal, stone, fabric or other material

... When an idea becomes embodied into tangible form it is called a product." Different types of ideas and their associated creativity have also been distinguished within this formulation. *Ideas in theory* hold the position of the highest order or type of product in the scale of creativity, followed by *ideas for inventions*, and finally *ideas for innovations* to existing inventions (Rhodes, 1961).

In attempting to understand how best to evaluate the creativity associated with a product, several categorical distinctions have been proposed. In the scientific domain, Kuhn distinguished between "normal science" and "revolution in science" where the latter reflects "those non-cumulative developmental episodes in which an older paradigm is replaced in whole or in part by an incompatible new one" (1970, 92). Gardner (1994) explicitly developed a scheme of creative activities that applies to all domains. He distinguished between five kinds: (a) the solution of a well-defined problem (e.g., Watson and Crick's discovery of the double helix structure of DNA), (b) the devising of an encompassing theory (e.g., Freud's formulations on the unconscious), (c) the creation of a "frozen work" where a distance exists between the creation and evaluation of the work (e.g., Kandinsky's paintings), (d) the performance of a ritualized work where the performance in itself is the work, which makes for little to no distance between the creation and evaluation of the work (e.g., Martha Graham's dance choreography), and (e) a "high stakes" performance where the details of the performance cannot be worked out in advance and are necessarily dependent on the reactions of the collective (e.g., Gandhi's non-violent protest movement).

To date, the only theory to focus solely on the creative product (as opposed to the product in conjunction with person, process, or place) is the Propulsion Model of Creative Contributions (Sternberg, 1999; Sternberg, Kaufman, & Pretz, 2001). The central idea behind this theory is that acts of creativity per definition propel a field forward from one point to the next, and the kind of creative contribution differs in accordance with the specific manner in which the ideas propel a field forward. Sternberg identified eight distinct ways in which creative contributions can be made, with room within each type for quantitative differences. *Replication* is an effort to show where a field currently is and thereby strengthens the field, whereas *redefinition* is an effort to redefine where a field currently is, which amounts to changing the perception of where that field is. This is distinguished from attempts to move a field forward in the currently taken direction to a point where others in the field want to go (*forward incrementation*) or beyond where others in the field want to go, which in doing so are "ahead of their time" (*advance forward incrementation*).

Attempting to move a field in a new and different direction from the present (*redirection*) is distinguished from attempts to move a field back to where it used to be before and to then proceed in a hitherto unexplored direction (*reconstruction/redirection*). *Reinitiation* refers to attempts that take a field to an as yet undefined starting point in order to move toward a new direction thereafter, away from the fully exhausted or undesirable current direction. The final category, *integration*, attempts to move a field by bringing together two distinct, unrelated or even opposing ideas.

This classification system is most valuable when qualitatively gauging specific creative contributions. For example, Kaufman and Skidmore (2010) classified "Mahjong" as a reconstruction/redirection creative contribution as the person who devised the game reconceptualized "the traditional Chinese high-stakes, male-oriented mix of dice and dominos … as a low-stakes, female-oriented leisure time activity," paving the way for its indubitable popularity in the US in the 1920s (Panati, 1999, cited in Kaufman & Skidmore, 2010, 380).

What about when having to determine creativity quantitatively as, for instance, when judging between two different products in order to determine which of the two is more creative? Is Salman Rushdie at his creative best in *The Moor's Last Sigh* (1995) or in *Midnight's Children* (1981)? The most widely used method for this purpose is the consensual assessment technique (described in more detail in Section 2.4) (Amabile, 1982), where the products in question are evaluated by experts within that domain whose combined assessment is used to deem the level of creativity associated with each of the products. An example of the use of this kind of technique in an applied setting is in the sport of Artistic Gymnastics, where competitions see two panels of judges rate the gymnasts on every single routine (floor, two-vault, single vault, uneven bars, balance beam) by providing each a D-score (difficulty score that reflects the combined difficulty of every skill in the routine) and an E-score (execution score that indexes the artistry of the routine), which then are summed across judges to give a total score for each individual gymnast.

With regard to the neuroscientific study of product-based creativity, there are only limited avenues, if any, to explore that could lead to meaningful insights. One rare example where it can be argued that such an approach was utilized was in a neuropsychological case study of the Canadian artist Annie Adams, who developed primary progressive aphasia (PPA), a neurodegenerative disorder characterized by the deterioration of speech and language (Seeley et al., 2008). Routine magnetic resonance imaging (MRI) scans of her brain were taken between 1997 and 2004 to monitor her acoustic neuroma (benign tumor of the auditory nerve). As a result, rather serendipitously, brain scans exist from the time when she was pre-symptomatic all the way to the period when she was diagnosed with PPA. Throughout this period, she was an active artist who produced several works, and it was therefore possible to render a timeline of her artistic output in relation to the appearance and intensification of her PPA symptoms and brain atrophy. The trajectory of change in expressive style shows a clear shift over the course of 6 years from avowedly abstract forms during the pre-PPA phase to "increasing photographic realism" in the form of more concrete and extremely detailed renderings. It is, of course, difficult to ascertain whether this change in style is directly attributable to the pattern of deteriorated versus preserved tissue across different brain regions given that most artists change and evolve in terms of expressive direction several times over their lifetime. Nonetheless, it remains an intriguing case study that provides much food for thought.

2.1.3 Press/Place

This approach refers to press (from *press*ures) factors that are present in an individual's place, situation, or environment that influence their capacity to be creative. "Studies of press attempt to measure congruence and dissonance in a person's ecology" (Rhodes, 1961, 308) and this is done by means of estimating "the specifications of the creative situation, the life circumstance, or the social, cultural, and work milieu which facilitate and encourage the appearance of creative thought and action" (MacKinnon, 1970, 17).

   While following the place approach in the study of creativity can take on many forms, because there are several different types of press factors that can be taken into account in any given context, the approach has been largely directed by two distinct research methodologies in psychology (Amabile & Pillemer, 2012). The historiometry approach championed by Dean Keith Simonton utilizes archival data of creators and creative outputs across cultures along different points in history to determine how environmental factors – social, cultural, and political – influence creative success in terms of eminence, originality, and productivity (Simonton & Ting, 2010). While this is seen as a manifestation of "macro-level" investigations within the social psychology of creativity, the alternative approach would be at the "micro-level" as championed by Teresa Amabile, which focuses on how the different parameters within the social environment around task engagement impact on the everyday creativity of people. The dominant method of investigation in this context is by means of the consensual assessment technique (Amabile, 1982) (described in Section 2.4).

In an influential paper on organizational creativity, Amabile (1998) identified that work environments that are designed to maximize their employees' intrinsic motivation are likely to spawn a more creative workforce. This kind of motivation is called "intrinsic" because what motivates people to carry out their work is the joy, interest, and challenge inherent in the task itself beyond extrinsic rewards and pressures. The six environmental factors that have been identified as stimulating intrinsic motivation at the work place are: (a) *challenge* or matching the right employee to the right task given their capabilities, (b) *freedom* by giving employee autonomy in how they choose to approach their work, (c) *resources* in terms of the optimal allocation of time, money, and space, (d) *work-group features* in the form of mutually supportive and diverse groups, (e) *supervisory encouragement* not merely in the form of rewards or punishment but by serving as role models, and (f) *organizational support* by valuing creativity and promoting information sharing and collaboration.

Some of these environmental factors have also been identified as being key in promoting creativity in completely different contexts, such as in academic research and education. Kevin Dunbar (1997), for instance, identified that the diversity of a collective, in terms of background and expertise of group members, is a key factor in promoting scientific creativity. Creative collaboration has also been identified as a relevant factor to focus on when encouraging creativity in the classroom, as has giving children the autonomy to choose their own strategies when deciding how to solve problems, providing encouragement for idea generation and sensible risk taking, allocating resources in terms of time devoted to creative thinking, and maintaining a psychologically safe classroom environment (Sawyer, 2014). Micro-level investigations using the press/place approach in creativity thus suggest that there are certain commonalities in the kinds of environmental factors that boost or impede creativity even when comparing across heterogeneous domains of human enterprise. However, such parallels are viable only up to a point. Complex interactions often surface when a wider spectrum of variables is taken into consideration. For instance, creative individuals are disproportionately likely to stem from two opposing types of family environment: optimal experience backgrounds and pathological experience backgrounds (Csikszentmihalyi & Csikszentmihalyi, 1993).

Macro-level analyses have also resulted in an abundance of insights and support for our intuitions of the importance of context in understanding creativity. There are countless examples throughout history of both systemic and sporadic patronages in the arts and letters that allowed for the fruition of creative achievement and eminence. A prime example of systemic patronage is the Medici family's exceedingly wide-ranging support during the Renaissance as patrons of a number of Florentine artists including Michelangelo Buonarroti and Leonardo da Vinci, as well as the scientist Galileo Galilei. Even more common is sporadic patronage, such as in the case of the poet, Rainer Maria Rilke, who received support from several patrons at different stages in his life, including Princess Marie von Thurn und Taxis and Werner Reinhart. Such acts of patronage meant vital environmental support was provided to meet a range of needs from basic sustenance to providing the space and means through which it would be possible for the work to be carried out. It is clear that, without such support, the probability of lasting and consistent output on the part of many talented individuals would be low because of the sheer lack of opportunity. This is also evidenced by lower creative accomplishment in times of war and political instability across Eastern and Western cultures (Simonton & Ting, 2010).

In contemporary times, there are several far-reaching avenues for environmental support in the form of government-funded initiatives (e.g., National Endowment for the Arts in the USA) or tax incentives to creative industries (e.g., creative sector tax relief in the UK). The need to promote creativity on a global scale by providing for optimal environments is being increasingly recognized. The Global Innovation Index 2012 (Dutta, 2012), for instance, highlighted the impact of press/place factors on a country's innovation. The income level of a country was positively correlated with its provision of enabling environments, which in turn was associated with an unambiguous increase in innovative outputs (ibid.). A clear example of a supremely enabling environment is the city of Vienna. Dubbed the "City of the Century" by the *Economist* in December 2016, it was the epicenter of the most seismic creative advances across all major spectrums of human endeavor in politics and economy, science and philosophy, and the arts (Kandel, 2012).

Few neuroscientific studies have adopted the press/place approach to investigating creativity to date. While several studies have examined the impact of negative environments on behavior and brain function (Hackman, Farah, & Meaney, 2010; Kishiyama, Boyce, Jimenez, Perry, & Knight, 2009; Marshall & Kenney, 2009; Tomalski & Johnson, 2010), none are specific to understanding the impact of such factors on creativity. So the place/press perspective on creativity has been all but unexplored from the purview of neuroscience.

2.1.4 Process

This approach involves the study of the mental operations that underlie
creative thought, and it "applies to motivation, perception, learning,
thinking and communicating" (Rhodes, 1961, 308). As it involves the study
of the intricacies of the creative mind, the process approach readily aligns
itself to the neuroscientific perspective, as neuroscience is the study of the
structure and function of the human nervous system. Although the term
"process" is always in the singular, one would be mistaken to consider
the creative process as single or unitary in any sense. It is merely "a con-
venient summary label for a complex set of cognitive and motivational
processes, and emotional processes too, that are involved in perceiving,
remembering, imagining, appreciating, thinking, planning, deciding, and
the like" (MacKinnon, 1970, 18). Central to the process approach is the
assumption that all persons are creative but that they differ with regard
to the "quality of these processes as well as in the degree to which persons are creative" (ibid.).

The two central themes within the process approach are (a) the stages
of the creative process, and (b) the components of the creative process. Key issues include the role of prior knowledge in creativity (also
see Box 3.2), the similarities and distinctions between creative and non-
creative thinking, divergent versus convergent thinking in creativity (see
Box 2.2), and the role of unconscious and conscious operations in creative thinking (Kozbelt, Beghetto, & Runco, 2010).

Box 2.2 Does Creativity Involve Both Divergent and Convergent Thinking?

In a word – yes. The common notion that divergent thinking, or the generation of multiple solutions to a problem, is synonymous with creative
thinking is profoundly mistaken. The importance of divergent thinking was
highlighted by Joy Paul Guilford (1950, 1959, 1967), with reference to its
relevance to creative potential, as conceptualizations of intelligence until
then focused only on convergent thinking, or the generation of a single
solution to a problem. But the output of divergent thinking is not necessarily creative given that the mere production of multiple solutions does
not guarantee the generation of original and useful solutions. Moreover,
there are open-ended contexts where divergent thought strategies would
be employed (e.g., during hypothetical reasoning when thinking about
the future) and creativity would not be a necessary feature of the ideas
generated in such situations. On the other end of the spectrum, convergent

thinking is often neglected and even portrayed as uncreative, particularly in the popular media. But, again, this is simply untrue. There are no grounds to support the notion that contexts involving the generation of a single solution during creative problem solving would be tantamount to an uncreative act.

In addition, although creativity in some contexts may be more influenced by divergent thinking (Guilford, 1957), divergent thinking without convergent thinking "runs the risk of generating only quasicreativity or pseudocreativity" (Cropley, 2006). The emphasis therefore ought to be on the importance of both divergent and convergent thinking styles in creative ideation and evaluation (Brophy, 2001; Runco & Acar, 2012).

Following the introspective accounts of great thinkers like Henri Poincaré and Hermann von Helmholtz on the progression and development of their own thought cycles when coming up with original ideas, Graham Wallas outlined a 4-stage theory of the creative process (Wallas, 1926; see also Box 3.1). The first stage is *Preparation* and it is considered to be a fully conscious phase where the problem for which an original solution is being sought is investigated intensively and extensively. The second stage is *Incubation* and it is a phase that is unconscious with reference to engagement with the problem at hand as no conscious effort is directed toward the problem during this period of rest or when carrying out unrelated activities. The third stage, *Illumination*, is marked by the solution consciously emerging fully formed in one's mind in a sudden flash of insight. The last stage is *Verification* and it involves conscious deliberation and working out of the details of the solution. It should be noted that empirical evidence has resulted in several challenges to the Wallas 4-stage model (Lubart, 2001), such as a lack of support for the discrete stages. There are also alternative ideas regarding the phases of the creative process, such as the Geneplore model where a generative phase in which preinventive structures are brought forth is followed by an explorative phase in which the structures are evaluated in terms of their utility (Finke, Ward, & Smith, 1996).

The challenge of empirically charting out the stages of the creative process is that it is exceedingly difficult to do so under laboratory conditions owing to the variable timescale for each problem to be solved and the unpredictable nature of the creative response. For instance, the occurrence of a creative insight cannot be predicted or prompted so one cannot estimate when exactly the phase of illumination will begin. In any event, psychological (and neuroscientific investigations) tend to focus on components that can be seen as specific to each of these stages individually or the transition between two stages.

One of the prominent debates of important factors in the preparation stage, for instance, has been on the association between knowledge and creativity (Weisberg, 1999). On the question of how much prior knowledge is optimal for creativity, the "tension" view holds that an inverted-U function best characterizes the association; that is, intermediate levels of knowledge provide the best condition as high levels of knowledge can lead to inflexibility of ideas and inability to change established schemas of thought. The "foundation" view, however, argues for a simple positive correlation in emphasizing that extensive knowledge is essential for creativity as the ability to generate original ideas stems from a clear and comprehensive understanding of prevailing ideas.

Incubation is perhaps the most widely studied of all the stages, with several investigations confirming the positive effect of an incubation phase on creative problem solving (Dijksterhuis & Meurs, 2006) and others reporting otherwise (Segal, 2004). Recent analyses have painted a more nuanced picture that reveals how many factors within the incubation phase need to be considered, such as the levels of cognitive demand associated with the incubation task or the delay associated with incubation (Gilhooly, 2016; Sio & Ormerod, 2009). High cognitive demand tasks lead to smaller incubation effects but low cognitive demand tasks show stronger incubation effects than periods of rest. Immediate incubation also has a more positive influence on creative problem solving compared to delayed incubation.

The moment of creative insight within stage of illumination is the most extensively investigated process-specific phenomenon within both the psychological and neuroscientific domains (Gilhooly, Ball, & Macchi, 2015; Kounios & Beeman, 2014; Weisberg, 2015b). Insightful solutions that come about through a sudden perspective shift owing to overcoming functional fixedness induced by the problem elements are differentiated from incremental or non-insight solutions that are reached through logical analysis. The case for qualitative differences between the operations underlying insight and incremental problem solving comes from evidence showing that the former is more dependent on unconscious processes. For instance, verbalization of problem-solving strategies disrupts insight but not incremental problem solving (Schooler, Ohlsson, & Brooks, 1993), and metacognitive awareness of closeness to the solution space is far less predictable in the case of insight problems (Metcalfe & Wiebe, 1987). With regard to brain structures that are preferentially engaged in relation to insight in problem solving, the findings are quite heterogeneous. A region in the anterior aspect of the superior temporal lobe has been highlighted as being especially relevant (Jung-Beeman et al., 2004), as has the dorsolateral prefrontal cortex. Disruptions of the latter have been shown to lead to enhanced performance in insight problem solving (Reverberi, Toraldo, D'Agostini, & Skrap, 2005).

Just as with insight, several creativity-relevant mental operations have been scrutinized from psychological perspectives, including conceptual expansion, creative imagery, overcoming knowledge constraints, analogical reasoning, and metaphor processing (Finke et al., 1996; Ward, Finke, & Smith, 1995; Ward, Smith, & Vaid, 1997). These processes (detailed in Section 2.3 and Box 5.3) have also been investigated from the neuroscientific perspective where the overarching goal is to understand the neural and information-processing mechanisms that underlie creative cognition (Abraham, 2014a, 2018). Brain structures such as the anterior prefrontal or frontopolar cortex (Brodmann area 10), anterior lateral inferior frontal regions (Brodmann areas 45 and 47), and the dorsolateral prefrontal cortex (Brodmann areas 8, 9, and 46) are consistently implicated in different componential processes of creativity (Abraham, Pieritz, et al., 2012; Beaty, Benedek, Kaufman, & Silvia, 2015; Ellamil, Dobson, Beeman, & Christoff, 2012; Green, Kraemer, Fugelsang, Gray, & Dunbar, 2012; Limb & Braun, 2008). These brain structures are known for their critical role in relational and conceptual integration, as well as the access, monitoring, retrieval, and maintenance of conceptual knowledge (Badre & Wagner, 2007; du Boisgueheneuc et al., 2006; Ramnani & Owen, 2004).

Another dominant approach is to evaluate divergent thinking (many potential solutions to a problem) and convergent thinking (one correct solution to a problem) in creativity and look for similarities and differences between the two in terms of information-processing operations (see Box 2.2). For instance, convergent thinking has a negative impact on subsequent mood whereas divergent thinking enhances positive mood (Chermahini & Hommel, 2011). Induced stress inhibits divergent thinking but has no discernable impact on convergent thinking (Krop, Alegre, & Williams, 1969). Attentional depletion prior to creative performance improves fluency (increases the number of ideas generated) in divergent thinking but has no significant impact on convergent thinking (Radel, Davranche, Fournier, & Dietrich, 2015). Increased fluency in divergent thinking and reduced performance in convergent thinking was reported following the consumption of ayahuasca, a brew with psychedelic properties (Kuypers et al., 2016).

The neuroscientific evidence on this count is relatively sparse given that few studies have contrasted divergent and convergent thinking in creativity within the same experimental paradigm. Neuropsychological findings indicate that the brain structures and networks involved in both can be differentiated (Abraham, Beudt, Ott, & von Cramon, 2012) (Chapter 4). Divergent thinking has been the main focus of most studies and the default mode network (DMN) of the brain, which is highly active under conditions of rest and internal mentation (Buckner, Andrews-Hanna, & Schacter, 2008), has been consistently implicated (Abraham, Pieritz, et al., 2012; Beaty et al., 2015), as has the central executive network (CEN), which is engaged in situations that call for goal-directed action (Niendam et al., 2012).

2.1.5 Issues for Further Consideration

Two further approaches have been proposed following the "alliterative scheme," which now renders it possible to speak of the "six Ps of creativity" (Kozbelt et al., 2010). One was to approach creativity from the perspective of *persuasion*, as creative people tend to fundamentally alter the way people think and can therefore be regarded as persuasive (Simonton, 1990). The factor *potential* was also added to the mix to reflect the need to consider creative potential exhibited in situations (e.g., from the behavior of young children) where it would be difficult to demonstrate creative performance in the form of ostensible products (Runco, 2007a). These are relatively recent ideas and so they have yet to generate the kind of critical discourse or body of empirical work necessary to gauge whether they form whole approaches in their own right that can be added to the "four Ps" conceptualization or whether they can instead be subsumed under the existing framework with little restructuring.

Another point to note is that studies rarely adopt only one approach in their investigations on creativity. More often than not, a confluence of approaches is championed by investigations. Again, it was Rhodes who stated: "Each strand has unique identity academically, but only in unity do the 4 strands operate functionally" (1961, 307). An ideal case in point can be made by referring to an influential paper the title of which addresses this very issue: "Decreased latent inhibition [process approach] is associated with increased creative achievement [product approach] in high-functioning individuals [person approach]" (Carson, Peterson, & Higgins, 2003). Adopting a neuroscientific approach in the study of creativity in itself necessitates a confluence of approaches given that it is cross-disciplinary, and it allows for the added brain-based perspective in the study of creativity (Figure 4.1).

2.2 Assessing Creativity: Person Measures

In this section, an overview will be presented of some of the most widely used measures available to evaluate creativity using the person approach (Figure 2.2). These fall into two categories: divergent thinking test batteries and self-report measures.

2.2.1 Divergent Thinking Test Batteries

Divergent thinking test batteries are rooted in the psychometric approach, within which the purview of individual and differential psychology involves estimating an individual's mental capacities. Historically, the objective of adopting the psychometric approach was to be able to determine how creative capacity relates to intelligence (Plucker & Renzulli, 1999; Sternberg & O'Hara, 1999). Divergent thinking test batteries consist of a range of different tasks that are jointly scored to give (a) an overall creativity index, and/or (b) sub-scores in relation to specific creativity-relevant factors (e.g., fluency, originality). These are deemed to be tests of divergent thinking as they are open-ended with regard to the number of possible responses as well as the permissibility of the responses. The responses are subjective and qualitative in nature, and quantitative information is derived from them. This is in contrast to convergent tasks, which are, for instance, typically used in intelligence testing where there is only a single objective and correct solution that a person's problem-solving thought processes need to "converge" on (see Box 2.2).

The idea of measuring divergent idea generation was launched by the seminal work of Guilford, whose Structure-of-Intellect (SOI) model was the catalyst for subsequent theories in this domain as well as research using or adapting his tasks of divergent production (Guilford, 1950, 1967, 1970, 1975, 1988; Wilson, Guilford, Christensen, & Lewis, 1954). Guilford proposed three dimensions of intelligence that form a cuboid structure: operations (e.g., divergent production, convergent production, evaluation), content properties (e.g., symbolic, semantic, behavioral), and products (e.g., relations, transformations, implications). Divergent production was considered the most relevant for creativity, and its central factors included *fluency* (number of ideas), *originality* (uniqueness of ideas), and *flexibility* (category shifts in ideas) in idea generation, among others. These ideas and metrics were adapted in subsequent test batteries (Getzels & Jackson, 1962; Wallach & Kogan, 1965).

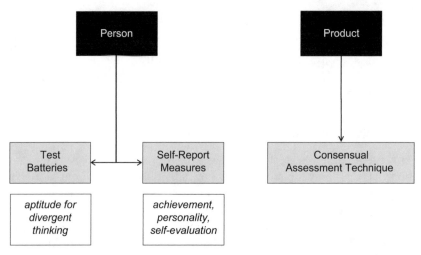

Figure 2.2 Measures of creativity using person-based and product-based approaches

The most widely used of these in current behavioral research is the Torrance Tests of Creative Thinking (TTCT) (Torrance, 1974; Torrance & Haensly, 2003). It includes verbal and non-verbal (or figural) tasks, which assess levels of fluency, originality, flexibility, and elaboration (details of ideas), as well as creative qualities such as expressiveness, synthesis, fantasy, humor, imagery, and visualization. The TTCT is also the most extensively studied divergent test battery in terms of its reliability and validity in assessing creative potential (Cropley, 2000; Kim, 2006a, 2006b; Plucker & Renzulli, 1999; Silvia et al., 2008; Swartz, 1988). Although it is not without its problems regarding such issues, the TTCT has proven to be a reasonably acceptable index of creative potential insofar as it is a moderate predictor of personal achievement (Runco, Millar, Acar, & Cramond, 2010) and creative achievement (Cramond, Matthews-Morgan, Bandalos, & Zuo, 2005). The critical issues of note associated with the TTCT and other divergent test batteries include variability in scoring as a function of the experience of the raters, and variability in performance as a function of testing conditions, problems in the scoring of originality, and the use of composite creativity scores over the more meaningful sub-scores (Baer, 2011; Kim, 2006a; Plucker & Renzulli, 1999).

2.2.2 Self-Report Measures

There are several self-report measures of creativity (LeBoutillier & Marks, 2003; Silvia, Wigert, Reiter-Palmon, & Kaufman, 2012). Examples include the Creative Personality Adjective Checklist, which estimates the degree of creativity-relevant traits exhibited by an individual (Gough, 1979), the revised Creativity Domain Questionnaire, which assesses an individual's subjective belief about their level of creativity in different domains (Kaufman et al., 2010), and the Creative Behavior Inventory, which provides an index of a person's creative behavior and accomplishments (Dollinger, 2003).

The most widely employed test of creative achievement is the Creative Achievement Questionnaire (CAQ; Carson, Peterson, & Higgins, 2005), which provides measures of domain-general creative achievement alongside domain-specific creative productivity in 10 domains: visual arts, music, creative writing, dance, drama, architectural design, humor, scientific discovery, inventions, and culinary arts. Among the critical issues associated with this test are the highly skewed distribution of scores, which is to be expected given the rarity of creative achievements, but which nonetheless pose challenges in terms of data analysis techniques and data interpretation (Silvia et al., 2012). Another important factor to consider is that the samples of most psychological and neuroscientific studies comprise university undergraduates. It is highly unlikely that substantial levels of creative accomplishment would be exhibited and evidenced by the earliest phase of young adulthood. The nature of sampling is a significant limiting factor of the CAQ, and findings associated with it need to be interpreted cautiously in light of this issue.

2.3 Assessing Creativity: Process Measures

In this section, an overview will be presented of some of the most widely used measures available to evaluate creativity using the process approach. There are three categories: convergent thinking tasks, process-general divergent thinking tasks, and process-specific divergent thinking tasks (Figure 2.3).

In the popular media, convergent thinking is often neglected and even portrayed as fundamentally uncreative. But this is mistaken as convergent thinking is an integral part of the creative process together with divergent thinking (Brophy, 2001; Cropley, 2006). The primary characteristic of convergent thinking problem-solving tasks is that there is only a single solution to the problem and problem-solving strategies are deployed to reach or converge on this solution. The creative component within convergent thinking tasks of creativity is that the problem-solving process is not linear, logical, or obvious (see Box 2.3). In tasks of

Box 2.3 Convergent Creative Thinking Tasks: Contemporary Paradigms

The Remote Associates Test (RAT) is the most widely used task of convergent thinking in creativity (Bowden & Jung-Beeman, 2003; Mednick, 1962). It is also one of the oldest tasks of creativity that are still in active use. A fair number of novel experimental paradigms using convergent tasks of creative thinking have been developed more recently. These fall under the category of *process-specific* convergent thinking tasks and all gauge the ability to glean novel semantic connections between seemingly unrelated concepts, which is a vital strategy that has been widely reported as significant in creative problem solving (Boden, 2004). Process-specific convergent thinking tasks include:

- *Analogical reasoning tasks* (Bunge, Wendelken, Badre, & Wagner, 2005; Green, Kraemer, Fugelsang, Gray, & Dunbar, 2010; Green et al., 2012; Wendelken, Nakhabenko, Donohue, Carter, & Bunge, 2008)
- *Conceptual expansion tasks* (Kröger et al., 2012, 2013; Rutter, Kröger, Hill, et al., 2012; Rutter, Kröger, Stark, et al., 2012)
- *Semantic association tasks* (Benedek, Könen, & Neubauer, 2012; Kenett, Anaki, & Faust, 2014; Mohr, Graves, Gianotti, Pizzagalli, & Brugger, 2001; Rossmann & Fink, 2010)

convergent creative thinking, problems need to be redefined or reframed, and the problem-solving process requires a perspective shift to move off the beaten track to find the correct solution (Ohlsson, 1984; Sternberg & O'Hara, 1999). The primary characteristic of divergent thinking problem-solving tasks is that there is no definable upper limit to the number of potential solutions that can be generated to solve the problem, and flexible problem-solving strategies are deployed to reach or diverge toward many different solutions.

2.3.1 Convergent Thinking Tasks

The most widely used task of convergent thinking is the Remote Associates Test (RAT), based on Sarnoff Mednick's (1962) idea that the creative process involves generating new and useful combinations from associative elements. In this task, participants are given a list of unrelated word triads (e.g., age–mile–sand) and asked to determine which fourth word is associated with each of them (e.g., stone)

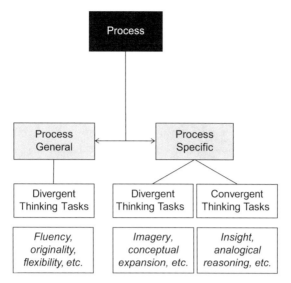

Figure 2.3 Measures of creativity using the process-based approach

so as to form a compound associate or compound phrase (e.g., stone age/milestone/sandstone). The original 30-item test has since been extended to a repository of 144 compound remote associates (Bowden & Jung-Beeman, 2003), which is widely used to investigate the process of insight in creative problem solving (Bowden, Jung-Beeman, Fleck, & Kounios, 2005). This is done by means of comparing cognitive or neural processing when performing remote associate problems that are accompanied by a feeling of insight ("a-ha" experience) upon solving compared to those that are solved without a feeling of insight (Jung-Beeman et al., 2004).

Insight in convergent problem solving has also been investigated by means of analytical problems, which can take on a multitude of forms – riddles, mathematical, geometrical, and manipulative (Weisberg, 1995). A classic example of a manipulative insight problem is the candle task (Duncker, 1945). In this task, participants are given materials (candle, matchbox, tacks) and required to find a way to fix a candle to a wall such that it burns safely without dripping wax on the ground (solution: empty out matchbox, use tacks to fix empty matchbox to wall, use empty matchbox as candle holder). Performance on insight analytical problems is contrasted with performance on non-insight or incremental analytical problems (Abraham, Beudt, et al., 2012). An example of a manipulative incremental problem task that could serve as a comparison to this insight problem is the Tower of Hanoi (adapted from Metcalfe & Wiebe, 1987). For the 3-ring version of this task, participants are instructed to find the fastest way to move the rings from the first tower to the third tower with the fewest possible moves (solution: seven moves) following a set of rules (e.g., only one ring can be moved at a time).

The singular advantage of convergent tasks is that, because they are objective, they are simple to score. The primary disadvantage is that the "creativity" associated with the tasks in question is often merely implicitly assumed with inadequate justification. For instance, in the case of testing the process of insight, the unquestioned assumption is that some problems are *de facto* insight problems while others are non-insight problems. But there is very rarely a check of whether the solving of an insight problem was actually accompanied by the feeling of insight. It has therefore been recommended that, when studying convergent creative thinking, self-report protocols should be employed such that participants are asked after each RAT or insight problem they solve to indicate whether the feeling of insight accompanied the problem-solving process (Bowden et al., 2005). This is to establish validity, that is, that the participants underwent a creative process while solving the task.

Another problem that is specific to the use of the RAT is that translated non-English versions of this test do not necessarily have the required fidelity to the original English version as they tend to be closer to free association tasks where more than one solution is possible (Abraham, Beudt, et al., 2012). Such fundamental differences are rarely acknowledged within the methods sections of papers, and are of real concern given that the specific solution search strategies associated with the RAT are constrained by the very nature of the task demands (Davelaar, 2015). More recent convergent creative thinking paradigms assess other creativity-relevant processes, such as analogical reasoning and conceptual expansion (see Box 2.3).

2.3.2 Process-General Divergent Thinking Tasks

Single tasks from divergent thinking test batteries, which were discussed earlier (Section 2.2.1), are often used in isolation to assess process-general divergent thinking ability. The phrase "process-general" is utilized here as these tasks estimate the general creative capacity or creative potential of an individual and stem from the psychometric approach. The most widely used divergent thinking task in this context is the Alternate Uses task (Guilford, Christensen, Merrifield, & Wilson, 1960; Wallach

& Kogan, 1965). Here, participants think of as many uses as they can for common objects such as a brick, shoe, or newspaper. The generated output is scored in terms of one or more of the following metrics: fluency (number of discrete uses), originality (degree of uniqueness of uses), flexibility (number of discrete categories of uses), and elaboration (level of detail associated with the uses).

There are a few different versions of this task in current use and these differ in terms of factors within task administration, such as task duration (brief times, lengthy times or untimed) and number of trials (usually ranging from 1 to 5). The choice of task administration protocol depends on the aims and objectives of the study. For instance, lengthy durations or untimed tasks often need to be used when evaluating creativity in clinical or atypical populations (Abraham, Windmann, McKenna, & Güntürkün, 2007), and the lack of time constraints is more conducive to originality in idea generation (Plucker & Renzulli, 1999; Wallach & Kogan, 1965).

Scoring protocols for the originality measure can also differ substantially between studies: (a) only focusing on extreme scores (uses generated by 1 or 5% of the sample) and disregarding the rest; (b) subjective evaluations of all uses by 2 trained raters, which are then averaged; (c) proportional weighting of each use by the frequency of its occurrence; and (d) top 2 uses selected by participants, which are then rated further (Guilford et al., 1960; Runco, Okuda, & Thurston, 1987; Silvia et al., 2008; Wallach & Kogan, 1965; Wilson, Guilford, & Christensen, 1953).

The advantage of process-general divergent thinking tasks is that they have been widely used across a range of contexts and there is a substantial repository of literature from which to infer consistent patterns. The chief disadvantage is that, just as in the case of divergent thinking test batteries (Section 2.3.1), the "apparent susceptibility of divergent thinking tasks to administration, scoring and training effects" is uncomfortably high (Plucker & Renzulli, 1999, 40). A troublesome example is the potential for fluency to act as a "contaminating factor" on originality scores, as the higher the fluency, the higher the originality (Plucker, Qian, & Wang, 2011). It is not always clear whether or when a corrective score (e.g., originality = originality/fluency) has been applied from the studies using this task, and fluency scores are rarely, if ever, partialled out when estimating effects in relation to originality. Also problematic is the emphasis on fluency-related findings, although originality and flexibility are more relevant indices of creativity (Runco & Acar, 2012).

2.3.3 Process-Specific Divergent Thinking Tasks

Process-specific divergent thinking tasks are rooted in the cognitive approach and these particular assessment tools prove useful when the aim is to gauge different components of the creative process (Abraham & Windmann, 2007; Finke et al., 1996). These components include conceptual expansion, overcoming the constraints of examples, and creative imagery, among others.

Conceptual expansion refers to the capacity to widen the boundaries of knowledge structures, a process that is at the crux of generating original ideas as novelty can only come about from broadening existing concepts to take on new elements. The first task to evaluate conceptual expansion was the animal task; here, participants are asked to imagine and draw an animal that lives on a planet that is very different from earth (Ward, 1994). The greater the degree to which the drawn animal differs in term of specific generic features of most animals on earth (bilateral asymmetry, lack of sense organs and appendages, presence of unusual sense organs and appendages), the greater the conceptual expansion.

Another process that has an impact on our ability to generate ideas is our capability to overcome the constraining influence of prior knowledge as it often gets in the way of our conceiving of an idea in a manner that is uncustomary, atypical, or distinct. This can be investigated by studying the effect of salient examples in the generation of new ideas (Smith, Ward, & Schumacher, 1993). When subjects are asked to generate novel ideas for toys after being shown exemplars of novel toys by the experimenter, the ideas they produce tend to conform to the ideas in the examples. This conformity is induced by exposing the participants to the same fundamental features across all the toy exemplars (e.g., ball, electronics, physical activity). The degree to which the ideas generated by the subjects incorporate these features from the exemplars is an indication of their propensity to override the constraining effect of recently activated knowledge when generating new ideas.

Creative imagery refers to the vividness of abstract imagination during the generation of an idea. The creative imagery task explores innovation and inventiveness under laboratory conditions (Finke, 1990). In the latter, participants are required to put together an object that falls into a predetermined category (e.g., transportation) using 3 figures from an array of 15 simple 3-dimensional figures (e.g., a sphere, a cone, and a cross). Participants are not allowed to change the essential form of the figures, but may vary the figures provided in any way with regard to size, orientation, position, texture, and so on. The invented object is then judged on two measures – originality, or how unusual the object is, and practicality, or how functional the object is.

The core advantage of process-specific divergent thinking tasks is that they allow a more precise examination of the neural and information-processing foundations of complex creative thought (Abraham, 2014a). The primary disadvantage is that, because they are context specific, it is unclear how the findings can be generalized to different domains of creativity.

2.4 Assessing Creativity: Product Approach

By and large, there has been only one dominant assessment tool within the product approach to investigating creativity (Figure 2.2). Stemming from a social psychological perspective of creativity testing, Amabile (1982, 1983, 1996) developed the consensual assessment technique (CAT) for evaluating creative products from different domains. Here,

a product or response is creative to the extent that appropriate observers independently agree it is creative. Appropriate observers are those familiar with the domain in which the product was created or the response articulated. Thus, creativity can be regarded as the quality of products or responses judged to be creative by appropriate observers. (Amabile, 1996, 33)

The CAT is the most widely utilized set of empirical protocols to gauge the creativity associated with products, and depends on experts' agreement or consensus concerning the same.

The main advantage of the CAT is its enormous flexibility; it can be adopted in a range of contexts and applied to numerous domains and product types, such as stories, collages, poems, musical compositions, mathematical equations, and personal narratives (Baer & McKool, 2009; Baer, Kaufman, & Gentile, 2004). Moreover, since the CAT is not tied to any particular theoretical framework, its validity is not threatened by changes in the dominance and veracity of different theories in the field (Baer & McKool, 2009). The key limiting factor is that, owing to its highly subjective nature, the validity of the ratings is exceedingly dependent on the level of expertise of the raters, as there are significant inconsistencies between the ratings of non-experts (Kaufman, Baer, Cole, & Sexton, 2008).

2.5 Issues for Further Consideration

You will notice that specific measures have not been outlined to assess creativity following the press/place approach. This is because the effects of place are typically studied as a mediating variable in terms of creativity.

So the effect on creativity in terms of person, process, or product can be investigated as a function of any press/place factor. These can take the form of distal press factors (evolution, zeitgeist, culture) or immediate place factors (direct environment) (Runco, 2007a). In fact, an alternative sociocultural and ecological five As framework (actor, action, artifact, audience, affordances) has been proposed as a contrast to the psychological four Ps (person, process, product, press) framework of creativity (Glăveanu, 2013).

Several measures of creativity have been outlined in the previous sections. Many lend themselves to being investigated from different perspectives as a function of the aims of the study, the set up of the experimental design, the rationale behind the metrics of interest within the selected creativity measure, and, as a consequence, the data analysis techniques that are employed to evaluate performance. With regard to general recommendations, reviews of divergent thinking tests have delivered the verdict that they are worth using to assess creative potential as they are indicative of creative achievement (Kim, 2008; Runco & Acar, 2012) but using more than one test is recommended to improve validity (Cropley, 2000; Kim, 2006a). An example of such a guideline being heeded in neuroscientific research is the use of a confluence of techniques – that is, a mixture of several divergent thinking tasks – and applying CAT protocols when evaluating the output to derive a composite creativity index (CCI; Jung et al., 2010). Running a battery of different divergent process-general and process-specific tasks on the same sample of participants and evaluating the similarities and differences in creative performance is another such approach (Abraham, Beudt, et al., 2012). The use of creativity tasks within neuroscientific studies has thus far been exceedingly heterogeneous as there are substantial differences in the experimental designs and tasks employed across the studies; this makes it difficult to glean any consistent picture of the neural bases of creative thinking (Arden, Chavez, Grazioplene, & Jung, 2010).

Finally, one of the more serious issues in the investigation of creativity is the very question of whether creativity can be measured at all. While creativity researchers have pet peeves over one or the other type of creativity test, the more critical concern is to come to terms with what we are measuring when we measure creativity. The influential account of different types of creativity argues for distinguishing between spontaneous and deliberate forms of creativity (Dietrich, 2004b). It is clear that, when we assess creativity under laboratory conditions, we are mainly assessing deliberate forms of creativity. Spontaneous forms of creativity are too ephemeral and unpredictable to be tested in a valid or reliable manner in controlled laboratory settings. It is absolutely vital that we are cognizant of and alert to the limitations of our perspectives and measures when we investigate creativity so as to avoid overgeneralizations and stay firm-footed on the path of real and accurate discovery.

Chapter Summary

- One can adopt different perspectives or approaches when assessing creativity.
- The person approach focuses on individual factors that impact creative ability.
- The product approach is used to evaluate any form of output in terms of quantitative or qualitative levels of creativity.
- The process approach is about uncovering the mental operations that are involved when we come up with creative ideas.
- The press/place approach focuses externally on environmental factors that influence creative ability.
- Measures of process approach are divided into convergent versus divergent thinking and, within the latter, on process-general versus process-specific forms.
- The creative achievement questionnaire is the most widely used measure within the person approach whereas the consensual assessment technique is the most extensively utilized measure following the product approach.

Review Questions

1. Can creativity be measured? And in what way?
2. Describe the six approaches used to investigate creativity.
3. How do process-general and process-specific tasks differ?
4. Which creativity approach is best suited to the neuroscientific perspective?
5. Can creativity be evaluated using divergent and convergent thinking tasks?

Further Reading

- Abraham, A., & Windmann, S. (2007). Creative cognition: The diverse operations and the prospect of applying a cognitive neuroscience perspective. *Methods*, *42*(1), 38–48.

- Amabile, T. M. (1982). Social psychology of creativity: A consensual assessment technique. *Journal of Personality and Social Psychology*, *43*(5), 997–1013.
- Arden, R., Chavez, R. S., Grazioplene, R., & Jung, R. E. (2010). Neuroimaging creativity: A psychometric view. *Behavioural Brain Research*, *214*(2), 143–156.
- Carson, S. H., Peterson, J. B., & Higgins, D. M. (2005). Reliability, validity, and factor structure of the Creative Achievement Questionnaire. *Creativity Research Journal*, *17*(1), 37–50.
- Plucker, J. A., & Renzulli, J. S. (1999). Psychometric approaches to the study of human creativity. In R. J. Sternberg (Ed.), *Handbook of creativity* (pp. 35–61). New York: Cambridge University Press.

CHAPTER THREE

Cognitive Explanations of Creativity

"All that we are is the result of what we have thought: it is founded on our thoughts, it is made up of our thoughts."

(Gautama Buddha)

Learning Objectives

- Understanding what is meant by cognitive explanations
- Distinguishing between the frameworks of individual differences in creativity
- Recognizing the intra-individual frameworks of creativity
- Outlining the creative process in terms of its stages
- Differentiating the creative process in terms of its operations
- Grasping the intricate relationship between knowledge and creativity

3.1 Explanations of Creativity

Ideas, frameworks, and theories that seek to explain how our creativity comes about are plentiful (Kozbelt et al., 2010; Runco, 2007b). But before we delve into them, let us take a moment to appreciate just how onerous this task of explanation is given that the fruits of creative labor can manifest in innumerable different ways. Take the well-known example of Wolfgang Amadeus Mozart, who was born in 1756 in Austria to a family steeped in musical tradition. Mozart began composing at the age of 5 and, in the following year, began performing as a child prodigy during his family's grand tour. His extraordinary talent was recognized right at the outset and, owing to his remarkable productivity, he occupied the spotlight throughout his lifetime until he died at the age of 35. In stark contrast is the case of Hilma af Klint, the Swedish artist and mystic, who was born a century later, in 1862, to a naval family with little interest in art. With her group of fellow female artists, *de Fem* ("The Five"), she engaged in experimental automatic drawing and produced works that are now considered to be among the earliest depictions of abstract art that predated the works of Kandinsky and Mondrian, the veritable masters of that form. However, af Klint was relatively unknown throughout her lifetime. She died in 1944 at the age of 81 and her body of work included 1200 paintings.

How do we explain the commonalities and differences in these manifestations of creativity? Apart from an exuberance of output, these cases appear to share little in common. But we need to look closer to tease apart the different factors at play, and to evaluate which of these are relevant to creativity.

Theories of creativity provide a foundation from which to explore and test our assumptions regarding the grounds for the multitudinous manifestations of creativity. An extremely useful overview was provided by Kozbelt et al. (2010), who classified theoretical explanations of creativity into 10 category-clusters: developmental, psychometric, economic, stage and componential, cognitive, problem solving and expertise based, problem finding, typological, systems, and evolutionary. *Developmental* theories focus on how the development of creative thinking skills over the early period of the human lifespan are mediated by individual and environmental factors. *Psychometric* theories derive from the measurement of creative aptitude in a valid and reliable manner, and consider its relation to other intellectual capacities. *Economic* theories estimate how market forces and cost–benefit analyses play a role in bringing about creative achievement. *Stage and componential* theories outline the stages of the creative process as it unfolds in the mind, and the multiple mental components that lead to higher creativity. *Cognitive* theories focus on characterizing creative thought processes as distinct from non-creative thought processes. *Problem solving and expertise based* theories seek to outline how domain-general cognitive skills and domain-specific expertise are drawn upon in ill-defined situations to generate creative strategies and solutions. *Problem finding* theories take a more open-ended and explorative view on the creative process as involving the discovery of novel problems that beg solutions. *Typological* theories distinguish between types of creator across different domains of human enterprise. *Systems* theories emphasize the need to consider the relation between multiple factors – cultural, personal, and societal – to understand creativity. *Evolutionary* theories examine how creativity arises as a function of evolutionary principles.

In the sections that follow, the focus will be primarily limited to cognitive theories or explanations as these are directly relevant with regard to developing an understanding of the neuroscience of creativity. In this context, it is worth bearing in mind that several of the constructs and theories that will be explored from the standpoint of cognitive explanations also overlap with those of other theoretical frameworks, such as psychometric theories (e.g., convergent creative thinking in remote associations), stage and componential theories (e.g., geneplore model), and problem solving and expertise based theories (e.g., insight, flow).

3.2 Focus on Individual Differences

What makes you more creative than some of the people you know and less creative than others? Is it possible to identify the factors that lead to greater creativity? This has been a central question that guides much of creativity research and a number of explanations have been put forward to explain the information processing mechanisms that underlie individual differences in creativity. Three dominant theoretical cognitive frameworks attribute such differences to (a) wider associative hierarchies in stored conceptual knowledge, (b) defocused attention during access to stored conceptual knowledge, and (c) reduced cognitive inhibition and arousal.

3.2.1 Knowledge Storage: Associative Hierarchies

The phrase "off the beaten track" refers to the search for novelty by moving away from well-known or well-trodden paths. This also applies to mental life, as generating a new idea requires, as a first step, existing knowledge from which to diverge. Theoretical ideas regarding conceptual knowledge and how it is represented and stored in the mind are therefore of paramount relevance to creative cognition, particularly in relation to unrelated concepts. This is a topic that unfortunately receives little focus compared to the gargantuan efforts made to chart the known conceptual space through similarities and related concepts in stored knowledge (De Deyne, Navarro, Perfors, & Storms, 2016).

In general terms, the central idea across different theoretical frameworks is that conceptual knowledge is represented within an extensive semantic network, in which concepts are represented by nodes that are linked to each other via connections such that closely related concepts are directly connected (Figure 3.1). Newer models emphasize that connections between nodes can be either excitatory, where the activation of one node increases activation of another node, or inhibitory, where the activation of one node decreases the activation of another node (Griffiths, Steyvers, & Tenenbaum, 2007).

Older models on which creativity-relevant theoretical ideas were based referred only to excitatory connections such that, when one concept is

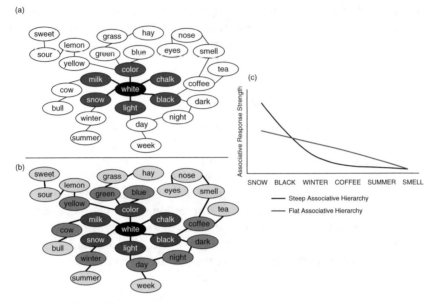

Figure 3.1 Knowledge storage model

(a) Steep associative hierarchies that characterize low-average creative individuals.
(b) Flat associative hierarchies that characterize highly creative individuals.
(c) Hypothetical associative hierarchies around the word "white." Adapted from
Mednick (1962).

activated, other concepts that are immediately linked to it are also activated
via spreading activation (Collins & Loftus, 1975; Collins & Quillian, 1969).
This explains why activation of a concept like "milk" would directly *prime*
(or lead to the faster retrieval of) strongly semantically related concepts
like "white" more than moderately semantically related concepts like
"exploit" and less semantically related concepts of "chimney."

This is where the creativity theorist Sarnoff Mednick steps in. He
postulated that what differentiates highly creative from less creative
people is the structure of their semantic networks in terms of strengths
in the connections between concepts in the network (Mednick, 1962).
The semantic network of a less creative person displays a *steep associative hierarchy* such that the activation of a concept (e.g., milk) in turn
leads to the activation of mainly closely associated representations (e.g.,
white, tea). So the hierarchy is steep because the concepts are strongly
related to one another given the narrow search space, as they fall within
similar semantic classes of node (e.g., color, beverage). A highly creative

person, in contrast, possesses a *flat associative hierarchy* such that the activation of a concept (e.g., white) also activates moderately and weakly associated representations (e.g., white, exploit). Having a flat associative hierarchy therefore allows the retrieval of more remote associations or representations. This gives one an advantage when attempting to go off the beaten track during the generation of ideas as access to unusual associations increases the likelihood of being able to come up with ideas that have a higher than average degree of originality. So the assumption here is that more creative people should demonstrate flat associative hierarchies as indicated by the performance on word association tasks, for example. So how does the evidence bear out in favor of this theory?

Mednick developed the Remote Associates Test (RAT), one of the most widely used tasks of convergent creative thinking (see Section 2.3.1), which involves reading word triads (e.g., same–head–tennis) and finding the solution word (match) that can form an association with each word within the triad via synonymy ("same" = match), compound word ("matchhead") or strong semantic association (tennis match) (Bowden & Jung-Beeman, 2003). It should be noted, though, that while performance on the RAT is taken as a measure of creative potential, the RAT does not in itself provide data that would constitute a test of Mednick's theory, and indeed that is not its purpose. There are actually few direct tests of Mednick's theory and the available evidence is mixed (Benedek & Neubauer, 2013; Brown, 1973; Gupta, Jang, Mednick, & Huber, 2012; Kenett et al., 2014). The use of computational network tools to generate association clouds from free association responses has indicated that less creative people appear to have more rigid semantic networks compared to highly creative people whose conceptual networks are more spread out (Kenett et al., 2014). The enhanced flexibility of thought that typically characterizes high creativity is associated with greater robustness of their semantic networks (Kenett et al., 2018). Other evidence, in contrast, has shown that higher associative fluency and more uncommon responses among highly creative people were not explained by differences in associative hierarchies within conceptual knowledge (Benedek & Neubauer, 2013). Indeed, the authors suggested that how knowledge is accessed might better explain differences in creative ability.

3.2.2 Knowledge Access or Retrieval: Defocused Attention

Another early creativity theorist who was interested in understanding individual differences in creativity was Gerald Mendelsohn. His focus was also on conceptual knowledge in explaining such differences but he

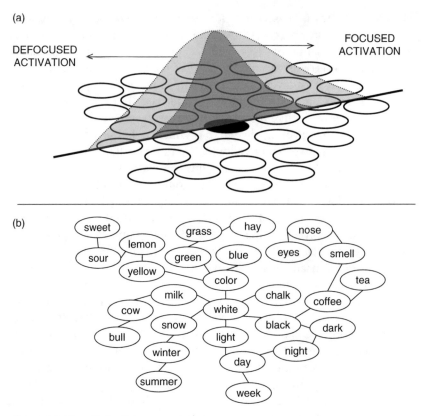

Figure 3.2 Knowledge access model

(a) Focused attentional spotlight characteristic of low-average creative individuals and defocused attentional spotlight characteristic of highly creative individuals. Based on Mendelsohn (1974). **(b)** Hypothetical semantic network around the word "white."

emphasized the role of access to or retrieval from conceptual knowledge (Mendelsohn, 1974; Mendelsohn & Griswold, 1964). What differentiated highly creative from less creative people was the type of attentional control they exerted when accessing knowledge (Figure 3.2). Relative to less creative people, highly creative people are characterized by a widened attentional capacity or *defocused attention*.

Following a spotlight metaphor, during the retrieval of information from memory the spotlight of one's attentional stream is tightly focused on accessing the target information. The thinner the spotlight, the smaller the focus of one's attentional stream and the fewer the number of conceptual elements retrieved. This is optimal for goal-directed action, as focused attention leads to higher accuracy in reaching a target as the number of distracters that are also retrieved will be low under such conditions. However, the number of associative elements present in one's attentional stream directly limits how many associations can be derived from combining those elements, which is consequential for generative tasks of creative ideation. A larger number of elements within one's attentional stream allows for a larger number of resulting combinations. For instance, if one is able to attend to only two elements at the same time (A, B), only one combination would arise (AB), but if one is able to attend to three elements at the same time (A, B, C), four permutations would be possible (AB, BC, AC, ABC). There is therefore an exponential increase in the number of potential combinations with each added element. So, according to this theory, highly creative people have defocused attention or a wider attentional spotlight that gives them access to more elements. Owing to this, they have a greater potential to generate more unusual ideas, as they have a wider array of elements that can be combined within the focus of their attention. Fluency is directly related to the uniqueness of a response as increased fluency is linked to an increased likelihood of more remote or unusual associations. Indeed, ideational fluency (number of responses) has been shown to be positively correlated with ideational creativity (Jung et al., 2015).

As Mendelsohn's ideas in relation to defocused attention are closely related to the following cognitive explanation account of individual differences in creativity (Section 3.2.3), the weighing of evidence in relation to this framework will be jointly discussed there. The reason for discussing Mendelsohn's account separately was due to the fact that his formulation was among the earliest to concretely emphasize the importance of the manner in which information from conceptual networks can be retrieved in relation to creativity and argued for a central role for *attentional control* in the same. It also pointed to the importance of operations that are relevant to *working memory* by highlighting that free manipulation of representations occurs within the attentional stream. This relates to important findings with reference to associative processing that have evaluated how low versus high cognitive load (or demands on working memory) differentially affects the remoteness of associations that are retrieved. For instance, high cognitive load negatively impacts the ability to retrieve remote associations by narrowing attentional control whereas, under conditions of low cognitive load, the activation of wider associations is an exploratory process by default (Baror & Bar, 2016). Such findings have important implications for how we necessarily conceptualize the interplay between knowledge access-based and knowledge organization-based accounts of creative ideation.

3.2.3 Attentional States: Disinhibition

Another prominent idea used to explain individual differences in creativity is that of disinhibition. This idea does not reflect a clear model in the classic sense of one theorist proposing a cohesive framework but is instead a constellation of very similar ideas that have been proposed either independently or co-dependently by several people. The terms that have been bandied around in this context include cognitive disinhibition, attentional disinhibition, latent disinhibition, diffuse attention, defocused attention, and overinclusive thinking, among others. Although the terms are varied, the phenomena they intend to capture strongly overlap, and the general underlying principles that are propounded are very similar. The central assumption here is that biased information processing in terms of poor attentional control or increased distractibility gives rise to an increased propensity for creativity.

These ideas have their roots in the psychoanalytic tradition. Ernst Kris (1952) proposed that creativity results from being able to effortlessly vacillate between "primary process" and "secondary process" cognition. Primary process cognition refers to free-associative, analogical, and concrete thought processes, which normally occur in states of distractibility like fantasy, reverie, and dreaming, but also sometimes feature during abnormal states, as in some forms of psychosis. In contrast, secondary process cognition reflects the abstract and logical thought processes that are grounded in conscious reality. The ability to be creative within this formulation occurs due to a "regression" to primary process states (ibid.). This enables wider associative thinking, which, in turn, allows for more novel combinations of elements.

Colin Martindale drew upon these and related ideas extensively in formulating his idea of the "conceptual–primordial cognition continuum," where states of mind can vary from one end of the continuum, marked by "ordinary, wakeful, reality-oriented, rational, problem-solving, conceptual cognition," to the other end, which extends "through several types of fantasy and reverie to [the] dreaming" of primordial cognition (Martindale, 2007, 1778). The further one moves away from goal-directed conceptual cognition, the more disinhibited, free-associative, open-ended, seemingly purposeless and irrational one becomes. Martindale also notes that first-person accounts from eminent creators across the arts and sciences have delivered a consistent message; namely, that states

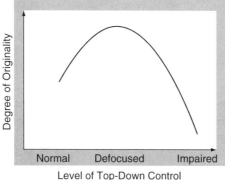

Figure 3.3 Disinhibition model

An inverted-U function is envisioned where too much and too little inhibition/ top-down control result in low levels of creativity. Defocused top-down control or moderate levels of disinhibition are associated with higher levels of creativity. Reproduced with permission from Abraham, A. (2014). Is there an inverted-U relationship between creativity and psychopathology? *Frontiers in Psychology*, 5, 750.

of disinhibited and defocused cognition outside of conscious control and not directly guided by purpose or design are most strongly associated with creative inspiration (Ghiselin, 1985). However, he emphasizes that the relation between the conceptual–primordial cognition continuum and creativity is best understood as an inverted-U function such that intermediate levels of disinhibition (as in states of reverie) are associated with enhanced creativity compared to extreme primordial cognition (as in states of dreaming) or conceptual cognition (as in states of externally-guided action) (Figure 3.3).

The idea that mild, but not severe, insufficiencies in attentional inhibition or inhibitory control can confer advantages in terms of creativity is one of the earliest tested hypotheses cited in the scientific literature (Dykes & McGhie, 1976); it has been frequently extended as a rationale to explain the link between mental illness and creativity (Abraham, 2014b; Carson, 2011; Eysenck, 1995). Indeed, much behavioral evidence has shown that decreased cognitive inhibition (or cognitive disinhibition) is associated with greater levels of creative ability or achievement (Carson et al., 2003; Dorfman, Martindale, Gassimova, & Vartanian, 2008; Kwiatkowski, Vartanian, & Martindale, 1999; Vartanian, Martindale, & Kwiatkowski, 2007; Zabelina & Robinson, 2010). However, opposing findings – that higher levels of creativity are associated with superior inhibitory control (Benedek, Franz, Heene, & Neubauer, 2012; Golden, 1975; Groborz & Nęcka, 2003) or no differences in inhibitory control (Burch, Hemsley, Pavelis, & Corr, 2006; Stavridou & Furnham, 1996) – have also been reported.

Owing to the extreme heterogeneity across studies in the use of tasks to measure creativity and cognition inhibition, it is not possible to evaluate the root of these divergent findings. Some researchers have emphasized that a more nuanced view is necessary, which distinguishes between creative potential and creative achievement, as well as considering flexibility in cognitive control as a key variable in this regard (Zabelina, O'Leary, Pornpattananangkul, Nusslock, & Beeman, 2015; Zabelina & Robinson, 2010). Another important factor to bear in mind is that most studies investigate a linear relationship between cognitive disinhibition and creativity and not the propounded inverted-U function in relation to the same (Abraham, 2014b; Martindale, 2007). This could go some way in explaining the extent of the disparities in the literature as the heterogeneity between studies in capturing different levels of cognitive disinhibition (from "mild" through "moderate" to "severe") is likely to be vast.

3.2.4 Summary: Individual Differences-Based Cognitive Explanations

The three models explicated here share commonalities in terms of the kind of information processing biases that have an impact on creative expression. All three accounts conceptualize creativity as the ability to activate remotely represented ideas and concepts; although this activation process is described with reference to the type of structural organization of long-term semantic memory networks in Mednick's flat associative hierarchy model, type of semantic retrieval wielded when accessing one's knowledge stores in Mendelsohn's defocused attention model, and levels of trait cognitive disinhibition in the third model. Central to all these conceptualizations is the significance of "loosened associational thinking," which is purportedly brought about by these different information processing biases. Unfortunately, as most creativity tasks are not designed to tease apart such closely coupled cognitive capacities, what one can conclude about the precise dynamics of the underlying mental operations when carrying out such tasks is limited. This is why the brain correlates of the same have yet to be established.

However, the putative brain correlates are worth exploring in more detail from a hypothetical standpoint. Which brain regions are likely to be the functional or structural neural markers of these biases in information processing? Given that the first two ideas – flat associative hierarchies and defocused attention – are centered on representation and access to conceptual knowledge, regions of the semantic cognition brain network (SCN) would be implicated (Figure 5.3). Brain areas that underlie the representation of multimodal conceptual knowledge (anterior temporal lobe or temporal pole: BA 38), the controlled retrieval of conceptual knowledge (ventrolateral PFC or inferior frontal gyrus, BA 45/47), or both (posterior lateral middle temporal gyrus) would be especially relevant (Binder & Desai, 2011; Jefferies, 2013; Lau, Phillips, & Poeppel, 2008). With regard to the disinhibition hypothesis, the central executive brain network (CEN) (see Figure 5.2) would be implicated. Regions that are critical in orchestrating inhibitory processes fall within fronto-striatal tracts and include the basal ganglia as well as dorsolateral and ventrolateral aspects of the prefrontal cortex (Aron, 2007, 2011; Munakata et al., 2011; Robbins, Gillan, Smith, de Wit, & Ersche, 2012).

3.3 Focus on Intra-Individual Dynamics

Another set of theories following the cognitive approach focuses on understanding the creative process itself within an individual in terms of the components and stages of the creative process. These theories seek to characterize the distinctions between creative and non-creative aspects of cognition (Abraham, 2013). Understanding the dynamics and specificity of the information processing mechanisms of creative and non-creative cognition, in terms of whether they are mutually exclusive, partially overlapping or wholly distinct, lies at the heart of such theories. Two of the most dominant cognitive frameworks that have been put forward to explain intra-individual aspects of creativity will be discussed in the following sections, namely, the Wallas model and the Geneplore model.

3.3.1 Stages of the Creative Process: Wallas Model

Graham Wallas outlined a four-stage theory of the creative process based on introspective reflections of great thinkers like Henri Poincaré (Ghiselin, 1985) on their thought processes when engaged in creative idea generation (Wallas, 1926) (see Box 3.1 and Section 2.1.4). The stages occur in the following order: preparation, incubation, illumination, and verification. The *preparation* stage is viewed as fully conscious, where the problem which triggers the search for an original solution or strategy is investigated thoroughly. The *incubation* stage, in contrast, is regarded as wholly unconscious with reference to the problem-solving process as no conscious effort is expended toward the problem during this period of rest, disengagement, or distraction. The *illumination* stage sees the sudden conscious emergence of the fully formed solution in one's mind in a flash of insight. The *verification* stage is associated with conscious deliberation with reference to evaluating and ironing out the details of the solution.

Box 3.1 From Stages of Creativity to Dual Systems Theories

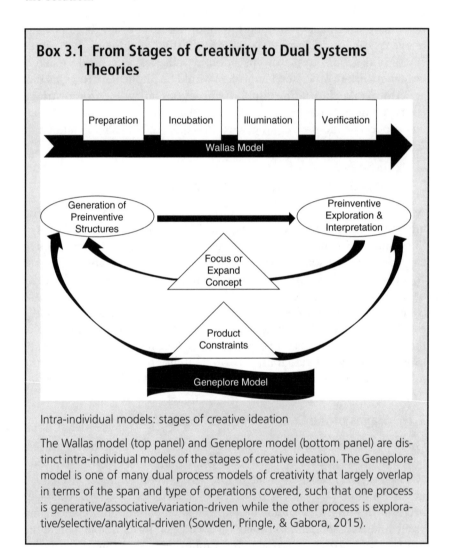

Intra-individual models: stages of creative ideation

The Wallas model (top panel) and Geneplore model (bottom panel) are distinct intra-individual models of the stages of creative ideation. The Geneplore model is one of many dual process models of creativity that largely overlap in terms of the span and type of operations covered, such that one process is generative/associative/variation-driven while the other process is explorative/selective/analytical-driven (Sowden, Pringle, & Gabora, 2015).

The Wallas model remains a popular and resonant idea despite strong challenges to some aspects of it, such as the lack of empirical support for the discrete stages (Lubart, 2001). Among the most controversial of these is whether an accurate understanding is in place about the level of conscious and unconscious processing across all stages. Some accounts have stressed that a closer reading of Wallas's ideas indicates that there are five stages; that is, a missing *intimation* stage takes place just prior to the illumination stage. These two stages each represent a different type of consciousness associated with the emergence of the insightful idea – fringe and focal consciousness, respectively (Sadler-Smith, 2015). However, these challenges to the Wallas model tend to suffer from the same problems. By deeming some stages to be conscious versus unconscious, what is missed is the fact that most aspects of information processing are unconscious insofar as we have no voluntary access to or awareness of the workings of these operations (Custers & Aarts, 2010). As this would be true across all stages of the creative process, the stages of preparation, verification, and illumination are undoubtedly also associated with unconscious processing, and to emphasize that they are not is erroneous.

Each of these stages receives differing levels of empirical engagement. One of the prominent issues of consequence in the preparation stage, for example, has been the association between knowledge and creativity (Weisberg, 1999) (see Boxes 3.2 and 3.3). Incubation is a relatively well-studied phase that is associated with conflicting findings: some studies point to the positive consequences of incubation in facilitating better creative problem solving (Dijksterhuis & Meurs, 2006), while others find no such effect (Segal, 2004). Contemporary investigations indicate that specific factors within the incubation phase need to be taken into consideration in order to understand the precise manner in which this phase influences problem solving. Such factors include the levels of cognitive demand associated within the task undertaken during the incubation phase and the delays associated with the incubation period (Gilhooly, 2016; Sio & Ormerod, 2009). Low cognitive demand tasks show stronger incubation effects than periods of rest, but at the same time, high cognitive demand tasks lead to smaller incubation effects, which is illustrative of an inverted-U pattern. Having a phase of immediate incubation has a positive impact on creative problem solving compared to having a delayed phase of incubation. The illumination stage is arguably the most widely investigated, as a large number of studies have focused on the phenomenon of insight, the cognitive operation that is integral to this stage (for further details, see Section 3.4.1). The verification stage is the least explored of the four, possibly because the cognitive processing occurring during this phase is assumed to be virtually synonymous with the kind of processing that accompanies many forms of non-creative problem solving.

Box 3.2 Knowledge and Creativity

In exploring the question of how much prior knowledge is optimal for creativity (Weisberg, 1999; Wiley, 1998), the "tension" view holds that an inverted-U function best characterizes the association. Intermediate levels of knowledge are held to provide the best conditions for creative ideation. Low levels of knowledge would be suboptimal as would high levels given that the latter can lead to an inflexibility of ideas and inability to change established schemas of thought. The "foundation" view, however, argues for a linear positive correlation in emphasizing that extensive knowledge is essential for creativity, as the ability to generate original ideas stems from a clear and comprehensive understanding of prevailing ideas. Another factor to consider is type of knowledge, as there are different types of contextual knowledge and these may have wide-ranging effects on different aspects of creative cognition (see Box 3.3). There is also evidence to suggest that we optimize our cognitive-search strategies in terms of both effort and variation depending on the distance between the knowledge domain in question and the individual's expertise. Analyzing solutions generated in a science competition revealed that, while high cognitive-search effort was common to both, individuals were more creative using high cognitive-search variation strategies across several different knowledge domains when their expertise was close to the knowledge domain being tested; in contrast, individuals were more creative using low cognitive-search variations in a focused knowledge domain when their expertise was far from the knowledge domain being tested (Acar & van den Ende, 2016).

Box 3.3 Types of Knowledge and Contextual Influences on Creativity

The influence exerted by knowledge, in the form of top-down control, can be separated into different types, including temporal or spatial, tonic or phasic, inhibitory or facilitatory, and arising through contextual priming or executive control (Hemsley, 2005). The last category is similar to the concept of cognitive contexts, relative to socioaffective contexts and perceptual contexts, in another classification (Park, Lee, Folley, & Kim, 2003). One type of cognitive context includes contextual effects provided by stored representations in long-term memory, which can be direct or indirect and explicit or implicit. Another type of cognitive context is the kind provided by task-relevant information, which is actively held in working memory.

Within creative cognition, three contexts have been differentiated (Abraham, 2014c; Abraham et al., 2007). *Active contexts* refer to the influence of knowledge that is best described as conditionally salient representations in short-term memory. This kind of top-down control influences performance in tasks that assess overcoming knowledge constraints. *Passive contexts* refer to the influence of knowledge that is best described as implicitly activated generic representations from long-term memory. This kind of top-down control influences performance in most creativity tasks, such as in those that assess conceptual expansion. *Goal-directed contexts* refer to the influence of knowledge that typically occurs during convergent creative thinking where there is only one correct solution and where both the initial state and the end state are stipulated. This kind of top-down control influences performance in tasks that assess insight in problem solving, for which the Einstellung effect (or mental set) is a well-known phenomenon that results in mental blocks and functional fixedness (Bilalić, McLeod, & Gobet, 2008).

3.3.2 Stages of the Creative Process: Geneplore Model

An alternative idea regarding the phases of the creative process was called the Geneplore (*Gene*rate and Ex*plore*) model (Finke et al., 1996; Ward et al., 1995, 1997) (see Box 3.1). The first phase is a generative one in which "preinventive" or internal precursor structures are produced. These preinventive ideas can be generated either in an open-ended exploratory manner or triggered by goal-directed inquiry. Depending on the task context and requirements, they can be simple or complex, conceptually focused or relatively ambiguous. This generative phase is followed by an explorative phase where the generated structures are evaluated in terms of their usefulness and feasibility. The generate-and-explore cycle repeats until a satisfying solution is reached in the form of a creative idea, which needs to be optimal given the product constraints on hand.

The initial generation of potential ideas or preinventive structures occurs through the mental synthesis of associations between conceptual structures in memory, the analogical transfer of information from one knowledge domain to another, and so on. Symbolic visual patterns, three-dimensional representations, mental blends of concepts, instances of hypothetical categories, and surprising verbal combinations are some examples of preinventive structures. The second phase of exploration and interpretation of the preinventive structures under consideration occurs by means of discovering the desired attributes and conceptual limitations of the generated structures, evaluating the structures from multiple perspectives, examining their emergent properties as well as their potential implications, and so on. Preinventive structures are then modified and regenerated in the light of the discoveries that have occurred.

It is important to note that both phases are associated with processes of discovery. In addition to outlining these stages of the creative process, this approach went further in specifying several mental operations that are centrally involved in creativity. Some of these processes of creative cognition are detailed in Section 3.4. So the focus of the Geneplore model (also known as the creative cognition approach) was to characterize the creative processes themselves, which would be the same for every person regardless of their inherent capacity for creativity. In emphasizing that several types of cognitive operation are involved in creative thinking, which can be assessed by examining normative cognitive processes under explicitly generative conditions, this was an approach that duly acknowledged the truly multifaceted nature of creativity. What was common to the various processes underlying creative thinking was that all of them drew on this generate-and-explore cycle.

3.3.3 Summary: Intra-Individual-Based Cognitive Explanations

The commonalities between the two models expounded here are that both constitute formulations about the stages of the creative process. However, their time scale is vastly different. What is implicit within the Wallas model is that the time scales involved are highly variable depending on the type of problem being tackled. The stages of the creative process can thereby range anywhere from minutes (such as tested within laboratory settings) to weeks, months, and years (as they occur in the real world). The time scale in the case of the Geneplore model is more short term, and as such lends itself to testing in laboratory contexts.

For both models, though, the brain basis of the different stages is virtually impossible to test as extant neuroscientific techniques can only be used in the context of testing over exceedingly brief periods of time (see Chapter 7). So there is very little that can be said about brain correlates of each of the stages of creativity or the transition between them. In the one well-known study that attempted to experimentally decouple the generative and evaluative phases of creativity, this was done by top-down instruction whereby participants were asked to generate ideas in a first phase and evaluate ideas in a second phase (Ellamil et al., 2012). What is important to note, though, is that while such experimental paradigms seem to have face validity, they neither acknowledge nor adequately take into account the essentially spontaneous nature of creative thinking where the generation of an idea is rapidly, immediately, and involuntarily accompanied by the evaluation of the idea. This is beyond our control under ordinary circumstances given the fundamentally associative, predictive, and proactive nature of neural and information processing (Bar, 2007; Bubić, von Cramon, & Schubotz, 2010). Indeed, artificially separating the two phases is not representative of the iterative nature of the generate-and-explore cycle that is central to the Geneplore model.

3.4 Creative Cognition: Relevant Operations

Operations relevant to creative cognition will be explored in this section. Some of these operations have been explicitly outlined from the perspective of the Geneplore model (Abraham & Windmann, 2007; Finke et al., 1996). These include conceptual expansion, overcoming the constraining influence of recently activated knowledge, and creative imagery. Others are directly pertinent to specific stages of the Wallas model (e.g., insight is relevant to the illumination stage). And still others are implicitly relevant to both (e.g., analogical reasoning, metaphor processing, flow). Some of these operations have been investigated from the neuroscientific perspective. The brain-based findings in relation to these processes are discussed in Section 5.3. In the subsections that follow, the theoretical views and empirical evidence will be discussed from the cognitive standpoint. These can inform and guide neuroscientific investigations of the same.

3.4.1 Insight

The experience of having a moment of "insight" is known to us all. It occurs with the sudden recognition of a previously unknown conceptual connection and it is experienced as the unexpected dawning of a new realization. Central to this experience is a fundamental restructuring or perspective shift in the manner in which one views a situation. Indeed, without the restructuring, there is no insight as it is the restructuring [parallax shift] of a context that leads to the discovery of new conceptual relations embedded within it. The process of insight as it applies to creativity has been extensively studied in the context of problem solving within both the psychological and neuroscientific domains (Gilhooly et al., 2015; Kounios & Beeman, 2014; Weisberg, 2015b).

Problems are situations for which an immediate solution is unclear. All problems are characterized by an initial state (the problem itself), a goal state (the solution to be reached), and the operations state (the path from the initial state to the goal state). The problem-solving process during non-insight-based problems (e.g., making oneself a cup of coffee) proceeds in a logical, incremental, and algorithmic manner. In contrast, the problem-solving process during insight-based problems (e.g., the RAT – see Section 3.2.1) is non-incremental and the solutions result from a perspective shift that allows one to overcome the "functional fixedness" induced by the problem elements. *Functional fixedness* refers to our overwhelming propensity to view an object or event only in terms of its most salient or common properties, and this *mental set* constrains our ability to consider alternate and unconventional perspectives (Duncker, 1945).

What evidence is there for fundamental differences between the operations underlying insight and incremental problem solving? Actually, evidence does show that insight in problem solving is more rooted in unconscious processes than is the case in incremental problem solving. Among some of the most well-known findings are that verbalization of problem-solving strategies during the problem-solving process disrupts the ability to solve insight problems but has no discernable impact on the solving of incremental problems (Schooler et al., 1993), and that metacognitive awareness of closeness to the solution space is less predictable in the case of insight problems relative to incremental problems (Metcalfe & Wiebe, 1987). Other metacognitive processes like intuition are held to precede the moment of insight (Zander, Öllinger, & Volz, 2016; Zhang, Lei, & Li, 2016). More recent evidence points to improvements in insight problem solving when covert (and overt) shifts of attention are experimentally induced to shift focus away from the external environment and toward one's internal milieu (Salvi, Bricolo, Franconeri, Kounios, & Beeman, 2015; Thomas & Lleras, 2009). While some have argued for an almost exclusive role of unconscious processes in facilitating insight during incubation in creative problem solving (Gilhooly, 2016), others have stressed the need to consider both conscious and unconscious processes (Yuan & Shen, 2016).

3.4.2 Analogy

"One should not think of analogy-making as a special variety of reasoning … rather, it's the very blue that fills the whole sky of cognition – analogy is everything, or very nearly so, in my view" (Hofstadter, 2001, 499). The phenomenon of insight discussed above results when one forges novel associations between two previously unconnected conceptual frameworks. But the word "association" does not adequately capture what this process entails. The term "bisociation" was coined "to point to the independent, autonomous character of the matrices which are brought into contact in the creative act, whereas associative thought operates among members of a single pre-existing matrix" (Koestler, 1969, 656). So the associative processes during the creative act occur across multiple planes at the same time. Associative mapping in contexts that call for creative thinking has been explored in relation to analogical relations between two dissimilar semantic domains (A:B::C:D) (Holyoak & Thagard, 1995). The distance that needs to be traversed is directly dependent on the extent of the semantic distance between the two domains. Processing relevant to near mapping analogies (e.g., furnace:coal::woodstove:wood) is typically contrasted with that of far mapping (e.g., furnace:coal::stomach:food), and findings specific to the latter are viewed as being relevant for creativity.

There is evidence to show that engaging in analogical reasoning biases and changes the information processing system and makes it more conducive to creative ideation. For instance, generating solutions for far analogies, but not near analogies, was accompanied by an increased transfer of relational mappings to a novel and unrelated transfer task (Vendetti, Wu, & Holyoak, 2014). Indeed, engaging in analogical reasoning can even alter the memory representation of a stored associative relation and enables memory recognition thereafter to be guided by the novel relational schema (Vendetti, Wu, Rowshanshad, Knowlton, & Holyoak, 2014), which comes about as a result of the seamless integration of the stored and novel relations (Blanchette & Dunbar, 2002). The fundamental importance of analogical reasoning has been emphasized in both artistic and scientific creativity (Boden, 2004; Dunbar, 1997).

3.4.3 Metaphor

A closely related form of associative processing to that of analogy is metaphors, which also lead to insights during problem solving (Keefer & Landau, 2016). The chief distinction between the two is that the relational structure between two domains in the case of analogy can only be mapped if specific parameters (e.g., direction of relation) are preserved. A metaphor is less constrained in its relational mapping between two dissimilar domains because it "operates by the imaginative realization and traversal of connections which exist in the 'latent field' of possible associations for the tenor of the metaphor" (Crowther, 2003, 83). This is why the metaphor "'Juliet is the sun' leads us to see various ways in which Juliet is, literally, like the sun. Since there is no stage at which all illuminating points of comparison have been exhausted, there is a sense in which a metaphor like this is ineliminable; something would be lost if we replaced it with a finite list of comparisons or other literal paraphrase" (Taylor, 1989, 71).

The most dominant idea in play regarding the nature of metaphor is that of George Lakoff, who holds that metaphorical thought is held to be independent of language (Lakoff, 2014; Lakoff & Johnson, 2003), and indeed that it organizes our knowledge structure by forming unconscious correspondences between concepts (for contrary views, see McGlone, 2007). Regardless of how exactly metaphor relates to language or whether it is the conceptual glue that binds our knowledge, the manner in which we process metaphors is relevant for creativity (Allan, 2016), which is why metaphor-based paradigms have been employed in the study of creative cognition (Beaty & Silvia, 2013; Kounios & Beeman, 2014; Rutter, Kröger, Stark, et al., 2012; Vartanian, 2012). Recent studies have provided evidence for the facilitative effect of engaging in the processing of metaphors on creative ideation. Mere exposure to novel metaphors leads to more creative interpretations of sentences that follow (Terai, Nakagawa, Kusumi, Koike, & Jimura, 2015), and embodying metaphors physically or psychologically leads to improvements in originality, fluency, and flexibility across tasks of convergent and divergent creative thinking (Leung et al., 2012).

3.4.4 Imagery

A great deal of anecdotal evidence points clearly to the relevance of imagery to creative invention and ideation, and this has been reported by eminent creators across the domains of science, art, literature, and music (Chavez, 2016; LeBoutillier & Marks, 2003). Tasks that tap creative imagery typically necessitate that abstract forms such as geometrical shapes be rearranged to form figures or objects in a particular category, and these inventions are assessed in terms of their originality (unusualness or novelty), practicality (relevance or appropriateness), and transformational complexity (Abraham & Windmann, 2007; Finke, 1996; Jankowska & Karwowski, 2015; Palmiero, Cardi, & Belardinelli, 2011).

Through the novel combination of simple parts, this kind of mental synthesis leads to creative visual discoveries (Finke & Slayton, 1988). In fact, performance of creative imagery tasks correlates positively with visuospatial ability (Burton & Fogarty, 2003; Palmiero, Nori, Aloisi, Ferrara, & Piccardi, 2015). Investigations of individual differences in creative imagery have revealed that people with an enhanced capacity for creative imagery are faster and better at reinterpreting ambiguous figures than those with a weaker propensity for creative imagery (Riquelme, 2002). Moderate and severe cognitive deficits in relation to inhibitory control and executive function have a negative impact on the ability to generate practical inventions in creative imagery (Abraham et al., 2007; Abraham, Pieritz, et al., 2012; Abraham, Windmann, Siefen, Daum, & Güntürkün, 2006).

Although most research on creative imagery has focused on the visual domain, imagery extends across and beyond all sensory domains, and each is associated with the capacity for imagery (Perky, 1910). This can extend cross-modally, which might be grounds for understanding why blind people have been reported to have greater originality in creative imagery (Johnson, 1979), and why engaging in mental imagery (visual and auditory) prior to music composition leads to greater compositional creativity (Wong & Lim, 2017).

3.4.5 Conceptual Expansion

At the crux of the formation of an idea that is considered original or novel is the meaningful addition of new elements or perspectives, or associations with existing concepts in our knowledge stores. This leads to a widening of the concept. So conceptual expansion is central to the formation of creative ideation across all domains (Abraham, 2014a; Abraham, Pieritz, et al., 2012; Ward, 1994). Let us take the example of the concept "moon." Its immediate meaning is derived from the fact of its being a celestial body but the concept has been coopted in several dissimilar metaphorically contexts (e.g., fertility symbol; werewolf controller; over the moon, i.e., to feel happy; to moon someone, i.e., to insult someone by baring one's backside) and it will continue to assume more connotations as long as the human species remains a communicative collective. Each added association to the concept "moon" will lead to the further expansion of that concept.

Conceptual expansion can be assessed in different ways. One is by having participants draw a meaningfully and semantically congruent connection between two previously unconnected ideas (Kröger et al., 2012, 2013; Rutter, Kröger, Hill, et al., 2012; Rutter, Kröger, Stark, et al., 2012) (also see Section 5.3.4). Another is by having participants expand a specific concept (Ward, 1994). The latter approach was the first adopted to assess conceptual expansion. In one of the earliest tasks designed for this purpose, participants were required to imagine another planet that is very different from Earth and then to imagine an animal that lived on this alien planet. Participants' drawings of their animal creations were then evaluated in terms of how far they departed from typical animals on earth in terms of their features. The more the alien animal displayed bilateral asymmetry of form, the lack of typical sense organs and appendages (e.g., eyes, legs) and the presence of unusual sense organs and appendages (e.g., infra-red sensitive pores, wheels instead of feet), the better the participants' conceptual expansion (Ward, 1994).

Behavioral evidence of conceptual expansion reveals that our concepts exert a powerful influence in determining the limits that are imposed during creative ideation. For instance, when asked to generate a creature with feathers, other category-congruent features (e.g., wings, beak) also accompanied the creature (Kozbelt & Durmysheva, 2007; Ward, 1994; Ward, Patterson, & Sifonis, 2004; Ward, Patterson, Sifonis, Dodds, & Saunders, 2002). The dynamics of creative imagination are therefore not chaotic but, in reality, quite structured by category relations. With regard to individual differences in conceptual expansion, advantages in the ability to do so are associated with populations that demonstrate mild insufficiencies in cognitive inhibition, such as in healthy participants with a high degree of psychoticism traits (Abraham, Windmann, Daum, & Güntürkün, 2005). But this advantage is lost in cases of extreme insufficiencies of the same, such as in populations that exhibit severe psychosis like schizophrenia (Abraham et al., 2007).

3.4.6 Overcoming Knowledge Constraints

Let us try out an imaginative exercise. Your task is to not think of a pink elephant. Are you able to do this? If not, don't worry. You are in good company as few among us are able to ignore this instruction. It's a simple yet powerful demonstration of the annoying fact that the mere instruction to not think about something salient or that could grab your attention gets in the way of you being able to do so. One of the biggest impediments when trying to generate a novel idea in a specific context is the difficulty in overcoming the influence wielded by our existing knowledge about that context (see Box 5.2). This is true across all contexts of creative ideation. In certain situations, though, like that of the pink elephant, the constraining context actively impinges on one's ability to think of something different, which in turn affects the capacity to create something new. In order to perform well, one needs to overcome the constraining influence imposed by this recently activated knowledge that is conveyed in the form of salient information. This is almost a reverse situation of a working memory task. In tasks of working memory, salient information has to be maintained in mind in order to perform optimally. The opposite is true in the case of overcoming knowledge constraints in creative cognition, as salient information needs to be ignored in order to perform well (Chrysikou & Weisberg, 2005; Marsh, Landau, & Hicks, 1996; Smith et al., 1993). In fact, being very distractible confers a substantial advantage in such a context. Creativity comes about by zoning in on task relevance over salience, and our "executive control system needs to be biased by salience but to override salience when something less intense, surprising, or emotional is more task-relevant" (Perlovsky & Levine, 2012, 296).

For instance, when asking participants to invent a completely new toy, showing participants distracting exemplars of novel toys engineered to have key features in common led to the invented toys bearing more similarity to the examples (Smith et al., 1993). But populations that are distractible owing to insufficiencies at the level of inhibitory control, such as healthy participants with elevated levels of schizotypal traits, adolescents with attention deficit hyperactivity disorder (ADHD) and neurological patients with lesions of the basal ganglia, show superior performance to matched control groups in creative ideation under these conditions (Abraham et al., 2007, 2006; Abraham, Beudt, et al., 2012). This is an example of an information processing bias (cognitive disinhibition), which confers a disadvantage in contexts of non-creative cognition (goal-directed attentional control) but an advantage in generative contexts of creative cognition.

3.4.7 Flow

The experience of flow has been described as "an almost automatic, effortless, yet highly focused state of consciousness" (Csikszentmihalyi, 1997), which is associated with optimal performance across all creative endeavors in writing, music, the fine arts, and the performance arts. A flow state occurs when specific dynamics between internal and external conditions are met while engaging in a sensorimotor task. Deep immersion or absorption in the task as well as high motivation and passion during its performance are some of the critical parameters that are prerequisites for the flow experience. The task itself needs to be challenging at a level that is perfectly matched to one's current ability and for which one receives immediate feedback during performance. One of the core features of flow is the absence of a clear sense of time when having this "peak experience," accompanied by a state of absolute contentment in the moment. The most prominent theoretical framework to explain flow experience is the "transient hypofrontality" hypothesis (Dietrich, 2004a), which emphasizes the critical role played by implicit and unconscious information processing and neural systems in facilitating the experience of flow. This is believed to occur as a result of a temporary weakening of executive or cognitive control, as orchestrated by the frontal lobe, over other cognitive and neural systems (see Section 5.2.2).

The importance of perceptual and mental feedback in the experience of flow as well as its influence on motivational perseverance and positive affect has received some empirical support (Cseh, Phillips, & Pearson, 2015, 2016). The experience of flow can occur simultaneously across individuals who perform together, which results in a state of combined flow or group flow such as during musical jam sessions (Hart & Di Blasi, 2015). However, the conditions that lead to flow differ considerably across domains (Cseh, 2016). Even within specific domains of haptic performance, accounts of flow "differ between activities that differ in their haptic or performative nature but are similar among haptically similar activities" (Banfield & Burgess, 2013, 275). It is as yet unclear precisely how flow relates to creative performance or achievement. Some of the evidence suggests that it is mainly primarily linked to self-perception of competence (Cseh, 2016), while other sources show a clear correspondence between the experience of flow and creativity (Byrne, MacDonald, & Carlton, 2003; Chemi, 2016; MacDonald, Byrne, & Carlton, 2006). Individual differences in the experience of flow are not associated with intelligence (Ullén et al., 2012); they are, however, positively linked to personality traits such as novelty-seeking, persistence and self-transcendence, and negatively associated with self-directedness (Teng, 2011).

3.5 Issues for Further Consideration

Several important operations of creative cognition were outlined in Section 3.4. While this is not an exhaustive list, the most pertinent processes in relation to neurocognitive investigations of creativity have been covered. Although it is as yet not possible to outline precisely how these operations interact with each other, what is clear is that they do and even strongly overlap. Tasks and experimental designs need to be precisely tailored in order to capture the process in question. Merely defining conditions as creative and uncreative is unhelpful if the processes being targeted are not explicitly outlined. In this context, what needs to be reckoned with is the issue of the "path-of-least-resistance," which is the overwhelming tendency – possibly due to our cost-effective brains – to take the least cognitively demanding route available when faced with situations that call for information processing (Finke et al., 1996; Ward, 1994).

There are examples in the creativity literature that demonstrate how the same task can be implemented differently across experimental designs to tap different operations of interest. For instance, contrasting brain activity and behavioral indices in relation to performance during the Alternate Uses task (e.g., think of as many uses as you can for the object "newspaper") and the Object Location task (e.g., think of as many objects as you can that belong in the location "office") reveals key insights about the neural basis of conceptual expansion (alternate uses > object location) because only the former necessitates the expansion of conceptual structures (Abraham, Pieritz, et al., 2012). Findings relevant to overcoming knowledge constraints were uncovered in an experimental design in which participants were tasked with carrying out the Alternate Uses task (e.g., think of as many uses as you can for the object "shoe") but their phase of creative ideation was preceded by salient examples of unusual uses generated for that object (e.g., plant pot) compared to non-salient examples of common uses generated for that object (e.g., stamp on an insect) (Fink et al., 2012). So, by modifying either the conditions surrounding a creativity task or the parameters of the task itself in inventive ways, one can better uncover the neural and information processing mechanisms underlying creative cognition. This, in turn, will lead to deeper and better-informed cognitive explanations of creativity.

[handwritten margin note: creativity as goal instead of process]

Chapter Summary

- Cognitive explanations are directed at understanding the mental operations or processes that are central to creativity.
- The associative hierarchies model, the defocused attention model, and the disinhibition model are explanations of individual differences in creativity.

- Individual differences-based models locate cognitive biases in organization of knowledge, retrieval of knowledge, or levels of cognitive disinhibition.
- The Wallas model and the Geneplore model are explanations of the dynamics of creative ideation within each individual.
- Intra-individual models outline the stages and components of the creative process across different contexts.
- The most widely investigated operations of creative cognition that bear relevance to the neuroscience of creativity include insight, analogy, metaphor, imagery, conceptual expansion, overcoming knowledge constraints, and flow.
- All cognitive explanations zone in on the relevance of conceptual knowledge in creative ideation across different types of context of generativity.

Review Questions

1. In what way are cognitive explanations similar to and different from other theoretical frameworks?
2. What are the commonalities and distinctions between the individual differences-based frameworks of creativity?
3. What differentiates individual differences and intra-individual accounts of creativity?
4. Summarize different conceptualizations of stage theories. Identify which operation(s) of creative cognition are relevant to stage theories.
5. What are the similarities and differences between each of the different operations of creative cognition in terms of temporal factors, spatial contexts, and stimulus/response modalities?

Further Reading

- Abraham, A., & Windmann, S. (2007). Creative cognition: The diverse operations and the prospect of applying a cognitive neuroscience perspective. *Methods, 42*(1), 38–48.
- De Deyne, S., Navarro, D. J., Perfors, A., & Storms, G. (2016). Structure at every scale: A semantic network account of the similarities between unrelated concepts. *Journal of Experimental Psychology: General, 145*(9), 1228–1254.

- Finke, R. A., Ward, T. B., & Smith, S. M. (1996). *Creative cognition: Theory, research, and applications*. Cambridge, MA: MIT Press.
- Kozbelt, A., Beghetto, R. A., & Runco, M. A. (2010). Theories of creativity. In J. C. Kaufman & R. J. Sternberg (Eds.), *The Cambridge handbook of creativity* (pp. 20–47). Cambridge: Cambridge University Press.
- Runco, M. A. (2007). *Creativity: Theories and themes: Research, development, and practice*. Amsterdam: Elsevier Academic Press.

CHAPTER FOUR

Brain-Based Global Explanations of Creativity

"Civilization occurs and maintains itself when the two forces – the striving and the ordering – approach equipoise."

(Clark Emery, quoted in Lewis Hyde's *The Gift*)

Learning Objectives

- Delineating the physiological approach to creativity
- Understanding the persistent notion of the creative right brain
- Grasping the relation of reduced concept-driven/top-down control to creativity
- Recognizing models of interacting brain networks in creativity
- Distinguishing between evolutionary models of creative neurocognition
- Evaluating the advantages and disadvantages of global explanations

4.1 The Physiological Approach to Creativity

We learned in Chapter 2 about approaches to studying creativity in terms of the person, place, process, and product (P-approaches). So what kind of approach is one taking when one seeks to answer questions that have to do with the brain basis of creativity? One way to think about brain-based approaches is that it is an extension of the "process approach" to exploring creativity. After all, the process approach is about understanding mental operations that underlie creative thinking, and the nervous system is the physical hardware through which these processes are instantiated. However, as we will see within this and later chapters in the book, the correspondences between operations of the mind and operations of the nervous system are far from linear (Dietrich, 2015).

Take the example of the process of "insight," which we often experience when we try to solve a problem for which a solution is not readily apparent. After a period of trying to work out the problem, often a solution will just simply pop into our minds, somewhat unexpectedly and seemingly out of the blue. This phenomenological experience (the "a-ha" feeling or the "eureka" effect) occurs as a result of a sudden perspective shift that allows for the restructuring of a problem and consequently leads to a solution. The operation of this mental process, which is highly relevant to creativity, is not consistently localizable in any one specific site in the brain. In fact, not only do the range of brain regions involved in the experience of insight *only partially overlap* between studies, but each of these regions is also *not exclusive* to insight-specific information processing as other non-insight-specific cognitive functions also recruit the very same brain regions (Dietrich & Kanso, 2010).

Moreover, it is possible to investigate issues central to the P-approaches to creativity through the lens of neuroscience, specifically, and physiology, generally. For instance, investigations following the "person approach" consistently identify the relevance of specific traits like "openness to experience" and "intellect" to creativity (Kandler et al., 2016; Kaufman et al., 2016). Neuroscientific studies have, in turn, sought to identify how the relation between creative performance and brain structures is influenced by such person-based factors (Jauk et al., 2015; Li et al., 2015).

So a mere extension of the "process approach" to include brain-based perspectives would not only be too simplistic but also erroneous. The adoption of a biological or neuroscientific or nervous system-based perspective in the study of creativity is unique in terms of its singular complexities and questions. There are ample grounds to argue that this "physiological approach" is a unique and fruitful one as it has led to fundamental insights in the way we understand creativity that were not obvious from a purely person, place, product, or process-based study of the same. Indeed, the book you are reading is a testament to this claim. It is indeed serendipitous, then, that the word "physiology" fits the alliterative "P" scheme of the approaches (Figure 4.1).

The physiological approach to understanding creativity has a very long tradition, beginning in the 1940s when investigations were conducted to examine the consequences to creativity – positive, negative, or unchanged – of prefrontal leucotomies (Ashby & Bassett, 1949; Hutton & Bassett, 1948; Reitman, 1947); a controversial procedure that involved severing the connections to and from the prefrontal cortex. The 1970s and 1980s saw the use of electroencephalography (EEG) to measure the type and pattern of brain activity exhibited during creative thinking (Martindale & Hasenfus, 1978; Martindale & Hines, 1975; Orme-Johnson & Haynes, 1981). Fast forward to the present day and the latest trend in the physiological approach to understanding creativity is to characterize the mechanisms underlying the same from the context of brain networks (Abraham, 2014a; Beaty, Benedek, Silvia, & Schacter, 2016;

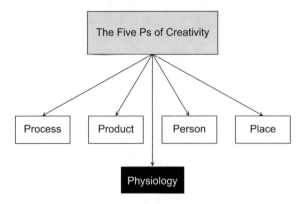

Figure 4.1 The Five Ps of creativity

A modification of Rhodes (1961) Four Ps model to include the physiological approach

Jung, Mead, Carrasco, & Flores, 2013). The range of paradigms, tasks, and techniques that have been used in the physiological approach have led to a diverse constellation of findings, and these have been used in different ways to "explain" the basis of creativity from the perspective of the nervous system (Jung & Vartanian, 2018; Vartanian, Bristol, & Kaufman, 2013). The physiological approach to creativity has explored the relation of creative engagement to peripheral nervous system activity, such as enhanced sympathetic cardiac activity during divergent thinking (Silvia, Beaty, Nusbaum, Eddington, & Kwapil, 2014) and increased pupil dilation in relation to music-induced aesthetic "chills" (Laeng, Eidet, Sulutvedt, & Panksepp, 2016). However, as the vast majority of empirical investigations and theories concerning such physiological correlates of creative thinking are focused on the central nervous system, and the brain in particular, this chapter will explore brain-based explanations of creativity. These can fall into one of two categories: global and local (Abraham, 2018). Global explanations of creativity will be covered in this chapter.

Explanations regarding the physiological basis of creativity that center on the workings of large and widely dispersed systems in the brain are referred to as "global" in the context of this book. Global explanations have two key features in common: they typically draw on dualistic or triadic models of brain function, and these functions map on to large brain networks (e.g., DMN) or minimally differentiated large brain structures (e.g., left versus right hemisphere). Let's explore the basis of the dual notions first.

4.2 Dual-Factor Models

Many of the theoretical frameworks afloat in psychology are essentially dualistic characterizations that conceptualize the human mind as having two general purpose systems that facilitate various functions of perception, action, emotion, and cognition (Evans, 2008; Evans & Stanovich, 2013; Schneider & Shiffrin, 1977). We speak of *explicit versus implicit systems* (attitudes: Rydell & McConnell, 2006; long-term memory: Squire, 1992); *top-down versus bottom-up processes* (visual attention: Kastner & Ungerleider, 2000; decision making: Miyapuram & Pammi, 2013); *spontaneous versus deliberate operations* (play: Pesce et al., 2016; mind-wandering: Seli, Risko, Smilek, & Schacter, 2016); *automatic versus controlled processes* (behavior: Hikosaka & Isoda, 2010; language: Jeon & Friederici, 2015); *unconscious versus conscious operations* (goal-directed thinking: Dijksterhuis & Aarts, 2010; emotion: Smith & Lane, 2015); *intuitive versus analytical styles* (problem solving: Pretz, 2008; decision making: Rusou, Zakay, & Usher, 2013); *reflexive versus reflective systems* (action control: Lengfelder & Gollwitzer, 2001; social cognition: Satpute & Lieberman, 2006; learning: Weiskrantz, 1985); and many more.

At the heart of dual-process and dual-systems theories in psychology and neuroscience is the notion that the operations of the mind can be classified as undertaking one of two broad modes of information processing. One mode is automatic, implicit, unconscious, bottom-up, spontaneous, intuitive, or reflexive. The other is controlled, explicit, conscious, top-down, deliberate, analytical, or reflective. Such conceptualizations have been extended and applied within theoretical frameworks that seek to explain creativity. The opposing modes are referred to as primary process-based, right brain-based, open-mode, generative, associative, spontaneous, or divergent on one hand, and secondary process-based, left brain-based, closed-mode, explorative, evaluative, executive, deliberate, or convergent on the other hand (Abraham, 2014a; Beaty, Silvia, Nusbaum, Jauk, & Benedek, 2014; Dietrich, 2004b; Finke, 1996; Finke et al., 1996; Jung et al., 2013; Martindale, 1999; Taft & Rossiter, 1966). The three most dominant of these frameworks are explored in more detail below (Figure 4.2).

4.2.1 Right Brain over Left Brain

To date, the most ubiquitous notion in our understanding of the brain basis of creativity is that the right hemisphere in the human brain is the seat of creativity. The idea of the "creative right brain" is a powerful one

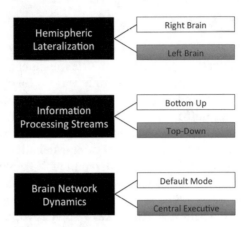

Figure 4.2 Dual-factor models

as it is extremely resistant to any form of revision and has proved to be virtually immovable from cultural consciousness. This is why, across domains of human enterprise, this understanding of the creative right brain is held as fact, and it informs lay beliefs about what we need to do to nurture our creativity to aid us personally and professionally (e.g., Edwards, 1982; Freed & Parsons, 1998). So is there any truth to this enduring idea of the creative right brain versus the uncreative left brain?

The differences in the functional roles played by the two hemispheres of the brain are primarily informed by split-brain studies on animals and humans that have revealed that the two hemispheres are quite separable in their functionality in many ways (Gazzaniga, 1967, 2000; Sperry, 1961). Split-brain patients undergo corpus callosotomies in order to mitigate the severity of epileptic seizures. In this surgical procedure, the corpus callosum, which is the white matter tract that connects the left and right hemispheres of the brain, is severed in part or completely. The functional specializations of the two disconnected hemispheres can thereby be assessed in split-brain patients.

Several studies have consistently revealed that lateralization of function is most apparent in language and perception where "the left hemisphere has marked limitations in perceptual functions and … the right hemisphere has even more prominent limitations in its cognitive functions" (Gazzaniga, 2000, 1294). While the disconnected left hemisphere can comprehend and produce language, the disconnected right hemisphere has lexical knowledge but only limited grammatical knowledge. The right brain, in turn, shows superiority for perceptual grouping processes and matching for visual stimuli. Such patterns have also been confirmed when evaluating information processing in the intact brain. In fact, studies have even indicated that the two hemispheres can be differentiated in terms of their functional patterns of communication. The left hemisphere demonstrates "a preference to interact more exclusively with itself, particularly for cortical regions involved in language and fine motor coordination," whereas cortical regions of the right hemisphere "involved in visuospatial and attentional processing interact in a more integrative fashion with both hemispheres" (Gotts et al., 2013, E3435).

Interestingly, the functionality of the left and right hemispheres has also been distinguished in terms of their "approaches" to information processing. The left hemisphere is seen as an interpreter and hypothesis generator during problem solving, whereas the right hemisphere is seen as an accurate record keeper of the current situation based on the simple frequency of events:

The right hemisphere maintains a veridical record of events, leaving the left hemisphere free to elaborate and make inferences about the material presented. In an intact brain, the two systems complement each other, allowing elaborative processing without sacrificing veracity. (Gazzaniga, 2000, 1317)

The functional lateralization of creativity has mainly been investigated in people with intact brains, and what is typically assessed is which hemisphere is more dominant or active in relation to creativity. The means by which this is determined can be "relatively direct" (e.g., patterns of brain engagement during creative thinking as engaging left, right, or bilateral hemispheric activity) or "relatively indirect" (e.g., determining levels of hemispheric dominance on a behavioral task of perceptual or language function and correlating this with behavioral performance on creativity tasks). The veracity of the creative right brain hypothesis is a virtual battleground for creativity researchers. There is vigorous opposition to the idea (Dietrich, 2015; Zaidel, 2013b) on account of the fact that the evidence thus far is ambiguous or mixed at best (Mihov, Denzler, & Förster, 2010). Contemporary advocates of the idea mainly lean on the behavioral evidence that indicates a right hemisphere bias for metaphor processing and other aspects of cognition that benefit from wider, more fluid, or "coarse semantic coding" of incoming stimuli (Beeman & Bowden, 2000; Kounios & Beeman, 2014).

So how does one decide between these rival viewpoints? Indeed, how can weighing of the same evidence lead to opposing conclusions?

Is it possible that, in trying to deliver a binary verdict on this hypothesis, some fundamental features of this line of research have escaped notice?

When perusing the literature that has been used to promote the idea of the creative right brain, it becomes apparent that most derive from relatively indirect (and largely behavioral) investigations of functional lateralization in relation to creativity. Moreover, relatively direct investigations using functional brain imaging of patterns of brain activity during visual and verbal forms of "divergent creative thinking" (where there are many potential responses/answers/solutions in a given context) have not supported the right brain hypothesis (Abraham, Pieritz, et al., 2012; Aziz-Zadeh, Liew, & Dandekar, 2012). In fact, the selectivity of right hemisphere processing has largely been reported in relation to "convergent creative thinking" (where there is only one potential response/answer/solution in a given context), and specifically in relation to the experience of "insight" during problem solving (Jung-Beeman et al., 2004). So the nature of the context in which creative idea generation is called for (here, the creativity task being employed and the mental operations involved during task engagement) cannot be disregarded. For more information on divergent versus convergent forms of creative thinking, refer to Section 2.1.4).

The persistence of the creative right brain idea is altogether remarkable, especially when considering that even the earliest advocates of lateralization research highlighted the importance of *both* hemispheres in creativity (Bogen & Bogen, 1969; Hoppe, 1988; Miran & Miran, 1984). This emphasis is also evident among contemporary voices (Goel, 2014; Gold, Faust, & Ben-Artzi, 2012; Lindell, 2011), with many pointing to the additional need to consider individual differences in creativity. For instance, more creative subjects tend to exhibit bilateral hemispheric activity whereas less creative subjects show more right lateralized activity (e.g., Atchley, Keeney, & Burgess, 1999; Carlsson, Wendt, & Risberg, 2000). Indeed, when estimating differences in the structure of brain networks using Bayesian procedures, it has been shown that "highly creative individuals display a higher propensity to form inter-hemispheric connections" (Durante & Dunson, 2016).

So, while there is a powerful resonance to the idea that mental operations specific to the right brain are more relevant for creativity, the evidence clearly indicates that no easy conclusions can be made about the nature of hemispheric differences as a function of creativity. While information processing in relation to different aspects of creative cognition (e.g., insight, conceptual expansion) may be biased with regard to hemispheric lateralization, regions in both hemispheres are involved in creativity.

4.2.2 Reduced Concept-Driven Thought or Top-Down Control

Another powerful idea that has been put forward to explain why some people are more creative than others is that dysfunctions of the mind can give rise to creativity. The logic behind this view is as follows. One of the classical theoretical divisions in our understanding of the mind is that top-down and bottom-up systems work in unison during the processing of any information (e.g., viewing a picture of a lotus). Bottom-up information processing is "sensory-driven" and therefore refers to processing that is driven by the characteristics of the stimulus (e.g., the hue and structure of the petals). Top-down information processing is "concept-driven" and thereby refers to processing that is driven by knowledge and prior experience (e.g., category-based knowledge that enables you to recognize the stimulus as a flower and, if you have encountered it before, as a lotus). If we were only reliant on bottom-up processing, it would take an exceedingly long time to recognize any stimulus, as each would have to be scanned for every single feature, every time around. If we were only reliant on top-down processing, we would be unable to categorize or develop an understanding of novel stimuli. As a result of having both systems in place, we can rapidly, accurately, and seamlessly process the external world. This is owing to "ascending feedforward" and "descending feedback" neural circuits that interact from very early on in the information processing cycle to guide and constrain one another (Bar, 2007).

So why would a break in this top-down versus bottom-up system (for contemporary ideas on this distinction, see Awh, Belopolsky, & Theeuwes, 2012) be considered advantageous for creativity? Our receptive–predictive information processing systems are in place to enable perception–action operations, the outcomes of which take place in the known space and need to be both fast and accurate. To be creative, though, one needs to generate novelty, which per definition is unknown or unpredictable. So a hyper-efficient system that is designed to reach the "correct" answer may not be as well suited to generating a "novel" idea. This is where some form of disruption to the well-oiled system might be advantageous.

Insufficiencies at the level of top-down control or concept-driven processing allow for wider access to raw and unprocessed sensory information. Having this form of unique access to stimulus features would enable one to generate more unusual associations and develop uncustomary perspectives (Snyder, 2009). Analogous ideas of information processing biases in association with heightened creativity include cognitive disinhibition, defocused attention, overinclusive thinking, and flat associative hierarchies of conceptual knowledge (Carson et al., 2003; Eysenck, 1995; Martindale, 1999; Mednick, 1962; Mendelsohn, 1974) (also see Chapters 3 and 5).

The empirical basis for the notion that reduced top-down or concept-driven processing leads to enhanced creativity comes from a range of sources. The most compelling of these is the study of individuals with savant skills, which are defined as the presence of exceptional or prodigious capabilities in at least one domain (e.g., art, music, speed calculation, memory) that far surpass any level that would be considered typical. These include people with savant syndrome who display such skills despite the presence of concomitant neurodevelopmental disorders or brain injuries (Treffert, 2014; Treffert & Rebedew, 2015). Around 10% are classified "acquired savants" as their skills suddenly manifest following a stroke, dementia, or head injury. The vast majority, then, are classified "congenital savants" as their skills manifest very early during development. The developmental disability that is overwhelmingly associated with this condition (estimated between 50–75%) is autism spectrum disorder (ASD). Conversely, 1 in 10 people with ASD also exhibit savant skills (Treffert, 2009). There are many captivating case studies that showcase the presence of savant skills alongside psychological deficits (Code, 2003). A striking one is the case of Nadia Chomyn, an autistic savant with profound language and social deficits, who began drawing at the age of 3. The aesthetic value of her sketches as a 7 year old was deemed comparable by some to those of Leonardo da Vinci (Ramachandran & Hirstein, 1999). While Nadia inexplicably lost her ability to draw realistically before she reached puberty, most savants do not show this pattern. A case in point is Stephen Wiltshire, whose extraordinary draftsmanship skills show no signs of decline.

Parallel to these ideas are case studies of individuals with frontotemporal dementia (FTD) where the onset of brain damage is sometimes associated with the release of artistic and musical abilities (Miller, Boone, Cummings, Read, & Mishkin, 2000; Miller, Ponton, Benson, Cummings, & Mena, 1996; Zaidel, 2010). This is a rare manifestation, however, that is only seen with a subset of patients, such as in FTD where the degeneration of brain tissue affects the temporal lobe but not the frontal lobe. It is important to note that, unlike in the case of savants, the skills displayed in this context of neurodegenerative disorders are seldom prodigious. However, they are wholly unexpected given the level of the said skills exhibited by the person prior to the neurological insult. So, again, brain injury leads to deficiencies in certain aspects of functioning (such as loss of semantic understanding, lack of social awareness, or speech production difficulties) and is accompanied by enhanced de novo abilities that are relevant to visual art or music.

A third line of evidence that has a bearing here is the link between mental illness and creativity. The idea that specific forms of mental illness are associated with a heightened propensity for creativity is a ubiquitous one. This is primarily informed by the higher incidence of mental illness in people who work in creative professions, such as writers and artists (Kyaga et al., 2011). A great many empirical studies have also examined creative thinking in association with specific forms of mental illness, such as schizophrenia and bipolar disorder, as well as their subclinical variants (Abraham, 2015; Andreasen, 2006; Kaufman, 2014). Here, again, the rationale for explaining the apparent advantages in specific aspects of creative cognition associated with such groups comes from arguing that skewed information processing biases (e.g., in the form of cognitive disinhibition or overinclusive thinking) that ordinarily lead to insufficiencies in goal-directed thought and action in some contexts (negative biases) can lead to particular advantages in open-ended contexts that call for generativity in thought and action (positive biases).

These quite distinct strands of evidence have one feature in common. They all seek to understand the information processing mechanisms that explain both the deficits in normative cognitive function and the enhanced creativity-relevant abilities. And the general idea is that a breakdown of top-down control or concept-driven thinking can be beneficial for releasing creative potential (for an alternative conceptualization of top-down and bottom-up control in relation to creativity, see the "matching filter hypothesis" in Chrysikou, Weber, & Thompson-Schill, 2014). What must be kept in mind, though, is that the creativity-relevant advantages exhibited across all groups are quite dissimilar but the underlying mechanisms that purportedly give rise to the same are very similar. Little attention has been given to explain the diversity in the manifestation of such abilities. Factors to consider include the degree to which such abilities, be it savant skills (see Box 4.1) or the mere fact of engaging in the arts (see Box 4.2), can be regarded as analogous to creativity, or indeed how to account for the fact that mental wellbeing is also associated with creativity (see Box 4.3).

Box 4.1 Savant Abilities: Exceptional Skill or Creativity?

The case of musical and artistic savants is often presented as indicative of heightened creativity-relevant skills. But are we justified in making this assumption? Musical and artistic skills are, after all, but two of the many types of savant skill that are seen in such populations – which include rapid math calculation skills, as exhibited by Daniel Tammet, and the astonishing photographic memory of Kim Peek. However, the information processing biases that have been proposed to underlie these diverse prodigious skills, both the (seemingly) creativity-relevant and (seemingly) creativity-irrelevant ones, are the same. Indeed, the commonality between the different savant skills is held to be an extraordinary capacity for memory, which manifests in different ways across domains. According to Treffert (2014, 564), "Whatever the skill it is always associated with massive memory of a habit or procedural type – very narrow but exceedingly deep within the confines of the special skill. In some cases massive memory is the special skill." So it seems unlikely that we can lean heavily on these explanations to deliver a comprehensive understanding of creativity without considering several other factors (also refer to Section 10.4.3).

Box 4.2 Does Engaging in Artistic Pursuits Equal Creativity?

In a word – no. Not according to the definition of creativity, which necessitates the presence of originality in that which is being produced. The mere practice of artistic skills (in the form of painting and playing music, for instance) in and of itself is not sufficient to be characterized as a "creative" act. The distinction to apply here is that "creating something" is not the same as "creating something creative" (see Box 1.2). This has been explicitly discussed in the case of de novo artistic skills, which is the sudden emergence and display of artistic abilities that were not expressed previously, which have been shown to develop on occasion following neurological insult or neuronal degeneration, such as in the case of specific forms of frontotemporal dementia (FTD). It has been observed that, while "in such neurological cases, the turning to art is itself innovative; the produced art, however, is not necessarily creative" (Zaidel, 2014, 2). An intriguing suggestion that has been put forward to explain such behaviors is that they reflect the motivation or drive to continue to communicate despite the inability to do so effectively owing to the deficits in language and communication skills that accompany such conditions. So the turning to art is viewed as an alternative means of expression, which serves the purpose of communication (Zaidel, 2014).

Box 4.3 Creativity: Mental Illness versus Mental Wellbeing

Alongside anecdotal accounts, much empirical evidence (particularly from the field of psychology) indicates an association – albeit a modest and complex one – between mental illness and creativity (Abraham, 2015; Kaufman, 2014). There is, however, growing evidence for the opposite association (particularly from the field of public or community mental health), which indicates that engaging in creative pursuits improves mental wellbeing (Bungay & Vella-Burrows, 2013; Cuypers et al., 2012). Indeed, this is the rationale behind using art therapies in the management of a wide range of health-relevant conditions (Forgeard & Eichner, 2014). While it seems counterintuitive that both these ideas can co-exist, it turns out that this may be possible as they reflect different aspects of the same associative link (Simonton, 2014). Furthermore, they actually refer to different levels of functionality. First, the need to be creative which was identified early on within the hierarchy-of-needs theory is part of the human self-actualization need, which is the innate drive to realize one's own unique potential (Maslow, 1943). Obstacles to engaging this drive can lead to negative outcomes for the individual, as indicated by the aforementioned public health research, and as such stands to impact any individual. Second, the predisposition for higher levels of creativity, through biases in information processing mechanisms like cognitive disinhibition, can be accompanied by an increased risk for psychopathological traits, which would explain shared characteristics, such as a high tolerance of ambiguity. Third, creative professions are associated with an exceedingly high degree of uncertainty and corresponding insecurities at every level, from the lack of guarantees in personal creative output to chronic job instability and rarity of continued success. Such consequences are potent psychosocial stressors and can easily lead to poor mental health.

4.2.3 Brain Networks Perspective

The overarching objective of cognitive neuroscience is to elucidate the manner in which psychological functions map on to specific features of brain regions (structural mapping) or specific activity within brain regions (functional mapping). While its early phase saw the mapping of functions to "locally segregated brain regions," the trajectory has now shifted toward the mapping of functions to the "integrated activity of large-scale, distributed networks of brain regions" (Meehan & Bressler, 2012, 2232; also see Bressler & Menon, 2010). Correspondingly, network theories of psychological function are increasingly more dominant and influential than modular theories. This is also true of the field of research on the neuroscience of creativity.

Empirical support for the involvement of different brain networks in creativity is largely derived from neuroimaging studies whereby creative thinking has been assessed using a range of different experimental paradigms from problem solving to improvisation (Abraham, Pieritz, et al., 2012; Beaty, Benedek, Kaufman, & Silvia, 2015; Limb & Braun, 2008). Dual-system ideas are virtually superimposed on the workings of these brain networks, such that each network is wed to one side of the system. In general, the open, divergent, or generative mode of creativity is held to engage the *default mode network*, whereas the closed, convergent, or evaluative mode of creativity recruits the *central executive network* (Beaty et al., 2016).

The DMN encompasses five core brain areas: (i) the ventral and dorsal medial prefrontal cortex; (ii) the medial parietal regions, including the retrosplenial and posterior cingulate cortices; (iii) the anterior lateral temporal cortex, including the temporal poles; (iv) the inferior parietal cortex and the temporoparietal junction; and (v) the medial temporal lobe structures, such as the hippocampal formation (Andrews-Hanna, Smallwood, & Spreng, 2014; Buckner et al., 2008; Raichle, 2015) (see Figure 5.2). The DMN came to prominence as a "task-negative" system as it is engaged during periods of rest and during conditions of low task demand, whereas it is disengaged during tasks that involve high cognitive demand (Gusnard, Raichle, & Raichle, 2001). Retrospective thought sampling questionnaires of the content of internal mentation during periods of rest have revealed that participants experience feeling "blank" only 5% of the time. Instead, they are actively engaged in free internally-directed thoughts about their past, the future, their goals, and so on (Andrews-Hanna, Reidler, Huang, & Buckner, 2010).

Indeed, this brain network is actively engaged during tasks that tap different types of deliberative imaginative thinking, such as autobiographical and episodic memory (e.g., reminiscing about my last birthday), episodic future thinking (e.g., imagining what my next birthday might be like), mental state reasoning or theory of mind (e.g., inferring what someone else is thinking about), self-referential thinking (e.g., reflecting on my own thoughts, feelings, and behaviors), and moral reasoning (e.g., judging the permissibility of my own or someone else's actions) (Andrews-Hanna et al., 2014; Mullally & Maguire, 2013; Schacter et al., 2012; Spreng, Mar, & Kim, 2009). Such operations can therefore be directly prompted or spontaneously elicited under conditions of rest (Andrews-Hanna et al., 2010; Fox, Spreng, Ellamil, Andrews-Hanna, & Christoff, 2015).

The DMN is primarily discussed in neuroscientific literature in the context of reasoning about the perception, cognition, or behavior of one's self and/or others (Bubić & Abraham, 2014). However, it is clearly also involved in non-social and non-personal aspects of imaginative thinking, such as semantic future thinking (Abraham, Schubotz, & von Cramon, 2008), counterfactual reasoning (Levens et al., 2014), and creative thinking (Abraham, Pieritz, et al., 2012). For these reasons, its role in mental operations relevant to intentionality-based imagination and novel combinatorial imagination has been emphasized (Abraham, 2016).

While the DMN is held to underlie the open/divergent/generative mode of creative information processing, the closed/convergent/evaluative mode of creative information processing is held to be orchestrated by the CEN, which includes a wide set of brain regions that closely corresponds to the fronto-cingulo-parietal network (see Figure 5.2). It encompasses (i) the lateral prefrontal cortex, (ii) the anterior prefrontal cortex, (iii) the anterior cingulate, and (iv) the posterior parietal cortex and intraparietal sulcus, alongside the connections of these broad regions to structures in the basal ganglia and cerebellum (Aarts, van Holstein, & Cools, 2011; Blasi et al., 2006; Cole & Schneider, 2007; Niendam et al., 2012; Robbins et al., 2012; Seeley et al., 2007; Spreng, Sepulcre, Turner, Stevens, & Schacter, 2013).

Of these, the regions that are relevant to creative cognition are the frontal pole (Brodmann area 10) and lateral aspects of the prefrontal cortex (dorsal: Brodmann areas 8, 9, 46; ventral: Brodmann areas 45, 47). These brain areas facilitate all aspects of cognitive control with a concrete–abstract division of information processing along the posterior–anterior continuum, with the anterior-most regions catering to the most complex and abstract aspects of cognition (Badre, 2008; Badre & Wagner, 2007; Donoso, Collins, & Koechlin, 2014; Koechlin, 2015; Ramnani & Owen, 2004; but also see Nee & D'Esposito, 2016). Evidence for the involvement of these prefrontal structures in creative thinking is both considerable and consistent across different experimental paradigms that have assessed creativity in problem solving, analogical reasoning, conceptual expansion, metaphor processing, musical improvisation, lyr- ical improvisation, and story generation (Abraham, Pieritz, et al., 2012; Fink, Grabner, et al., 2009; Green et al., 2012; Kröger et al., 2012; Limb & Braun, 2008; Liu et al., 2012; Rutter, Kröger, Stark, et al., 2012; Shah et al., 2011; Vartanian, 2012).

So the brain network explanation of creativity is that the dual systems corresponding to the open, generative, and divergent mode relative to the closed, evaluative, and convergent mode are subserved by the default mode and central executive brain networks, respectively. This has all the elements of a neat story, so it begs the question – is there anything prob- lematic about it?

The most obvious issue to clarify is the relation between these enor- mous brain networks. From a functional neuroanatomical point of view, the DMN and the CEN are shown to be anticorrelated (Fox et al., 2005; Fox, Zhang, Snyder, & Raichle, 2009). Furthermore, the engagement of these networks – or the decision about which network is involved at a particular point in time – is held to be mediated through the *salience network* of the brain (Chand & Dhamala, 2015; Chen et al., 2013; Goulden et al., 2014; Sridharan, Levitin, & Menon, 2008), which includes the dorsal anterior cingulate and orbital frontoinsular cortices (Seeley et al., 2007; Uddin, 2015). Regions of the insula, in particular, are held to mediate "dynamic interactions between other large-scale brain networks involved in externally oriented attention and intern- ally oriented or self-related cognition" (Menon & Uddin, 2010, 655). Does this bear out when examining neuroscientific investigations of creativity?

There is some evidence of insular involvement in creativity (Beaty et al., 2015; Boccia, Piccardi, Palermo, Nori, & Palmiero, 2015; Ellamil et al., 2012), but how this region facilitates the switch between networks as a function of creativity is as yet unclear. The insula is characterized by its sensitivity to bottom-up salience (Menon & Uddin, 2010), but the studies that attempt to experimentally decouple the generative and evaluative phases of creativity do so via top-down instruction. Participants are, for instance, asked to generate ideas in a first phase and evaluate ideas in a second phase (Ellamil et al., 2012). So we do not as yet know how the activity of the DMN and CEN is coupled to facilitate creative thinking. And our hypotheses regarding the same cannot blindly be drawn from the published literature on aspects of psy- chological function that are not specific to creativity. One needs to also consider that "salience" in the case of creativity is likely to be differen- tially impacted by bottom-up versus top-down factors, as well as explicit versus implicit factors, as it is fundamentally about going against the grain of what is known and generating novelty.

In fact, creativity may be a special case in point in terms of the manner in which it engages these large-scale brain networks. Functional connect- ivity studies indicate that high creative ability is associated with a brain network that consists of hubs within the central executive, default mode, and salience networks (Beaty et al., 2018).

4.2.4 What Speaks against Dual-Factor Global Explanations?

The unmistakable appeal of dual models lies in their apparent tidiness and simplicity. However, this belies the reality, which is that no one duality can capture the full extent of any aspect of psychological function. This is in fact why multiple dual systems have been proposed (e.g., top-down/bottom-up, global/local, spontaneous/deliberate conscious/unconscious, internal/external, intrinsic/extrinsic, automatic/controlled, implicit/explicit). However, these simplistic divisions blur instantly when dualities interact.

A good example of this was provided by a review of the brain basis of externally directed cognition and internally directed cognition. Researchers examined how the brain activity in relation to both types of cognition are differentially impacted as a function according to whether the states were spontaneously or intentionally prompted (Dixon, Fox, & Christoff, 2014). When spontaneously elicited, externally directed cognition (e.g., "attentional re-orienting in response to a salient external stimulus") and internally directed cognition (e.g., "mind wandering without awareness") activate mostly distinct brain areas and co-occur with little interference. Externally directed cognition engages primary sensory, primary motor, and modality-specific association areas, whereas limbic and paralimbic regions are involved during internally directed cognition. However, the picture changes under circumstances of intentional processing, as externally directed cognition (e.g., "attention orienting to a task-relevant external stimulus") and internally directed cognition (e.g., "directed thinking about future plans") then compete for cognitive resources. This causes the lateral prefrontal cortex, which facilitates cognitive control, to become engaged during both forms of cognition. So what this study demonstrates is that the engagement of two or more dualities complicates the more neat and tidy portrayals that emerge when considering dualities in isolation. This is testament to a sense of false comfort that comes from studying cognition in laboratory contexts where such systems can be teased apart artificially. Implementing contexts that are a closer representation of how we operate in our natural environments reveals the need to consider complex interactions between systems if the aim is to develop an accurate understanding. Indeed, more recent theories such as the dual pathway model of creativity proposes that creative ideation comes about through both flexibility and persistence, and these are differentially impacted by individual/dispositional and environmental/ situational variables (Boot, Baas, van Gaal, Cools, & De Dreu, 2017; Nijstad, Dreu, Rietzschel, & Baas, 2010) (see Box 10.2).

Another problem with the global view is that its foundation is solely based on brain networks. The contemporary emphasis in cognitive neuroscience is to move toward interpreting findings in terms of brain networks and away from the classic focus on single brain regions (Poldrack, 2012). The significance and utility of the brain network-based approach is clear given the sheer degree of interconnectedness between brain regions (Ioannides, 2007; Medaglia, Lynall, & Bassett, 2015; Petersen & Sporns, 2015; Sepulcre, Sabuncu, & Johnson, 2012; Smith, 2012). What is rarely discussed, though, is the unique problem that comes from interpreting findings as drawing on a vast network when only a few parts of the network are actually significantly engaged in relation to a specific task (also see Box 5.1).

Brain imaging findings in relation to creativity indicate that it is the rule rather than the exception that any given creativity task will activate only limited parts of the brain network of interest, be it the DMN or CEN. Under the circumstances, is it justified to talk about a whole network's involvement if it is only partially engaged? As yet, there are no published consensus-based guidelines that specify the extent of a network (e.g., the number of core regions, Brodmann areas, etc.) that need to be involved to be able to advocate network-derived interpretations of findings. These are vital issues to consider as the legitimacy of global views on creativity is necessarily impacted by the answers to such questions.

4.3 Multiple-Factor Models

More recent models that propose global explanations of creative thinking have recognized the necessity to take multiple factors into account in understanding the brain basis of creative thinking. In doing so, they have gone well beyond dual models of creativity by considering the parallel

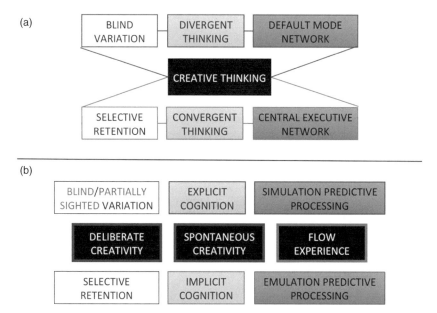

Figure 4.3 Multiple-factor models

(a) Rex Jung's model. **(b)** Arne Dietrich's model. The colors code for systems of factors that work separately (blue versus red) or systems of factors that are commonly drawn upon regardless of the type of creativity (black). A black and white version of this figure will appear in some formats. For the color version, please refer to the plate section.

workings of three (or more) systems that work in unison. The two models that have been put forward so far postulate the information processing mechanisms underlying (a) different aspects of the creative-thinking process in general (Jung's evolutionary brain networks perspective) or (b) the many operations underlying different types of creative insight (Dietrich's evolutionary predictive perspective) (Figure 4.3).

4.3.1 An Evolutionary Brain Networks Perspective

In 2013, Rex Jung proposed an integrated theoretical framework that brought together three different perspectives or frameworks on creativity (Jung et al., 2013: (a) divergent thinking versus convergent thinking, (b) the default mode versus central executive networks of the brain, and (c) the Blind-Variation–Selective-Retention (BVSR) model.

The BVSR model refers to an evolutionary theory of thought processes relevant to creativity as advocated by Donald Campbell. The essence of the theory is that creativity comes about by means of three mechanisms that operate during thought trials. The first mechanism of "blind-variation" enables the generation of idea variants. These variants are "blind" in that they originate at random and without intention from the mind, and are not induced by the environment, previous thought trials, or even the two mechanisms that follow. The "selective-retention" phase sees the working of the second mechanism of selection, where viable and fitting idea variants are chosen, and a third mechanism "for preserving and reproducing the selected variations" (Campbell, 1960).

In Jung's model, the three explanations, which are at different levels of analysis (cognitive, neural, evolutionary), are proposed to directly map onto one another. This is in fact the unique feature of this theory, in which the "structure of creative cognition" is outlined. Blind-variation gives rise to divergent thinking, which is instantiated by the DMN. Selective-retention, on the other hand, gives rise to convergent thinking, which is subserved by the CEN.

In accommodating multiple levels of explanation within one mold, this is certainly a very tidy theory of creative neurocognition that is inspired by evolutionary principles. It has been criticized, however, for being too simplistic on theoretical grounds (Dietrich, 2015). With regard to the empirical evidence, the jury is out as the picture is mostly incomplete. When reviewing the existing relevant findings, though, the picture does not align seamlessly with this model. For instance, regions of the CEN have been found to be involved during divergent creative thinking (e.g., left inferior frontal gyrus: Abraham, Pieritz, et al., 2012) and default mode regions have been found to be engaged during convergent creative thinking (e.g., right anterior superior temporal gyrus: Jung-Beeman et al., 2004). It must be noted, though, that a clear verdict on the theory can only be delivered from studies in which the brain activity profiles generated during divergent creative thinking and convergent creative thinking are assessed within a single experimental design. No published functional neuroimaging study has implemented this to date. This is unsurprising, as it is indeed difficult to design technically similar tasks that tap divergent and convergent forms of creativity due to their inherent differences (see Chapter 2). So, investigating them in a methodologically sound manner within one experimental design that can be used in a neuroimaging environment remains a challenge (see Chapter 6).

Another issue that remains unclear is how one could test for the evolutionary elements of the model given that these mechanisms are extremely fast in terms of processing speed and are unlikely to be captured using the neuroscientific techniques we have on hand. Indeed, studies that attempt to dissociate brain activity patterns during generative and evaluative components of the creative-thinking process have found engagement of the default mode and central executive networks in both components (Ellamil et al., 2012). The larger issue to ascertain is whether blind-variation could conceivably apply only to divergent thinking while selective-retention applies only to convergent thinking, as both forms of thinking necessitate the generation and selection of idea variants in order to reach a creative solution.

4.3.2 An Evolutionary Predictive Perspective

Another evolution-based neurocognitive model was proposed around the same period (Dietrich, 2015; Dietrich & Haider, 2015). While this framework also draws its underlying principles from the BVSR theory, similarities between this and the previous theory end there. For one, Dietrich rejects the divergent–convergent distinction outright, and proposes that the mechanisms of blind-variation and selective-retention are the general all-purpose underlying principles that give rise to creative thought across all contexts of human endeavor. The critical feature of his drawing from the BVSR theory is in arguing that the processing of variant generation during thought trials is not blind, but partially sighted, which is an opinion held by many experts (e.g., see commentaries on Simonton, 1999, 2010). He goes much further, though, in that he expands from this idea to postulate how different cognitive mechanisms might provide differing "degrees of sightedness" during the variant-generation phase that give rise to different forms of creativity.

Dietrich has put forward a number of ideas in relation to creative cognition since the early 2000s. His first global theoretical model was a two-by-two system, where he distinguished between two processing modes (spontaneous, deliberate) and two knowledge domains (cognitive, emotional) that give rise to four types of creative insight (Dietrich, 2004b). The systematic incremental discovery of DNA is an example of *deliberate-cognitive* insights, and this form was proposed to involve the prefrontal cortex acting on the temporal-occipital-parietal areas. Reaching personal insights via psychotherapy is an example of *deliberate-emotional* creativity, and purportedly involves the prefrontal cortex acting on limbic regions. An example of *spontaneous-cognitive* creativity is the kind where the solution suddenly pops into one's awareness seemingly out of nowhere (e.g., Friedrich Kekulé's discovery of the ring structure of the benzene molecule allegedly after a period of daydreaming). Such operations are held to derive from the temporal-occipital-parietal areas with the involvement of brain regions relevant to implicit cognition, such as the basal ganglia, alongside the periodic down-regulation of the prefrontal cortex. Finally, the *spontaneous-emotional* forms of creative insight supposedly arise when "the neural activity of structures that process emotional information is spontaneously represented in working memory" (1019) and thereby enter consciousness. This form is believed to underlie works such as Picasso's *Guernica* (Dietrich, 2004b).

Although exceedingly speculative and based on very little in the way of direct empirical evidence, this was the first proposal for a comprehensive brain-based model of creativity. Dietrich has expanded significantly, though, in his latest take on the neurocognition of creativity and some of the elements of the original theory are still in place. The distinction between spontaneous (or bottom-up) and deliberate (or top-down) forms of creativity are, for instance, still paramount, and the possibility that "the central-executive network is the crank behind the deliberate creativity mode, whereas the default network powers the spontaneous creativity mode" is given consideration (Dietrich, 2015, 161). But the meat of the model lies elsewhere.

The current multiple factors model by Dietrich proposes the existence of three creativity modes: deliberate, spontaneous, and flow experience. These modes come about by coupling (a) aforementioned evolutionary models of partially sighted or blind-variation and selection algorithms to (b) predictive processing mechanisms of simulation and emulation within these thought trial cycles as instantiated in (c) explicit or implicit cognitive systems. The deliberate and spontaneous modes of creativity arise from the explicit system of cognition, which acquires and represents content that is consciously accessible, verbalizable, and rule-based. Dietrich holds that it is in fact these features of the explicit system that allow information to be represented in abstract formats that can be maintained separately from one's own experiential knowledge structure (e.g., allowing us to imagine movements we cannot generate from our own bodies such as the drift of ocean waves). The explicit system can therefore run "offline" iterations of variation-selection thought trials. This is in contrast to the implicit system of cognition through which the third mode of creativity, flow experience, is instantiated. The implicit system is skill-based and it is neither consciously accessible nor verbalizable. It also cannot form abstract representations, and is inaccessible to the explicit system, which is why the implicit system can only run "online" iterations of variation-selection thought trials.

So how do these online and offline variation-selection thought trials take place? Dietrich draws heavily from predictive processing models of sensorimotor control (e.g., Wolpert, Ghahramani, & Jordan, 1995) in proposing that this occurs through the mechanisms of "simulation" and "emulation" (which ordinarily run "online" in the case of sensorimotor control) such that "forward models" are behind the variation component and "inverse models" underlie the fitness function of the selection component. Fitness criteria vary across domains and can, accordingly, take on different forms: wonder, curiosity, surprise, goodness-of-fit, and so on.

Simulations are essentially characterized by two features (Moulton & Kosslyn, 2009). First, they generate knowledge or make knowledge available and this allows one to consider novel questions (e.g., how does my son's laugh differ from my own?) and make predictions. Second, they "operate by sequential analogy," such that the steps of the simulation run in an analogous pattern to that of the represented situation. The sequence is also functional in that each step constrains subsequent steps. There are two types of simulation – first-order or instrumental simulations (these are referred to as simulations) and second-order or emulative simulations (these are referred to as emulations) – which differ in terms of exactness or fidelity in relation to the situation being simulated. Simulations mimic content (e.g., imagining the changing scenery when running through the park without also imagining the steps corresponding to the leg movements which cause the scene changes) whereas emulations are more exacting in that they imitate both the content and process that led to the changes in content.

According to Dietrich, the three modes of creativity differ in the type and extent of predictive processes they are driven by. Spontaneous and deliberate modes of creativity involve thought trials that run via both simulation and emulation in the explicit system. The difference between the two is the degree of sightedness that characterizes the variant-generation process as well as the strength of the selection process. There is a substantial degree of sightedness in the case of the deliberate mode and only modest levels of sightedness in the spontaneous mode. Sightedness comes about through the potential for goal representation and task-set maintenance and these are referred to as ideational representations of predicted goals (RPGs). By having the twin processes of the variation-selection algorithm operate in the same computational system, the ideational RPG enables the selection process to be coupled to the variation process (via operations such as task-set inertia, fringe working memory and cognitive scaffolding), and this gives rise to differing degrees of partial sightedness. In contrast, the flow experience mode of creativity only draws from emulation mechanisms in the non-representational implicit system. So the variation-selection thought trials here are blind.

Dietrich is a vehement advocate against the orthodoxy of creativity theory and research and he views virtually all previous investigations and theoretical formulations about the brain basis of creativity as being fundamentally flawed and, consequently, quite useless in terms of being able to deliver any truths about the phenomenon in question. His own theoretical approach is unique in that the mechanisms that underlie the very fabric of the neuroscience of creativity are stitched very firmly to noteworthy models that have been proposed in dominant fields in cognitive neuroscience.

One of the weaknesses of this theory is that, as it currently stands, it proposes the existence of innumerable systems and toolboxes in the service of different aspects of creativity, the specifics of which are confusingly outlined. What is more, as it currently stands, it does not generate testable hypotheses that empiricists could use to attempt to affirm or disconfirm the theory. Another concern is that it is not possible to glean what exactly is specific about this theoretical model to understanding creativity as opposed to cognition in general. In fact, it smacks of a "creativity is not so special" hypothesis, which is certainly a plausible idea, but it has not been articulated or defended in that manner. What needs to be clarified is whether creativity is merely an extension of predictive brain mechanisms, and, if so, in what manner it extends. How does a predictive system that has evolved to ensure fast, accurate, seamless, and goal-directed action in order to select the "correct" action give rise to novelty or originality when goals are unclear or the situation is open-ended and unpredictable? If, instead, creativity is purported to be something more, the grounds for this must be explained in a clear manner as well. This is a truly exciting theory of creativity and has much to offer. But it needs to be fleshed out far more clearly so as to be accessible and coherent. Also necessary are specific suggestions on how it could be empirically tested using the tools of psychology, neuroscience, or any other discipline.

4.3.3 What Speaks against Multiple-Factor Models?

These are still early days in the case of global explanations as afforded by multiple-factor models, so it is not as yet possible to review them extensively in terms of their benefits and pitfalls. Multiple-factor models have yet to spur the kind of concerted empirical investigations that are necessary to establish how well the theories (or different aspects of the theories) hold up vis-à-vis the evidence. The usefulness of multiple-factor models of creativity clearly lies in the fact that they are attempts to account for some of the complexities of the phenomenon in question. What is equally apparent, though, is that a crucial shortcoming associated with both models is that it is not clear how they can be tested or verified. As they stand, they look to be purely theoretical models that serve to stimulate and inform views rather than guide empirical investigations in the neuroscience of creativity.

4.4 A Final Word

This chapter explored many explanations ranging from classical to contemporary that have been proposed to explain the brain basis of creativity. These explanations were dubbed "global" as creativity is explained from the context of large-scale interacting brain networks or information processing systems. The global approach is particularly useful when trying to draw the big picture concerning creativity (Abraham, 2018). It is a highly accessible approach to understanding the creative brain as it lends itself to easy translation, which accounts for the enduring appeal of many of the notions stemming from global explanations among the lay public and in popular culture. It is important, though, to be alert to the necessary simplicity of global explanations, as they cannot but compromise accuracy in their depiction of the physiological basis of creativity.

Chapter Summary

- The neuroscientific or brain basis of creativity is part of the larger physiological approach to investigating and understanding creativity.
- Global explanations are those that conceive of the brain basis of creativity as arising from extensive information processing systems or brain networks. They can be further classified as systems of dual models or multiple-factor models.
- The supremacy of the right brain is the most pervasive notion that has been peddled in relation to creativity, although the involvement of both hemispheres is unmistakable.
- Reduced concept-driven thinking or lowered top-down control, as evidenced by some neurological and psychiatric populations, are proposed to underlie increased creative ideation.

- The two brain networks that are held to orchestrate creative thinking are the DMN and the CEN.
- The evolutionary brain networks perspective proposes that creative thinking arises through the mechanisms of blind-variation and selection, which map on to divergent thinking by means of DMN activity and convergent thinking via CEN activity, respectively.
- The evolutionary predictive perspective model proposes that three different modes of creativity – spontaneous, deliberate, and flow experience – emanate from the interaction of variation-selection mechanisms with different degrees of sightedness, explicit versus implicit cognitive systems, and simulation versus emulation operations.

Review Questions

1. Can the physiological approach to creativity be considered a unique one?
2. How are global brain-based explanations of creativity characterized?
3. Describe the three dominant dual-system models of the creative brain.
4. What differentiates the two multiple-factor models of creative neurocognition?
5. Consider and outline the conceptual developments that have come about with each global explanation, from classical to contemporary.

Further Reading

- Abraham, A. (2018). The forest versus the trees: Creativity, cognition and imagination. In R. E. Jung & O. Vartanian (Eds.), *The Cambridge handbook of the neuroscience of creativity* (pp. 195–210). New York: Cambridge University Press.
- Beaty, R. E., Benedek, M., Silvia, P. J., & Schacter, D. L. (2016). Creative cognition and brain network dynamics. *Trends in Cognitive Sciences*, 20(2), 87–95.
- Dietrich, A. (2015). *How creativity happens in the brain.* New York: Palgrave Macmillan.
- Jung, R. E., Mead, B. S., Carrasco, J., & Flores, R. A. (2013). The structure of creative cognition in the human brain. *Frontiers in Human Neuroscience*, 7, 300.
- Snyder, A. (2009). Explaining and inducing savant skills: Privileged access to lower level, less-processed information. *Philosophical Transactions of the Royal Society B: Biological Sciences*, 364(1522), 1399–1405.

CHAPTER FIVE

Brain-Based Local Explanations of Creativity

"Creativity is that marvelous capacity to grasp mutually distinct realities and draw a spark from their juxtaposition."

(Max Ernst)

Learning Objectives

- Differentiating between brain-to-process and process-to-brain explanations
- Grasping the intricacies of frontal lobe function in relation to creativity
- Recognizing non-frontal brain regions and wider brain systems of relevance to creative cognition
- Delineating the brain correlates of insight, analogy, and metaphor processing
- Distinguishing between the brain correlates of processing conceptual expansion, constraining influence of examples, and creative imagery
- Advantages and disadvantages of local explanations of creativity

5.1 The Local Approach to Creativity

An alternative set of views to global explanations (detailed in Chapter 4) within the physiological approach of creativity can be dubbed "local" explanations. Unlike global explanations where the focus when explaining creative function is on widely distributed brain networks (e.g., DMN) or large expanses of brain area (e.g., right hemisphere), local explanations are exemplified by an emphasis on circumscribed brain regions (e.g., the frontal pole corresponding to Brodmann Area 10) or narrowly defined brain activity patterns (e.g., EEG alpha waves) (see Box 5.1). Local explanations derive from specific physiological markers or indices to characterize how the brain facilitates particular mental operations that are relevant to creative thinking (e.g., analogical reasoning, conceptual expansion). Specificity is therefore the credo of local explanations, both in terms of zoning in on the particular creativity-relevant cognitive processes under study and the engagement of select brain regions or activity patterns (Abraham, 2014a; Abraham & Windmann, 2007).

Box 5.1 Problems of Interpretation: From My-Favorite-Brain-Region to My-Favorite-Brain-Network

Global explanations of creativity (see Chapter 4) are based on network-based models of neurocognition, the current dominant trend in cognitive neuroscience that guides interpretations of brain activity in relation to psychological function. These enable one to counter the previous trend in the functional localization practice of local explanations, which was to ascribe single functions to single regions. This led to the problem of oversimplifications in the interpretation of data, looking for patterns that fit preconceived notions, and ignoring potentially important data patterns in other brain regions. The currently accepted mode of network-based explanation is, however, not without the same problems. By focusing on whole brain networks that overlap in terms of brain regions, attributing a functional role to one's chosen whole network when the data only shows activity in one or two of its nodes is also based on preconceived notions. And it results in the ubiquitous tendency toward overgeneralization and lack of specificity. So only leaning on global or local explanations runs the risk, in both cases, of serious confirmation biases. We stand to miss important patterns that are revealing of the actual nature of the operation in question by focusing only on the forest (global explanations) or only on the trees (local explanations) in our attempts to make sense of the findings (Abraham, 2018).

The overarching goal when following the local approach is to uncover the specific dynamics of the complex information processing mechanisms that give rise to creativity. Theoretical and empirical works that employ the local approach aim to reach this objective by adopting two directional paths of analysis. One is to commence with specific brain regions or brain systems to reach conclusions about the operation being studied (brain-to-process). An example of this direction of approach is the finding of increased alpha power in EEG patterns during divergent creative thinking, which is the basis of why alpha brain activity is touted to be one of the potential biomarkers of creative ideation (Fink & Benedek, 2014). The second is when the interpretation is led from the standpoint of the specific creativity-relevant operation being studied (process-to-brain). An example of this is interpreting the mechanisms underlying "creative conceptual expansion" in relation to processes of controlled semantic retrieval based on the involvement of anterior inferior frontal gyrus during controlled semantic retrieval in non-creative thought processes

(Abraham, Pieritz, et al., 2012). Both directional approaches are complementary and necessarily interact with one another. They have nonetheless been separately detailed in the sections that follow in order to aid comprehension.

The mental processes that have been examined from the perspective of local explanations include analogical reasoning (Green, 2016; Green et al., 2010), attentional control (Zabelina et al., 2015), episodic cognition (Beaty et al., 2016), executive function (Abraham, Beudt, et al., 2012), metaphor processing (Faust & Kenett, 2014; Mashal, Faust, Hendler, & Jung-Beeman, 2007), problem solving (Fink, Grabner, et al., 2009; Reverberi et al., 2005), and semantic cognition (Kenett et al., 2014; Kröger et al., 2012; Rutter, Kröger, Stark, et al., 2012), among others.

The brain structures of note in the context of local explanations are regions that can be primarily characterized as belonging to either the CEN, the DMN, or the semantic cognition network (SCN). The central executive network closely corresponds to the fronto-cingulo-parietal network (Aarts et al., 2011; Cole & Schneider, 2007; Niendam et al., 2012; Power et al., 2011; Robbins et al., 2012; Spreng et al., 2013) and includes several frontal regions, such as the dorsal and ventral lateral prefrontal cortex, frontal pole, and anterior cingulate (Figures 5.1 and 5.2). Other CEN nodes within the fronto-parietal and fronto-striatal tracts include the posterior parietal cortex, intraparietal sulcus, basal ganglia, thalamus, and cerebellum. The CEN as a whole facilitates attentional control in the service of goal-directed thought and action, whereas the DMN is engaged under conditions of internally directed mentation (Andrews-Hanna et al., 2014; Buckner et al., 2008; Raichle, 2015). Default mode network brain regions include the ventral and dorsal medial prefrontal cortices; retrosplenial and posterior cingulate cortices; anterior lateral temporal cortex and temporal poles; inferior parietal cortex and temporoparietal junction; and hippocampus and other medial temporal lobe structures (Figures 5.1 and 5.2). The third network of regions that has been discussed in the context of creative information processing operations is the SCN (Binder & Desai, 2011; Binder, Desai, Graves, & Conant, 2009; Jefferies, 2013) (Figure 5.3). The regions of the SCN that overlap with the DMN include the ventral medial PFC, dorsal medial PFC (medial extent of the superior frontal gyrus), posterior cingulate cortex, posterior middle temporal gyrus, and the angular gyrus. The regions of the SCN that overlap with the CEN include the ventrolateral PFC, dorsolateral PFC (lateral extent of the superior frontal gyrus), and the supramarginal gyrus (which is part of the posterior parietal cortex). There are several to consider

when interpreting the role of a brain region that is implicated in two or
more brain networks (see Box 5.2).

Box 5.2 Problems of Interpretation: Which Network-Based Interpretation to Choose?

A serious problem that has received almost no attention in methodological
discussions within cognitive neuroscience is how to ascribe functional roles
to single brain regions that are part of two or more brain networks – all of
which are theoretically relevant to the particular psychological operation
under study. One example of implicated brain regions across networks in the
case of creative neurocognition includes lateral and medial parts of the most
posterior and dorsal extent of Brodmann area 8 in the superior frontal gyrus
(SFG), which is the brain area that is part of the dorsolateral PFC in the CEN
(Figure 5.2), the dorsomedial PFC in the DMN (Figure 5.2), and the SFG in
the SCN (Figure 5.3). Another example is the angular gyrus (Brodmann area
39) along the lateral parietal cortex, which is part of the semantic control
network (Figure 5.3) and overlaps with the inferior parietal lobe in the DMN
as well as the posterior parietal cortex in the CEN (Figure 5.2). There are few
guidelines on how to go about deciding which network-level interpretation
to lean on when these regions are engaged, particularly in the context of
explorative investigations. Instead of choosing thoroughness and explicating
all relevant interpretations, the practice tends to be a compromise of sorts in
that the authors pick one or other interpretation of interest and simply disre-
gard the rest of the possibilities. The problem of interpretation in relation to
brain networks is a matter of legitimate concern in research in creative (and
non-creative) neurocognition (Fedorenko & Thompson-Schill, 2014), and it
is one in dire need of further attention.

5.2 Brain-to-Process Explanations

Most brain-to-process explanations have their basis in the frontal lobe
generally and the prefrontal cortex (PFC) in particular. This is probably owing to the fact that the PFC is known to be involved in all forms
of complex cognition and is consistently engaged across a wide array
of creativity paradigms (Dietrich & Kanso, 2010). So two of the four
local explanations described below lean on frontal lobe-related function
(Sections 5.2.1 and 5.2.2). The remaining two focus on non-frontal
regions of interest (Section 5.2.3) and other indices of brain activity
(Section 5.2.4).

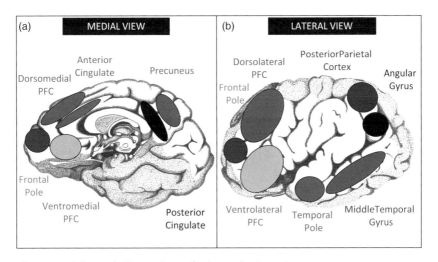

Figure 5.1 Schematic illustrations of relevant brain regions

(a) Medial view of the brain. **(b)** Lateral view of the brain. © Greig Abraham. A black and white version of this figure will appear in some formats. For the color version, please refer to the plate section.

5.2.1 Frontal Lobe Function/Dysfunction

Investigations of creativity have indicated that the areas of the PFC that are of especial relevance are the lateral and anterior regions (Petrides, 2005; Stuss, 2011). Based on neuroanatomical and functional evidence, the role of the frontal pole (also referred to as the anterior PFC, rostral PFC, or frontopolar cortex), which encompasses Brodmann area 10 (BA 10) is regarded to be that of an integrator which synthesizes the output of multiple cognitive operations (Ramnani & Owen, 2004). This brain region is active during creativity tasks that call for the integration of unrelated or weakly related concepts, such as during creative idea generation, conceptual expansion, musical improvisation, analogical reasoning, and metaphor processing (Abraham, Pieritz, et al., 2012; Beaty et al., 2015; Green et al., 2010; Kröger et al., 2012; Limb & Braun, 2008; Rutter, Kröger, Stark, et al., 2012) (Figure 5.2).

Located just posterior to the frontal pole are the ventrolateral and dorsolateral PFC. The ventrolateral PFC, or lateral inferior frontal gyrus (IFG: BA 45 and 47), is involved in semantic aspects of cognitive control, such as the lexical selection and controlled retrieval of conceptual knowledge (Badre & Wagner, 2007; Thompson-Schill, 2003), and

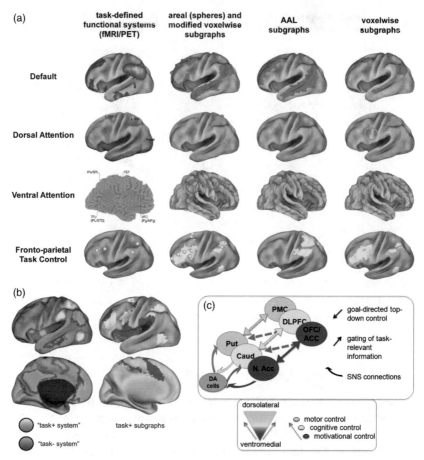

Figure 5.2 The default mode network (DMN) and the central executive network (CEN) Key regions of the DMN [**(a)** top row and **(b)** task-negative network] and the CEN fronto-parietal task control network [**(a)** bottom row and **(b)** task-positive network]. Reprinted from *Neuron, 72*(4), Power JD, Cohen AL, Nelson SM, Wig GS, Barnes KA, Church JA, Vogel AC, Laumann TO, Miezin FM, Schlaggar BL, & Petersen SE, Functional network organization of the human brain, 665–678, © 2011, with permission from Elsevier. **(c)** Three frontostriatal loops involved in top-down control (red: motivational; yellow: cognitive; blue: motor). Reprinted with permission from Aarts E, van Holstein M & Cools R (2011). Striatal dopamine and the interface between motivation and cognition. *Frontiers in Psychology, 2*, 163. [ACC: anterior cingulate cortex; Caud: caudate nucleus; DLPFC: dorsolateral prefrontal cortex; N. Acc: nucleus accumbens; Put: putamen; OFC: orbitofrontal cortex; PMC: premotor cortex; SNS: striato-nigral-striatal]. A black and white version of this figure will appear in some formats. For the color version, please refer to the plate section.

is consistently engaged during creative story writing and conceptual expansion, and when processing novel metaphors (Abraham, Pieritz, et al., 2012; Kröger et al., 2012; Mashal et al., 2007; Rutter, Kröger, Stark, et al., 2012; Shah et al., 2011). Direct comparisons using suitable control tasks have, in fact, indicated that the ventrolateral PFC is more engaged during creative ideation than during cognitive control (Abraham, Pieritz, et al., 2012).

The role of the dorsolateral PFC, which includes parts of the superior and middle frontal gyri (BA 8, 9, and 46), is in the monitoring and maintenance of task-set information in working memory (du Boisgueheneuc et al., 2006; Eriksson, Vogel, Lansner, Bergström, & Nyberg, 2015; Wager & Smith, 2003). Activity in this region has been associated with creativity, such as during the evaluation stage in creative ideation (Ellamil et al., 2012). The dorsolateral PFC, however, plays a more complex role in creative cognition as "deactivations" of this region have also been shown to characterize the creative idea generation stage during poetry composition as well as musical and lyrical improvisation (Limb & Braun, 2008; Liu et al., 2012, 2015).

Indeed, such findings highlight one of the complexities about the role of the PFC in creativity. It is clear that different parts of this vast structure are activated during creative thinking (Dietrich & Kanso, 2010), although the engagement of specific brain regions across paradigms is somewhat erratic and therefore challenging to interpret meaningfully. This is partly attributable to the lack of consistency between experimental paradigms that investigate creativity (Arden et al., 2010). While lesions to the PFC are associated with impoverished performance on many aspects of creative cognition, such as fluency and originality in idea generation, they have also been linked to specific advantages (Abraham, Beudt, et al., 2012). For instance, lesions of the lateral PFC (predominantly dorsolateral) have been associated with superior performance on insight problem-solving tasks (Reverberi et al., 2005), and lesions of the frontopolar and orbitofrontal regions have been associated with an enhanced ability to overcome the constraining influence of salient examples during creative idea generation (Abraham, Beudt, et al., 2012).

So how best can these divergent findings of advantages and disadvantages in relation to frontal lobe damage be integrated and understood? One postulation that has been put forward is that the information processing advantages that accompany frontal lobe deactivation or dysfunction are specific to "active contexts" (Abraham, 2014c).

These are immediately salient contexts that actively, automatically, and inadvertently impinge on one's thought processes. In order to perform optimally on specific tasks of creative thinking (e.g., overcoming knowledge constraints, improvisation, insight), such actively salient contexts need to be inhibited or overcome in order to move away from the path-of-least-resistance and generate truly original responses. Downregulation of the frontal lobe leads to reduced cognitive control, which in turn allows for the loosening of conceptual constraints and consequent access to less salient or more unusual conceptual associations (Abraham, 2014a; Ansburg & Hill, 2003; Chrysikou, Novick, Trueswell, & Thompson-Schill, 2011; Reverberi, Laiacona, & Capitani, 2006). This would enable better performance on these specific aspects of creative cognition where active contexts abound, but not in other contexts. Such ideas about the specificity of frontal lobe function in orchestrating aspects of creative thinking can be aligned to another local explanation, which is discussed next.

5.2.2 Basal versus Transient Hypofrontality

Beginning in the 1970s, in his pursuit of unraveling the biological correlates of creativity, Martindale conducted a series of EEG-based investigations to examine brain activity elicited during creative thinking. He proposed that brain activity patterns during creative inspiration in highly creative individuals are marked by a state of defocused attention (see Section 3.2.2). This is held to occur by means of lower levels of cortical arousal and reduced frontal lobe activation, which brings about loose associational thinking and results in the activation of more remote associates than is ordinarily the case (Martindale, 1999). There is some evidence that "hypofrontality"' is associated with creative ideation and diffuse attentional control. For instance, comparable levels of EEG complexity over frontal brain regions are found during divergent creative thinking and mental relaxation compared to convergent non-creative thinking (Mölle et al., 1996). Venturing down this line of reasoning, then, investigations were conducted to verify whether this potential marker of hypofrontality or reduced frontal engagement in relation to creativity could explain individual differences in creativity. However, evidence that highly creative subjects exhibited lower levels of trait or basal cortical activation is equivocal, at best (Martindale, 1999; Mölle et al., 1996).

An alternative idea – that of state, or "transient hypofrontality" – was popularized by Arne Dietrich based on his analysis of flow experience,

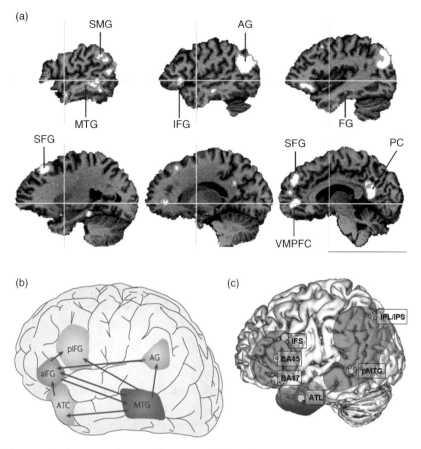

Figure 5.3 The semantic cognition network (SCN)

(a) Key regions of the SCN as indicated by a meta-analysis. Reprinted from *Trends in Cognitive Sciences*, *15*(11), Binder JR & Desai RH, The neurobiology of semantic memory, 527–536, © 2011, with permission from Elsevier. **(b)** A model for semantic cognition where pIFG and aIFG mediate controlled access and retrieval, respectively, of lexical representations that are stored in the MTG. The ATC and AG integrate incoming information with current context representations. Reprinted by permission from Springer Nature. *Nature Reviews Neuroscience*. A cortical network for semantics: (De)constructing the N400. Lau EF, Phillips C & Poeppel D. © 2008. **(c)** A distributed brain network for semantic cognition. Reprinted from *Cortex*, *49*(3), Jefferies E, The neural basis of semantic cognition: converging evidence from neuropsychology, neuroimaging and TMS, Pages 611–625, © 2013, with permission from Elsevier. [a: anterior; AG: angular gyrus; ATC/ATL: anterior temporal cortex/lobe; FG: fusiform gyrus; IFG/IFS: inferior frontal gyrus/sulcus; IFS: inferior frontal sulcus; IPL/IPS: inferior parietal lobule/sulcus; MTG: middle temporal gyrus; PS: posterior cingulate; p: posterior; SFG: superior frontal gyrus; SMG: supramarginal gyrus; VMPFC: ventromedial prefrontal cortex]. A black and white version of this figure will appear in some formats. For the color version, please refer to the plate section.

which is "an almost automatic, effortless, yet highly focused state of consciousness" (Csikszentmihalyi, 1997). Any activity can lead to a flow state as long as certain internal and external conditions are met. Flow occurs under conditions of deep task absorption and passion in performance of a challenging task that is perfectly matched to one's ability and for which one receives immediate feedback. This "peak experience" is accompanied by a melting away of the sense of time and a state of absolute contentment in the moment. The brain mechanisms underlying flow, which is believed to be integral to creativity, occur through the dynamic interplay between the explicit system, which is subserved by frontal and medial temporal lobe structures, and the implicit system, which is undertaken by the basal ganglia to facilitate the flexibility–efficiency tradeoff during information processing (Dietrich, 2004a). The temporary lapse of the explicit system via transient hypofrontality allows for entering into a state of flow, which involves seamless sensory-motor integration processes that would be advantageous during extended acts of creative feats, such as during musical improvisation, writing, and athletic performance. While there is behavioral evidence of the link between flow and creative performance (Section 3.4.7), the idea that transient hypofrontality is the basis of (or conducive to) getting into flow states has yet to be empirically verified (for indirect evidence, see Wollseiffen et al., 2016).

5.2.3 Alpha Wave-Related Brain Activity

The aforementioned studies of Colin Martindale constituted the very first EEG investigations of creativity, and the focus on alpha wave activity as being especially relevant (Martindale, 1999). Alpha wave brain activity is held to reflect cortical arousal in the form of an inverse relation such that high alpha activity reflects reduced cortical arousal. An early study, for instance, found that good performers on a creativity task exhibited reduced cortical arousal in the form of enhanced alpha wave activity but that this was limited to the inspiration phase of creative thinking, not the elaboration phase (Martindale & Hasenfus, 1978).

Alpha waves are characterized as those falling in the 8–12Hz frequency band, which are further subdivided in two sub-bands, lower alpha (8–10Hz) and higher alpha (10–12Hz), reflecting different aspects of information processing (Fink & Benedek, 2014). Event-related desynchronization (ERD) and event-related synchronization (ERS) refer to event-related power decreases and increases, respectively, from an activation interval reference point. Both these indices are sensitive to higher-order cognitive abilities. The lower alpha ERD (8–10Hz), for instance, is held to reflect attentional processes like vigilance and arousal, while the higher alpha ERD (10–12Hz) is modulated by specific task parameters, such as semantic memory processes (Klimesch, 1999). In contrast, the ERS, or increases in alpha band power, is held to be indicative of a state of "cortical idling" or diminished information processing (Pfurtscheller, Stancák, & Neuper, 1996).

While the manner in which each alpha band and the different brain regions implicated in generating such activity respond across the generation and evaluation stages of creative ideation is as yet unclear, increased ERS (or an absence of ERD) in alpha power has been consistently reported in relation to creative idea generation, particularly when using tasks of divergent creative thinking (Fink & Benedek, 2014). Moreover, the greater the level of originality associated with creative ideation, the higher the levels of alpha synchronization, particularly in the right hemisphere (Schwab, Benedek, Papousek, Weiss, & Fink, 2014). In fact, temporarily enhancing alpha power over frontal sites by means of transcranial alternating current stimulation (tACS) led to demonstrably improved performance on a creative aptitude test battery (Lustenberger, Boyle, Foulser, Mellin, & Fröhlich, 2015). A special case is being increasingly made for alpha wave activity as not only reflecting internally directed attention, but also a form of neural gating mechanism that keeps distractions in the external world from impinging upon internal imaginative mentation (Benedek, Schickel, Jauk, Fink, & Neubauer, 2014).

The message delivered within the scientific literature in relation to creativity and alpha synchronization is relatively homogenous, but one major caveat needs to be kept in mind. Problems with interpretations of alpha wave activity have been extensively noted in the wider EEG literature. This is partly attributable to the fact that "alpha is not a unitary phenomenon, rather it is comprised of different oscillations with different frequencies across a broad range" (Bazanova & Vernon, 2014, 106). Experts have gone so far as to state that "alpha does not generally reflect 'passive states' or 'idling of the brain'" (Başar, 2012, 21) and instead that "synchronization in the alpha frequency range … plays an important role in top-down control of cortical activation and excitability" (Bazanova & Vernon, 2014, 106). Such observations have serious implications for interpretations of what exactly alpha brain activity is indicative of in relation to creative cognition.

5.2.4 Other Specific Brain Regions of Interest

Apart from the frontal lobe, other regions that have received special focus in the context of creativity include the precuneus, the hippocampus, and the basal ganglia. The precuneus occupies the dorsal regions in the medial parietal cortex (BA 7) and is involved in a wide range of functions, including episodic memory retrieval, self-related operations, and visuo-spatial imagery (Cavanna & Trimble, 2006). It is also often positively associated with divergent creative thinking (Beaty et al., 2015; Chen et al., 2015; Jauk et al., 2015). Along with the neighboring posterior cingulate cortex (PCC), the precuneus is widely regarded as being part of the DMN of the brain, and this shapes interpretations of its specific role in creative ideation. Interestingly, it was stated in one of the seminal papers that delineated the DMN that "connections do exist between area 7m and the PCC, which may be the basis for the extensive activation patterns sometimes observed along the posterior midline, but we suspect that area 7m is not a core component of the network" (Buckner et al., 2008, 9). The debate surrounding the functional role of the precuneus, which is associated with both the DMN and the CEN, is seldom acknowledged in the creativity literature. For instance, the finding that increased connectivity is seen between the precuneus and the DMN during rest whereas increased connectivity is found between the precuneus and the CEN during task performance (Utevsky, Smith, & Huettel, 2014) has critical implications for the connectivity-based studies of creativity, which largely only interpret the involvement of the precuneus in relation to its role within the DMN (e.g., Zhu et al., 2017).

Another region of the DMN that is increasingly gaining more attention is the hippocampus within the medial temporal lobe. The role of the hippocampus in operations relevant to episodic memory is well established (Cabeza & St Jacques, 2007; Svoboda, McKinnon, & Levine, 2006), and the potential role of this region in creative thinking is based on its involvement in flexible cognition (Rubin, Watson, Duff, & Cohen, 2014) and operations of the imagination (Abraham, 2016). Studies on five patients with hippocampal lesions showed that they display poor performance in convergent creative thinking, as well as in verbal and figural forms of divergent creative thinking (Duff, Kurczek, Rubin, Cohen, & Tranel, 2013; Warren, Kurczek, & Duff, 2016). The engagement of the hippocampus in creative ideation is, however, rarely reported in neuroimaging studies. The limited evidence on hand suggests that the hippocampus may be sensitive to the processing of appropriateness (but not novelty) in creativity (Huang, Fan, & Luo, 2015).

A final region of focus is the basal ganglia, which is a core structure within the CEN and is involved in inhibitory control in cognition and action (Aron, 2007). Several neuroimaging studies have indicated that larger gray and white volumes of the basal ganglia (Jauk et al., 2015; Takeuchi et al., 2010a, 2010b) and increased functional engagement and connectivity within the structure (Erhard, Kessler, Neumann, Ortheil, & Lotze, 2014a; Lotze, Erhard, Neumann, Eickhoff, & Langner, 2014) are correlated with better performance or ability on a range of creativity tasks. On the other hand, though, one study found the opposite pattern (Jung et al., 2010), which fits better with the pattern of findings from behavioral studies that have, for instance, shown that poor cognitive inhibition (or cognitive disinhibition) is linked with better creative achievement (e.g., Carson et al., 2003). This indicates that engaging inhibitory control is associated with better creativity but that insufficiencies in inhibition also lead to enhanced creativity. Here, again, we have the problem of understanding how these conflicting ideas can be aligned. One possibility is that advantages in information processing that occur through cognitive disinhibition are specific to particular contexts of creative idea generation. That is indeed what some neuropsychological evidence suggests: patients with basal ganglia lesions demonstrated poorer performance on some facets of creative cognition (e.g., "practicality in creative imagery" or the ability to generate functional inventions). But on other aspects of creative cognition, they showed unchanged performance (e.g., "originality in creative imagery" or the ability to generate unique inventions) and even superior performance (overcoming constraints of examples during creative idea generation) (Abraham, Beudt, et al., 2012) (see Section 5.3.2).

5.3 Process-to-Brain Explanations

The alternative path to take when applying local explanations in the physiological approach to understanding the creative mind is to begin by focusing on processes specific to creative cognition (Abraham & Windmann, 2007; Finke et al., 1996) and to evaluate the brain basis of these processes in order to understand their underlying mechanisms by relating them to the wider functions of the implicated brain regions. The mental operations of relevance to creative neurocognition (also see Section 3.4) include the "a-ha" experience that accompanies the solving of analytical problems (insight), the widening of existing conceptual knowledge structures to include novel elements (conceptual expansion), getting past the distracting influence of salient information (overcoming knowledge constraints), envisioning novel and usable objects by combining simple abstract elements (creative imagery), and applying the knowledge of one domain to another domain in order to solve problems (analogical reasoning) or reap a deeper conceptual understanding of a particular phenomenon across different contexts (metaphor processing) (see Box 5.3).

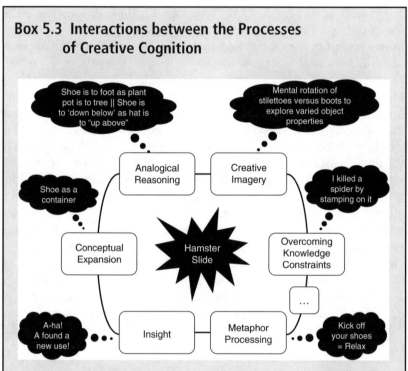

Box 5.3 Interactions between the Processes of Creative Cognition

Processes of creative cognition

In order to uncover the information processing and neural mechanisms that underlie creativity, the different operations of creative cognition have been necessarily examined in isolation. This is the standard approach that is adopted in empirical investigations on all aspects of perception, cognition, and action. It must therefore be noted that it would be invalid to reach the conclusion that these operations are mutually exclusive and do not interact with one another. The opposite is, in fact, the case. These (and other) processes work in unison when we engage in creative pursuits in any domain of human endeavor. The schematic diagram above uses a hypothetical example to illustrate the dynamic and integrated workings of the mental operations that have been studied following the "physiological" approach to creativity and that are involved in creative idea generation (adapted from Abraham, 2014a).

5.3.1 Insight

All of us have had the experience of being at an impasse, being unable to solve a problem. A sense of frustration ensues and often, when temporarily distracted from the context, a solution suddenly pops into one's consciousness seemingly out of nowhere. This "eureka" moment or "a-ha" experience is often referred to as insight. It is the most widely studied mental operation in relation to the neurocognition of creativity (Kounios & Beeman, 2014). The feeling of insight is indexed by the phenomenology of suddenness in the arrival of a solution during the problem-solving process. Insight is held to be especially relevant for creativity as this involuntary feeling that accompanies the reaching of the solution emerges as a result of overcoming functional fixedness and engaging in a perspective shift. The brain region that is held to be particularly relevant in the context of insight is the right anterior temporal lobe (one of the core regions of the DMN as well as the SCN), a brain area that encompasses parts of the superior and middle temporal gyri (Chi & Snyder, 2011; Jung-Beeman et al., 2004).

Regions of the CEN, such as the dorsolateral PFC, ventrolateral PFC, and anterior cingulate cortex, have also been reported in relation to insight in problem solving. However, the picture is somewhat complicated, with some studies showing the engagement of ventrolateral regions in the same (Aziz-Zadeh, Kaplan, & Iacoboni, 2009) while others indicate that disruptions to dorsolateral regions are associated with better performance on insight tasks (Reverberi et al., 2005). So the role played by the different frontal structures within the CEN in insight problem solving has yet to be clarified.

Due to the temporal specificity involved in the feeling of insight, this operation lends itself to investigation using EEG-based approaches and these can be used to uncover its neural signature. EEG power indices that are held to be relevant in this regard include the alpha activity over right parietal-occipital regions prior to the response and gamma activity over right temporal regions at the point of the response (Kounios & Beeman, 2014). The "alpha insight effect" is held to reflect neural inhibition in the form of "transient sensory gating that reduces noise from distracting inputs to facilitate retrieval of the weakly and unconsciously activated solution," whereas the "gamma insight effect" is believed to index "a mechanism for binding information" as one becomes conscious or aware of the solution (ibid., 79–80). Increases in alpha power are specific to the intrinsic or self-generation of insight during problem solving, as decreases in alpha power are associated with extrinsically induced insights (by means of hints or providing the solution) (Rothmaler, Nigbur, & Ivanova, 2017).

5.3.2 Analogical Reasoning

Complete this sentence: *Kitten is to cat as puppy is to* ___. This is an example of a simple analogy (also see Section 3.4.2) where the relational mapping (A:B::C:D) between concepts is made within two very similar contexts [kitten:cat] and [puppy:dog]. By varying the semantic distance between the contexts, though, the analogical transfer can be made more challenging. *Blindness is to sight as poverty is to* ___. This is an example of a more complex analogy where a relational mapping needs to be formed across quite seemingly different contexts [blindness:sight] and [poverty:money]. What is important to note, however, is that the surface dissimilarity between the domains belies the potential for gleaning deep similarities in the way their concepts relate to one another (Green et al., 2012).

Reasoning by analogy typically refers to processing of information where the nature and relationships between the nodes of conceptual knowledge in a highly familiar domain are applied to another, less familiar, domain in order to solve a problem or better understand a situation therein (Holyoak & Thagard, 1995; Speed, 2010). The iconic example is the analogical mapping made by Ernest Rutherford between the structure of the solar system and that of an atom, which was a revolutionary conceptual advance that laid to rest the then-dominant plum pudding model of the atom proposed by Joseph John Thomas, English physicist and Nobel laureate. Analogical reasoning is held to be central to understanding creativity, as creative ideas occur via the establishment of novel conceptual connections between previously unconnected or only weakly associated concepts. As such, it is associated with key advances in scientific creativity (Dunbar, 1997) (Section 12.2.2).

Much evidence supports the case that the frontal pole (BA 10) is the key structure implicated in the processing of analogical reasoning (Urbanski et al., 2016) in general. This fits with the functional role ascribed to this brain region during information processing (especially when taking into account its unique anatomical features), which is to integrate the output of multiple cognitive operations (Ramnani & Owen, 2004). This is necessitated when engaging in complex relational reasoning and relational integration of concepts (Christoff et al., 2001; Parkin, Hellyer, Leech, & Hampshire, 2015; Wendelken et al., 2008). There is evidence to suggest that this functional specificity of the frontal pole extends to creative analogical reasoning (Green, 2016; Green et al., 2012). The study that would constitute definitive proof of this would be to evaluate brain activity patterns during the discovery or generation of novel analogies, but this is difficult to pin down given the unpredictability of the creative process. So far, the approach has been to contrast the brain correlates underlying inference generation when making analogies between more and less dissimilar semantic contexts.

5.3.3 Metaphor

Another domain that deals with learning, expressing, or discovering by mapping similarity between different contexts is that of metaphor processing (also see Section 3.4.3). The difference between metaphors and analogies lies in the fact that the relational nature of the associations in the case of a metaphor (e.g., *Your words are hollow*) is less directionally prescribed than an analogy. Linguistic metaphors are "the application of a word or expression that properly belongs to one context to express meaning in a different context because of some real or implied similarity in the referents involved" (Anderson, 1964, 53). A notion of conceptual metaphors goes beyond this, in that metaphors are primarily seen as conceptual and only secondarily as linguistic, gestural, or visual (Lakoff, 2014). The relevance of metaphor processing to creativity was noted early on by Arthur Koestler (1969), who postulated that originality in science, art, and humor stems from the bisociation or juxtaposition, as opposed to the mere association, of two unrelated thought matrices.

With regard to the brain regions involved in metaphor processing, the overall picture is less clear-cut relative to other processes of creative cognition, with several brain regions implicated. The focus here will be limited to the most consistent findings across paradigms. Abundant research on semantic aspects of language processing have indicated that the processing of novel metaphors consistently engages specific regions of the semantic cognition brain network (Binder et al., 2009; Bookheimer, 2002), particularly anterior aspects of the inferior frontal gyrus (BA 45 and 47) and the left angular gyrus (BA 39) (Beaty, Silvia, & Benedek, 2017; Benedek, Beaty, et al., 2014; Rapp, Leube, Erb, Grodd, & Kircher, 2004; Rutter, Kröger, Stark, et al., 2012; Stringaris, Medford, Giampietro, Brammer, & David, 2007). As to the specific roles of these regions within semantic processing, the role of the anterior inferior frontal gyrus (also known as the ventrolateral prefrontal cortex) is in controlled semantic retrieval whereas the angular gyrus (parts of which are also referred to in the neuroscientific literature as the temporo-parietal junction) is held to subserve the detection of conceptual associations via the integration of multisensory information (Badre & Wagner, 2007; Lau et al., 2008; Seghier, 2013).

5.3.4 Conceptual Expansion

Try this imaginative exercise. I want you to imagine an egg. And not just any egg. The kind of egg no one has ever seen before, a completely new type of egg. In fact, it should be nothing like a typical egg. Once you've imagined it, draw your invention. Your task, then, is to think about how different your invented egg is from a typical egg in terms of shape, size, texture, density, and so on. A typical egg you find on Earth is rounded, symmetrical, fragile, pale in color, and so on. The further away your invented egg is from a typical egg, the better your ability to engage in conceptual expansion (also see Section 3.4.5).

A central mental operation of creative cognition is conceptual expansion, which refers to the ability to broaden our concepts or go beyond the limitations of established conceptual structures of semantic knowledge (Ward, 1994). It is the very basis of creative idea generation, as the ability to come with an original idea necessitates the modification of existing concepts through the addition of novel elements. Neuroimaging studies have shown the involvement of CEN regions, such as the frontal pole (BA 10) and ventrolateral PFC (BA 45 and 47), as well as DMN regions, such as the temporal poles (BA 38), during conceptual expansion (Abraham, 2014a). These regions are discussed in unison as part of the SCN (Binder & Desai, 2011) and are more strongly engaged across different experimental paradigms that assess conceptual expansion relative to general divergent thinking and high cognitive demand (Abraham, Pieritz, et al., 2012) and during conceptual expansion (semantic novelty and semantic appropriateness) relative to the processing of mere semantic novelty or mere semantic appropriateness (Kröger et al., 2012; Rutter, Kröger, Stark, et al., 2012). EEG studies of conceptual expansion indicate that two event-related potential (ERP) components are of key relevance. The N400, which indexes semantic novelty (Kutas & Federmeier, 2011), and a late positivity ERP, which indexes the integration of semantic knowledge (Brouwer, Fitz, & Hoeks, 2012), jointly provide a coupled neural signature for conceptual expansion (Kröger et al., 2013; Rutter, Kröger, Hill, et al., 2012). So, the SCN plays a key role in facilitating this creative cognitive operation.

5.3.5 Overcoming Knowledge Constraints

Here's another imaginative activity. Your task now is to not think about your mom. Can you do that? I suspect that this is a difficult task for you as it is for almost everyone. The mere instruction of telling someone not to think of something has induced the opposite effect. This simple exercise is revealing of one of the obstacles we face when we try to generate a new idea; that is, it is difficult to see past what we already know. Our knowledge can impose conceptual constraints, limiting our ability to create. An important cognitive faculty, then, in the context of creativity is to be able to overcome knowledge constraints in order to make something new. Our propensity to be limited by knowledge can be investigated by assessing our ability to inhibit the distracting influence of salient examples that activate a knowledge context that gets in the way when trying to generate something new (Smith et al., 1993) (also see Section 3.4.6). Neuropsychological evidence has revealed that lesions to parieto-temporal areas of the brain (of relevance to the DMN and the semantic control network), are accompanied by a reduced ability to overcome knowledge constraints (Abraham, Beudt, et al., 2012). Lesions of this brain region are typically associated with perseverative responses that are commonly reported when faced with semantic distractors (Corbett, Jefferies, & Ralph, 2009, 2011). In fact, structural neuroimaging studies have indicated that greater cortical thickness in this region is associated with better creative performance and creative achievement (Jung et al., 2010).

Interestingly, though, lesions to circumscribed areas of the CEN, namely, the basal ganglia and the frontal pole, were associated with an enhanced capacity to overcome the constraining influence of examples during creative idea generation (Abraham, Beudt, et al., 2012). The advantage was specific to this process of creative cognition as neither of these neurological groups demonstrated advantages on any other aspect of creativity. This information processing advantage was also specific to these brain regions, as lesions to other parts of the CEN, such as the lateral prefrontal cortex, did not have a significant positive or negative impact on the ability to overcome the constraining influence of examples during creative ideation. The hypothesis that immediately salient or "active contexts" that intrude on one's thought processes and inhibit creative ideation would be less potent following damage to parts of the CEN and thereby lead to advantages in creativity was discussed earlier (Section 5.2.1), and it applies to the present context as well as those of insight and improvisation in creativity.

5.3.6 Imagery

Mental imagery has been a topic of broad interest from the earliest phases of neuroscientific research, where much of the impetus was directed at identifying whether the brain regions that are involved in sensory perception are also involved in the mental imagery of the same. Considerable evidence suggests that this is the case (Pearson & Kosslyn, 2015). Mental imagery is thought to play a central role in reaching creative insights in both discovery in the sciences and expression in the arts, as has been suggested by much anecdotal evidence. For instance, Kekule's insight into the structure of the benzene atom was allegedly derived from the imagery he generated while daydreaming of a snake biting its own tail. Creative imagery typically refers to the vividness of abstract and mainly visual imagination that serves as an aid in the generation of a novel idea (Finke, 1990) (also see Section 3.4.4).

This operation of creative cognition has not been as well studied in a concerted manner using neuroscientific techniques as other operations of creative cognition, but when viewed for consistency, the limited evidence on hand is suggestive of a number of patterns. The tasks can vary greatly in that some test the ability to create novel but usable combinations from a set of simple geometrical elements (Abraham, Beudt, et al., 2012; Aziz-Zadeh et al., 2012), while others are more concrete tasks that require people to generate a book cover or a work of art, for instance (De Pisapia, Bacci, Parrott, & Melcher, 2016; Ellamil et al., 2012; Li, Yang, Zhang, Li, & Qiu, 2016).

There is evidence for the dynamic interplay between the DMN and the CEN during tasks that call for creative imagery (De Pisapia et al., 2016; Ellamil et al., 2012). Some researchers have attempted to be more focused in that they have more specifically argued for the role played by distinct parts of the CEN, such as the dorsolateral and ventrolateral PFC. Creative imagery compared to noncreative imagery leads to activations in these regions (Aziz-Zadeh et al., 2012; Huang et al., 2013). A large neuropsychological study indicated that patients with lesions of the basal ganglia (CEN) and the lateral temporal-parietal cortex (DMN, SCN) show poor creative imagery with reference to only the practicality index, which refers to the functionality of the generated product. However, lesions of the lateral prefrontal cortex (CEN) were accompanied by poor performance on both the originality and practicality indices of the creative imagery task (Abraham, Beudt, et al., 2012).

5.4 Critical Evaluation of Local Explanations

If you look back over the previous sections of this chapter, the first problem with the local view should be apparent. The chief problem with local explanations is that, because they are focused at the level of detail, one faces an ever-growing list of brain regions of interest, cognitive processes of note, diversity in the operationalization of these processes, and the complex interactions between different types of creative cognitive operation within any particular brain region (frontal lobe), brain system (alpha activity), or brain network (default mode or central executive or semantic cognition networks). This makes getting a clear grasp of what it all means very challenging. Even detecting dominant patterns within the abundant findings can be overwhelming when having to deal with innumerable details. To make the enterprise more manageable, researchers often have to compromise by focusing even more precisely on the one process or brain region of interest while ignoring the rest. This often leads to serious oversights, particularly on account of the very real possibility of confirmation biases.

So why take a process-based approach at all? The truth of the matter is that one cannot but take on the local view if the overarching aim is to outline the information processing and neural mechanisms that underlie creative thinking across different contexts of human life, and to be able to generate powerful and valid theories regarding the same. The local view is necessarily handicapped at present because it can only flourish with momentum. Other fields of cognition and imagination, such as memory or social cognition, manage far better because of the sheer number of research groups and scientists the world over that are dedicated to the study of the key topics within these expansive fields of research. Added to that are the proactive research environments that are conducive to advances being made in the field, and the abundance of funding opportunities and initiatives available to support such research. Such a situation is not true of creativity research, which, although rapidly growing, generates nowhere near the kind of research impetus and critical discussion required for real and timely progress to be made.

So the main case against taking the view of local explanations is a logistical one. Developments happen at the pace of a slow drip owing to current deficiencies in the research infrastructure and investment associated with the neuroscience of creativity. The consequence of this state of affairs is a lack of innovation on the theoretical side, particularly in contrast to the global view where newer ideas are network-based

(Abraham, 2014a; Beaty et al., 2016) and/or derive from evolutionary principles (Dietrich, 2015; Jung et al., 2013). The field is in need of new ideas that are empirically testable while also being ecologically and biologically valid, as well as revelatory of underlying mechanisms. It is little wonder, then, that few choose to follow the directions of investigation afforded by the local view.

Chapter Summary

- Local explanations of the physiological approach to creativity are those that center on explicating the specific brain regions that are involved in specific processes of creative cognition.
- Brain-to-process local explanations focus on characterizing neural indices that can be taken as specific biomarkers of creative cognition.
- The frontal lobe is the central region that has been implicated in brain-to-process explanations in terms of both frontal lobe function and dysfunction, as well as in relation to transient hypofrontality.
- Electrophysiological approaches indicate the relevance of alpha power increases in brain activity to creative cognition.
- Process-to-brain local explanations focus on specific creative cognitive operations and seek to uncover their underlying neurocognitive mechanisms.
- The frontal poles are consistently implicated in analogical reasoning and conceptual expansion, and the ventrolateral PFC is notably involved in conceptual expansion and metaphor processing.
- Dysfunctions in parts of the CEN are shown to lead to advantages in insight during problem solving and in overcoming the constraining influence of salient examples during creative ideation.

Review Questions

1. How are local brain-based explanations of creativity characterized?
2. What are the dominant brain-to-process explanations?
3. Describe the many process-to-brain explanations.
4. What are the problems that emerge when interpreting brain activity patterns in relation to creativity?
5. Consider and outline the conceptual developments that have come about with each local explanation.

Further Reading

- Abraham, A. (2014). Creative thinking as orchestrated by semantic processing vs. cognitive control brain networks. *Frontiers in Human Neuroscience*, *8*, 87–95.
- Fink, A., & Benedek, M. (2014). EEG alpha power and creative ideation. *Neuroscience and Biobehavioral Reviews*, *44*, 111–123.
- Green, A. E. (2016). Creativity, within reason semantic distance and dynamic state creativity in relational thinking and reasoning. *Current Directions in Psychological Science*, *25*(1), 28–35.
- Kounios, J., & Beeman, M. (2014). The cognitive neuroscience of insight. *Annual Review of Psychology*, *65*, 71–93.
- Martindale, C. (1999). Biological basis of creativity. In R. J. Sternberg (Ed.), *The Cambridge handbook of creativity* (pp. 137–152). New York: Cambridge University Press.

CHAPTER SIX

Neuroscientific Methods in the Study of Creativity

"It is an earth, its fibres wrap things buried ... I am created in you somewhere as a complex filament of light."

(Margaret Atwood)

Learning Objectives

- Understanding how neuroscientific methods are used in the study of creativity
- Identifying the breadth of focus afforded by functional neuroimaging methods
- Grasping the strengths associated with structural neuroimaging methods
- Recognizing the advantages of electrophysiology-based methods
- Distinguishing between neuromodulation methods and their efficacy
- Considering the unique insights afforded by the neuropsychological approach

6.1 Mapping the Brain: Gross Anatomy, Electrical Activity, and Blood Flow

Human beings seem to have a penchant for amassing knowledge about all aspects of the world and generating summaries of the same in representative and accessible forms. A common way to do this is by constructing maps and this can be done across a wide array of physical and cultural landscapes (Brunn & Dodge, 2017). The human brain has long been included in such human endeavors and the mapping of the structures and functions of the brain date back to antiquity, with the oldest known illustrations emerging in the third century BCE within the "Alexandrian Series" (Harp & High, 2017). The dominant pre-scholastic account of brain anatomy was that of Galen (129–210 CE), whose description of human neuroanatomy as being a net-like structure was derived from the dissection of other mammals as human dissection was prohibited in ancient Rome. This strongly influenced early Christian thinkers like St Augustine (354–430 CE), who formulated the Cell Doctrine where three ventricles of the brain were referred to as cells and were each believed to contain the core abilities of the mind. René Descartes (1596–1650) extended these maps to include the eyes and limbs from which sensations were sent to the brain. In doing so, he fundamentally extended the relationship between brain structure and function. It was Andreas Vesalius (1514–1564), hailed as the founder of modern human anatomy with his seminal book, *On the Fabric of the Human Body*, who produced exquisitely detailed illustrations to depict the gross anatomy of brain including the gyri of the neocortex, the corpus callosum, the optic chiasm, the cerebellum, and the basal ganglia.

With advances in techniques that allowed better visualization of finer anatomical details, the focus shifted from mapping macrostructures in the brain to mapping microstructures in the brain. This paved the way for the Neuron Doctrine as expounded by Santiago Ramón y Cajal (1952–1934) who published *Texture of the Nervous System of Man and the Vertebrates* and other works, which contained a large collection of his beautiful illustrations of microscopic structures of brain cells. Cajal's fundamental insight was that the brain is made up of cells that are not interlinked in a net, but are spatially separated. The differences in the structural properties of cells across regions of the brain were utilized by Korbinian Brodmann (1868–1918) to create a cytoarchitectonic map of 52 distinct brain areas. The "Brodmann area" convention is still used today when referring to specific brain regions. For instance, the frontal pole corresponds to Brodmann area 10 or BA 10.

Although the mapping of psychological function to brain structure began limitedly with the invention of crude devices, such as Mosso's circulation device (see Box 6.1), they were mainly driven at the outset by neuropsychological studies (see Box 6.2), where an association is made between specific brain injuries and insufficiencies in particular psychological functions. Seminal to this approach were the investigations by Paul Broca (1824–1880), which revealed that lesions to specific regions of the frontal lobe (inferior frontal gyrus) resulted in significant difficulties in speech production; a condition that was from then on referred to as "Broca's aphasia." One of the most famous early single case reports was that of Phineas Gage, who survived an accident when a tamping iron was shot clean through his head owing to an explosion. The rod entered from the bottom of his left cheek and moved in an upward direction behind his eye, damaging his left frontal lobe from ventral orbitofrontal regions to dorsal medial and lateral regions. This case was examined by John Harlow (1819–1907), who noted permanent personality changes as a result of this brain injury. Box 6.3 explores how the neuropsychological approach has been employed in the study of creativity.

Box 6.1 Angelo Mosso (1884): The First Neuroscientific Technique

The first device designed to measure cerebral blood flow was invented by Angelo Mosso, who hypothesized in 1884 that engaging in cognitive tasks would lead to an increased blood flow to the brain (cited in Sandrone et al., 2014). In explaining what is ostensibly the first neuroscientific technique used to measure functional brain activity, William James reported the following:

> The subject to be observed lay on a delicately balanced table which could tip downwards either at the head or the foot if the weight of either end were increased. The moment emotional or intellectual activity began in the subject, down went the balance at the head-end, in consequence of the redistribution of blood in his system. (1891, 98)

While many have understandably voiced skepticism regarding the validity and reliability of the original explorations, there has in fact been a contemporary replication of Mosso's historical investigation using a similar "circulation balance" apparatus (Field & Inman, 2014).

Box 6.2 The Neuropsychological Approach

The very utility of neuroimaging approaches in delivering key theoretically relevant insights about behavioral and brain function has been called into question by some neuropsychologists (Coltheart, 2013; Page, 2006); others, however, have outlined specific contexts in which both neuroscientific and neuropsychological approaches can be used in a complementary fashion (Shallice, 2003). Synthesizing information from both approaches is the usual perspective taken by clinical, systems, and cognitive neuroscientists, who generally seek to better understand psychological function in relation to physiological factors. The field of neuropsychology aims to understand human psychological function in terms of physiology by examining dysfunctions of the brain (Ellis & Young, 2000; Gurd, 2012; Heilman & Valenstein, 2012; Schwartz & Dell, 2010). This can be done via *single case studies* of individuals with specific neurological damage or *group studies* on populations of interest that reflect specific neurological disorders or psychiatric conditions. In both situations, the guiding factor is that psychological dysfunctions that accompany brain injury or insufficiencies are exceedingly informative about the healthy human brain. While the advantage of the neuropsychological approach is its ability to be theoretically informative, the disadvantage is the inability to fully control for the impact of co-morbidities (emotional, motivational, motoric, etc.) that often accompany brain dysfunctions. Also lacking are clear ideas about the neural reorganization and plasticity following brain injury. These automatic healing and coping mechanisms of the brain have the capacity to profoundly impact our understanding of psychological and brain function.

Box 6.3 Neuropsychological Studies of Creativity

The field of creativity has seen a medley of different types of study design to assess creative processes following a neuropsychological approach; for example:

- *Single case studies* of individuals with specific neurological damage (de Souza et al., 2010; Liu et al., 2009; Miller et al., 2000, 1996; Pring, Ryder, Crane, & Hermelin, 2012; Treffert, 2014; Zaidel, 2010). The most common of these have been examinations of neurological patients with specific forms of frontotemporal dementia who develop de novo creative abilities or people who have savant-like capabilities (see Sections 4.2.2 and 10.4.3).
- *Neurological group studies* of creativity, which so far have largely examined the impact of lesions in distinct parts of the frontal lobe, temporo-parietal cortex, basal ganglia, and hippocampus on creative cognition (Abraham, Beudt, et al., 2012; Duff et al., 2013; Mayseless, Aharon-Peretz, & Shamay-Tsoory, 2014; Reverberi et al., 2005; Shamay-Tsoory, Adler, Aharon-Peretz, Perry, & Mayseless, 2011; Warren et al., 2016).
- *Psychiatric group studies* of creativity, which have mainly examined creative neurocognition in relation to bipolar disorder, schizophrenia, ADHD, and autism (Abraham et al., 2007, 2006; Andreasen, 1987; Craig & Baron-Cohen, 1999; Power et al., 2015; Soeiro-de-Souza, Dias, Bio, Post, & Moreno, 2011).
- A *quasi-neuropsychological approach*, which marks the grounding behind the study of subclinical personality traits in relation to creativity, such as psychoticism and schizotypy (Abraham, 2014b; Fink et al., 2013; Nettle & Clegg, 2006; Park, Kirk, & Waldie, 2015).

Wilder Penfield (1891–1976) was the first to stimulate brain activity in real time. He developed the Montreal procedure, whereby neurons along the cerebral cortex of an anesthetized patient could be stimulated with electrodes. This signal would evoke a behavioral response, thereby guiding surgical incision. Using this technique, Penfield strengthened the empirical foundations of functional localization by creating "maps of cortical connections to limbs and organs in the body, which remain in use today" (Harp & High, 2017, 133). Modern-day brain stimulation techniques such as transcranial magnetic resonance imaging (TMS) and transcranial direct current stimulation (tDCS) seek to disrupt or modulate neural activity (see Section 6.5).

Lengthy recordings of brain activity from awake subjects began with the development of electroencephalography (EEG) by Hans Berger (1873–1941) (see Section 6.4). The first human EEG was carried out in 1924, where the recording of cellular signals was made possible through the use of extracranial scalp electrodes. The utility of this non-invasive technique to measure the brain's electrical activity was clear early on as it allowed for the detection of interictal spike waves later identified as the focal physiological signature of epilepsy.

Brain mapping technology as currently used for the purpose of brain research began with technological advances in tomography, which refers to imaging or reproducing an object's form by sections. It is performed using specific types of penetrating wave, such as X-rays in computed tomography (CT), radio-frequency waves in magnetic resonance imaging (MRI), electron-positron annihilation in positron emission tomography (PET), and gamma rays in single-photon emission computed tomography (SPECT) (see Section 6.3). The waves differentially penetrate an object as a function of its density and composition. Images can thereby be generated from the sections using reconstruction algorithms. By taking advantage of the fact that an increase in brain activity leads to increased blood flow to the implicated regions from which this activity emanates, brain mapping technology can be used for functional imaging of the hemodynamic response in real time (see Section 6.2). Classic functional neuroimaging studies using PET (e.g., the neural basis of the visual and auditory processing of single words, as described in Petersen, Fox, Posner, Mintun, & Raichle, 1988) saw the birth of modern cognitive neuroscience, and the relentless pace of advances has continued ever since (Raichle, 2009; Savoy, 2001).

In the sections that follow, a brief overview of the methods used in the neuroscientific study of creativity will be explored with representative examples to enable a clearer understanding of the "whys" and "hows" of such investigations.

6.2 Functional Neuroimaging Methods

The earliest functional neuroimaging studies in the field of creativity saw the use of regional cerebral blood flow (rCBF) techniques using radioactive tracers, such as Xenon-enhanced computed tomography, PET and SPECT (Bechtereva et al., 2004; Carlsson et al., 2000; Chávez-Eakle, Graff-Guerrero, García-Reyna, Vaugier, & Cruz-Fuentes, 2007). While some investigations relevant to the study of creativity have been conducted using near-infrared spectroscopy (NIRS; Folley & Park, 2005; Gibson, Folley, & Park, 2009), functional MRI is by far the most dominant method used in the study of creativity (Dietrich & Kanso, 2010), just as it is in cognitive neuroscience more generally (Huettel, Song, & McCarthy, 2014; Otte & Halsband, 2006; Rinck, 2017; Shibasaki, 2008).

Techniques of rCBF measure the rate of the cerebral blood flow to a specific brain region at a given time by means of thermal diffusion. In the case of techniques using radioactive tracers, a small dose of radioactive isotopes is injected into or inhaled by participants and the radioactivity emitted can be detected outside the body. Functional MRI, in contrast, does not involve the ingestion of any foreign matter. Instead, it works through the detection of *in vivo* changes in blood oxygenation. The body's hemodynamic response works through homeostatic principles and enables the rapid delivery of blood (containing nutrients like oxygen and glucose) to active body tissues, including the neuronal tissues of the brain. The fMRI response reflects changes in the ratio of oxygenated hemoglobin to deoxygenated hemoglobin, as the difference in their magnetic properties can be detected when a strong magnetic field is applied to the brain. fMRI boasts several advantages over other functional techniques, such as its noninvasiveness and the possibility of lengthier testing durations (Raichle, 2009; Savoy, 2001). Neurophysiological investigations have confirmed the coupling of neural activity to regional cerebral blood flow using fMRI (Logothetis, Pauls, Augath, Trinath, & Oeltermann, 2001).

6.2.1 rCBF via Radioactive Tracer Techniques

In 2000, Ingegerd Carlsson, Peter Wendt, and Jarl Risberg conducted the first ever neuroimaging study on creativity, in which they examined the brain correlates of individual differences in creative thinking. They explored the veracity of the hypothesis detailing the dominance of the right brain over the left brain in relation to creativity (see Section 4.2.1 on brain-based global explanations). Specifically, they predicted that highly creative individuals would demonstrate bilateral frontal lobe engagement during creative ideation whereas low creative individuals would show only unilateral left frontal lobe engagement (Carlsson et al., 2000).

Their results largely confirmed their expectations: the high creative group showed mainly bilateral increases or unchanged activity relative to the low creative group, who demonstrated mainly decreases in anterior prefrontal regions (frontal poles), frontotemporal regions (ventrolateral PFC, temporal poles), and superior frontal regions (dorsolateral PFC) (see Sections 4.2.3 and 5.1 for the relevance of these brain regions in creative neurocognition; also see Figure 6.1).

So how were the high and low creative people identified? Participants were pre-selected based on their performance on the Creative Functioning Test (CFT), a Swedish test of creative visual perception (ibid.). High creative and low creative participants (all male, 12 per group) underwent brain imaging while carrying out three verbal tasks: Automatic Speech (count aloud in sequence beginning at the number 1), Word Fluency (call aloud as many words as you can that begin with the letters "f", then "a", and finally "s"), and Alternate Uses (call aloud as many uses as you can for a brick, both common and uncommon). The dependent measures included number of words generated per minute (omitting the responses from the first minute and the last minute) for the Word Fluency task and the number of categories generated (corresponding to "flexibility" in divergent thinking) for the Alternate Uses task. Data relevant to important measures of creativity, such as "fluency" or "originality" of the generated uses was not provided. Importantly, the high and low creative groups did not differ significantly in their behavioral performance on the measures of the word fluency and Alternate Uses task. But ideational flexibility on the CFT (which was significantly more prominent in the high creative sample) significantly correlated with flexibility on the Alternate Uses task.

While Carlsson et al. (ibid.) examined the brain basis of individual differences in creative ideation within a sample of undergraduate students (magnitude of creativity – see Box 2.1 – estimated as ranging from "mini-c" to "little-c"), another team, led by Rosa Aurora Chávez-Eakle, explored the same but within a population that boasted far higher levels of creative aptitude (magnitude of creativity estimated as ranging from "Pro-c" to "Big-C"). Participants were pre-selected from a screening sample of 100 individuals, which included 40 nationally or internationally awarded artists and scientists, based on their performance on one of the figural forms of the Torrance Tests of Creative Thinking (TTCT; see Section 2.2.1). Individuals were allocated to the high creative group if they obtained a TTCT Creativity Index of very high or "gifted" (levels that only occur in 1 in 100 people), and their brain activity and

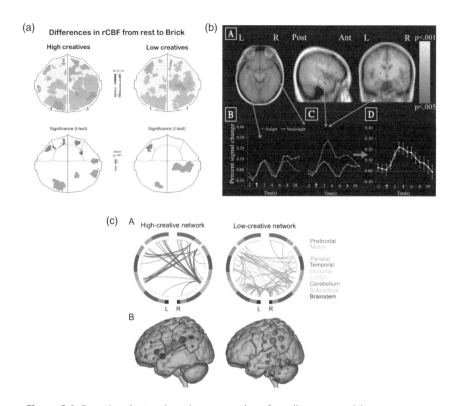

Figure 6.1 Functional neuroimaging: examples of studies on creativity

(a) A PET study showing differences in the regional cerebral blood flow (rCBF) of high and low creative people when generating alternate uses for a brick. Reprinted from *Neuropsychologia*, *38*(6), Carlsson I, Wendt PE & Risberg J, On the neurobiology of creativity: Differences in frontal activity between high and low creative subjects, pages 873–885, © 2000, with permission from Elsevier. **(b)** An fMRI study focusing on differences in functional brain activity across single brain regions in anterior (Ant) and posterior (Post) parts of the left (L) and right (R) hemispheres during insight compared to non-insight problem solving. Reprinted from Jung-Beeman M, Bowden EM, Haberman J, Frymiare JL, Arambel-Liu S, Greenblatt R, Reber PJ & Kounios J (2004). Neural activity when people solve verbal problems with insight. *PLoS Biology 2*(4): e97. **(c)** An fMRI study using functional connectivity analyses reveals high and low creative brain networks across the left (L) and right (R) hemispheres. Reprinted with permission from Beaty RE, Kenett YN, Christensen AP, Rosenberg MD, Benedek M, Chen Q, Fink A, Qiu J, Kwapil TR, Kane MJ & Silvia PJ (2018). Robust prediction of individual creative ability from brain functional connectivity. *Proceedings of the National Academy of Sciences*, 201713532. A black and white version of this figure will appear in some formats. For the color version, please refer to the plate section.

behavioral performance were then contrasted with those of an average creative group who had scores indicating an average TTCT Creativity Index (Chávez-Eakle et al., 2007).

High creative and average creative participants (12 per group, gender distribution not reported, distribution of creative professionals in each group not reported) carried out one verbal TTCT task during brain imaging: *unusual uses* (think of as many "fun, unusual, interesting, and intelligent" uses as you can for cardboard boxes). When contrasting the brain activity of these groups, high creatives demonstrated greater rCBF activity in two of the same regions reported in the previous study – the middle frontal gyrus (frontal pole: BA 10) and the frontal orbital gyrus (ventrolateral PFC: BA 47), but only in the left hemisphere. Other implicated brain regions included the bilateral premotor cortex, right orbitofrontal cortex, left inferior temporal cortex, and right culmen in the cerebellum. They also went on to correlate the degree of originality, fluency, and flexibility of the generated uses to the levels of brain activity in different regions, regardless of the individuals' level of creativity. So, for instance, level of blood flow to the frontal pole was positively correlated with the ideational originality whereas blood flow to the ventrolateral prefrontal cortex was positively correlated with ideational fluency and flexibility. The behavioral evidence indicated that the high and average creatives differed significantly on all TTCT measures of creative potential (figural creativity index, verbal creativity index, fluency, flexibility, and originality; Chávez-Eakle et al., 2007).

The Carlsson et al. (2000) landmark study paved the way for all future neuroimaging studies and was noteworthy for several reasons. For one, it was *theory-driven* in its hypotheses. In comparison, the Chávez-Eakle et al. (2007) study is largely explorative. The Carlsson et al. study also included two *control conditions* and *control variables* (anxiety and intelligence) whereas the Chávez-Eakle et al. study examined only creative ideation, which makes it impossible to verify how comparable the groups were on other aspects of (non-creative) psychological function. The remarkable feature of the Chávez-Eakle et al. study is the sample itself. *Creative potential, creative achievement*, and *creative performance* are captured by recruiting highly accomplished creative professionals, taking estimates of psychometrically based creative potential, and examining brain activity during creative ideation. In contrast, even the behavioral evidence in Carlsson et al.'s study did not significantly differentiate the groups, which raises questions about the kind of conclusions that can be reached as a result. The Chávez-Eakle et al. study also carried out *correlational analyses* between brain activity and creativity indices, but the findings are challenging to interpret as they were conducted separately for the high and average creative groups. Common to both studies is the fact that each constitutes an examination of *individual differences in creativity*. A significant shortcoming is that the findings in both studies are based on only a *single trial* of the creativity task – an unavoidable problem given the nature of such brain imaging techniques and the speed with which the radioactive tracer loses potency.

6.2.2 fMRI

Mark Beeman led a landmark study using fMRI in the neuroscience of creativity in which he examined the brain correlates of insight in problem solving (Jung-Beeman et al., 2004) (see Figure 6.1). The creative cognitive process of insight could be precisely targeted because its phenomenological properties include a feeling of the sudden arrival or onset of the solution, and this allows for the time-locking of the response to the brain activity. In evaluating the patterns of brain activity just prior to the onset of the solution, the objective of the study was to pinpoint the brain basis of the insight process and to verify whether the right hemisphere contribution in this regard was significantly greater than that of the left hemisphere (see Section 4.2.1 on brain-based global explanations). For this purpose, the Compound Associates Test (derived from the Remote Associates Test (RAT); see Section 2.3.1) was used whereby participants were presented with three words (e.g., pine | crab | sauce) for which they needed to find the solution word (e.g., apple) that forms a compound associate with all three given words (e.g., pineapple | crabapple | apple sauce). Brain activity that occurred during trials in which the participants successfully generated the solution with the experience of having an insight (suddenness in the arrival of the solution, accompanied by a feeling of confidence in the correctness of the solution) was compared with the brain activity that occurred in trials in which participants did not experience insight during problem solving.

The findings revealed that insight problem solving engaged inferior frontal regions bilaterally (ventrolateral prefrontal cortex) alongside lateral aspects of the left frontal pole and the right anterior superior temporal gyrus (STG). While these regions are commonly seen as being part of the SCN, regions of the DMN, such as the posterior cingulate and the amygdala and parahippocampal regions, were also implicated (see Sections 4.2.3 and 5.1 for the relevance of these brain regions in creative neurocognition). The authors focused on the right anterior STG as being especially relevant to the process of insight because of the pattern of brain activity across the time course of the trial as well as the corresponding EEG evidence (discussed in Section 6.4). With regard to the behavioral data, participants (13 in total: 6 men and 7 women) solved 59% of the 124 problems they were presented with and, of these, 56% of the solutions were experienced as arising through insight. So the average number of problems/trials per participant was high (41 for the insight problems and 30 for the non-insight problems), which allows for robust brain activity patterns to be derived.

While Jung-Beeman et al. focused on insight in creative cognition as the operation of interest, Abraham, Pieritz et al. (2012) examined conceptual expansion in creative cognition. Here, participants carried out two divergent thinking tasks: the Alternate Uses task (e.g., think of as many uses as possible for a shoe) and the Object Location task (e.g., think of as many objects as possible that are found in an office). Two control tasks (2-Back and 1-Back Working Memory tasks) were also included to partial out brain activity related to cognitive control components.

The brain correlates of conceptual expansion were uncovered by comparing the differences in brain activity when undertaking these tasks as the Alternate Uses task requires forging novel associations between unrelated concepts (e.g., shoe as a plant pot) and the Object Location task merely requires recalling generic associations to concepts (e.g., office: desk, chair, computer, table lamp). The authors hypothesized that brain regions that were involved in the retrieval of semantic knowledge (ventrolateral prefrontal cortex), the storage of semantic knowledge (temporal pole), and the relational integration of knowledge (frontal pole) would be engaged during conceptual expansion based on the theoretical and empirical literature on semantic cognition and executive function. The findings supported these predictions (Abraham, Pieritz, et al., 2012).

With regard to the behavioral data, participants (19 in total: 8 men and 11 women) carried out 20 trials of each task. The average number of uses generated for the Alternate Uses task was 4 and the average number of objects reported for the Object Location task was 8. Similar to the Jung-Beeman et al. (2004) study, brain activity prior to the generation of each use was examined. So the average number of responses per participant was very high (80 for the Alternate Uses task; 160 for the Object Location task). This enabled the detection of robust brain activity patterns as a *greater number of trials* contributes to more reliable average responses.

The Jung-Beeman et al. (2004) and Abraham, Pieritz et al. (2012) studies constitute examinations of *intra-individual dynamics in creativity*. Both focus on different *operations of creative cognition*, with Jung-Beeman et al. adopting a *convergent* creative thinking paradigm to study insight and Abraham, Pieritz et al. adopting a *divergent* creative thinking paradigm to study conceptual expansion. Both were *theory-driven* in hypothesis testing and employed closely matched tasks or stringent *control conditions*. A key difference in the two studies was that the Jung-Beeman et al. study required *verbal responses* (significant potential for motion artefacts in the data arises in this context), whereas the Abraham, Pieritz et al. study saw *silent response generation* during imaging and post-imaging reporting of uses/objects (significant potential for forgetting or elaboration effects arises in this context).

6.2.3 fMRI Connectivity

Given that the brain is always active and exhibits specific patterns of activity even under conditions of rest, the question arose of whether the brain basis of individual differences in creativity may be rooted not only during the active generation of ideas (see Sections 6.2.1 and 6.2.2), but also in the state levels of brain activity at rest. This idea was explored by Beaty, Benedek et al. (2014), in that they examined the relationship between divergent thinking skills and resting state functional connectivity (i.e., correlated patterns of activity between regions during rest). Participants were selected from a sample of 91 individuals and classified as belonging to a high creative group (top 33% of scorers) or a low creative group (top 33% of scorers) based on their performance on three Alternate Uses tasks (e.g., generate creative uses for a hairdryer) and three Instances tasks (e.g., what can be elastic). The differences in the resting state connectivity patterns of the high creative (12 people in total: 5 men and 7 women) and low creative group (12 people in total: 5 men and 7 women) were contrasted. The findings revealed that the high creative group showed significantly greater functional connectivity between the bilateral inferior frontal gyrus (ventrolateral prefrontal cortex) and brain regions within the DMN, such as the ventromedial and dorsomedial prefrontal cortex, the posterior cingulate, and the inferior parietal lobule (see Sections 4.2.3 and 5.1). This was interpreted as potentially indicating "a greater ability of creative individuals to govern their imaginations, by executing complex search processes, inhibiting task-irrelevant information, and selecting ideas among a large set of competing alternatives" (Beaty, Benedek, et al.,

2014, 96). This idea was expanded much further following the results of a large functional connectivity study of 163 people that indicated that high creative ability was associated with brain network hubs across the default mode, central executive, and salience networks (Beaty et al., 2018) (see Figure 6.1).

While Beaty, Benedek et al. (2014) examined individual differences in creative potential in relation to resting state functional connectivity, De Pisapia et al. (2016) examined functional connectivity during creative performance itself. In addition, they also examined individual differences in functional connectivity during the same in the brains of professional artists demonstrating significant creative achievement compared to non-artists. The experimental session during brain imaging comprised 8-minute blocks divided into three: (i) the *resting state* block, in which participants merely rested and were given no task to perform; (ii) the Alphabet task, where participants were instructed to mentally visualize letters of the alphabet in sequence from A to Z; and (iii) the Creative task, where participants were instructed to mentally create a novel image that would fit into the category of "landscape," which they would have to manually reproduce after the brain imaging session. The 15 brain regions of interested selected for the functional connectivity analyses were those belonging to the DMN (e.g., medial prefrontal cortex, precuneus) and the CEN (e.g., frontal pole, dorsolateral prefrontal cortex, ventrolateral prefrontal cortex).

Across all participants, comparisons of functional connectivity patterns in brain activity during the Creative task compared to both the resting state block and the Alphabet task revealed significantly stronger connectivity during creative visualization between the default mode and CEN, but decreased connectivity within the CEN, which they interpreted as indicating "the need to balance convergent and divergent thinking during creativity" (De Pisapia et al., 2016, 8). The right ventrolateral prefrontal cortex (BA 47) was held to be the hub node as it formed the "highest number of significant functional connections" with other nodes (ibid., 6). These findings parallel those of Beaty, Benedek et al. (2014). Comparisons of the brain activity of the artists and non-artists (12 people per group: 14 males and 10 females) during the Creative task indicated stronger functional connectivity of the precuneus along the medial parietal wall, the posterior cingulate cortex, and the left dorsolateral prefrontal cortex, as well as several other brain regions that do not fall within the DMN or CEN, such as the premotor cortex. The latter finding was interpreted in terms of significant expertise in the physical making of art and greater capacity for visual imagery on the part of the professional artists.

These two studies indicate that functional connectivity analyses can be carried out across a range of situations – at rest and during task performance – and can be used to examine individual differences and intra-individual dynamics in creativity. Although the selection of brain regions of interest is derived from the published literature, functional connectivity studies – as they currently stand – are largely *explorative* in nature, as they rarely make predictions about which particular brain structures are likely to be especially relevant to creative thinking and under what conditions they are expected to be coupled to other specific brain regions. This also means that there is *rarely any testing for competing hypotheses*.

6.3 Structural Neuroimaging Methods

Magnetic resonance imaging (MRI) is the only method that has been used in volumetric or structural neuroimaging studies of creativity. The physics behind MRI is based on the detection of the time taken by highly polar molecules (like water) to align themselves to the axis of a strong magnetic field after they have been knocked away from the axis by radio waves. A range of different analysis techniques, that are widely used in other fields of cognitive neuroscience (Johansen-Berg & Behrens, 2014; Rinck, 2017; Zatorre, Fields, & Johansen-Berg, 2012), have been employed across studies on creative neurocognition to detect levels of white matter and gray matter concentration in the brain. Diffusion tensor imaging (DTI) measures the diffusion of water molecules in multiple directions. Directional estimates enable "diffusion tractography" through the generation of maps of white matter tracts in the brain.

There are also surface-based approaches to morphometry (e.g., using the *FreeSurfer* image analysis suite for surface-based cortical reconstruction and volumetric segmentation), where morphometric measures such as cortical thickness and surface area are derived from geometric models of the two-dimensional outer cortical surface of the brain. Voxel-based approaches to morphometry, in contrast, involve the spatial normalization of individual brain images to a group template, enabling a common metric of correspondence between participants in terms of concentration, density, or volume of brain regions. It should be noted, though, that the use of such anatomical terms using structural MRI "do not relate in a straightforward way to underlying neuronal densities" (Zatorre et al., 2012, 529). Differences between surface-based and voxel-based approaches need to be considered when deciding which approach to adopt as there are significant disparities associated with the use of these

structural neuroimaging methods (Greve, 2011; Grimm et al., 2015) and
software toolboxes to implement them (Rajagopalan & Pioro, 2015).

6.3.1 Surface-Based and Voxel-Based Approaches

Rex Jung carried out the first structural neuroimaging study in relation
to creativity by examining correlations between cortical thickness and
performance on two measures of creativity (61 participants: 33 men and
28 women). One was the Creative Achievement Questionnaire (CAQ),
which gives an indication of the level of creative output over 10 domains
(see Section 2.2.2). The other was a composite creativity index of divergent creative thinking, which was derived from behavioral performance
on three divergent thinking tasks – an Alternate Uses task (think of as
many uses as you can for a paperclip in 1 minute), the Free Condition
of the Design Fluency test (draw as many unique designs as possible
within 5 minutes), and the Four Line Condition of the Design Fluency
test (draw as many designs as possible using prespecified types of line
within 4 minutes) – the output of which was rated by 3 independent raters
following the consensual assessment technique (CAT) (see Section 2.4).

These measures of creativity were associated with very dissimilar
findings with regard to gross neuroanatomy. Cortical thickness in the
right angular gyrus (BA 39), for instance, was negatively correlated
with divergent creative thinking but positively correlated with creative
achievement (Figure 6.2). The angular gyrus is a key node in the DMN
and the SCN (see Sections 4.2.3 and 5.1). Superior divergent creative
thinking was mainly associated with decreases in cortical volume across
parts of the occipital lobe while greater creative achievement was also
related to reduced cortical volume in an orbitofrontal region. As few theoretical ideas are afloat concerning the nature of the relationship between
creative potential and creative achievement, grasping what these findings
could potentially reflect is challenging. Within this study, a significant but
weak positive correlation was found between creative achievement and
divergent creative thinking (Jung et al., 2010).

In focusing on representational drawing abilities, Chamberlain et al.
(2014) compared art school undergraduates (21 participants: 14 women
and 7 men) with non-art university undergraduates (23 participants: 16
women and 7 men). All completed two observational drawing tasks, which
were judged by 10 non-expert raters on the basis of accuracy (not aesthetic
appeal) and the average of the ratings constituted the drawing ability score
for each participant. The aim of the study was to identify which regions of
the brain would be differentiated in terms of white matter and gray matter

volume using voxel-based morphometry (VBM) as a function of drawing ability and artistic training (Chamberlain et al., 2014). Only one brain region, the left anterior cerebellum, was associated with significant findings (after correction for multiple comparisons). Both the level of drawings skills and the depth of artistic training were positively correlated with gray matter volume in the left anterior cerebellum, which the authors interpreted as potentially reflecting differences in fine motor control capacities.

Neuroimaging studies like that of Chamberlain et al. (2014) are often automatically deemed as being highly relevant to understanding creativity as the sample being studied ostensibly derives from contexts or professions associated with creativity. The process of interest in itself, though, is not necessarily central to creativity as, unlike the Jung et al. (2010) study, it focuses neither on the originality of the responses nor the level of creative achievement on the part of the participants. The emphasis on representational drawing abilities indicates that the findings are specific to visuomotor skills in the context of copying an image. So yet another factor to be kept in mind is the need to *consider and specify the manner in which the operation being studied is of relevance to creativity* in light of the definition of creativity employed in academic theory and research (see Figure 1.3).

6.3.2 Diffusion Tensor Imaging (DTI)

In examining white matter architecture using diffusion tensor imaging (DTI), Takeuchi et al. (2010a, 2010b) sought to identify the relationship between creative ability and structural brain network connectivity. The S-A creativity test of divergent thinking was used, whereby participants (55 participants: 42 men and 13 women) were required to generate as many responses as possible during three tasks: *generate unusual uses* ("Other than reading, how can we use newspapers?"), *imagine desirable functions of objects* ("What are the characteristics of a good TV?"), and *imagine consequences of unimaginable events* ("What would happen if all the mice in the world disappeared?"). Measures of fluency, flexibility, originality, elaboration, and total creativity (originality + elaboration) were derived from these tasks. White matter integrity within or adjacent to the bilateral prefrontal and anterior cingulate cortices, bilateral basal ganglia, bilateral temporo-parietal junction, corpus callosum, and right inferior parietal lobule were positively correlated with total creativity after controlling for age, sex, and IQ (Takeuchi et al., 2010b) (Figure 6.2). These findings therefore suggest that increased white matter connectivity in several regions of the brain is associated with enhanced divergent creative ability.

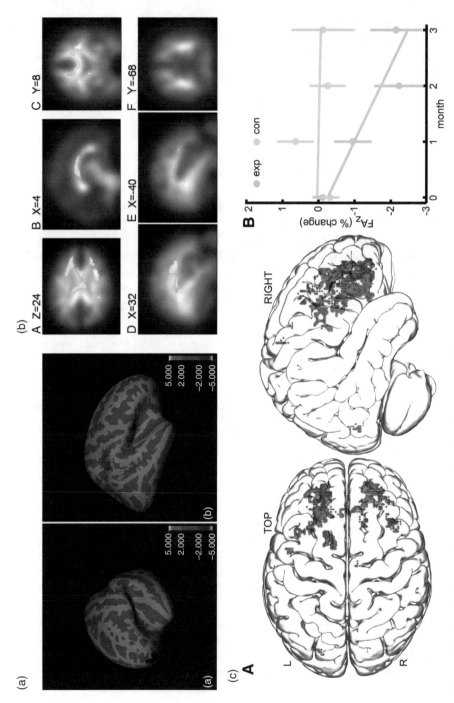

Figure 6.2 Structural neuroimaging: examples of studies on creativity

(a) A surface-based MRI approach showing increased cortical thickness (red) and decreased cortical thickness (blue) in relation to higher levels of creativity. Reprinted from *Human Brain Mapping*, *31*(3), Jung RE, Segall JM, Jeremy Bockholt H, Flores RA, Smith SM, Chavez RS & Haier RJ, Neuroanatomy of creativity, pages 398–409, © 2010, with permission from Wiley. (b) A DTI study showing greater structural integrity (yellow) within specific white matter tracts in relation to higher levels of creativity. Reprinted from *NeuroImage*, *51*(1), Takeuchi H, Taki Y, Sassa Y, Hashizume H, Sekiguchi A, Fukushima A & Kawashima R, White matter structures associated with creativity: Evidence from diffusion tensor imaging, pages 11–18, © 2010, with permission from Elsevier. (c) A longitudinal DTI study showing reductions over time in white matter integrity (indexed by FA/fractional anisotropy) as a function of artistic training. Reprinted from *NeuroImage*, 105, Schlegel A, Alexander P, Fogelson SV, Li X, Lu Z, Kohler PJ, Riley E, Tse PU & Meng M, The artist emerges: Visual art learning alters neural structure and function, pages 440–451, © 2015, with permission from Elsevier. A black and white version of this figure will appear in some formats. For the color version, please refer to the plate section.

A compelling example of an investigation using DTI was a longitudinal study that examined individual differences in the organization of white matter as a function of visual art training (Schlegel et al., 2015). An experimental group of art undergraduates who completed an introductory observational drawing course (17 participants: 13 women and 4 men) and a control group of chemistry students (18 participants: 9 women and 9 men) were tested on the Figural Form A of the Torrance Tests of Creative Thinking (TTCT; see Section 2.2.1) at the start and at the end of the study from which the creativity index measure was derived. The study took place over the course of 4 months during which the participants had monthly structural and functional brain imaging scans. During functional neuroimaging, participants performed two tasks. In the first, they were required to make judgments about physical features (length and brightness) of visual illusions as they were presented. In the second, participants made gestural drawings in 30 seconds upon observing photographs of human figures. Art students showed significant improvements in their divergent creative thinking skills over the course of the 4 months. There was evidence of reorganization of white matter in the prefrontal cortex, such that the art students relative to controls demonstrated steady reductions in white matter integrity in this region (Figure 6.2). This finding was attributed to their artistic training over the study period. The art students also showed improvements in their gestural sketching abilities (but not on their perceptual judgments), over time, which was related in particular to discriminant activity patterns in the right anterior cerebellum.

The problems of low sample size and unmatched control group notwithstanding (which are difficult to guarantee owing to the longitudinal nature of the study), the Schlegel et al. (2015) study is a rare example of an investigation in which the brain correlates of *domain-specific* (gestural drawing) and *domain-general* (divergent thinking) aspects of creative ability are brought together and explored from the dynamic perspective of measuring the effect of experience in creative or creativity-relevant pursuits on our physiology.

6.4 Electroencephalogram (EEG) Methods

In measuring "the electrical activity of large, synchronously firing, populations of neurons in the brain" using scalp electrodes, EEG-based methods constitute non-invasive and direct measurements of brain activity (Light et al., 2010, 1) and have been widely used in creativity research (Srinivasan, 2007). The temporal resolution of brain activity afforded by EEG is vastly superior to those of functional neuroimaging methods (whose advantage lies in greater spatial resolution in the mapping of brain activity). Voltage fluctuations as detected over the scalp are held to reflect postsynaptic activity emanating from ensembles of neurons as opposed to a summation of action potential signals from individual neurons (Nunez & Srinivasan, 2006). So EEG signals index "electrical potentials generated in the extracellular fluid as ions flow across cell membranes and neurons talk to one another via neurotransmitters" (Woodman, 2010, 2032). EEG signals, or waveforms, are mainly categorized on the basis of their frequency, amplitude, and position of scalp electrode. Frequency bands are classified as reflecting delta (0.1–4Hz), theta (4–8Hz), alpha (8–13Hz), beta (13–30Hz), or gamma (30–100 Hz) activity. Each of these EEG bands corresponds to distinct arousal, attentional, cognitive, and behavioral states (Kumar & Bhuvaneswari, 2012; Nidal & Malik, 2014).

An evoked or event-related potential (ERP) refers to changes in EEG activity that are triggered by, and therefore time-locked to, particular stimuli (Luck, 2014). The unique opportunity that is gifted in ERPs is the ability to visualize the unfolding of operations of information processing through the course of a trial. There are several well-studied ERP components that index specific attentional, perceptual, or cognitive operations and "are defined by their polarity (positive or negative going voltage), timing, scalp distribution, and sensitivity to task manipulations" (Woodman, 2010, 2034).

6.4.1 Power

Most EEG investigations in the field of creativity have zoned in on alpha activity as being especially relevant, as task-related alpha synchronization is presumed to reflect cortical idling or low arousal states that are conducive to creative ideation (see Section 5.2.3). This is what was reported in an EEG study by Andreas Fink and his team (2009). Participants (47 in all: 22 women and 25 men) carried out four tasks: the Alternate Uses task (think of unusual uses for a tin), the Object Characteristics task (think of the typical characteristics of a shoe), the Name Invention task (invent original names that have the abbreviation KM), and the Word Ends task (think of words with the suffix "-ung") (Fink, Grabner, et al., 2009). The trial events were separated so that the 20-second Idea Generation phase preceded a 9-second Response phase. Comparison of the levels of alpha activity across conditions revealed stronger synchronization in the upper and lower alpha band activity during the Alternate Uses task and Object Characteristics task. Individual differences were also found such that participants who generated highly original responses on the Alternate Uses task demonstrated more upper alpha band synchronization in the right hemisphere than in the left hemisphere compared to their low original counterparts (Figure 6.3).

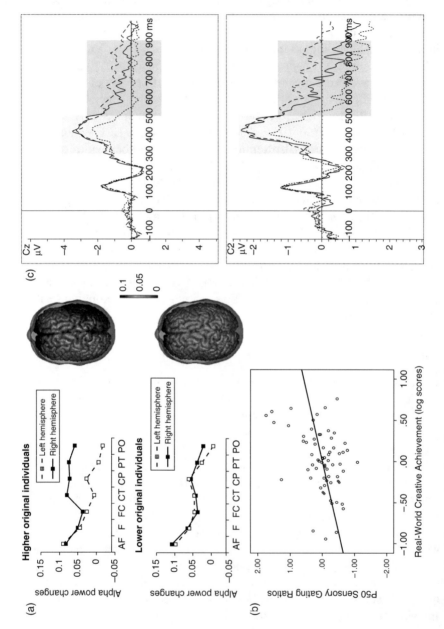

Figure 6.3 EEG: examples of studies on creativity

(a) An EEG study looking at the alpha power differences in high and low creative people across different scalp electrode sites. Reprinted from *Human Brain Mapping, 30(3)*, Fink A, Grabner RH, Benedek M, Reishofer G, Hauswirth V, Fally M, Neuper C, Ebner F & Neubauer AC, The creative brain: Investigation of brain activity during creative problem solving by means of EEG and FMRI, pages 734–748, © 2009, with permission from Wiley. (b) An ERP study showing the correlation between the P50 attentional attenuation response and self-reported creative achievement. Reprinted from *Neuropsychologia, 69*, Zabelina DL, O'Leary D, Pornpattananangkul N, Nusslock R & Beeman M, Creativity and sensory gating indexed by the P50: Selective versus leaky sensory gating in divergent thinkers and creative achievers, pages 77–84, © 2015, with permission from Elsevier. (c) An ERP study showing the grand average brain activity patterns elicited in two central scalp electrode sites (top: Cz; bottom: C2) when determining uses to be creative (solid line), nonsensical (dashed lines), and common (dotted line). The N400 (light gray box) and post-N400 (dark gray box) time windows index the discrimination of creative from common uses and creative from nonsensical uses, respectively. Reprinted from *Brain Research, 1527*, Kröger S, Rutter B, Hill H, Windmann S, Hermann C, & Abraham A, An ERP study of passive creative conceptual expansion using a modified alternate uses task, pages 189–198, © 2013, with permission from Elsevier. A black and white version of this figure will appear in some formats. For the color version of this figure, please refer to the plate section.

By focusing on upper alpha band activity (10–12 Hz), an investigation into the brain correlates of individual differences in musical improvisation assessed skilled musicians with formal institutional training in
improvisation (10 participants: 3 women and 6 men) and those without
such training (12 participants: 6 women and 6 men) (Lopata, Nowicki, &
Joanisse, 2017). All participants carried out six 80-second long musical
tasks: *listen* (hear the melody without playing); *learn* (learn to play the
melody on a keyboard); *imagine playback* (imagine playing the melody
after listening); *actual playback* (physically play back the melody after
listening); *imagine improvisation* (imagine improvising over chord
changes); and *actual improvisation* (physically improvise over the chord
changes). Heightened upper alpha band activity over frontal lobe sites
was found during the improvisation tasks that required more creativity
compared to other tasks, an effect that was stronger for musicians with
formal improvisation training.

6.4.2 Evoked Potentials

One of the few studies to use ERP to assess creative cognition evaluated
the operation of conceptual expansion using a modified Alternate Uses
task (Kröger et al., 2013). Participants (20 in total: 11 women and 9 men)
were presented with object–use combinations that were individually
classified as common (shoe–clothing), nonsensical (shoe–Easter bunny),
or creative (shoe–plant pot). With a minimum of 30 trials per condition,
the brain responses generated as a function of processing the object–
use stimuli were evaluated in terms of two ERP components: the N400
(occurring 300–500 ms after stimulus presentation) and a later ERP
(occurring 300–500 ms after stimulus presentation). The N400 is sensitive to semantic mismatches or violations of world knowledge whereas
later post-N400 components are sensitive to interpretative processes
and conceptual integration. Both ERP components were found to
index creativity-relevant processing in unison, as the N400 component
was responsive to the novelty of the object–use combinations (nonsense = creative > common), whereas the post-N400 ERP component
was responsive to the appropriateness of the object–use combinations
(nonsense > creative = common) (Figure 6.3).

In contrast, Zabelina et al. (2015) tested how attentional factors vary
as a function of divergent thinking and creative achievement by examining sensory gating though the P50 ERP component, which indexes sensory inhibition of meaningless stimuli when there are no task-relevant

goals to attend to. The P50 is an automatic early attentional response that occurs 50 ms after the onset of stimuli that capture attention. The P50 is typically assessed in experimental paradigms where two auditory clicks are presented to participants one after the other. The degree to which the brain response to the second click is attenuated compared to the brain response to the first click (P50 of second click/P50 of first click) is taken to be a marker of sensory gating. Participants (84 in total: 27 men and 57 women) filled out two creativity tasks: the Abbreviated Torrance Tests for Adults (ATTA), which is a divergent thinking test battery from which fluency and originality scores were used to derive a divergent thinking measure; and the Creative Achievement Questionnaire (CAQ). Correlational analyses revealed a dissociation in the findings such that higher divergent thinking was accompanied by "selective sensory gating" in the form of lower P50 scores whereas higher creative achievement was accompanied by "leaky sensory gating" in the form of higher P50 scores (Figure 6.3).

The Kröger et al. (2013) study examines the brain basis of passively induced creative conceptual expansion as it unfolds in real time and reflects intra-individual dynamics in creative cognition. The Zabelina et al. (2015) study, in contrast, reflects an individual differences approach whereby its correlational analysis between creativity measures and an ERP index of attentional capture reflects biases in information processing as a function of individual differences in divergent thinking ability and creative achievement.

6.5 Neuromodulation Methods

Techniques of neuromodulation (Kadosh, 2014; Lewis, Thomson, Rosenfeld, & Fitzgerald, 2016; Miniussi & Ruzzoli, 2013; Reti, 2015) are increasingly being used in the study of creative neurocognition. Transcranial magnetic stimulation (TMS) is the more established technique, but is less used in creativity research. During TMS, small electrical currents are produced in regions of the brain by means of electromagnetic induction using a handheld magnetic field generator, in the form of a coil, over the scalp (Wasserman, Epstein, & Ziemann, 2008; Ziemann, 2017).

Unlike TMS and like transcranial electrical stimulation (TES), transcranial direct current stimulation (tDCS) does not induce neuronal action potentials as the technique does not produce the necessary rapid depolarization that would be required to produce the same (Antal, Ambrus, & Chaieb, 2014; Reinhart, Cosman, Fukuda, & Woodman, 2017). Instead, tDCS "modifies spontaneous neuronal excitability and activity by a tonic de- or hyperpolarization of resting membrane potential" (Nitsche et al., 2008, 208), where anodal stimulation is believed to increase cortical excitability while cathodal stimulation decreases the same. Several grave concerns have been raised about tDCS, however (Horvath, Carter, & Forte, 2014; Horvath, Forte, & Carter, 2015), including the intensity and duration of stimulation, and type point of task performance (during stimulation or directly after stimulation).

6.5.1 Neuromodulation and Creative Cognition

The only published study of creative neurocognition that employed TMS assessed the impact of low frequency magnetic pulses over fronto-temporal regions of the brain on drawing abilities (Snyder et al., 2003). This small qualitative study was designed to test whether reductions in concept-driven thinking would facilitate creative performance (see Section 4.2.2). Eleven participants (all men) received 15 minutes of placebo stimulation in one session and 15 minutes of real stimulation in a separate session. Nine of the participants received stimulation at 0.5Hz frequency while two received stimulation at 1Hz frequency. Participants were asked to draw either a dog or a horse four times: before TMS, during TMS, immediately after TMS, and 45 minutes after TMS. While this form of stimulation did not improve artistic performance as a whole, the drawings of 4 out of the 11 participants were judged as showing significant changes in the convention or scheme of the drawings (as judged by undefined "committees" in the study) such that they became more complex, detailed, or lifelike. Despite the fact that these changes were noted in a minority of the participants, the authors concluded that this constitutes proof of the inhibiting influence of TMS, which has the potential to release savant-like skills in healthy individuals.

Other studies of neuromodulation use tDCS (Weinberger, Green, & Chrysikou, 2017) and have better controls in place and improved consistency in experimental design. Chi and Snyder (2011), for instance, evaluated whether brain stimulation over the anterior temporal lobe (ATL) could facilitate insight in problem solving. For this purpose, they assigned 60 participants (29 women, 31 men) to 1 of 3 treatment conditions: sham stimulation, left ATL anodal stimulation, or right ATL anodal stimulation. The "matchstick arithmetic problem" was used as the cognitive task of insight. Repeatedly solving an insight problem using one type of strategy hinders one's ability to solve another type of insight problem requiring an alternative strategy as the first strategy induces functional fixedness. The aim of this study was to determine whether administering tDCS over the right ATL prior to the switch in problem type would lead to improved performance. The findings confirmed these predictions, as problem-solving accuracy and speed were improved following right ATL stimulation. All stimulation groups were comparable in their performance in the first minute of problem solving; however, after 150 seconds, only the right ATL group continued to successfully solve problems. Moreover, 60% of the right ATL anodal stimulation group solved the Type 2 insight problem within the 6-minute time limit allotted for problem solving compared to only 20% of the sham stimulation and left ATL anodal stimulation groups. The one factor that this study did not control for was whether the participants actually underwent an insight experience while solving the problems.

In targeting the role of the frontal poles in the relational integration of distant concepts, Green et al. (2016) carried out a tDCS study in which the participants were assigned to the tDCS group (14–15 participants depending on the analysis; gender distribution unknown) or the sham stimulation group (12–16 participants depending on the analysis; gender distribution unknown). tDCS was delivered over the left frontal pole while participants performed an Analogy Finding task and a Thin Slice Creativity Verb Generation task. In the former task, participants are instructed to generate creative and valid analogies by combining word-pairs on one side of a grid with word-pairs along the top of the same grid to make a valid analogy. In the latter task, participants are presented with a noun and asked to provide a verb that is related in any way to the noun. In half the trials, they are asked to think creatively while performing the tasks. Using latent semantic analysis (LSA), it was possible to generate measures of semantic distance from both tasks to obtain an indication of the degree of semantic association between the prompts and the participants' responses. tDCS over the left frontal pole was associated with greater semantic distance in both analogy finding and cued verb generation, indicating a prominent role for this structure in relational integration of conceptual knowledge (Green et al., 2016).

While TMS is certainly better established as a method than tDCS transcranial direct current stimulation, it has rarely been used in the study of creative neurocognition. So far, methods of neuromodulation have shown modest improvements in component processes of creativity, such as the aforementioned studies that revealed a greater propensity to overcome functional fixedness during insight problem solving and better creative analogical reasoning following anodal stimulation of the ATL and frontal poles, respectively. Other studies have found that other factors need to be taken into consideration, such as the effect of expertise

(Rosen et al., 2016) or the interplay of both hemispheres in creative ideation (Mayseless & Shamay-Tsoory, 2015). These are still early days in the
investigation of creative neurocognition via neuromodulation methods,
and the larger critical discussion concerning the utility and validity of
these methods in delivering key insights about brain function will necessarily have an impact on how we come to view the relevance of these
findings for the field of creativity.

6.6 Issues for Further Consideration

This purpose of this chapter was to give the reader a closer look at the
neuroscientific methods used in the study of creativity, with examples
to illustrate how this is instantiated. There are a number of issues to
bear in mind when considering which techniques to use in the study
of creative neurocognition (also refer to Chapter 7). Some established
neuroscientific methods and imaging analysis techniques have yet
to be widely employed in creativity research. For instance, combined
methods (e.g., simultaneous fMRI and EEG; see Ullsperger &
Debener, 2010) have not been implemented in the study of creativity.
Magnetoencephalography (MEG) has also yet to be used in the direct
investigation of creative neurocognition, although there are a smattering
of studies evaluating indirectly related facets of cognition (Marinkovic
et al., 2011). The implementation of longitudinal approaches (Skup,
2010) and multivariate pattern analyses (MVPA; see Haxby, Connolly, &
Guntupalli, 2014) are also rare in the study of creativity (Schlegel
et al., 2015).

Even if one decides to opt for one of the customary methods, an issue
that remains a grave point of concern is the sheer variety of the creativity
tasks employed and the diversity of experimental paradigms that are
employed both within and across neuroscientific methods (Arden et al.,
2010). Careful consideration needs to accompany the choice of task,
sample under study, type and magnitude of creativity being tested, the
logistics of the method, and so on. There are also unique problems that
beset the neuroscience of creativity that cannot be swept aside in this
context, and these are detailed in the next chapter (Chapter 7).

Chapter Summary

- Mapping of brain structure and function is a long tradition that began
  in the third century BCE and continues to the present day.

- Functional neuroimaging methods are used to characterize creative ideation as it unfolds in real time in the form of a brain map with high spatial resolution.
- Structural neuroimaging methods allow for the generation of associations between gross anatomy and creative ability or achievement.
- The neuropsychological approach establishes correspondences between brain structure and function by evaluating the psychological consequences of brain insult.
- EEG methods allow for the direct study of brain activity, and the major focus in creativity EEG research has been on alpha band frequency activity.
- The use of brain stimulation or neuromodulation techniques, such as TMS and tDCS, is slowly gaining popularity in the field of creativity.
- Among the many challenges facing the neuroscience of creativity is the issue of enormous heterogeneity in tasks and experimental designs across studies.

Review Questions

1. Identify the similarities and differences between the many functional neuroimaging methods.
2. How do structural neuroimaging studies abet our understanding of creative neurocognition?
3. Describe the neuropsychological approach in terms of its advantages and disadvantages.
4. Which method can be used to visualize operations of information processing as and when they occur within a trial?
5. Consider and outline the different techniques of neuromodulation. Which one is more widely employed in creativity research?

Further Reading

- Amaro, E., Jr, & Barker, G. J. (2006). Study design in fMRI: Basic principles. *Brain and Cognition*, *60*(3), 220–232.
- Gurd, J. M. (Ed.). (2012). *Handbook of clinical neuropsychology* (2nd edn.). Oxford: Oxford University Press.
- Huettel, S. A., Song, A. W., & McCarthy, G. (2014). *Functional magnetic resonance imaging* (3rd edn.). Sunderland, MA: Sinauer Publishers.

- Johansen-Berg, H., & Behrens, T. E. J. (Eds.). (2014). *Diffusion MRI: From quantitative measurement to in-vivo neuroanatomy* (2nd edn.). London: Elsevier/Academic Press.
- Lewis, P. M., Thomson, R. H., Rosenfeld, J. V., & Fitzgerald, P. B. (2016). Brain neuromodulation techniques: A review. *The Neuroscientist: A Review Journal Bringing Neurobiology, Neurology and Psychiatry, 22*(4), 406–421.
- Nidal, K., & Malik, A. S. (Eds.). (2014). *EEG/ERP analysis: Methods and applications.* Boca Raton, FL: CRC Press.
- Rinck, P. A. (2017). *Magnetic resonance in medicine: The basic textbook of the European Magnetic Resonance Forum* (10th ed.). E-version 10.1 beta.

CHAPTER SEVEN

Unique Problems in the Neuroscientific Study of Creativity

"All the soarings of my mind begin in my blood."

(Rainer Maria Rilke)

Learning Objectives

- Identifying why unique problems accompany the neuroscience of creativity
- Distinguishing between the different methodological and conceptual problems
- Grasping the problems of low trial numbers and lengthy trial durations
- Recognizing response-based problems like subjectivity and movement
- Differentiating task-based problems from group-based problems
- Evaluating the problems of validity in investigating creativity

7.1 Problems? What Problems?

Each technological advance in neuroscientific methods and techniques allows for clearer and more detailed exploration of the relationship between brain factors and psychological functions (see Chapter 6). Like virtually all others fields of psychology, the widespread establishment of neuroimaging facilities for the purpose of research saw the exponential rise of neuroscientific studies in the field of creativity. The environments in which these techniques can be used lead to limits in the manner in which studies can be designed. For instance, the environment in which functional neuroimaging studies can be run using magnetic resonance imaging (MRI) requires that participants lie supine in a very confined space in which they are not supposed to move their heads even slightly over the entire testing period. This poses limits on the type of tasks that can be carried out in that environment as well as the duration of the tasks. As the environment involves magnetic fields, the kind of hardware used within those environments cannot be made up of ferromagnetic components, limiting the types of response hardware that can be implemented in that setting. For the most part, it is neither impossible nor exceedingly challenging to adapt empirical paradigms from experimental psychology to fit neuroscientific settings to allow for meaningful research. Unfortunately, the same cannot be said for empirical paradigms of creativity where methodological difficulties are not inconsequential and they range from methodological to conceptual. Unusually for the field, although these issues of significance are well-documented (Abraham, 2013; Dietrich, 2007b, 2015; K. Sawyer, 2011), empirical work continues with little engagement or acknowledgment of the same. This is, of course, a serious problem.

In the sections that follow, central issues of concern will be outlined to illustrate the unique problems associated with the neuroscientific study of creativity, and not neuroscience research generally, which are covered very well elsewhere (Bennett & Hacker, 2003; Legrenzi & Umilta, 2011) (to understand which aspects of creativity cannot be directly tapped by current neuroscientific approaches, see Boxes 7.1, 7.2, and 7.3). To aid comprehension, comparisons will be made between paradigms of creativity and those of other higher-order "non-creative" cognition that are employed in functional MRI-based research. While reading this chapter, it is important to bear in mind that the highlighted issues are not the only ones of note, and also that it is not the case that every single neuroscientific study is marred by every single one of the listed problems. Knowledge of potential factors of concern will serve to aid with the ready identification of issues of note in the published studies so far, and the studies to come. This is vital as more informed research practice paves the way for better research outcomes.

Box 7.1 What is Left Out? Spontaneous Creativity

The differentiation between deliberate and spontaneous forms of creativity (Dietrich, 2004b) is relevant when considering neuroscientific approaches to investigating creativity. Most neuroscientific studies – particularly those employing functional neuroimaging, EEG, and neuromodulatory methods – are investigations of deliberate forms of creativity. This is because unpredictable and spontaneous aspects of creative ideation, which arise effortlessly and without prior warning, cannot (per definition) be reliably prompted. This is certainly a factor to not lose sight of when making any generalizations about the implications of the findings from any one study on creativity to wider contexts. And it is also worth noting that studies that use methods of structural neuroimaging and functional neuroimaging of resting state dynamics cannot claim to have a specific bearing on either deliberate or spontaneous forms of creativity as these are trait-based investigations.

A key factor to bear in mind, though, is that creative ideation across virtually all contexts of human enterprise, regardless of whether the context involves the creation of an original painting, poem or principle, involves a complex and dynamic interplay between both deliberate and spontaneous forms of information processing. Claims that are made otherwise are usually based on anecdotal evidence, and should not be left unchallenged.

Box 7.2 What is Left Out? Temporally Extended Forms of Creative Ideation

All neuroscientific investigations of creativity examine the brain correlates of creative processing as instantiated in the present moment (functional neuroimaging, EEG, and neuromodulatory methods) or in terms of the output of creative ideation (functional neuroimaging-resting state and structural neuroimaging studies). What is entirely left out of this picture is the brain basis of creative ideation across all its stages from start to finish. The classical stage theory in the context of creativity is that of Graham Wallas, whose four-stage model began with "preparation," involving deliberate and conscious ideation (Wallas, 1926) (see Section 3.3.1). This was followed by a period of "incubation," of switching off from consciously deliberating on the problem, which allows unconscious forces in the mind to facilitate idea generation that one becomes consciously aware of in the third stage," illumination," in the form of a sudden insight. The last stage, "verification," involves the deliberate instantiation of the idea in terms of a tangible output or product. The temporal duration encompassing the stages of creative ideation is extremely variable as it can run over several days or months or even extend to years.

Box 7.3 What is Left Out? Motorically Complex Forms of Creativity

For many of the reasons detailed in this chapter, forms of creativity that cannot be directly studied in an optimal manner using current neuroscientific methods include contexts where (a) complex bodily movement is central to creative ideation (e.g., dance choreography), (b) creative performance involves engaging with multiple participants who interact with one another in real time (e.g., improvisation in theater, synchronized group dance) , and (c) multiple action effectors and/or performance domains are called upon in unison (e.g., musical, verbal, and kinesthetic skills in musical theater). To get around such seemingly insurmountable problems, innovative experimental designs that are tantamount to oblique or indirect approaches need to be developed to investigate these forms of creativity (see Chapters 8–11, which explore musical, literary, visual artistic, and kinesthetic creativity).

7.2 The Problem of Trials

All empirical paradigms are comprised of conditions (one or more) and trials to capture the processes that are evoked by each condition. The number of trials per condition differs substantially depending on the process under study across perceptual, emotional, cognitive, and motor domains of psychological function because the different tasks used to elicit the processes are associated with widely varying durations. The first thing to note about creativity paradigms is that, because the task response is one of generativity, as opposed to reactivity, trials typically have lengthy durations. As people cannot be assessed for overly extended periods of time in an fMRI environment owing to the strain of having to stay perfectly still, this means that creativity paradigms are typically marked by fewer trials than other paradigms of cognition and "non-creative" imagination (Figure 7.1).

Functional run(s), where brain activity is mapped to task performance or rest, are usually limited to around 40 minutes. Every trial within a functional run is composed of all the events that take place within a trial, each of which has a temporal duration. These include the presentation time for the stimuli, capture time for responses, and the many pauses of varying duration (which can extend to a few seconds), which are a necessary part of every paradigm. So the trial length of an experimental paradigm in an fMRI setting is typically longer than that of the same paradigm within a behavioral setting. Due to the upper limit of the duration of a functional run, the length of a trial directly limits how many trials can feature in a run and therefore has a considerable impact on the power and efficiency of an experimental design. It is crucial to properly consider the efficiency–power tradeoff when devising fMRI paradigms (Liu, Frank, Wong, & Buxton, 2001). "Power" refers to the capacity to detect brain activity and "efficiency" refers to the degree of accuracy in determining the shape of the hemodynamic response function of the brain activity in relation to

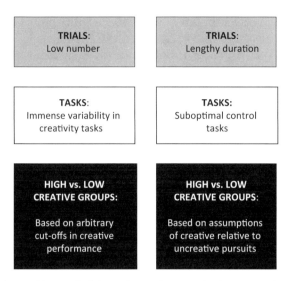

Figure 7.1 The problems of trials, tasks, and groups in the neuroscience of creativity

the eliciting stimuli. The power of an fMRI experimental design varies as an exponential function of the number of trials per condition (until 100–150 trials). The efficiency of the same is deemed to be acceptable at around 25 trials per condition (Desmond & Glover, 2002; Huettel & McCarthy, 2001).

7.2.1 Number of Trials

Just as the average reaction time taken to respond "yes" to a picture (e.g., to indicate whether a presented picture is one that has been seen before) is derived from the average of all the reaction times to every picture one responded to in the affirmative, the average brain response to a condition is derived from all the trials that belong to that particular condition. The robustness, or the average response, regardless of whether it is reaction time or hemodynamic brain activity, is incumbent on the number of trials for each condition. Although no exact guidelines can be prescribed regarding the minimum number of trials necessary per condition, the general rule is that the greater the number of trials, the more robust is the average response. So paradigms with fewer trials per condition are necessarily compromised. Early functional neuroimaging studies assessing regional cerebral blood flow using radiotracers (e.g.,

PET, SPECT) were especially susceptible to this problem, with many studies using only one trial per condition (Carlsson et al., 2000; Chávez-Eakle et al., 2007). But even fMRI studies often implement fewer than 20 trials per condition within experimental paradigms (Fink, Grabner, et al., 2009; Howard-Jones, Blakemore, Samuel, Summers, & Claxton, 2005). Some studies have found ways to incorporate a greater number of trials by reducing the number of contrasting conditions under study (Benedek, Beaty, et al., 2014; Jung-Beeman et al., 2004) or devising novel designs that utilize multiple responses from each trial (Abraham, Pieritz, et al., 2012) (also see Section 6.2.2).

7.2.2 Duration of Trials

The number of trials per condition in an experimental paradigm is determined in large part by the duration of a trial. Most behavioral paradigms of creative thinking involve lengthy trial durations (2–5 minutes), which cannot be meaningfully implemented as such in neuroimaging settings. Even when devising special creativity paradigms that can be implemented within an "event-related" design, the trial length is usually well over 10 seconds (Abraham, Pieritz, et al., 2012; Chrysikou & Thompson-Schill, 2011). This is inevitable given that tasks typically involve the generation of ideas and the formation of complex conceptual associations as opposed to mere reactivity to presented stimuli. Moreover, the responses themselves can necessitate an extended temporal duration as they can involve verbal or non-verbal (musical, drawing) articulation (Aziz-Zadeh et al., 2012; Limb & Braun, 2008; Shah et al., 2011).

One means by which some studies have dealt with lengthy duration of trials is to conduct "epoch-related" analyses based on a "block design" of the relevant trial event where the creativity-relevant information processing is taking place. For instance, the average brain activity across the idea generation phase (10 seconds in duration) within a trial was compared for metaphor generation (condition 1) relative to synonym generation (condition 2) (Benedek, Beaty, et al., 2014). This single trial execution of epoch analyses, however, is not entirely comparable to how block designs are usually implemented in neuroscientific studies as they typically involve several trials of the same condition (condition 1) presented sequentially in a single block (Amaro & Barker, 2006). The brain activity across this whole block of condition 1 is averaged and then compared to brain activity across this whole block of condition 2 (Beaty et al., 2017). Moreover, such comparisons also necessitate taking other factors into

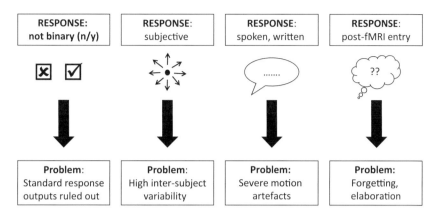

Figure 7.2 The problem of responses in the neuroscience of creativity

consideration, such as the nature of the differences between the creative and non-creative/control conditions (Section 7.4), and response-related factors, which are explored next.

7.3 The Problem of Responses

The biggest challenge when implementing behavioral paradigms of creativity within neuroscientific set-ups is to ensure fidelity to the task and, more importantly, the processes being targeted. Tasks of creativity typically involve highly individual and subjective responses, which often take the form of elaborate motor responses by hand (through drawing and writing) or mouth (vocal responses). The fact that responses in creativity tasks are typically non-binary and/or non-objective makes it exceedingly challenging to design experimental paradigms that can tap creativity in an empirically sound manner in behavioral and neuroscientific settings (Figure 7.2).

7.3.1 Non-Binary and Subjective Responses

While there is abundant variety in types of stimuli and trial events used to prompt and evaluate psychological phenomena across empirical paradigms, the common denominator across the vast majority is the response outcome. This is usually instantiated by means of speed and/or accuracy response measures – reaction time (RT) for speed, and proportion of target hits, errors, misses, and false alarms for accuracy following signal detection theory (Green & Swets, 1966; Stanislaw & Todorov, 1999).

Several paradigms, particularly those involving questionnaires, also routinely employ rating scales, such as a Likert scale (Likert, 1932), to obtain scaling responses within a pre-specified range (e.g., 5-point scale ranging from 1 to 5).

Apart from a few convergent creative thinking tasks where an objectively correct solution needs to be found, such as the Remote Associates Test (RAT), the vast majority of divergent creativity tasks, such as the Alternate Uses task or the Creative Imagery task, are highly individual (see Section 2.3). Creativity neuroscientists therefore face unique problems in response implementation as responses to creativity tasks are non-binary (irreducible to yes or no decisions), open-ended (involve multiple responses), subjective (the criterion of "objective accuracy" does not apply, although "response validity" does), and involve temporally extended and complex movement (spoken, written, or drawn). The generated responses are qualitative and no two individuals are exactly comparable in the type or number of responses they generate. Indeed, measures of creativity are unique in that quantitative data (e.g., degree of originality, degree of conceptual expansion) are derived from qualitative responses (non-binary, subjective).

7.3.2 Response-Induced Movement

The great advantage of having such response measures, which are binary (yes/no) or constitute objective outcome measures, is that the motor response (using the fingers of one or both hands) can be recorded using standard hardware (e.g., keyboard, mouse, response button), which can be readily incorporated in a neuroscientific setting (e.g., response button) to enable responding with minimal movement of the head. This is exceedingly challenging with creativity tasks.

Most neuroscientfic paradigms of creativity separate the creative ideation phase from the response phase (Aziz-Zadeh et al., 2012; Fink, Grabner, et al., 2009; Jung-Beeman et al., 2004). Typically, participants are given a stimulus cue that informs them of the task that they have to mentally carry out over an extended period of time (e.g., think of as many uses as you can for a brick). After this ideation period has elapsed, they are given a response cue, which indicates to them that they can now respond in an overt manner, usually vocally (single word or more elaborate articulations). This manner of temporal lag between stimulus and response is for the purpose of minimizing movement-related problems (unspecific brain activations and potential motion artifacts) from affecting the pattern of findings during creative ideation.

The problem here is that the use of vocal responses has a critical impact on being able to ensure data quality because the variations on the magnetic field caused by jaw and head movements are known to lead to motion artefacts in fMRI data (e.g., Birn, Bandettini, Cox, Jesmanowicz, & Shaker, 1998; Chouinard, Boliek, & Cummine, 2016; Chouinard et al., 2016). While guidelines on how to optimally circumvent this issue when designing experimental paradigms are available (Birn, Bandettini, Cox, & Shaker, 1999; Diedrichsen & Shadmehr, 2005; Gracco, Tremblay, & Pike, 2005; Huang, Francis, & Carr, 2008), such as block designs with task and control durations of 10 seconds (Birn, Cox, & Bandettini, 2004), none of these proposals were made with divergent creativity tasks in mind, which are characterized by longer trial durations and involve multiple verbal responses. What is a matter of concern is that, apart from a paltry few studies (Fink et al., 2010), most neuroimaging studies of creativity neither explicitly acknowledge such issues nor indicate how they circumvent such problematic issues within their experimental designs.

7.3.3 Post-Neuroimaging Response Entry

As response isolation strategies in creativity neuroimaging designs are not foolproof, an alternative approach has been to avoid having participants generate overt responses involving complex movement inside the MRI environment and instead to have them overtly generate their responses directly after the neuroimaging (Abraham, Pieritz, et al., 2012; De Pisapia et al., 2016). The problem of this approach of post-neuroimaging response entry is that, unless the experimental paradigm instantiates valid forms of response checks that ensure that tasks set out for them are being carried out (Abraham, Pieritz, et al., 2012), one cannot be certain that they are actually following task instructions during the imaging session. Moreover, one can also not ascertain the level of correspondence between the "responses generated covertly" during the imaging session and the "responses generated overtly" following the imaging session. These could be impacted by forgetting (loss of responses) and/or post-experiment elaboration of the responses.

7.4 The Problem of Tasks

The issues of concern in relation to the tasks used in studies of creative neurocognition extend to both those that measure some aspect of creative thinking (see Chapter 2) *and* the control tasks that are used as a contrast or comparison measure (Figure 7.1).

7.4.1 Creativity Task Variability

One of the key problems in neuroscientific research in creativity is the staggering variety of tasks used to assess creative thinking both within and across its different methods (functional neuroimaging, structural neuroimaging, EEG, techniques of neuromodulation) (Arden et al., 2010). This makes it very difficult to interpret and even appropriately generalize findings beyond a specific context. While having many paradigms on hand to evaluate one or the other aspect of creativity is itself not a negative feature at all, and indeed could prove to be very helpful, what is missing in neuroscientific studies is a detailed task classification and description that would clarify which specific operations of interest are targeted in each study, and how the aims and findings of the study relate to other aspects of creative and non-creative cognition.

What is also lacking is specificity and clarity in the manner in which findings are reported in empirical papers. As it stands, studies are rarely circumscribed in terms of the implications of their results. Few explicitly delimit them to select aspects of creativity (e.g., fluency in creative idea generation). On the contrary, most reports are indiscriminately presented as concerning creativity as a whole, especially within the abstract section of journal articles (which are freely accessible to one and all). Other problems include faux equivalencies when adapting widely used creativity tasks for use in non-English speaking contexts (for a discussion of the Remote Associates Test (RAT), see Abraham, Beudt, et al., 2012).

7.4.2 Less-Demanding Control Tasks

The relevance of brain-based findings in relation to any creativity task, which is the experimental task, is entirely dependent on the appropriateness of the non-creative control task. Most neuroimaging studies of creativity compare brain activation that results during creative thinking (e.g., generate a story using three semantically unrelated words) compared to that of a far less cognitively demanding control task (e.g., generate a story using three semantically related words) or unspecific baseline states (e.g., rest). The latter option is highly problematic to employ as the contrasting control state given its absolute lack of specificity (Stark & Squire, 2001). In fact, an early neuroimaging study of episodic memory referred to the resting brain as "a resource not only for the creative process, but also for meditational states, religious experiences, and dreams" and stated that its activities reflect "substrates of the creative process" (Andreasen et al., 1995, 1577, 1583).

Less cognitively demanding control tasks are also suboptimal to employ as comparison tasks to creative tasks as it is not possible under such circumstances to tell which components of the ensuing brain activations are attributable to a mere increase in cognitive control and which of the components are specifically relevant for creative idea generation. While some studies have focused on explicitly and optimally controlling for differing levels of cognitive demand between the creative and non-creative control tasks through the use of different strategies, conditions, and analysis techniques (Abraham, Pieritz, et al., 2012; Aziz-Zadeh et al., 2012), it is often at the expense of having control tasks that are qualitatively very different from the creative task (for a case of an optimal match between creative and non-creative conditions, see Jung-Beeman et al., 2004).

7.5 The Problem of Groups

Two primary objectives guide investigations of the brain correlates of creative thinking (see Chapter 3): to understand it in terms of intra-individual dynamics and/or to uncover the physiological basis of individual differences in creativity. With regard to the latter between-subjects approach, differentiations are typically made between highly creative individuals relative to average or low creative individuals. Using this approach, higher creative ability has been associated with many brain-related factors such as reduced white matter integrity in the ventrolateral prefrontal cortex (Jung et al., 2010), increased gray matter density in the dorsolateral prefrontal and basal ganglia regions (Takeuchi et al., 2010a), more integrated white matter tracts of the corpus callosum, basal ganglia, and inferior parietal regions (Takeuchi et al., 2010b), increased functional brain activity in the frontal lobe (Carlsson et al., 2000), and increased functional connectivity at rest between regions of the DMN of the brain and the ventrolateral prefrontal regions (Beaty, Benedek, et al., 2014).

One of the questions that arises in these contexts is whether brain-based differences between high and low creative groups are specific to creativity such that they have little relevant impact on other aspects of cognition (Figure 7.1). The theoretical implications that derive from answering this question, either in the affirmative or negative, need to be openly discussed. If such differences have an impact on cognitive operations beyond creativity, in what other contexts would the high creatives be more or less adept than the low creatives? Alternatively, if such differences are limited to creativity, how is this domain-specific information processing toolbox for creativity characterized in the brain? The chicken-and-egg problem of what came first also looms large. Are highly creative people more creative because they have increased gray matter volume in specific brain areas or vice versa? Also, how generalizable are such findings within and across domains of creativity? For instance, would a positive correlation as seen between gray matter volume in region A and a verbal creativity task X also be expected when using another verbal creativity task Y, and would the results extend to non-verbal measures of creativity?

Which control group to match to the high creative group is also a key concern. Groups are usually classified on the basis of their performance on one or more creativity measures. However, as many of the most widely employed creativity tasks (e.g., Alternate Uses task, RAT) are not comprehensively standardized (in the manner of IQ measures, for instance), what the differing performance levels truly indicate is unclear. This is true even when one only carries out comparisons between the highest (e.g., top 25%) and lowest (e.g., bottom 25%) performers on the test. For instance, does low performance on the RAT reveal below average or average creative ability? The choice of which control group (low creative or average creative) would afford a better comparison is a critical one that impacts the interpretations of the findings. What is also unclear is how findings can be generalized to the wider population.

The implicit notion that creativity is primarily an inherent trait of sorts and other factors need not be given much consideration is potentially problematic. Examining the trajectory of output in eminently creative individuals (e.g., Picasso or Einstein) reveals that there is great variability in the degree and quality of output throughout their lifetimes. This suggests that creative output cannot be solely explained in terms of inherent traits; rather, fluctuating or state-based aspects of creative cognition also need to be considered (Harnad, 2006), even in cases of exceptional creative ability.

Many studies do away with using measures of creative ability to classify high and low creative groups and instead assess creative performance and brain correlates in high and low creative groups by comparing individuals who are highly proficient in ostensibly creative pursuits (e.g., art, music, dance) with those who are not. One of the major shortcomings faced in this context is failing to ensure homogeneity in the samples both within groups and between groups. Moreover, the implicit assumption that creativity can be comprehensively understood by making comparisons between artists and non-artists cannot be accepted at face value. For one, creativity is a highly valued trait across virtually all professions, including medicine, engineering, marketing, law, advertising, research, teaching, and even accounting. It is also entirely fallacious to presume that all individuals who pursue the fine arts or the performing arts are, by virtue of that fact alone, guaranteed to be highly creative.

7.6 The Problem of Validity

The unique problems faced by creativity researchers at the level of responses have already been noted in Section 7.3, and they are reiterated in part in this section because the problem of response is also relevant to the problem of validity in terms of: (a) often being unable to pinpoint the moment of creative insight, (b) being unable to prompt creativity reliably, and (c) equating trying to be creative with actually being creative (Figure 7.3). In general, creativity tasks are non-binary (can rarely be reduced to yes/no answers), open-ended (involve multiple responses), subjective (there are no correct or incorrect responses), and involve movement (spoken, written, or drawn). What is more, responses are rarely logged in "real-time" with a clear time stamp, i.e., as and when each creative response is generated. Typically, the participants are exposed to a stimulus cue (e.g., Uses $\longrightarrow$ Brick), which indicates the task that they have to undertake over an extended period of time without moving (e.g., think of as many uses as possible for a brick). After this silent generation period, participants are usually given a response cue, which indicates that it is time to reveal their responses (e.g., single word or more elaborate articulations).

The problem with not having responses logged and coded in real time is that there is no way of determining at which points during the extended trial period the creative responses were generated, much less determining when the most creative of all the uses was produced. The absence of online logging of responses in the form of a behavioral marker that guides brain-based analyses points to the problem of pinpointing the moment of creativity and being unable to uncover the brain basis of the same.

The unfortunate truth is that because creativity cannot simply be prompted in a manner that is reliable or necessarily valid, one is particularly dependent on behavioral responses in neuroscientific studies of creativity as the stimulus event or task cue does not automatically evoke the necessary cognitive processes under study. This is one of the chief factors that sets apart studies of creativity from most other aspects of cognition and renders it incredibly challenging to investigate. If asked whether you went to the dentist last week or can name the capital of

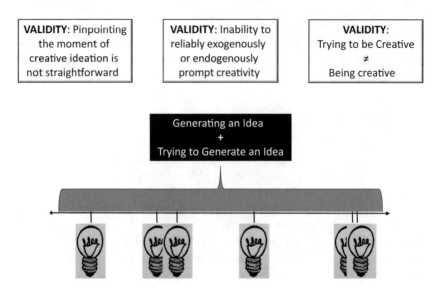

VALIDITY: Pinpointing the moment of creative ideation is not straightforward	**VALIDITY**: Inability to reliably exogenously or endogenously prompt creativity	**VALIDITY**: Trying to be Creative ≠ Being creative

Figure 7.3 The problem of validity in the neuroscience of creativity

Serbia, the question in itself suffices as a prompt to evoke a reliable and valid response (yes or no). This is not so when you have to generate new uses for objects, or create an original story, or manipulate geometrical figures to form a novel and meaningful gestalt. In the absence of a behavioral marker, we have no idea about the point of the cognitive event of interest (here, the generation of the creative idea). Analyses of the brain's functional response with reference to the actual point of creative ideation cannot be conducted without this information.

Moreover, within the extended period of time (that can range from a couple of seconds to almost half a minute) when subjects have to generate novel uses for an object, the brain activation during that period reflects the engagement of brain regions when (a) developing strategies to tackle the problem (i.e., trying to be creative), and (b) the actual generation of the original solution (i.e., being creative). So averaging the brain response over the entire period and claiming that it is indicative of creative idea generation is incorrect.

To make matters more problematic, the generated solutions or responses during the extended period of time may be valid or invalid as well as creative or uncreative. None of these factors can be effectively teased apart in such experimental designs. Several studies assume that such problems are inconsequential as they specifically instruct their subjects to "be creative" during idea generation. However, this is not a simple instruction to follow, as merely instructing people to be creative does not guarantee their success in doing so. Notwithstanding the problem of definition of what it means to be creative (which may not be understood by one and all to mean the same thing), our brains are highly susceptible to the "path of least-resistance" strategy. This refers to the overwhelming tendency of our cost-effective brains to follow the cognitively least demanding route in generative situations (Ward, 1994).

All of the aforementioned technical limitations within creativity experimental paradigms, which in themselves are wholly limiting, are related to a much larger conceptual problem. This is that "trying to be creative" is not the same as "being creative" – a fact that most people would be keenly aware of from personal experience. While it is certainly useful to assess the pattern of brain response when people are "trying to be creative" in order to understand what happens in the brain when people are "being creative" when generating original and fitting responses, it is important that we are cognizant of this crucial distinction at the level of implicated mental operations, and let it guide our interpretation of findings accordingly.

More studies using structural neuroimaging or functional neuroimaging of resting states may appear to circumvent some of these issues of validity by carrying out correlational analyses between performance on creativity measures and indices of brain structure volumes or resting state activity patterns. However, the issue of validity is more prominent in such contexts as they are even further removed from the process of interest.

7.7 How to Deal with Problems?

While the extension of most experimental paradigms in psychology toward that of neuroscience may not be unduly problematic, this simply cannot be done with the same degree of ease in the case of creativity. This does not mean that creative thinking cannot be subject to neuroscientific study. But any technique, regardless of its inherent promise, is going to be ineffectual if the experimental designs being used are suboptimal in terms of answering the questions being posed. When considering how to create an optimal experimental design in the study of creativity, the following three guiding principles may prove to be of utility in clarifying how best to set sail in our enquiries.

First, according to Dietrich (2007a, 2), "It is high time that researchers became more creative about creativity." This means, among other things, that clever and oblique strategies need to be applied to create experimental designs that are both suitable for use in neuroscientific setups and targeted at investigating specific aspects of creativity. Examples of the same include experimental designs devised to test musical improvisation (Limb & Braun, 2008), conceptual expansion (Abraham, Pieritz, et al., 2012), and insight (Jung-Beeman et al., 2004).

Second, it is absolutely imperative that academic publications clearly delineate the scope of the experimental design used in a creativity study in terms of both its strengths and limitations. For instance, approaches that come closer to tapping creative thinking as it occurs in the real world, such as during musical improvisation and story generation (Limb & Braun, 2008; Liu et al., 2012, 2015; Shah et al., 2011), are necessarily less controlled in their experimental designs, but the upside is that they assess creative idea generation in a manner that may be considered more ecologically valid. It would be enormously useful to have such tradeoffs explicitly acknowledged.

Third, a useful strategy is to employ multiple approaches and experimental designs to directly or indirectly investigate the same operations of creative cognition. Some researchers have done so by using multiple methods, like EEG and fMRI, within the same experimental design (Fink, Grabner, et al., 2009; Jung-Beeman et al., 2004). Others have designed multiple experimental paradigms to tap the same process (Abraham, Pieritz, et al., 2012; Kröger et al., 2012; Rutter, Kröger, Stark, et al., 2012). The utility of such approaches is that commonalities in the findings across paradigms are indicative of process-specific neurocognitive mechanisms.

It is vital to consider questions that are posed in the study of creativity in relation to wider questions about how we ought to bridge our understanding of psychological function and brain function. The "mind–brain correspondence problem" reflects the understanding that brain states and psychological states, such as thoughts and feelings, are not instantiated in an equivalent manner to one another (Barrett & Satpute, 2013; Bennett & Hacker, 2003; Bressler & Menon, 2010; Haueis, 2014), which points to the need to cultivate an understanding of how psychological states emerge from the interaction of more basic mental components (Barrett, 2009).

Open discussions about the conceptual and methodological weaknesses that seem unavoidable in the neuroscientific study of creativity, constructive challenges to prevailing orthodoxies, and concerted dialogue about how best to overcome the unique challenges faced within the field of creativity offer the best way forward for the neuroscience of creativity to be a thriving and fruitful enterprise.

Chapter Summary

- The neuroscientific study of creativity is associated with unique problems, both technical and conceptual, that pose limitations on the interpretation and generalization of findings.
- Trials may be problematic as a result of being limited in number or lengthy in duration.
- Responses may be problematic as a result of being non-binary and subjective and often involving complex movements.
- Creativity tasks may be problematic as a result of considerable variability between tasks; in addition, control tasks may be inadequate.
- Groups may be problematic in terms of how they are classified – high and low creative groups, for example – and the questionable rationale that guides such distinctions.
- The problem of validity refers to issues such as the inability to prompt creativity and failure to differentiate between trying to be creative and actually being creative.
- Another factor that bears consideration is the types of creativity that cannot be directly studied using neuroscientific approaches.

Review Questions

1. What makes the neuroscientific study of creativity distinct from the neuroscientific study of other forms of complex cognition?
2. How are the problems of trials and problems of response related to one another?
3. What can be done to optimize creativity and control tasks within single experimental designs?
4. Are the grounds for proposing high and low creative ability groups dubious or sound?
5. Describe the unique problems of validity in the neuroscience of creativity.

Further Reading

- Abraham, A. (2013). The promises and perils of the neuroscience of creativity. *Frontiers in Human Neuroscience*, 7, 246.
- Arden, R., Chavez, R. S., Grazioplene, R., & Jung, R. E. (2010). Neuroimaging creativity: A psychometric view. *Behavioural Brain Research*, 214(2), 143–156.

- Dietrich, A. (2007b). Who's afraid of a cognitive neuroscience of creativity? *Methods, 42*(1), 22–27.
- Dietrich, A. (2015). *How creativity happens in the brain.* New York: Palgrave Macmillan.
- Sawyer, K. (2011). The cognitive neuroscience of creativity: A critical review. *Creativity Research Journal, 23*(2), 137–154.

CHAPTER EIGHT

Musical Creativity

"Music is the effort we make to explain to ourselves how our brains work. We listen to Bach transfixed because this is listening to a human mind."

(Lewis Thomas)

Learning Objectives

- Evaluating which aspects of music and musicality are creative
- Recognizing the effect of expertise on music perception
- Distinguishing between the many components of musical performance
- Grasping the problems associated with the neuroscientific study of musical composition
- Understanding the brain's response during musical improvisation
- Identifying how music impacts brain plasticity and vice versa

8.1 Music and Musicality

There are two truths about music. One is that musicality (the capacity to create music or the sensitivity to music) is universal as it is expressed in every known human culture. The other is that, while musicality is a central feature in our species, the multitudinous forms of musical expression that exist within and across cultures as well as generations render the making of generalizations about the nature of music across the many instantiations of musicality challenging. We are still grappling with the dynamics of the biological and cultural origins, as well as the development and maturation, of this fundamental human capacity (Cross, 2001; Peretz, 2006).

"Musicality can be defined as a natural, spontaneously developing trait based on and constrained by biology and cognition. Music, by contrast, can be defined as a social and cultural construct based on that very musicality" (Honing, ten Cate, Peretz, & Trehub, 2015, 1). While these definitions clarify the distinction between musicality and music, they remain incomplete as the crucial term "sound" has been omitted. Cross (2001, 33) proposes a generalizable definition: "Music can be defined as

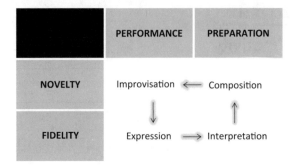

Figure 8.1 Types of musical creativity
Two orthogonal dimensions (novelty-fidelity; performance-preparation) give rise
to four types of musical creativity (adapted from Merker, 2006).

those temporally patterned human activities, individual and social, that
involve the production and perception of sound and have no evident and
immediate efficacy or fixed consensual reference." This description draws
attention to sound and movement, the central features of music.

How does music relate to creativity? This is a complicated question
given that we cannot but conceive of different types of musical creativity
(Figure 8.1). While the case for creativity in the inventive forms of musical
composition and musical improvisation is undisputed (Figure 8.2), can
the same be assumed for musical expression vis-à-vis creativity? At which
point does the creative process commence? While processes relevant to
communication and the imagination are triggered by the perception and
performance of music (Hargreaves, Miell, & MacDonald, 2012; Malloch
& Trevarthen, 2009), can this be generalized further to claim that the first
stirrings of the creative capacity begin with learning to play notes accurately on a musical instrument or singing in key? Or can one only speak of
creativity at the point of deliberate expression in performance where one
attempts to communicate specific feelings or emotions? Such theoretical
questions are rarely considered in detail within neuroscientific or behavioral studies of musical creativity (see Box 8.1).

The limited evidence on hand examining whether playing music
suffices to engender greater creativity has indicated that this is not necessarily the case. For instance, only expert musicians who created music
through the practices of composition or improvisation generated more
creative uses for musical items. This was not true for non-musicians or
expert musicians who do not create music (Sovansky, Wieth, Francis, &

Box 8.1 Are You Creative When You Merely Listen to Music?

This question can only be answered in the affirmative in the view of David Hargreaves. While the association between listening and other forms of musical creativity, such as composition, have been examined by others (Lerdahl, 2001), his is the most explicit avowal of the need to regard imaginative listening as a creative activity in and of itself (Hargreaves et al., 2012). The reciprocal-feedback model of response to music highlights the interplay between the music, the listening situation, and the listener, all three of which determine the response to music (Hargreaves, 2012). The first stems from the structural level of the pieces of music, which arise from the composer interacting with their personal inner musical library and using musical references to engage with the listener. The second refers to cultural associations, in the form of the contexts and typical situations in which one listens to music, which have a direct impact on one's experience of the same. The third refers to personal networks of associations that are generated by combining musical and cultural associations with their own associative networks of people, contexts, and events. The latter is closely coupled with the idea of the spreading activation theory of creativity (Schubert, 2011). Listening to music leads to the forging of a new associative pathway, a process that occurs spontaneously. This is related to the issue of recognizing creativity that was explored in Section 1.4.

McIlhagga, 2016). Moreover, musicians stemming from genres that are more typically associated with musical creativity, such as jazz owing to the emphasis on improvisation in practice, reveal a wider creative profile. In a study comparing the musical activities of students of classical, folk and jazz music, those studying jazz boasted more creative achievements and exhibited greater frequency in engaging in extracurricular musical activities. Jazz musicians also exhibited greater openness to experience, a personality trait that is central to creativity, as well as greater ideational originality in non-musical divergent thinking (Benedek, Borovnjak, Neubauer, & Kruse-Weber, 2014).

As generative processes are held to be inherent to music performance, music composition, and musical improvisation (Sloboda, 2000), the bulk of this chapter will be devoted to exploring the same. In the sections that follow, a summary of the field of music perception will be featured first, particularly with regard to the influence of musical experience on the same. Following this will be brief overviews of the neuroscientific and pertinent psychological literature in the fields of music performance, music composition, and musical improvisation with specific reference to creativity. The chapter ends with a reflective analysis of the relationship between music and brain plasticity.

8.2 Music Perception

What happens in the brain when we listen to music? It is clear that we don't hear music as a mere collection of sounds or noises. We perceive form, movement, themes, moods, and other abstractions. So there is an automatic and unconscious structuring of the acoustic information arriving at our senses through which we seem to make sense of and understand music. So what are these "musical structures" and how do they operate?

Musical structures are formed as a response to a sequence of notes that constitute the "musical surface" or "the array of simultaneous and sequential sounds with pitch, timbre, intensity, and duration" (Jackendoff & Lerdahl, 2006, 37). The musical structure of "grouping" takes the form of motives, phrases, and sections that arise through the segmentation of the musical surface. These largely derive from Gestalt perceptual principles that determine musical boundaries. Grouping is one component of "rhythm" in music; another is "metrical structure," the basic unit of which is a "beat" marking a point in time. The metrical grid constitutes "an ongoing hierarchical temporal framework of beats aligned with the musical surface" (ibid., 39). "Pitch" is the other major musical structure, the basic unit of which is a "note" that belongs to a tonal "pitch space" such as a musical scale. Tonality and pitch work in a congruent manner such that movement away from the tonic pitch raises "tension" whereas movement toward creates "relaxation." "Melodies" are constructed from the ordering of pitches and intervals at different levels of abstraction and arise as a function of a range of principles. Beginning with the musical surface, then, the construction of musical structures like pitch and rhythm lead to the experience of musical affect.

8.2.1 Rhythm, Pitch, and Affect

"One factor that appears to apply to almost all the world's musics is that there is a level of temporal organization that is regular and periodic, sometimes called the tactus. It is taken to correspond to the regular points in the music where one would tap one's foot or clap along ... Even when encountering previously unheard music from an unknown culture, a listener can still 'keep a beat.'" (Cross, 2001, 30–31)

Indeed, the innateness of beat perception can even be gleaned from the brain activity of newborn infants indicating a violation of sensory expectations after the omission of a downbeat which they had come to expect as a marker of the onset of a rhythm cycle (Winkler, Háden, Ladinig, Sziller, & Honing, 2009).

The perception of rhythm and pitch are orchestrated by separable brain systems that interact with one another to generate a musical percept (Peretz & Coltheart, 2003; Zatorre, Chen, & Penhune, 2007). Rhythm, in particular, is held to involve interaction between auditory and motor brain systems. Regions like the basal ganglia, the cerebellum, the dorsal premotor cortex, and the supplementary motor area (SMA) are frequently implicated. For instance, the basal ganglia is a key structure in rhythm detection as it is involved in the evaluation of temporal relations and temporal structure (Schwartze, Keller, Patel, & Kotz, 2011). Pitch perception activates different regions of the auditory cortex, with regions outside the primary auditory cortex engaged as a function of melodic and harmonic manipulations; regions rostral and ventral to the auditory cortex in the superior temporal gyrus and sulcus, however, are responsive during the perception of harmonies, melodic intervals. and melodic patterns (Janata, 2015).

The perception of musical structures like rhythm and pitch is intricately tied to the experience of musical affect. For instance, correlates of harmonic preferences, such as perceived consonance, can be detected at subcortical stages of musical processing, such as brain stem frequency-following response magnitude (Bidelman & Krishnan, 2011). The neural circuitry involved in reward processing in general "include[s] dopaminergic brainstem nuclei, especially the ventral tegmental area, the ventromedial and orbital frontal cortices, the amygdala, the insula, and the striatum" (Zatorre, 2015, 203). A study of music listening using positron emission tomography (PET) found key roles played by the brain's reward system, with endogenous dopamine release in the striatum accompanying states of peak emotional arousal where the nucleus accumbens was more engaged during the experience of peak emotional responses to music while the caudate nucleus was more engaged during the anticipation phase (Salimpoor, Benovoy, Larcher, Dagher, & Zatorre, 2011).

8.2.2 Post-Training Effects

Our implicit ability to detect music regularities is evidenced by behavioral and neuroscientific studies on untrained listeners like non-musicians and children who use the same principles as expert musicians in the manner in which the hearing of music is organized (Bigand, 2003; Koelsch & Friederici, 2003). Musically untrained listeners are similar to musicians in their ability to (a) "perceive musical tensions and relaxations in both melodies and harmonic sequences," (b) "anticipate musical events on the basis of subtle syntactic-like features of the prime sequence," (c) experience similar levels of "difficulty [in] integrat[ing] local structures in large-scale structures," and (d) "respond very consistently to music in an emotional (affective) way" with little difference in "the content of the emotional experience" (Bigand & Poulin-Charronnat, 2006, 119). Even the brain activity of musically untrained listeners evokes signature ERP indices, such as mismatch negativity (MMN; a pre-attentive response generated from the auditory cortex and elicited by sensory irregularities) and early right-anterior negativity (ERAN; generated from the inferior frontal gyrus and elicited by musical structural irregularities), indicating the automatic detection of the relations between temporally and spectrally complex musical sounds that engender musical expectancy (Koelsch, Gunter, Friederici, & Schröger, 2000; Tervaniemi, 2001).

With the onset of musical training, our innate musicality is honed in specific ways that are aligned with the context of musical development. Longitudinal studies have been employed to isolate and characterize neural markers in auditory discrimination in musicians and non-musicians from childhood into adulthood. The evidence indicates no pre-existing perceptual differences between the groups before commencing musical training, and that superior auditory perceptual skills in adult musicians develop over the course of musical training (Putkinen, Tervaniemi, Saarikivi, Ojala, & Huotilainen, 2014). So, for instance, musicians relative to non-musicians demonstrate larger MMN responses to changes in melodic contour or interval but not frequency of a pure tone. Such a pattern is suggestive of enhanced automatic encoding and discrimination of pitch contour and interval information (Pantev et al., 2003).

The processing of sounds among musicians is also influenced by instrument, performance practice, and level of expertise. In a study examining MMN activity in relation to six types of changes in musical feature across musicians playing three styles of music (classical, jazz, rock/pop), jazz musicians displayed larger MMN amplitude than the other groups across all sound features, indicating heightened sensitivity to auditory outliers overall. So the features of the style of music played by musicians influence their perceptual processing of acoustic information in music (Vuust, Brattico, Seppänen, Näätänen, & Tervaniemi, 2012).

A comparison of percussionists, vocalists, and non-musician controls indicated selective enhancements in perceptual encoding of speech as a function of the salient acoustic features of the primary instrument in question. Compared to non-musicians, percussionists demonstrated more precise encoding of fast-changing acoustic features whereas vocalists were better at frequency discrimination and speech harmonics encoding. Percussionists also showed enhanced performance on inhibitory control compared to both vocalists and non-musicians (Slater, Azem, Nicol, Swedenborg, & Kraus, 2017). So, this selectivity in perceptual skills can even extend to non-musical acoustic information.

Genre-based selectivity in perceptual sensitivity was also gleaned from the brain activity of classical, jazz, and rock musicians as well as non-musicians in terms of the accuracy of neural encoding (via the MMN response) in relation to the melody, which contained deviations within features of tuning, timbre, rhythm, melody transpositions, and melody contour. Only classical musicians were selectively attuned to tuning deviants while only jazz musicians showed the same for transposition. Both classical and jazz musicians demonstrated selectivity for timing, while both jazz and rock musicians indicated heightened sensitivity for melody contour (Tervaniemi, 2009; Tervaniemi, Janhunen, Kruck, Putkinen, & Huotilainen, 2015).

There is evidence of experience-based differences even at the conscious level of musical analysis. In line with the "more-experienced-listeners-understand-more-like-performers" hypothesis, listeners with more jazz experience as well as experience of playing the musical instruments of the performer were more likely to endorse statements given by the performers about their jazz improvisations than listeners who had less jazz experience and experience of musical instruments different to that of the performer (Schober & Spiro, 2016).

What is more, enhanced perceptual processing skills on the part of musicians also extend to musical imagery. Musically trained participants outperform non-musicians on both musical and non-musical behavioral tasks of auditory imagery. This advantage is limited to the acoustic domain as no significant advantage as a function of group are found on tasks of visual imagery (Aleman, Nieuwenstein, Böcker, & de Haan, 2000). There is also neuroscientific evidence that aligns well in this context. A magnetoencephalography (MEG) study contrasted the brain activity of musicians and non-musicians while they imagined familiar melodies. The task of all participants was to indicate whether or not a presented tone correctly continued the melody. An MMN response was elicited to incorrect tones but only in musicians, indicating the detection of a violation of an established rule even within an imaginative context as a function of musical training (Herholz, Lappe, Knief, & Pantev, 2009).

8.3 Music Performance

The feat of musical performance is highly unique for several reasons. There are few activities that we humans engage in for which (a) multimodal sensorial experience is necessarily closely coupled with complex and precise motoric coordination, in (b) contexts that involve an open-ended number of people ranging from one individual (solo musician) to a large group (ensemble performances), and (c) are carried out for extended periods of time ranging from brief (a few seconds) to lengthy (several hours) durations.

What is common to all types of musical performance is the necessary engagement of motor control systems in the brain that enable three core functions. These are "timing" in order to instantiate musical rhythm, "sequencing," and the "spatial organization of movement" that enables the playing of single notes on a musical instrument (Zatorre et al., 2007). An important factor to consider in sequencing is its time course as there is a temporal overlap between item retrieval of the note to be played that precedes movement preparation of the same (Palmer, 2005). While these reflect the technical aspects of musical performance, its expressive aspects are of especial relevance in the context of musical creativity. These are highly complex to investigate (Wöllner, 2013) as the expressive intentions of a musician during a performance are based on both trait (e.g., accumulated through practice and experience) and state (e.g., current emotional state, interplay with other musicians present) factors (De Poli, 2003). The technical and expressive sides of music performance cannot be teased apart when considering the aesthetic pleasure of music listening. These are held to largely stem from the generation of musical expectations (Huron, 2006; Zatorre & Salimpoor, 2013), although the principles by which music induces emotions in the listener are complex and draw from the interaction between innate auditory responses and learned associations (Huron, 2015).

In discerning factors that are distinctive to music compared to other forms of art, the presence of the musical instrument seems to stand out as a relevant variable, albeit that this is less applicable in the case of singing than when instruments external to the body are used in musical performance. Some have even pointed to the natural extension of the musical instrument to the body of the musician (Nijs, Lesaffre, & Leman, 2013).

Regardless of the type of "instrument," musical performance constitutes a sustained sensorimotor task where practice leads to a strong "coupling" between sensory brain regions (visual and auditory) and motor brain regions. This coupling is believed to serve two overarching functions. The first is that it enables the generation of equivalent predictions in both music perception and music performance about which event is likely to take place and when this event is likely to occur. The second is that coupling forms the foundation of the common coding between perception and action that enables multiple musicians to engage in joint musical tasks through training, which is instantiated via processes of reciprocal prediction and adaptation while working toward shared goals (Novembre & Keller, 2014).

8.3.1 Behavioral Characteristics

For a performer, the creative cycle commences with the preparation of the performance in studying and practicing the work in order to "work toward a congruence with the piece" that comes about by cultivating an understanding of the composer's intent while bringing one's own essence and individuality to the piece (Lund & Kranz, 1994). This is instantiated in the form of minute deviations that register as palpable individual differences. For instance, by extracting highly precise performance features of touch, pedaling, articulation, and dynamics among expert pianists it was found that pianists demonstrate both shared patterns for each timbral intention and unique signature patterns for different timbral intentions (Bernays & Traube, 2014).

Musical imagery is also central to musical performance. Musicians demonstrate an enhanced ability to engage in musical imagery both in terms of auditory imagery, where sounds are imagined, and motor imagery, which is "the imagination of the kinesthetics involved in actual movement" (Zatorre & Halpern, 2005, 10). Multimodal mental imagery is commonly evoked under conditions of musical performance across auditory, motor, and sometimes even visual domains. In line with evidence that supports the overlap of brain regions involved in auditory imagery and temporal prediction, it has been suggested that the information processing mechanisms underlying imagery include internal models, action simulation, and working memory. These "support the generation of anticipatory images that enable thorough action planning and movement execution that is characterized by efficiency, temporal precision, and biomechanical economy" (Keller, 2012, 206).

This multimodality lies at the heart of synchrony in music and its wider effects. The mere act of moving to an auditory rhythmic pattern synchronously with another person increases interpersonal synchrony and prosocial behavior (Trainor & Cirelli, 2015). Multimodal synchrony also impacts expressiveness in performance, with head movements being the differentiator in joint music performance compared to solo music performance (Glowinski et al., 2013). In fact, communication through body sway with ensemble performances influences perceived performance success (Chang, Livingstone, Bosnyak, & Trainor, 2017).

Flow states are commonly discussed in the context of musical performance, both with musical instruments and during singing. For instance, longer practice times increased the likelihood of flow experience during musical performance in vocalists, and the experience of flow was not related to specific musical genres (Heller, Bullerjahn, & von Georgi, 2015). On the basis of self-reported flow following the playing of a musical piece, the flow states in professional classical pianists were significantly correlated with indices of cardiovascular and respiratory systems as well as electromyography activity. Here, the experience of flow was related to "an increased activation of the sympathetic branch of the autonomic nervous system in combination with deep breathing and activation of the ZM," or the "smile muscle" (de Manzano, Theorell, Harmat, & Ullén, 2010, 306). The number of hours of practice and trait emotional intelligence also predict the propensity to experience flow during musical performance (Marin & Bhattacharya, 2013).

8.3.2 Brain Basis

Timing, sequencing, and spatial organization of action constitute the information processing triad of musical performance (Peretz & Zatorre, 2003; Zatorre et al., 2007). While parameters related to "movement timing" are subserved by processing within the cerebellum, the basal ganglia and the SMA, the learning, planning, and execution of sequences that require higher levels of control involve these and additional brain structures in the premotor cortex, the pre-SMA, and the prefrontal cortex. The neural correlates of spatial organization of movement during musical performance are less well understood, with the limited evidence suggesting that the dorsal aspect of the premotor cortex appears to play a significant role. This region is also associated with increased gray matter as a function of early musical training (approximately before the age of 6) (Brown, Zatorre, & Penhune, 2015).

The coupling between auditory and motor systems during music performance is orchestrated by feedback and feedforward interactions. Feedback interactions reflect the influence exerted by the auditory system on the motor system, such as tapping to the beat of ambient music. Feedforward interactions reflect the situations in which a movement leads to auditory information and this information can be used to modify further movements, such as during musical practice when motor adjustments are continually made in relation to auditory feedback. The cerebellum, in particular, plays a key role in the optimization of movements as it is involved in error correction and in the learning of new motor skills (Brown et al., 2015).

The auditory-motor pathways that facilitate this interaction are anatomically enhanced in musicians compared to non-musicians. The pathways are comprised of dorsal and ventral routes, with the latter involved in the representation of musical intervals, contours, and other melodic features. The dorsal route engages dorsal premotor and parietal pathways in transforming acoustic patterns into motor patterns. Long-term memory, which engages medial temporal lobe structures, and working memory, which engages frontal lobe structures, are also significant in relation to expert musical performance. Long-term memory skills are superior in expert musicians, allowing them to play from memory by recalling not only hundreds of pieces but also their own interpretations of musical work, which they have consciously chosen and extensively rehearsed beforehand. Working memory involves the retrieval, maintenance, and manipulation of musical segments, and the working memory skills of expert musicians reflect planning in advance and doing so in segments (ibid.).

Ensemble music performances necessitate sensorimotor coordination as audiomotor and visuomotor messages are dynamically communicated in real time between the musicians. The "mirror" and "echo" systems of the brain are commonly evoked in this context, as overlapping regions of the ventral premotor cortex and the inferior parietal lobule are engaged during action observation, action performance, and while listening to action-related sounds (Volpe, D'Ausilio, Badino, Camurri, & Fadiga, 2016; Zatorre et al., 2007). This is taken as evidence of such regions coding for the abstract properties of sensorimotor coupling in representing the meaning of actions. The relevance of such mirror systems is enhanced in the context of ensemble performance as it involves multimodal communication and coordination between several individuals in service of complementary joint action (Volpe et al., 2016).

8.4 Music Composition

The act of composition marks the origin of a piece of music and "may be described as the art of organizing sounds that by themselves do not have clear semantic associations in an original way that acquires or induces meaning either or both for the composer and the listener" (Brattico & Tervaniemi, 2006, 290). The conditions under which composition can take place vary widely as,

in principle the full score of a symphony might emerge in perfect silence, on paper alone, by fits and starts and constant revision, over a time-span of years. More typically, composition avails itself of performance at various stages of the process of finding, elaborating, varying, and selecting novel musical structures. (Merker, 2006, 28)

Peter Webster's (2003) model of creative thinking in music, which is of especial relevance in music composition (Burnard & Younker, 2004), places divergent and convergent thought processes at the center. It also includes Wallas's stages of creative ideation through preparation, incubation, and verification and adds "working through," or revising and editing, which is integral to music composition as elements are continually structured, combined, and refined. It additionally boasts a systemic focus as it takes into consideration enabling conditions, both personal (e.g., motivation) and socio-cultural (e.g., peer group), and enabling skills (e.g., aesthetic sensitivity, craftsmanship) in relation to the thought processes (Figures 8.2 and 8.3). Time perception is also held to be different under conditions of musical composition compared to musical improvisation. Composition is marked by temporality that is "expanding" in that "temporal projections may be conceived from any moment in a work to past and future time coordinates," whereas improvisation is characterized as inner-directed or "vertical" in its temporality such that "the present is heightened and the past and future are perceptually subordinated" (Sarath, 1996, 1).

Conceptualizations of music composition often showcase parallels and distinctions between the domains of music and language (Adorno & Gillespie, 1993), music and architecture (Young, Bancroft, & Sanderson, 1993), and music and math (Mode, 1962). "Patterning" is held to be essential to the composition of music cross-culturally (Wilson, 1989), and constructive forms of composition are distinguished from generative forms such that,

we speak about constructive creative ability in music where the composer gives a final form to an original opus by means of conscious work, employing

Characteristic	Improvisation	Composition
Context	Public or private	Private
Individual/group	Individual or group	Individual or group (less frequent)
Development	Continuous, linear, real-time act, extemporaneous creation	Continuous or discontinuous act, mediated creation
Experimentation	Extemporaneous experimentation; it can provide suggestions to composition	Reasoned experimentation
Abilities	Performing and compositional	Compositional
Processes	Anticipation, use of repertoire, emotive communication, feedback, and flow	Planning, translating from the sound to graph, idea generation, organization and construction, revision
Reversibility	Irreversible action, it cannot be changed	Reversible action, it can be changed until the final draft
Revision	It cannot be reviewed, but only adjusted in real-time during the performance with the feedback	It can be reviewed and improved
Control	Control of individual variables but not of group variables	Overall control of the score and of the complexity of the compositional process
Feedback	Real-time feedback	Feedback without real-time pressure
Process dynamics	Interactive process it has an adaptable nature, it allows you to answer to context variables, it can be adjusted instantly. Challenge between performers, taking risks	Fix product. The composition can be interpreted but it is not possible to change the notes of the score
Communication	The author has a direct communication with the audience. It is more authentic and real than composition	The author has a communication with the audience mediated by the performer(s) who interprets his/her ideas

Figure 8.2 Musical improvisation and composition

Commonalities and differences in their characteristics. Reprinted with permission from Biasutti M (2015). Pedagogical applications of cognitive research on musical improvisation. *Frontiers in Psychology*, *6*, 614.

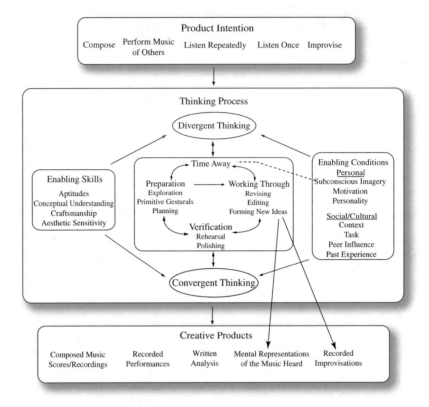

Figure 8.3 A theoretical framework for musical creativity

Model of creative thinking in music by Peter R. Webster. Reprinted with permission of the author.

and (partly) reshaping the elements and rules known to him. By generative composing we mean a largely unconscious or intuitive variational application of the elements and rules which does not result in a final opus of unchangeable form but merely in a new variant. (Sági & Vitányl, 2001, 3)

8.4.1 Behavioral Studies

Much of the empirical work in this field stems from examining the intrapersonal and interpersonal dynamics of young children during their engagement in music composition (Burnard, 2012; Webster, 2016). For instance, distinct bodily intentions, as defined by the interactions between preference for instrument, type of instrument, and body movement, have been identified in relation to music composition compared to musical improvisation. Improvisation was characterized in terms of the "perceiving" body as it involved meeting "the consequence of continuity through the interplay of visual, kinaesthetic and aural senses," while composition led to the engagement of the "knowing" body in that it involved accessing "a well-spring of existing ideas using known movement patterns already encoded in the kinesthetic memory" (Burnard, 1999, 170–171).

Behavioral studies have examined musical composition in music undergraduates particularly in relation to the experience of flow and its impact on creativity of the composition. In one study, participants were given a composition to work on in groups of 3, had to meet at least 3 times a week to do so, and were asked to fill out experience sampling forms to measure their flow experience at each meeting. The higher levels of flow reported within one group were also related to higher levels of creativity for that group's composition (MacDonald et al., 2006). Greater flow experiences also resulted from the creation of music compared to the mere performance of music among non-music undergraduates and retirees who created music compositions as part of a therapeutic songwriting experience, and this was true regardless of type of composition: song parody, lyric writing, or original songwriting. Moreover, compared to lyric writing and song parody, original songwriting was rated as more meaningful and was associated with higher levels of satisfaction as well as a greater sense of achievement and self (Baker & MacDonald, 2013).

Creativity in music composition also has a discerning impact on informational feedback. Relative to music students whose compositions were judged to be low in creativity, high creative composers were more likely to report using experimentation during composition, express optimism, employ expressive intent in the titles of their pieces, and engage critically in the analysis of their work (Priest, 2006). Moreover, high creative composers hold that creativity and craftsmanship in their compositions derive from temporal factors, or changes over time in the form of recurring themes, transitions, contrasts, developments, and so on, whereas low creative composers cite factors such as metaphors and agility instead (Priest, 2001).

Empirical explorations of musical creativity in professional composers are rare. Instead, mainly theoretical, historiometric, and case study examinations of musical composition in eminent populations exist (Hass

& Weisberg, 2009; Roels, 2016; Simonton, 1989b; Sloboda, 2000). This is unsurprising given the lack of access to such niche populations. But this is an unfortunate situation as we lack an enormous piece of the puzzle that is necessary in order to truly understand this vital form of musical creativity.

8.4.2 Neuroscientific Studies

Investigations of the brain basis of music composition are also surprisingly rare, and are largely limited to case explorations of eminent composers who suffered from clinical disorders (Altenmüller, Finger, & Boller, 2015). The few that were carried out were early EEG investigations in the 1990s, such as reports of dominant left hemisphere activity during musical composition compared to the conditions of music analysis and music memory among young adult music students (Beisteiner, Altenmuller, Lang, Lindinger, & Deecke, 1994). Increases in EEG coherence were also reported in a group of professional musicians while composing compared to listening to a piece of music, reflecting enhanced contralateral cooperation of distant parts of the parietal and frontal areas (Petsche, 1996).

A functional neuroimaging study that examined the brain basis of musical composition revealed the difference between functional connectivity in the brain during rest compared to during a 5-minute composing task (Lu et al., 2015). The study examined composers only so there was neither a control group nor a control condition to provide a contrast. Findings revealed reduced functional connectivity between visual and motor areas alongside increased functional connectivity between the anterior cingulate and the posterior cingulate during the composing state compared to a resting state. Another study correlated self-reported creativity with structural brain measures and revealed that those subjects who reported having "improvised or written original music" to a greater degree than other subjects, had a larger surface area in many parts of the "default mode network," including the dorsal medial PFC, the temporal pole, and the lateral temporal cortex, the "motor planning regions," including the SMA and pre-SMA, and the "limbic regions," such as the orbitofrontal cortex and the amygdala (Bashwiner, Wertz, Flores, & Jung, 2016). More concerted brain-based investigations of musical composition are necessary in order to develop a viable neuroscientific framework regarding the same (see Box 8.2).

Box 8.2 How to Better Study Musical Creativity?

A multi-pronged approach is necessary. One is to develop and/or adapt more techniques and methodologies to evaluate physiological responses under conditions of musical creativity. A new procedure to measure performers' skin conductance (SC) during musical improvisation that allows for continuous measurement during piano performances while detecting relevant changes during transitions between musical segments is one such example (Dean & Bailes, 2015). The challenge here is to see whether such a technique could be effectively adapted for use with other instruments.

It would also be useful to see the adoption of multiple measures of creativity when investigating musical creativity in order to evaluate how well the measures of such laboratory-based clinically developed tests correspond to musical creativity in the real world. It is also important to use these in conjunction with physiological measures. Several relevant scales relating to musical improvisation and collaboration are available, such as the Interpersonal Music-Communication Competence Scale (IMCCS; Hald, Baker, & Ridder, 2017), Webster's Measure of Creative Thinking in Music (MCTM II; Webster, 1987, 1994), and the Musical Expression Test (Bardot & Lubart, 2012).

Just as vital is the need to run more ecologically valid as well as scientifically sound studies using professional musicians across a range of contexts of musical generativity, both spontaneous and deliberate. This requires sustained collaboration and dialogue between neuroscientists and musicians (McPherson & Limb, 2013).

8.5 Musical Improvisation

Musical improvisation is where musical performance meets musical composition on the fly, and it varies considerably from the relatively constrained conditions in traditional jazz, featuring close adherence to a harmonic sequence and metrical structure, to the extremely indeterminate conditions of free improvisation. While it is mostly an oversimplification to aver that improvisation is marked by little preparation or planning during performance, it is clear that skilled and creative improvisation only emerges if one has amassed extensive musical experience in performance. Flea, bass player in the Red Hot Chili Peppers, captured the involuntary aspects of the process when he stated that,

The apparatus has to serve our improbability and improvisation … Being good and playing the songs is not enough. Being entertaining isn't enough …

We must improvise and we must experiment and we must do things that might go wrong and everything we bring – the people and the equipment – must serve us in that goal. (quoted in Fitzpatrick, 2011)

Caution must be exerted when considering what musical improvisation reflects as it is often assumed *de facto* to reflect musical creativity. This is not necessarily true. To improvise in a manner that pushes the envelope so as to display manifestly high levels of originality is actually exceedingly challenging. Every act of improvisation is not necessarily highly creative, a fact that is rarely explicitly acknowledged within behavioral or neuroscientific studies. Most brain-based studies on musical creativity get around this problem by contrasting conditions of musical performance with and without improvisation. Owing to the unpredictability of creative idea or response generation and the limitations of current technologies to record the brain response (see Chapter 7 and Box 8.2), we are not at the stage where we can adequately test questions concerning the degree of originality within musical improvisation. Nonetheless, some groundbreaking studies have allowed us to get much closer to understanding how such tremendous capacities are orchestrated. Musical improvisation, after all, epitomizes musical creativity at its most spontaneous.

8.5.1 Behavioral Characteristics

Of the many frameworks that have been proposed to explain musical improvisation (Biasutti, 2015; Biasutti & Frezza, 2009), the algorithmic demand model has been the most influential in the context of jazz (Johnson-Laird, 2002). In distinguishing between three algorithms for creativity – *neo-Darwinian* (random/arbitrary variation in generation and criterion-based selection), *neo-Lamarckian* (experience/criterion-based variation in generation and arbitrary selection), and a *compromise* between the two (neo-Lamarckian like generation, neo-Darwinian like selection) – Johnson-Laird averred that,

The composition of tonal chord sequences depends on a multistage algorithm that requires a working memory (or, equivalently, a notation) for intermediate results, whereas the tacit procedures for the improvisation of melodies depend on a neo-Lamarckian algorithm that requires no working memory for intermediate results. (2002, 423)

An even more detailed model of musical improvisation is that of Jeff Pressing (2001), who averred that improvisational skills are typified by "improved efficiency, fluency, flexibility, capacity for error correction, expressiveness ... inventiveness and the achievement of coherence" (50). These skills are brought about by specific cognitive changes, such as an enhanced memory store "of objects, features, and processes – in musical, acoustic, motor (and other) aspects," increased "accessibility of this memory store due to the build-up of redundant relationships between its constituents and the aggregation of these constituents into larger cognitive assemblies," and heightened "attunement to subtle and contextually relevant perceptual information" (ibid.).

Drawing on the different frameworks of musical improvisation, Biasutti and Frezza (2009) identified five factors of relevance for musical improvisation (Figure 8.2): (i) *anticipation*, or the ability to plan the development of the improvisation on melodic, rhythmic, and harmonic levels, (ii) *emotive communication*, or the ability to convey affective states, (iii) *flow*, which is the optimal experience of complete absorption during performance, (iv) *feedback*, which can be internal (as monitored within the musician themself) or external (as communicated from the outer world via fellow musicians, the audience, or the environmental context) and is used to make changes to improvisation in real time, and (v) *use of repertoire*, which refers to existing formulas, scripts, clichés, or licks. These were incumbent on two further elements being in place, namely: (vi) *basic skills*, such as pitch recognition and beat perception, and (vii) *musical practice*, as developed through continual exercise and study. Behavioral studies of musical improvisation have in fact focused on the effects of training duration and other individual factors, such as cognitive abilities, on improvisation skill. For instance, the number of hours of cumulative practice was a good predictor of improvisational creativity among jazz musicians. Moreover, improvisational creativity was also positively correlated with ideational originality in non-musical divergent thinking, while being negatively correlated with working memory capacity and inductive reasoning in fluid intelligence (Beaty, Smeekens, Silvia, Hodges, & Kane, 2013).

As musical improvisation can take place at both individual and group levels, the latter context brings with it the necessity to consider the impact of additional factors. Three elements are central to group creativity: improvisation, collaboration, and emergence (Sawyer, 2006), and an example of such principles at play can be gleaned from the following study. Nineteen expert improvisers with substantial years of experience were presented with several blocks of a free sorting task, each for a set of 25 sounds. These were to be organized into as many groups as they wished such that the groups reflected the pragmatic similarity of the sounds in a manner mirroring how the participants would react if they were to hear them in a collective free jazz setting. Musicians who frequently played together tended to "think" about improvised music in the same way, a finding that was ascribed to the degree of similarity in participants' mental models (Canonne & Aucouturier, 2016).

The importance of other group dynamics, such as perceived authenticity of communication, has also been examined in improvisation by means of non-verbal social feedback cues. Musicians performed duo improvisations with solo episodes in standard jazz style (regular pulsed rhythm) and free improvisation style (non-pulsed rhythm). The improvisations of both the soloist and the silent non-soloing musician were recorded using a motion capture system. Other musicians who observed the point light displays were more sensitive to the real duos compared to fake (mismatched) duos in the free improvisation condition, and this was unrelated to their musical experience or rhythm perception abilities. The need to consider the role of interpersonal dynamics is highlighted in such studies as picking up the non-verbal social cues in free improvisation is a general perceptual-cognitive ability that is not dependent on music-specific skills (Moran, Hadley, Bader, & Keller, 2015). Other researchers have highlighted the necessity to also consider the dynamics of the actual movement coordination between improvising musicians in order to comprehend how creative expression emerges (Walton, Richardson, Langland-Hassan, & Chemero, 2015).

Evidence that improvisation experience can lead to improvements in musical creativity is also mounting. The inclusion of improvisation training in music lessons over a period of 6 months for 6-year-old children compared to only teacher-centered and didactic activities was found to lead to increase in creative thinking with reference to the four musical parameters of extensiveness, flexibility, originality, and syntax (Koutsoupidou & Hargreaves, 2009). The enhancing effect of improvisation on creativity also extends to non-musical contexts. Comparisons between musicians with improvisation training, musicians without improvisation training, and non-musicians revealed that the first group outperformed the others in both ideational fluency (the number of ideas generated) and ideational originality (the uniqueness of the generated ideas) when performing divergent tasks of creative thinking, leading the authors to postulate the "releasing" effect of the deliberate practice of improvisation on creative thinking (Kleinmintz, Goldstein, Mayseless, Abecasis, & Shamay-Tsoory, 2014).

8.5.2 Brain Correlates

When reviewing neuroscientific studies of musical improvisation, what appears to be commonly indicated across investigations is that there is an interplay between the two large brain networks that orchestrate cognitive control and spontaneous thought, namely, the CEN and the DMN (Beaty, 2015) (see Section 4.2.3). What differs between the studies is the manner in which single regions within these brain networks are selectively engaged, with some studies showing stronger engagement or "activation" of core brain regions and others showing reduced engagement or "deactivation" of core brain regions.

The first published neuroimaging study of musical improvisation examined classically trained pianists and revealed that on-line improvisation relative to both rest and the reproduction of previously improvised music from memory resulted in activations within the dorsolateral PFC, the dorsal premotor cortex, and the right pre-SMA (Bengtsson, Csíkszentmihályi, & Ullén, 2007). While the latter two regions were seen as playing a role in the planning and timing aspects of motor responses, the dorsolateral PFC was specifically highlighted in terms of its function in the maintenance of working memory and other aspects of complex cognitive control that would be necessitated during musical improvisation.

Another early study that explicitly examined improvisation with reference to novel action generation revealed that both rhythmic and melodic motor sequence creation activated brain regions involved in movement sequence generation, voluntary selection of action sequences, and execution of the selected action sequence, namely, the inferior frontal gyrus, the mid-anterior cingulate cortex, and the dorsal premotor cortex, respectively (Berkowitz & Ansari, 2008). However, they reported task-relevant deactivations in relation to melodic improvisation (but not rhythmic improvisation) in parts of the lateral PFC as well as the angular gyrus, posterior cingulate, and supramarginal gyrus, but these were not discussed in much detail.

The first study to have paid especial interest to improvisation related deactivations was conducted with professional jazz pianists (Limb & Braun, 2008). They reported that, when compared to the reproduction of known musical sequences, improvisation led to a dissociated pattern of brain engagement within the prefrontal cortex itself. This was characterized by deactivation of lateral regions such as the dorsolateral PFC (CEN) with the simultaneous activation of medial prefrontal regions, such as the frontal pole (DMN). Limb and Braun (2008) found that:

Such a pattern may reflect a combination of psychological processes required for spontaneous improvisation, in which internally motivated, stimulus-independent behaviors unfold in the absence of central processes that typically mediate self-monitoring and conscious volitional control of ongoing performance. (2008, 1)

A related proposal, but in the context of another brain region, was put forward within a later study that reported the deactivation of the right temporoparietal junction (rTPJ) (a DMN region) among classically trained musicians compared to non-musicians during melodic improvisation (Berkowitz & Ansari, 2010). In interpreting the role of the rTPJ from the context of the ventral attentional network, such that its deactivation inhibits attentional shifts toward task-irrelevant stimuli, the authors speculate that a

potential interpretation of the musicians' deactivation of the rTPJ during improvisation is that they strategized in a more top-down fashion … thus inhibiting any sort of stimulus-driven response to what they played while they planned their next improvised sequence. (Berkowitz & Ansari, 2010, 717)

Evidence for deactivations also comes from EEG studies (Adhikari et al., 2016). When comparing differences in alpha (8–12 Hz) and beta (13–30 Hz) activity within musicians as they played or imagined brief learned melodies and improvised on the same showed that reduced network activity between brain regions involved in cognitive control, such as the superior frontal gyrus, supplementary motor area, and left inferior parietal lobule, was seen under conditions of improvisation.

One factor to bear in mind about studies that examine improvisation in classically trained musicians is that, as little information is provided about the levels of expertise in musical improvisation itself within such groups, it is challenging to interpret the findings as their musical expertise in musical performance may not be directly pertinent to musical improvisation if they have little experience in the same. This was taken into account in an EEG study in which alpha activity was taken as an index to relate creativity-relevant mental states to the generation of artistic works in skilled musicians with and without formal improvisation training. While all musicians showed greater frontal alpha activity during improvisation, this brain response was strongest for musicians with formal improvisation training (Lopata et al., 2017). One functional neuroimaging study with 39 professional pianists examined the correlations between the number of hours of musical improvisation experience and brain activity during musical improvisation (Pinho, Manzano, Fransson, Eriksson, & Ullén, 2014). Higher levels of experience were associated with lower activity in fronto-parietal executive networks, which plausibly suggests a greater degree of automaticity as a function of training, and higher activity in dorsal premotor, pre-supplementary motor, and dorsolateral pre-frontal regions, which they attributed to greater efficiency within associative networks relevant to musical creativity. The somewhat paradoxical responsiveness of the dorsolateral prefrontal cortex has been attributed to contextual factors because it was strongly coupled to the DMN during musical improvisation with pre-specified emotional content (happy/fearful) but strongly coupled to the premotor network during musical improvisation with pre-specified pitch-sets (tonal/atonal) (Pinho, Ullén, Castelo-Branco, Fransson, & de Manzano, 2015).

Novel directions of enquiry include whether musical experience in improvisation facilitates the perception of spontaneity in musical performance (Engel & Keller, 2011). While jazz musicians' accuracy when judging whether piano melodies they listened to were improvised or imitated was low but above chance, their performance was positively correlated with musical experience. Indeed, analysis of their brain responses indicated greater activity within the amygdala activation for improvisations relative to imitations, and that melodies judged to be improvised engaged parts of the "action simulation network" in that regions such as the pre-supplementary motor area, frontal operculum, and anterior insula were most strongly activated for melodies judged to be improvised. The accurate assessment of spontaneity in musical performance is held to be influenced by "whether an individual's action-related experience and perspective taking skills enable faithful internal simulation of the given behavior" (Engel & Keller, 2011, 1).

8.6 Music and Brain Plasticity

The term "brain plasticity" or "neuroplasticity" refers to changes in neural pathways that develop as a function of alterations in behavior (e.g., training induced), environment (e.g., enriched, impoverished), and physiological processes (e.g., maturation, brain insult). This chapter has already featured the plasticity or malleability of the brain in response to behavioral training in music (Schlaug, 2015). Another type of music-related brain plasticity occurs in the context of biofeedback training (see Box 8.3). This final section will focus on music and the disordered brain.

Box 8.3 Musical Training via Behavioral/Neurofeedback

- Musical training leads to heightened sensitivity via auditory feedback to music-related sensorimotor relationships or action–effect associations across a wide range of hierarchical levels (Pfordresher, 2012).
- Tonality or atonality of auditory feedback has discerning effects such that atonal feedback during the planning of a tonal melody is not treated as relevant whereas tonal feedback during the planning of an atonal melody has an impact on the planned sequence (Jebb & Pfordresher, 2016).
- Neural patterns that index violations of expectancies are stronger during music performance than music perception (Maidhof, Vavatzanidis, Prinz, Rieger, & Koelsch, 2010).
- EEG-based neurofeedback and biofeedback have been effectively used by musicians to self-regulate their physiological responses. Of the many training protocols used in this domain, including alpha/theta (A/T), sensory-motor rhythm, and heart rate variability training methods, A/T neurofeedback training, where one learns to reach a hypnagogic state that is conducive to unusual or dreamlike or lucid associative thought, is most consistently associated with improved creative musical performance (Gruzelier, 2014).
- Contemporary formats include technology-enhanced training that centers on virtual feedback. An example of the same is the Musical Interaction Relying on Reflection (MIROR) project using child–machine interactions where children can manipulate virtual copies of themselves within interactive reflexive musical systems for body performance, composition, and improvisation (Addessi, 2014).

Relations between brain disorder and music follow two directions (Sacks, 2008). One is where a heightened capacity for music suddenly emerges following the onset of the brain disorder (see Section 4.2.2), such as in frontotemporal dementia, or is a core feature of a brain disorder, such as in savant syndrome (Fletcher, Downey, Witoonpanich, & Warren, 2013; Miller et al., 2000; Treffert, 2009, 2010). Due to the fact that most individuals beset with such conditions do not display enhanced musical skills and the heterogeneity with reference to the brain correlates of such disorders and the extensive networks involved in the same (Seeley, Crawford, Zhou, Miller, & Greicius, 2009), it is not possible as yet to clearly pinpoint which specific regions of the brain are especially significant in the sudden emergence or unexpected presence of musical capacity.

The other direction is that the practices of music making and music listening are employed in the context of neurorehabilitation to improve deficits in speech, motor, and other psychological functions that have resulted from a brain disorder, such as following stroke or with the onset of neurodegenerative disease. Examples of the widely used techniques in this context (that overlap in part in terms of their workings) include melodic intonation therapy, auditory-motor mapping training, music-support therapy, and auditory rhythmic movement. There is also evidence of improvements in attention, memory, mood, and wellbeing in relation to neurorehabilitation as well as normal aging (Altenmüller & Schlaug, 2015; Särkämö & Soto, 2012; Schaefer, 2014; Schlaug, 2015; Thaut, 2015).

There are several interesting questions to explore when considering the specifics of the relation between music and brain plasticity as well as their wider impact. For instance, the power of music as a potent social glue in facilitating collective identity and sense of community has been noted across diverse academic disciplines (D'Ausilio, Novembre, Fadiga, & Keller, 2015; Malloch & Trevarthen, 2009). On the other side of the coin are disorders of music perception (Alossa & Castelli, 2009; Stewart, von Kriegstein, Warren, & Griffiths, 2006), which are not accompanied by severe deficits in social cognition (Gosselin, Paquette, & Peretz, 2015). A strong predisposition toward musicality has been noted in atypical populations, such as among those with autism spectrum disorders (ASDs) (Molnar-Szakacs & Heaton, 2012), which is somewhat counterintuitive given that the primary deficit in this case is severe impairments in communication and social interaction (American Psychiatric Association, 2013). There is, in fact, increasing evidence of the utility of music therapy in ASD rehabilitation in improving verbal and non-verbal communication skills and socio-emotional reciprocity (Geretsegger, Elefant, Mössler, & Gold, 2014). While the precise mechanisms underlying such interactions are unclear, a complex interplay between richly intertwined and interconnected brain networks can be assumed to be at work.

Gerard Edelman's (1989) theory of neuronal group selection, or "Neural Darwinism," has been touted as a good candidate framework for explaining how such interactions could emerge from processes of integration and differentiation that are fundamentally reconstructive in nature (Ballan & Abraham, 2016; Pearsall, 1999; Sacks, 2015). Indeed,

Edelman used a musical metaphor to convey the power of this theory in a BBC interview:

Think: if you had a hundred thousand wires randomly connecting four string quartet players and that, even though they weren't speaking words, signals were going back and forth in all kinds of hidden ways [as you usually get them by the subtle non-verbal interactions between the players] that make the whole set of sounds a unified ensemble. That's how the maps of the brain work by reentry. (cited in Sacks, 2015, 364)

We have only begun to skim the surface of understanding how musical creativity emerges in this context.

Chapter Summary

- Music and musicality reflect a fundamental human capacity.
- The multimodal nature of music begins at the level of music perception, the most widely studied facet of music from the neuroscientific perspective.
- Musical production or performance arises as a function of closely coupled auditory–motor interactions.
- The workings of the creative process are clearest in the case of music composition and musical improvisation compared to music performance.
- Few neuroscientific investigations have been directed at examining the brain correlates of music composition.
- Musical improvisation is associated with deactivation of brain networks that orchestrate executive function or volitional cognitive control.
- Brain plasticity occurs through musical training. Conversely, neurological changes can also lead to the emergence of musical skills.

Review Questions

1. Which forms of music engagement can be considered "creative" and why?
2. Outline the intersections between musical perception and performance.
3. Compare the characteristics of musical composition and improvisation.
4. What are the behavioral and brain correlates of musical improvisation?
5. Describe how music and music making can both induce and be caused by brain plasticity.

Further Reading

- Beaty, R. E. (2015). The neuroscience of musical improvisation. *Neuroscience and Biobehavioral Reviews*, *51*, 108–117.
- Biasutti, M. (2015). Pedagogical applications of cognitive research on musical improvisation. *Frontiers in Psychology*, *6*.
- Brown, R. M., Zatorre, R. J., & Penhune, V. B. (2015). Expert music performance: Cognitive, neural, and developmental bases. *Progress in Brain Research*, *217*, 57–86.
- Sacks, O. (2008). *Musicophilia: Tales of music and the brain*. New York: Vintage Books.
- Schlaug, G. (2015). Musicians and music making as a model for the study of brain plasticity. *Progress in Brain Research*, *217*, 37–55.
- Sloboda, J. A. (Ed.). (2000). *Generative processes in music: The psychology of performance, improvisation, and composition*. New York: Oxford University Press.

CHAPTER NINE

Literary Creativity

"A book must be the axe for the frozen sea within us."

(Franz Kafka)

Learning Objectives

- Identifying the principles underlying generativity in language
- Recognizing the factors, processes, and stages of literary creativity
- Understanding the brain networks of relevance in linguistic forms of creativity
- Distinguishing between verbal divergent thinking and creative cognition
- Grasping the neural underpinnings of story generation and creative writing
- Evaluating insights about literary creativity as delivered by the disordered brain

9.1 Creativity in Language and Literature

Kafka's words at the start of this chapter are remarkable and they capture how the inherent creativity of language is dynamically manifest at two levels. One is at the level of linguistic expression from the writer, which is virtually limitless, and the other is at the level of interpretation within the reader, which occurs when one is faced with the outputs of linguistic expression. The fundamental generativity of our linguistic capacities allows for varied expression within a space that is marked by fixed principles, such as the rules of sentence construction in any given language, as well as the ability to understand unfamiliar expressions that one has not previously encountered (Chomsky, 2006).

Creativity in language production can be evaluated in a variety of ways, including syntactic creativity (Lieven, Behrens, Speares, & Tomasello, 2003) and lexical creativity (Allan, 2016). But these are far from the only roots of literary creativity. The social context in which communication takes place must also be acknowledged as a key element.

Syntactic and semantic skills may be the engine underlying speech, but what is not so often remarked is that one has to have something to say with these marvellous skills, and that this creative something, evidencing the "openness" of language, arises not from linguistic skills narrowly conceived but from sociality and the social matrix in which one lives. One speaks not abstractly, but to someone about something of mutual concern. What we perhaps do most with language is not manipulate ideas, but manipulate each other. (Carrithers, 1990: 202)

Our need for sociality and the capacity to relate and communicate with members of our shared world also spurs another drive; namely, the drive to stand apart from the collective, to be recognized as distinct and noteworthy. Language is the prime currency that enables this need to be catered to because

it is precisely language that creates the human experience of individuality: Language makes subjectivity possible via universal systems of grammatical person, which force us to categorize the world into self and others. Through talk and other aspects of behavior, individuals display their individuality ... When people understand each other fairly easily it is because, for the most part, it is more practical to use familiar sounds, words, and syntactic patterns than to use unfamiliar ones that would require more interpretive work. People recognize each other as individuals, however, because each person has a unique set of linguistic resources on which to draw, and each person makes unique, creative uses of these resources. (Johnstone, 2000, 407)

Indeed, Brian Boyd holds that the confluence of these factors – the development of complex linguistic abilities and the need to communicate effectively with others and express oneself uniquely within complex collective social contexts – together with other complex human faculties form the building blocks that explain our immersion in and drive to create fictional narratives (Boyd, 2010). The key capacities that have been highlighted in this context include *event comprehension* ("the prehuman capacities to understand, recall, and communicate events"), *communication* ("the human preconditions for protolanguage and protonarrative" in "the mimetic phase"), *language* and *memory* ("the invention of language" and "the emergence of full linguistically enabled narrative and the difference it made to human cognition and sociality"), and *imagination* ("the emergence of fiction from factual narrative and play, and its impact in development and in modern hunter-gatherer societies" and "the extra impact of fiction through myth and religion") (Boyd, 2017, 2).

This leads us to another question, namely, determining the extent to which the concerted focus on language research in psychology and neuroscience has a significant bearing in understanding literature (Alexandrov, 2007). This is a question that has rarely received much consideration. In determining the essential elements of any message in an act of verbal communication, the structural linguist, Roman Jakobson (1960), identified six constitutive factors that serve specific functions (indicated in brackets): the context (referential), the addresser (emotive), the addressee (conative), the contact or channel between the addressee and addresser (phatic), the code within which the communication happens (metalingual), and the message itself (poetic). Even if only few appear to be visibly present, all six factors are inherent within an utterance, with one element being dominant. The "poetic function" is the most relevant factor from the standpoint of "literariness" as "a literary work is one in which the poetic function dominates the other five but does not necessarily eliminate any of them" (Alexandrov, 2007, 102). The creation of linguistic meaning derives from the "selection" of words that can be substituted for one another and the "combination" of words into larger linguistic elements like phrases and sentences. Meaning in language is expansively generated via the poetic function by integrating these components optimally such that "maximally developed similarity is superimposed on fully developed contiguity" (ibid.) through various means of establishing full or partial equivalences such as meter, sound repetitions, and rhyme.

In line with Jakobson's view, "the dominant characteristic of works that are called literary is the multiplication of the 'inner' relations among the words and the other linguistic elements that constitute them" (Alexandrov, 2007, 101). The potency of these dynamic and complex inner relations is further reinforced when considering that our knowledge stores are not only made up of lexical items and grammatical structures but also built on a vast repository of "institutionalized utterances" which allow for the generation of "improvised speech and premeditated literary composition" (MacKenzie, 2000, 179). The creative process of "conceptual integration" or "conceptual blending" is central to the poetics of literature as this mental operation allows for the generation of novel meaning out of existing or old concepts, and as such has a role to play in semantics, grammar, meaning, discourse, humor, poetry, and so on (Turner & Fauconnier, 1999).

9.2 Literary Creativity: Factors, Processes, and Stages

A brief examination of empirical work conducted specifically in relation to literary creativity will be presented in this section. These include person-based or individual factors that are strongly associated with creative writing, the cognitive processes, or mental operations that are of particular relevance to literary creativity, and some theoretical frameworks that outline components or stages of the ideation process during creative writing.

9.2.1 Person-Based/Individual Factors

What are the characteristics of a great creative writer? James Kaufman (2002) explored this very question in a review article and concluded that internal factors, or factors within the individual, such as motivation, intelligence, personality, thinking styles, and knowledge were more relevant than external or environmental factors. For instance, the development of domain-specific knowledge and skills is vital for writers to be able to attain significant creative achievements. Personality traits like instability and impulsivity are also associated with creative writers, with extremes of such traits being manifest at the level of specific mental illnesses (see Box 9.1). Motivational factors have also been shown to have a significant impact on creative writing in that intrinsic motivation, which is reflected when undertaking an activity for the sake of the enjoyment one derives from the task itself, is conducive to creativity in writing whereas extrinsic motivation, which is reflected in undertaking an activity for external rewards and public recognition, is detrimental to the same and is instantiated in the form of less creative writing (Amabile, 1985). While intelligence is a necessary but not sufficient condition to engender high levels of creativity, fluid intelligence ↰ appears to be an important factor in relation to literary creativity. One study reported that fluid intelligence explained a quarter of the variance in metaphor quality within a creative metaphor generation task (Silvia & Beaty, 2012).

Experts from a range of disciplines identified five factors vital in the development of creative writing skills – "observation, generation of description, imagination, intrinsic motivation and perseverance" – in contrast to other potential factors that were deemed to be of negligible relevance, namely, "intelligence, working memory, extrinsic motivation and penmanship" (Barbot, Tan, Randi, Santa-Donato, & Grigorenko, 2012, 218). Relevant skills, in turn, influence the quality of the products of creative writing. In an investigation of how individual factors influence a writer's ability to pen a story (Maslej, Oatley, & Mar, 2017), 93 writers and 113 non-writers were provided with a portrait and tasked with penning a character description for it. The character descriptions were then evaluated by 144 raters in terms of likeability, interest, and complexity. The characters created by writers were judged to be more

Box 9.1　Mental Illness, Substance Abuse, and Creativity

- The idea that creativity and mental illness are strongly associated has a long history and has been advocated from multiple perspectives (e.g., psychoanalytic, cognitive, clinical, genetic, evolutionary) (Eysenck, 1995; Ludwig, 1995; Nettle, 2001; Richards, 1981). The guiding rationale is that of "paradoxical functional facilitation" where direct or indirect neural insufficiencies can lead to facilitation of psychological functions (Kapur, 1996).
- While the field remains polarized on the nature of the creativity–mental illness link (Abraham, 2015), with some even questioning its validity (Dietrich, 2014; Rothenberg, 2006; Schlesinger, 2009), the empirical basis of this association is mainly derived from the elevated incidence of severe mental illness, particularly bipolar disorder and schizophrenia, among eminent and high achievers in creative professions (Kyaga et al., 2011, 2013; Lauronen et al., 2004; Ludwig, 1992; Post, 1994). Creative writers have been singled out as being especially vulnerable in this context, both in terms of mental illness and propensity toward substance abuse (Andreasen, 1987; Andreasen & Powers, 1975; Jamison, 1989; Kyaga et al., 2013; Ludwig, 1994; Post, 1996).
- There are several open questions about the nature of association between creativity and mental illness, three of which are highlighted here. One question concerns the shape of the association, with some researchers arguing for an inverted-U function of sorts (Abraham, 2014b; Carson, 2011; Richards, 1993). Another question concerns how to integrate what we know about the link between creativity and mental illness; some literature, for example, suggests that creativity is positively related to mental wellbeing (see Box 4.3). The chicken-and-egg question of what came first is of especial relevance in the context of vulnerability to substance abuse, use of psychostimulants, cultural contexts of use, and creative achievement (Smith, 2015).

interesting and complex than those of non-writers. Several other individual factors also had a significant impact on the character ratings. More interesting and likeable characters were created by participants who reported higher openness to experience as well as by those who were more engaged in fiction-writing and poetry-writing, and who read more poetry. This constitutes evidence that individual trait and practice-based factors impact a writer's likelihood of being able to create compelling fictional characters in their stories.

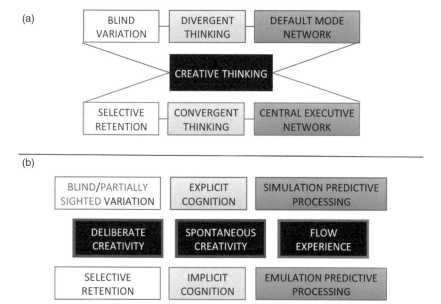

Figure 4.3 Multiple-factor models

(a) Rex Jung's model. **(b)** Arne Dietrich's model. The colors code for systems of factors that work separately (blue versus red) or systems of factors that are commonly drawn upon regardless of the type of creativity (black).

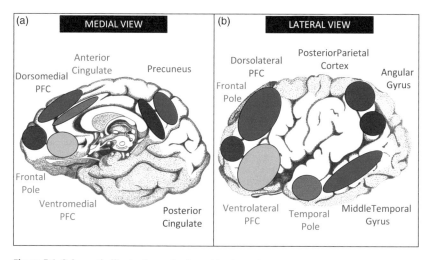

Figure 5.1 Schematic illustrations of relevant brain regions

(a) Lateral view of the brain. **(b)** Medial view of the brain. © Greig Abraham.

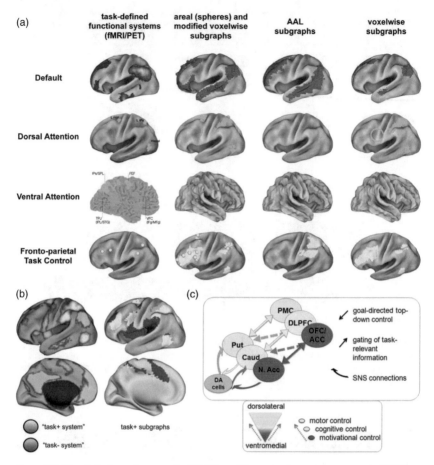

Figure 5.2 The default mode network (DMN) and the central executive network (CEN)

Key regions of the DMN (**(a)** top row and **(b)** task-negative network) and the CEN fronto-parietal task control network (**(a)** bottom row and **(b)** task-positive network). Reprinted from *Neuron*, *72*(4), Power JD, Cohen AL, Nelson SM, Wig GS, Barnes KA, Church JA, Vogel AC, Laumann TO, Miezin FM, Schlaggar BL, & Petersen SE, Functional network organization of the human brain, 665–678, © 2011, with permission from Elsevier. **(c)** Three frontostriatal loops involved in top-down control (red: motivational; yellow: cognitive; blue: motor). Reprinted with permission from Aarts E, van Holstein M & Cools R (2011). Striatal dopamine and the interface between motivation and cognition. *Frontiers in Psychology*, *2*, 163. [ACC: anterior cingulate cortex; Caud: caudate nucleus; DLPFC: dorsolateral prefrontal cortex; N. Acc: nucleus accumbens; Put: putamen; OFC: orbitofrontal cortex; PMC: premotor cortex; SNS: striato-nigral-striatal].

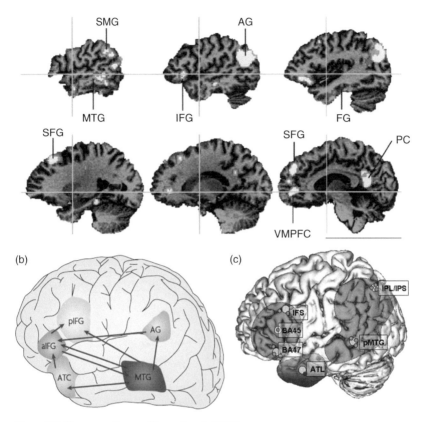

Figure 5.3 The semantic cognition network (SCN)

(a) Key regions of the SCN as indicated by a meta-analysis. Reprinted from *Trends in Cognitive Sciences*, *15*(11), Binder JR & Desai RH, The neurobiology of semantic memory, 527–536, © 2011, with permission from Elsevier. **(b)** A model for semantic cognition where pIFG and aIFG mediate controlled access and retrieval, respectively, of lexical representations that are stored in the MTG. The ATC and AG integrate incoming information with current context representations. Reprinted by permission from Springer Nature. *Nature Reviews Neuroscience.* A cortical network for semantics: (De)constructing the N400. Lau EF, Phillips C & Poeppel D. © 2008. **(c)** A distributed brain network for semantic cognition. Reprinted from *Cortex, 49*(3), Jefferies E, The neural basis of semantic cognition: converging evidence from neuropsychology, neuroimaging and TMS, Pages 611–625, © 2013, with permission from Elsevier. [a: anterior; AG: angular gyrus; ATC/ATL: anterior temporal cortex/lobe; FG: fusiform gyrus; IFG/IFS: inferior frontal gyrus/sulcus; IFS: inferior frontal sulcus; IPL/IPS: inferior parietal lobule/sulcus; MTG: middle temporal gyrus; PS: posterior cingulate; p: posterior; SFG: superior frontal gyrus; SMG: supramarginal gyrus; VMPFC: ventromedial prefrontal cortex].

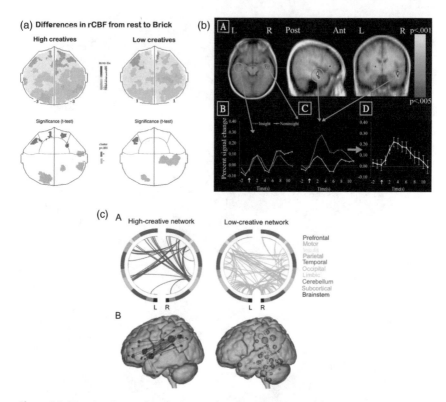

Figure 6.1 Functional neuroimaging: examples of studies on creativity

(a) A PET study showing differences in the regional cerebral blood flow (rCBF) of high and low creative people when generating alternate uses for a brick. Reprinted from *Neuropsychologia*, *38*(6), Carlsson I, Wendt PE & Risberg J, On the neurobiology of creativity: Differences in frontal activity between high and low creative subjects, pages 873–885, © 2000, with permission from Elsevier. **(b)** An fMRI study focusing on differences in functional brain activity across single brain regions in anterior (Ant) and posterior (Post) parts of the left (L) and right (R) hemispheres during insight compared to non-insight problem solving. Reprinted from Jung-Beeman M, Bowden EM, Haberman J, Frymiare JL, Arambel-Liu S, Greenblatt R, Reber PJ & Kounios J (2004). Neural activity when people solve verbal problems with insight. *PLoS Biology* 2(4): e97. **(c)** An fMRI study using functional connectivity analyses reveals high and low creative brain networks across the left (L) and right (R) hemispheres. Reprinted with permission from Beaty RE, Kenett YN, Christensen AP, Rosenberg MD, Benedek M, Chen Q, Fink A, Qiu J, Kwapil TR, Kane MJ & Silvia PJ (2018). Robust prediction of individual creative ability from brain functional connectivity. *Proceedings of the National Academy of Sciences*, 201713532.

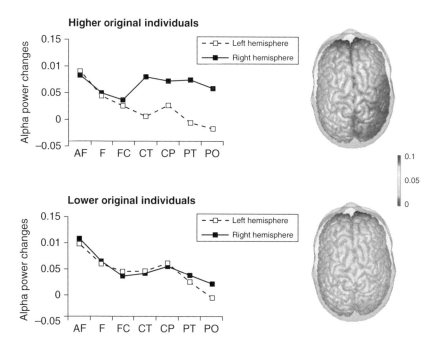

Figure 6.3 EEG: examples of studies on creativity

An EEG study looking at the alpha power differences in high and low creative people across different scalp electrode sites. Reprinted from *Human Brain Mapping*, *30*(3), Fink A, Grabner RH, Benedek M, Reishofer G, Hauswirth V, Fally M, Neuper C, Ebner F & Neubauer AC, The creative brain: Investigation of brain activity during creative problem solving by means of EEG and FMRI, pages 734–748, © 2009, with permission from Wiley.

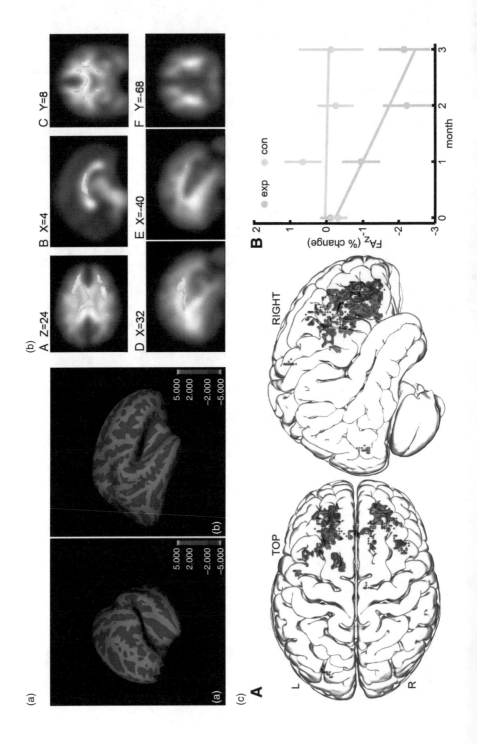

Figure 6.2 Structural neuroimaging: examples of studies on creativity

(a) A surface-based MRI approach showing increased cortical thickness (red) and decreased cortical thickness (blue) in relation to higher levels of creativity. Reprinted from *Human Brain Mapping,31*(3), Jung RE, Segall JM, Jeremy Bockholt H, Flores RA, Smith SM, Chavez RS & Haier RJ, Neuroanatomy of creativity, pages 398–409, © 2010, with permission from Wiley. (b) A DTI study showing greater structural integrity (yellow) within specific white matter tracts in relation to higher levels of creativity. Reprinted from *NeuroImage,51*(1), Takeuchi H, Taki Y, Sassa Y, Hashizume H, Sekiguchi A, Fukushima A & Kawashima R, White matter structures associated with creativity: Evidence from diffusion tensor imaging, pages 11–18, © 2010, with permission from Elsevier. (c) A longitudinal DTI study showing reductions over time in white matter integrity (indexed by FA/fractional anisotropy) as a function of artistic training. Reprinted from *NeuroImage*, 105, Schlegel A, Alexander P, Fogelson SV, Li X, Lu Z, Kohler PJ, Riley E, Tse PU & Meng M, The artist emerges: Visual art learning alters neural structure and function, pages 440–451, © 2015, with permission from Elsevier.

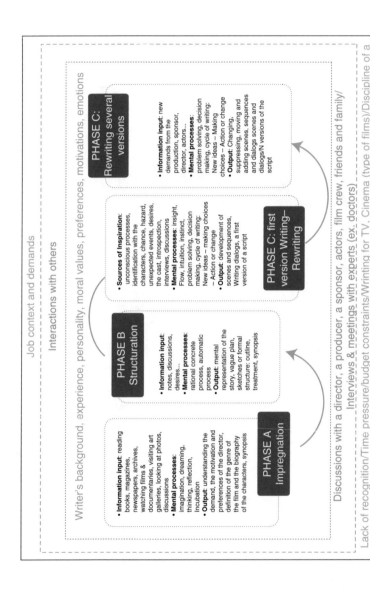

Figure 9.1 A model of the creative process during screenplay writing

Reprinted from Bourgeois-Bougrine S, Glaveanu V, Botella M, Guillou K, De Biasi PM & Lubart T (2014). The creativity maze: Exploring creativity in screenplay writing. *Psychology of Aesthetics, Creativity, and the Arts, 8*(4), 384–399.

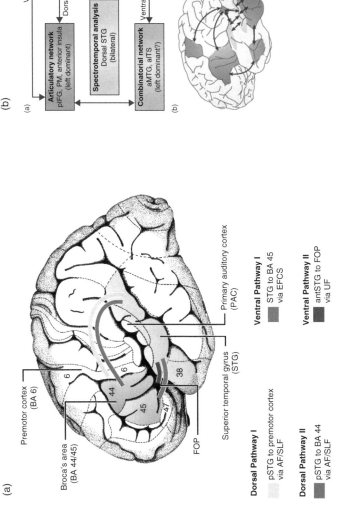

Figure 9.2 The language brain network

(a) Structural pathways between key regions of the language network. The arcuate fasciculus (AF) and the superior longitudinal fasciculus (SLF) connect posterior aspects of the superior temporal gyrus (STG) to the premotor cortex (dorsal pathway I) and BA 44 (dorsal pathway II). Anterior parts of the STG connect to BA 45 and the temporal cortex through the extreme fiber capsule system (EFCS) (ventral pathway I) and the frontal operculum (FOP) via the uncinate fasciculus (UF) (ventral pathway II). Reprinted with permission from Friederici AD (2011). The brain basis of language processing: From structure to function. *Physiological Reviews, 91*(4), 1357–1392. (b) The dual-stream model in the right and left hemispheres. Cortical speech processing begins with spectrotemporal analysis that interacts with the phonological network. Following this, ventral and dorsal streams are engaged, both of which interact with the widely distributed conceptual network [a: anterior; MTG: middle temporal gyrus; IFG: inferior frontal gyrus; ITS: inferior temporal sulcus; MTG: middle temporal gyrus; p: posterior; PM: premotor cortex; Spt: area in the sylvian fissure at the parietotemporal boundary; STG: superior temporal gyrus]. Reprinted by permission from *Springer Nature. Nature Reviews Neuroscience. The cortical organization of speech processing.* Hickok G & Poeppel D. © 2008.

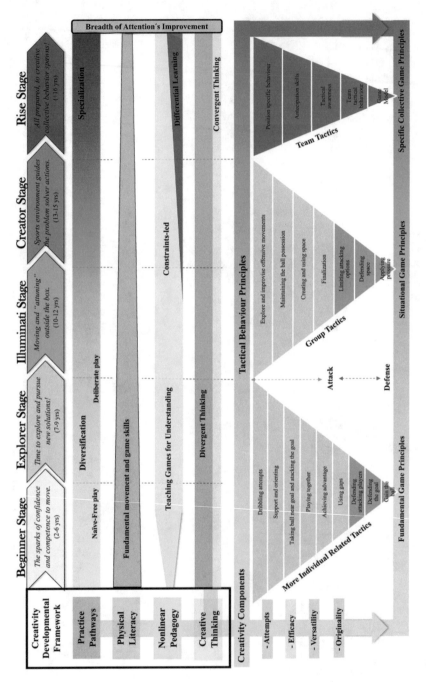

Figure 11.3 A model of creative behavior in team sports

The creativity development framework (CDF) structure. Reprinted with permission from Santos SDL, Memmert D, Sampaio J & Leite N. (2016). The spawns of creative behavior in team sports: A creativity developmental framework. *Frontiers in Psychology, 7*, 1282.

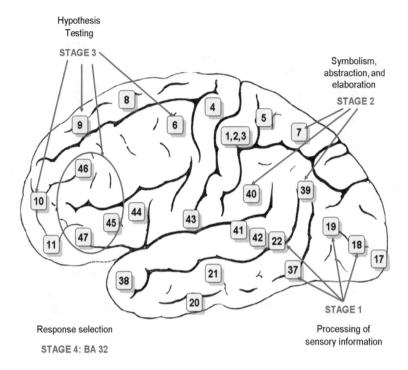

Figure 12.1 Information processing stages in the P-FIT model of intelligence

Reprinted from *Dialogues in Clinical Neuroscience* with the permission of the publisher (Les Laboratoires Servier, Suresnes, France): Colom R, Karama S, Jung RE, Haier RJ. Human intelligence and brain networks. *Dialogues Clin Neurosci.* 2010;*12*(4):489–501. © LLS.

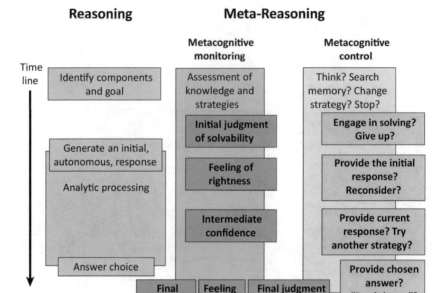

Figure 12.2 Models of reasoning

The purported time course for reasoning and metareasoning operations. Reprinted from *Trends in Cognitive Sciences*, *21*(8), Ackerman R & Thompson VA, Meta-reasoning: Monitoring and control of thinking and reasoning, pages 607–617, © 2017, with permission from Elsevier.

Moreover, specific emotional states of the writer at the time of creative ideation can induce the same emotional states in the reader when they read the product of this inspiration. When evaluating phenomenological states (like inspiration and awe) that were experienced by the writer when writing a poem in relation to the reader's phenomenological states when reading the same poem, evidence was found for "inspiration contagion" such that writers who were inspired elicited greater levels of inspiration in their readers. This effect of infectiousness of writer inspiration was mediated by the insightfulness and pleasantness of the text and moderated by the degree of openness to experience on the part of the reader (Thrash, Maruskin, Moldovan, Oleynick, & Belzak, 2016).

9.2.2 Process and Constraints

That ideation under conditions of contextual constraints can lead to greater originality than under conditions without constraints is sometimes affectionately referred to as the *Green Eggs and Ham* hypothesis (Haught-Tromp, 2017), the background story being that Theodor Geisel (aka Dr. Seuss) wrote this classic and bestselling children's book in 1960 in response to a bet he made with the book's publisher, Bennett Cerf, to write a compelling children's book from a set of 50 words that constituted simple vocabulary for beginning readers.

Mounting empirical evidence lends support to this "constraints improves creativity" hypothesis. The imposition of an external constraint (the instruction to incorporate concrete nouns provided by the experimenter in the generated rhyme) led to more creative rhyme generation compared to the situation in which no constraints were imposed. It even led to a carryover effect such that practicing with externally imposed constraints stimulated creativity in later contexts when external constraints were absent. This was presumed to reflect the fact that participants generated their own constraints during the ideation process following their successful experience with externally imposed constraints (ibid.). So the release of creative ideation in language is abetted by imposing constraints and rules, just as it is in the case of creative ideation through visual imagery (Finke, 1990), which is attributed to the inability to take the "path-of-least-resistance" under conditions of contextual constraints (Finke et al., 1996).

In fact, constraints have a positive effect on creativity and complexity during creative writing. For instance, high formal constraints (via acrostics) during creative writing lead to more complex and creative uses of language compared to loose formal constraints (via similes) (Tin, 2011).

The relation between linguistic complexity and creativity also holds for narrative performance, such that high levels of originality were associated with fewer stories but greater levels of complexity in the stories that were created (Albert & Kormos, 2011). Complexity also affords the possibility of taking semantic leaps during creative writing (see Section 9.4.2), such as in the case of humor. In a study examining factors that facilitate humor production, comparisons between semantically unrelated concepts led to a higher incidence of funny responses than semantically related concepts, as did responses that focused on differences between the concepts rather than the similarities, indicating a role for incongruity resolution as a central component of humor processing (Hull, Tosun, & Vaid, 2017). Humor is in fact seen as an important manifestation of literary creativity and is strongly associated with "openness to experience," a personality trait that is highly relevant to individual differences in creativity (Nusbaum, Silvia, & Beaty, 2017).

9.2.3 Stages/Components of Creative Writing

Following interviews with 22 established French screenplay writers, Bourgeois-Bougrine et al. (2014) proposed a 3-stage model of screenplay creative writing. The creative process is conceived of as a journey through a maze, with a first "impregnation" phase (preparation for the journey), a second "structuring" phase (creating a map of the maze), and a third "writing and rewriting" phase (navigating through the maze successfully by finding the correct path and avoiding the blind alleys). The exit of the maze is successfully reached upon finishing the final script. This theory also has a systemic focus as it accommodates a multitude of factors that interact with one another at each of these stages, including cognitive, conative, affective, and environmental (Figure 9.1). The need to consider unconscious and conscious cognitive processes is emphasized, as writers report the importance of activities such as mind wandering, reflection, reading, and the collection of information, particularly during the first phase. The spontaneity of idea generation during unrelated tasks (e.g., bathing a child) and the affective experience of joy during moments when intuitive, automatic, and unconscious processes deliver creative insights were also highlighted. So too were working styles adopted, such as choosing public spaces with ambient noise (e.g., cafés), and interactions with relevant others on personal and professional fronts.

Another interview-based analysis of the experiences of writers of fiction, which has several parallels with that of the previous study, identified a set of factors in the "creative episode" that was common to

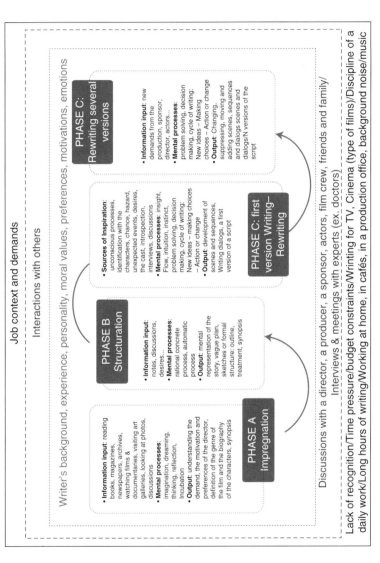

Figure 9.1 A model of the creative process during screenplay writing

Reprinted from Bourgeois-Bougrine S, Glaveanu V, Botella M, Guillou K, De Biasi PM & Lubart T (2014). The creativity maze: Exploring creativity in screenplay writing. *Psychology of Aesthetics, Creativity, and the Arts*, 8(4), 384–399. A black and white version of this figure will appear in some formats. For the color version, please refer to the plate section.

all authors (Doyle, 1998). The start of the creative process was often marked by a "seed incident," referring to an event the author personally experienced or encountered through someone else or read about. The seed incident was experienced as being overwhelming, haunting, touching, or intriguing and as such provides a mystery to explore further. In other situations, the seed incident is evoked from within when an author is ensconced purposefully in a "writingrealm" – a designated writing space in which the "form of sociality [is] solitariness; the experience of self [is] highly self-conscious; [and] thinking [is] intentioned, purposeful, reflective" (Doyle, 1998, 31). After the experience of a seed incident, writers enter the "fictionworld," which marks the start of the writing period in which the characters and events of the story gradually unfold. The writing period involves an interplay between the writingrealm and the fictionworld and features the workings of reflective (conscious) and nonreflective (unconscious) thought processes, and deep engagement with different elements of the fictional world. The influence of personal and professional interactions on the creative process was also highlighted, as was the distinction between writing, the intense task of continual revision, and the culmination of finishing and sharing the work.

9.3 Language and the Brain

There are several influential theories of language processing and brain function. Those that are actively generating hypotheses in contemporary research from a brain network perspective are explored briefly in this section. The dual-route model of speech perception (Hickok & Poeppel, 2015), for instance, proposes that two brain pathways, a ventral auditory-conceptual route and a dorsal auditory-motor route, are engaged during the processing of speech. These routes are instantiated in brain networks that only partially overlap (Hickok & Poeppel, 2007) (Figure 9.2). Following bilateral engagement of the auditory cortex on the dorsal superior temporal gyrus (green) and the mid-posterior superior temporal sulcus (yellow) for the initial stage of speech processing, the information is further processed along the two routes. The ventral stream is based in the temporal lobe (pink) and aids speech comprehension through lexical access and combinatorial processes. The left hemisphere-dominant dorsal stream receives input from other sensory modalities and aids sensory-motor integration through the sensorimotor interface in the Sylvian temporo-parietal junction (Wernicke's area) and the articulatory network, which encompasses the posterior inferior frontal gyrus (Broca's area), premotor cortex, and anterior insula. Both routes interact with one another and the larger conceptual network, which is widely distributed across the brain (Hickok & Poeppel, 2007, 2015).

Other models have elaborated on this dual motion idea to explore the dynamics of the roles played by each of the regions of the network and the many pathways that connect them. The language network regions or nodes include Broca's area (BA 44, 45) and other parts of the inferior frontal gyrus (BA 47), Wernicke's area (BA 42, 22) and other parts of the superior temporal gyrus (BA 22, BA 38), as well as regions in the middle temporal gyrus (BA 21, 37), inferior parietal lobule, and angular gyrus (BA 39). Several ventral and dorsal white matter tracts form pathways that connect different parts of these frontal, temporal, and parietal lobe regions (Friederici, 2011, 2015; Hagoort, 2014) (Figure 9.2).

Sentence comprehension begins with "acoustic-phonological analysis" of a sentence, which engages the auditory cortex (BA 41) bilaterally in the temporal lobes. Following this initial phase, the first phase of sentence-level processing sees the building of the words in the sentence, and the establishment of syntactic and semantic relations within the sentence occurs in the second phase of the same. A third phase may be necessary in situations where the mapping between semantic and syntactic relations does not entirely correspond and the situation calls for retrieval of world knowledge or contextual information. All three phases interact with linguistic prosody, which highlights phrase boundaries or the thematic focus of a sentence. These phases are undertaken by separable temporo-frontal brain networks, which are more strongly left lateralized in the case of syntactic processing and more right lateralized in the case of prosodic processing (Friederici, 2011).

There is one critical point to bear in mind in this context. To conceive of the language brain network as being purely domain-specific in that its different regions (e.g., Broca's area, BA 44) are only recruited for specific language-based processing (e.g., processing of complex syntactic structure) does not strictly hold when viewing the evidence on hand. This is because many of the regions are also actively engaged in non-linguistic contexts, which necessitate cognitive control and this constitutes evidence for domain-general processes being undertaken by the brain regions within this network. This suggests that there are domain-general mechanisms being undertaken by the same network. Calls are increasingly being made to identify the computations that underlie language processing in order to gain an accurate sense of the properties of the language network as we understand it and how similar computations may be required in non-linguistic contexts (Fedorenko & Thompson-Schill, 2014). Indeed, there is even evidence of domain-general and domain-specific

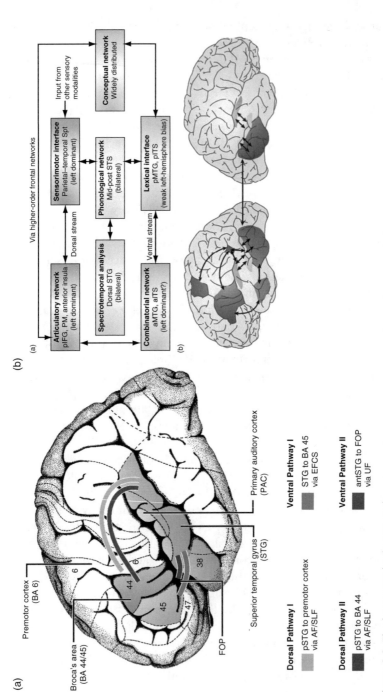

Figure 9.2 The language brain network

(a) Structural pathways between key regions of the language network. The arcuate fasciculus (AF) and the superior longitudinal fasciculus (SLF) connect posterior aspects of the superior temporal gyrus (STG) to the premotor cortex (dorsal pathway I) and BA

44 (dorsal pathway II). Anterior parts of the STG connect to BA 45 and the temporal cortex through the extreme fiber capsule system (EFCS) (ventral pathway I) and the frontal operculum (FOP) via the uncinate fasciculus (UF) (ventral pathway II). Reprinted with permission from Friederici AD (2011). The brain basis of language processing: From structure to function. *Physiological Reviews, 91*(4), 1357–1392. **(b)** The dual-stream model in the right and left hemispheres. Cortical speech processing begins with spectrotemporal analysis that interacts with the phonological network. Following this, ventral and dorsal streams are engaged, both of which interact with the widely distributed conceptual network [a: anterior; MTG: middle temporal gyrus; IFG: inferior frontal gyrus; ITS: inferior temporal sulcus; MTG: middle temporal gyrus; p: posterior; PM: premotor cortex; Spt: area in the sylvian fissure at the parietotemporal boundary; STG: superior temporal gyrus]. Reprinted by permission from *Springer Nature. Nature Reviews Neuroscience.* The cortical organization of speech processing. Hickok G & Poeppel D. © 2008. A black and white version of this figure will appear in some formats. For the color version, please refer to the plate section.

(language-selective) zones within the same region (e.g., Broca's area) of the language network (Fedorenko, Duncan, & Kanwisher, 2012).

There are also several models of language production, but these are primarily limited to contexts of speech production (making vocal utterances) (Hickok, 2012), and the act of writing mainly receives consideration in relation to reading skills and deficits thereof (Hulme & Snowling, 2014). Speech production has been approached from the very separate perspectives of psycholinguistics and motor control. Psycholinguistic models start at the conceptual representation level and work their way through different levels of phrasal level units, morphemes, and phonemes. They end at the phonological representation level, which feeds into motor systems. Motor control models, in contrast, start at the level of sensory input, which initiates systems for planning and feedback control via forward and inverse models that lead to motor output. These processes are orchestrated by regions of the language network (indicated above), and extend to the motor control brain network, which includes regions such as the somatosensory cortex, motor cortex, and cerebellum (Hickok, 2012). Psycholinguistic and motor control traditions are integrated in contemporary speech production models like the semantic–lexical–auditory–motor (SLAM) model (Walker & Hickok, 2016).

9.4 Literary Creativity and the Brain

The brain networks that have been most widely discussed in relation to creativity were described in detail in Chapters 4 and 5. They include the "default mode network" (DMN) for internal mentation, the "central executive network" (CEN; also referred to as the CCN: cognitive control network or FPN: fronto-parietal network) for goal-directed processing, and the semantic cognition network (SCN) for the processing of conceptual knowledge (Figures 5.2 and 5.3). The salience network (SN) involved in the processing of situational relevance is also gaining more attention. In terms of the general differences between the brain regions attributed to these networks (Figure 5.2), the DMN primarily comprises medial regions within the prefrontal cortex (BA 8, 9, 10) and the parietal lobe (BA 29/31), as well as lateral regions within the inferior parietal lobe and posterior middle temporal gyrus (BA 39) and the temporal poles (BA 38); the CEN is made up of lateral regions in the prefrontal cortex (BA 8, 44, 45, 46, 47, 9, 10) and the posterior parietal cortex (BA 40), as well as regions of the basal ganglia and the cerebellum (Figure 5.2). These networks partially overlap with the SCN, which encompasses, for instance, CEN lateral regions in the inferior frontal gyrus (BA 45, 47) and DMN medial prefrontal regions (BA 8, 9, 10) (Figure 5.3). Primary regions of the SN include the insula, orbitofrontal regions, and dorsal anterior cingulate. As language processing is inherent to verbal and linguistic forms of creativity, the aforementioned language processing networks of the brain are of utmost relevance (Figure 9.2).

Many of the earliest studies of creativity in relation to brain function were in relation to the creative right brain hypothesis (see Section 4.2.1). A meta-analysis of hemispheric lateralization studies in the field of creativity indicates that the evidence speaks for the case of right hemisphere dominance in creativity tasks in general (Mihov et al., 2010), which fits with "coarse coding" computations ascribed to this hemisphere that would lead to semantic overlap between distant or weakly-related concepts (Jung-Beeman, 2005). The pattern of right brain dominance, though, is very strong for figural tasks of creativity, but less so for verbal tasks of creativity (Mihov et al., 2010). In the following sections, neuroscientific evidence demonstrating the involvement of specific brain structures and networks in relation to literary creativity will be discussed. As verbal forms of creativity have been studied using a variety of tasks, each section will provide a brief overview of the chief findings that have been reported using a specific constellation of verbal creativity tasks (see Box 9.2 for critical issues in relation to the testing of literary creativity).

Box 9.2 Overcoming Confusion Regarding Literary Creativity

- It is inaccurate to claim that any task that uses linguistic material to measure creative thinking is a task of literary creativity. A *verbal task of creativity* does not constitute a *task of literary creativity*.
- A recent meta-analysis that demonstrated cognizance of such distinctions argued for a ventral/dorsal dissociation in the brain activity patterns within the lateral prefrontal cortex that were correspondingly elicited by verbal/non-verbal tasks of creative thinking (Gonen-Yaacovi et al., 2013).
- It cannot be assumed *prima facie* that verbal forms and non-verbal/figural forms of divergent thinking tests directly correspond to "literary creativity" and "visual artistic creativity," respectively.
- Any study that claims to evaluate verbal creativity needs to stipulate how verbal forms of creativity are similar to and differ from non-verbal forms of creativity. The study also then needs to uncover how the paradigm they use specifically targets verbal creativity.

- It would also be useful to consider how performance on verbal divergent thinking tasks that assess domain-general aspects of creativity reflect processes relevant to the many applied spheres of literary creativity.
- There is some evidence to suggest that aspects of creative writing are heritable and familial and these might be distinct from heritable factors that are associated with domain-general creativity (Tan & Grigorenko, 2013).

9.4.1 Verbal Divergent Thinking Tasks

Divergent thinking tasks have been widely used to investigate verbal creativity. One approach is to compare verbal and non-verbal forms of creativity tasks. What is a considerable challenge in this context is the ability to detect coherent patterns that allow for sound interpretations of the findings. Some examples are discussed below so that the reader can get a taste of this difficulty.

When exploring correlations between resting state functional connectivity between the DMN and the CEN and performance of the verbal and figural forms of the Torrance Tests of Creative Thinking (TTCT; see Section 2.2.1), a positive connectivity was established between the DMN and the CEN for both verbal and visual forms of creativity. In terms of domain-specific differences, verbal creativity was negatively correlated with functional connectivity within the medial prefrontal cortex of the DMN and this association between anterior aspects of the DMN and verbal creativity was mediated by the CEN (Zhu et al., 2017). A structural neuroimaging study by some of the members of that research group found another set of results in that they demonstrated that greater verbal creativity as measured by the TTCT was associated with larger gray matter volumes and white matter volumes in the bilateral inferior frontal gyrus (part of the language network and CEN: BA 45) (Zhu, Zhang, & Qiu, 2013).

In a study that examined both structural and functional brain correlates (Chen et al., 2015), higher verbal creativity was associated with lower functional regional homogeneity (synchrony between neighboring voxels in the brain in terms of their time series activity) in the precuneus (part of the DMN), but with higher structural properties of volume and thickness in the same brain region. While this pattern also held true for the subcomponents of ideational originality and ideational flexibility, it is difficult to make sense of these seemingly opposing findings from functional and structural neuroimaging, and they have not been discussed as such within this paper. While the precuneus has been highlighted by other researchers in terms of its especial relevance to verbal creativity

(Fink et al., 2014), training of verbal creativity was not associated with activation changes in this region but instead pointed to the relevance of other brain areas in the inferior parietal lobule and the middle temporal gyrus (Fink et al., 2015).

A series of studies on verbal creativity have been carried out by researchers at Tohoku University in Japan, led by Hikaru Takeuchi. A wide range of techniques has been employed to explore the brain correlates of performance on one verbal task of creativity, the S-A test. This is a divergent thinking test involving three tasks: an alternate uses task (e.g., think of different uses for a newspaper apart from reading), a desirable functions listing task (e.g., list all the characteristics of a good TV), and a counterfactual imagination task (e.g., imagine a world without mice; what would that be like?). Responses are scored following the protocol applied to standard divergent thinking tasks in terms of fluency, flexibility, originality, and elaboration, and the latter two are combined to give a total score. Structural neuroimaging studies confirmed the involvement of the CEN, DMN, and language networks in verbal creativity. They demonstrated positive correlations between verbal divergent thinking and white matter integrity in frontal, anterior cingulate, striatum, anterior IPL, occipital regions, corpus callosum, and arcuate fasciculus (Takeuchi et al., 2010b), as well as with gray matter volume in the dorsolateral PFC, striatum, precuneus, and several midbrain regions (Takeuchi et al., 2010a). The basal ganglia have been singled out as playing a particularly significant role with a negative correlation, as higher scores in verbal divergent thinking are associated with lower mean diffusivity in the globus pallidus (part of the CEN) (Takeuchi et al., 2015). Functional neuroimaging has indicated positive correlations between verbal divergent thinking resting state activity in the precuneus (Takeuchi et al., 2011). With regard to resting state functional connectivity, patterns of connectivity between the medial prefrontal cortex and the posterior cingulate cortex (both part of the DMN) were positively correlated with verbal divergent thinking (Takeuchi et al., 2012).

From this selection of findings in relation to the neuroimaging of verbal divergent thinking, it should be apparent that providing a summary of the findings in relation to verbal divergent thinking is very challenging. While this is primarily due to the wide assortment of findings implicated in several brain regions, the bigger and trickier question to consider is whether verbal divergent thinking tasks are capturing something that is specifically "verbal" about creativity (see Box 9.1). Few studies have directly contrasted verbal with non-verbal forms of creativity so as to be able to make any claim for the same. Moreover, the assessments of verbal creativity are made on the basis of response properties that are deemed relevant to creativity from a psychometric standpoint (e.g., fluency, flexibility), which are applicable across all modalities of creative ideation. These are not metrics that emerge from verbal creativity as instantiated in the applied sphere within genres of fiction or non-fiction, such as novels, poems, lyrics, standup comedy, speech writing, and so on.

9.4.2 Metaphor and Other Forms of Semantic Leaps

Examinations of verbal creativity have also been undertaken by examining the processing of cognitive operations that are especially relevant to the linguistic form. The processing of metaphors is one example of such (also see Sections 3.4.3 and 5.3.3) as it reflects figurative use in language given that, per definition, it refers to words or phrases that are used in contexts in which they are not literally applicable. Brain-based investigations of metaphor processing in the context of creative cognition can follow two directions.

One route is to examine the processing of novel metaphoric expressions relative to common, literal, or nonsensical expressions (Mashal et al., 2007; Rutter, Kröger, Stark, et al., 2012). For instance, processing novel metaphoric expressions compared to both literal and nonsensical expressions engaged the inferior frontal gyrus (part of SCN and LAN: BA 45, 47), temporal poles (part of SCN and DMN: BA 38), and lateral frontal pole (part of CEN: BA 10) in a functional neuroimaging study (Rutter, Kröger, Stark, et al., 2012). The other route is to examine the neural basis of novel metaphor production (Beaty et al., 2017; Benedek, Beaty, et al., 2014). For instance, the brain response when generating novel metaphors compared to literal assertions was centered on the dorsal medial prefrontal cortex (dmPFC, part of SCN and DMN: BA 8, 9), posterior cingulate (part of DMN and SCN: BA 23, 30), and angular gyrus (part of SCN and DMN: BA 39) (Benedek, Beaty, et al., 2014).

Interestingly, many of these regions, and in particular the dorsal medial prefrontal cortex (BA 8, 9, 10) have been discussed more widely in contexts in which "semantic leaps" are required. This includes inference generation during high-construal abstractions (Baetens, Ma, & Overwalle, 2017), such as during coherence testing in discourse comprehension (Ferstl & von Cramon, 2001; Siebörger, Ferstl, & von Cramon, 2007) as well as humor processing and appreciation in the verbal domain (Campbell et al., 2015; Chan et al., 2013). For instance, greater brain activity was found in the dorsal mPFC and other DMN regions during the processing of texts where coherent inferences could be generated (e.g., "Sometimes the truck drives by the house. That's when the dishes start to rattle.") compared to when no coherent inference generation was possible (e.g., "Sometimes the truck drives by the house. The car doesn't start.") (Ferstl & von Cramon, 2002, 1601). Inference generation is also necessary when processing metaphors (e.g., He is a snake in the grass) where there is a wider divide between associated concepts than in metonymy (e.g., He is the shoulder I cry on), another type of figurative language which involves the substitution of one term with another contextually related term. Behavioral research in fact supports the idea of greater cognitive distance in metaphors compared to metonyms (Rundblad & Annaz, 2010a) (see Box 9.3 for links between metaphor processing and developmental disorders).

Box 9.3 Metaphor Processing in Developmental Disorders

Following a hemispheric lateralization hypothesis where the right hemisphere (RH) is considered more important for metaphor processing, disruptions in RH processing are proposed to explain poor metaphor comprehension skills in the case of conditions like Asperger's syndrome (reduced) and schizophrenia (excessive) (Faust & Kenett, 2014). There is evidence to suggest that such theoretical stances may be painting an overly reductive picture. While children with ASDs demonstrate poor metaphor comprehension (Rundblad & Annaz, 2010b) and a reduced ability to generate conventional metaphors (Kasirer & Mashal, 2016b), there is evidence to show that such metaphor comprehension deficits tend to dissipate with time (Melogno, Pinto, & Orsolini, 2016), and that automatic processing of metaphors is intact in adults with Asperger's syndrome (Hermann et al., 2013). In fact, a comparison of adults with Asperger's syndrome and a typically developing control group showed that they performed similarly on tasks of conventional and novel metaphor comprehension. However, the Asperger's syndrome adults generated more creative metaphors than the control group (Kasirer & Mashal, 2014). Higher creativity in metaphor generation was also found in children and adolescents with Asperger's syndrome (Kasirer & Mashal, 2016b). A similar pattern of performance also applies to the case of dyslexia. While dyslexic children perform worse than typical children in processing conventional metaphors, they exhibit no such disadvantage during novel metaphor comprehension. In fact, they outperform their typically developing peers in metaphor generation (Kasirer & Mashal, 2016a).

9.4.3 Story Generation

A few neuroimaging studies have examined brain activity patterns
during the generation of stories and the composing of poems. In an early
PET study (Bechtereva et al., 2004), 16 participants were given lists of
words and asked to generate a story connecting them. The list for the
creative story generation condition used semantically unrelated words
(e.g., silence, mushroom, cow, to throw) whereas the list of the uncreative
story generation condition used semantically related words (e.g., school,
lesson, teacher, to solve). Two control conditions – reading and memory –
were also used. The only region that significantly engaged during creative
story generation compared to uncreative story generation was the left
posterior middle temporal gyrus (BA 39), a core region of the DMN and
the SCN. Relative to both control tasks, story generation (creative and
uncreative) led to greater activity in the dorsolateral prefrontal cortex
(part of CEN: BA 8) and the ventrolateral prefrontal cortex (part of
CEN, SCN, and language network: BA 44, 45, 47) .

A similar story generation paradigm using three words was used in an
fMRI study, albeit on a small sample of eight participants (Howard-Jones
et al., 2005). Story generation for semantically unrelated words were
judged to be more creative than those of semantically related words,
and this contrast was accompanied by greater activity in anterior cingulate regions (bordering the DMN: BA 24, 32). Moreover, the instruction
to "be creative" relative to "be uncreative" within the unrelated versus
related story generation contrast resulted in the activation of ventral
medial prefrontal regions (part of DMN: BA 9, 10).

So there is no real overlap between the findings of the Bechtereva et al.
(2004) and Howard-Jones et al. (2005) studies to suggest commonalities
in the brain correlates of the same. There are several methodological
differences between the two studies, though, such as the verbal generation of vocal responses during scanning in the former study whereas
the latter study followed a post-scanning recall protocol to avoid motion
artefacts. The limitations of such verbal creativity paradigms in delivering
a clear verdict in this regard are discussed in Section 9.5.

9.4.4 Prose

Three studies have examined the brain correlates of creative writing in
real time within a functional neuroimaging environment, all of which
were carried out by the same research group using overlapping participant samples (Erhard, Kessler, Neumann, Ortheil, & Lotze, 2014b; Lotze

et al., 2014; Shah et al., 2013). The studies were carried out in an MRI scanner in which, rather unusually, it was possible to have a participant's body (from chest downwards) remain outside the scanner (Figure 9.3). The writing hand of the participant was positioned to access an inclined plastic desk such that they could write on sheets of paper using felt pens. An assistant was present in the scanning environment to replace the sheets when necessary.

In the first study using this setup, participants carried out four tasks using excerpts from Thomas Bernhard's *The Loser*: (a) silent "reading" of an excerpt, (b) "copying" of an excerpt on a sheet of paper, (c) silent "brainstorming" to think of a creative continuation for an excerpt, and (d) "creative writing" of a continuation of an excerpt (Shah et al., 2013). So two conditions are "passive" processing conditions requiring no motor output (reading, brainstorming) and two are "active" processing conditions requiring complex movement (copying, creative writing). The trial events, as shown in Figure 9.3, indicate that the creative writing task was of 140 seconds duration while the other tasks were of 60 seconds duration. There are significant issues associated with dealing with extensive motor output in fMRI analysis as well as with comparison of trial events that differ considerably in length (see Chapter 7), and these need to be borne in mind when interpreting such findings.

The results pertaining to creative ideation without movement (contrast: brainstorming > reading) were not provided in the Shah et al. paper. Comparing the brain activity elicited during creative writing with that of copying revealed the engagement of the bilateral hippocampus, posterior cingulate (BA 31), and temporal poles (BA 38), brain regions that are part of the DMN and the SCN. Moreover, activity in the left IFG (BA 45) and temporal pole (BA 38) (both SCN regions) during creative writing, as compared to during copying, was positively correlated with higher trait creativity (as measured by a separate creativity index) (Shah et al., 2013).

Using the same experimental setup (but different texts: Ror Wolf's *Zwei oder drei Jahre später. Neunundvierzig Ausschweifunden* [*Two or Three Years Later: Forty-nine Digressions*] and Durs Grünbein's "Den teueren Toten" ["The Expensive Dead"]), a second study was conducted comparing expertise in writing (Erhard et al., 2014b). The group of expert writers included students who had completed 30 months of study on creative writing degree programs (Creative Writing and Cultural Journalism) by the time the functional neuroimaging study was conducted. The expert writers reported an average of 12 years' experience of writing (including the period of their creative writing study) and an average 21 hours of

(a)   Conditions per run:

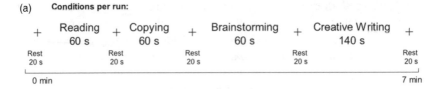

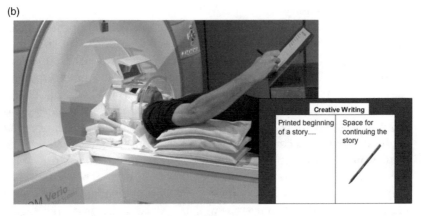

Figure 9.3 An example of a creative writing study in an fMRI environment

(a) Schematic diagram showing the trial events. (b) A picture of the experimental testing set up. Reprinted from *Human Brain Mapping*, *34*(5), Shah C, Erhard K, Ortheil H-J, Kaza E, Kessler C & Lotze M, Neural correlates of creative writing: An fMRI study, pages 1088–1101, © 2013, with permission from Wiley.

weekly writing practice, which was significantly more than the non-expert group comprising undergraduates from non-creative writing degree programs who reported an average of 3 years' writing experience and an average 30 minutes of weekly writing practice. Expert writers scored higher on trait creativity compared to non-experts and their generated texts in the creative writing condition during functional neuroimaging were also rated as more creative. In fact, there was a positive correlation between trait creativity and creative writing performance. Greater levels of practice were also associated with greater levels of trait creativity and performance in creative writing.

During brainstorming, expert writers relative to non-experts demonstrated enhanced brain activity in the mid-cingulate cortex (part of CEN: BA 24), putamen (part of CEN), and posterior insula (part of salience network: BA 13). During creative writing, expert writers relative to non-experts demonstrated enhanced brain activity in the dorsolateral prefrontal cortex (part of CEN: BA 9, 46), caudate nucleus (part of CEN), inferior frontal gyrus bilaterally (part of SCN and the language network: BA 45, 47), and dorsal medial prefrontal cortex (mPFC: BA 8, 9). The latter region is of especial interest as the more anterior dorsal mPFC (BA 9) is seen as a core region in the DMN whereas the more posterior dorsal mPFC (BA 8) is discussed in relation to the CEN. The authors of the study favor the latter rationale by arguing for the relevance of this region in working memory and cognitive flexibility (Erhard et al., 2014b).

In summary, then, while creative writing in general engages regions of the DMN and the semantic control network (SCN), expert writers additionally recruit the central executive network (CEN) during creative writing.

9.4.5 Poetry and Lyrics

Using similar empirical designs as those used in investigating the brain correlates of prose creative writing explored in the previous section, researchers are looking to expand to other realms of literary creativity, such as writing poetry and lyrics. One study compared the performance of 13 non-experts (with no experience or formal training in poetry) and 14 experts (who published their work in poetry journals and had completed at least one year of a Master's in Fine Art) on several tasks of verbal recall and generativity (Liu et al., 2015). Participants were given a list of 10 factual statements and two 10-line poems ("What are Years" by Marianne Moore and "Fall 1961" by Robert Lowell) to memorize in advance and recall during the functional neuroimaging session. The session also included a control condition in which participants made random typing movements, but the main conditions of interest were generating a new poem and revising it. Participants generated their responses across all three conditions by typing into an MRI-safe keyboard. Experts were found to generate poems of higher quality than those of non-experts in terms of craft ("incorporating elements of sound, form, figurative and sensory language"), linguistic creativity ("innovative use of craft terms"), and revision (improvements in the generated poem) (ibid., 3559).

Across all participants, brain activity elicited when generating a new poem compared to recalling a memorized poem, over a 60-second period, was found to involve an extensive set of brain regions. Increased activation was found across regions of the DMN (e.g., dorsal and ventral mPFC: BA 8, 9, 10), SCN (e.g., temporal poles: BA 38; angular gyrus: BA 39), language network (e.g., inferior frontal gyrus: BA 44, 45, 47; superior temporal gyrus: BA 21, 22), and CEN (e.g., basal ganglia; cerebellum; supramarginal gyrus: BA 40). Moreover, decreased activation was found across regions of the DMN (precuneus: BA 7), SCN (intraparietal sulcus), CEN (frontal pole and dorsolateral PFC: BA 10, 9), and salience network (insula). In contrast to this highly unspecific pattern of brain engagement, comparison of the neural activity in experts and non-experts during the generation of new poems indicated that only regions in the thalamus and basal ganglia, which are part of the CEN network, were more strongly engaged as a function of expertise.

A very similar pattern of findings was found using a quite different experimental paradigm – the brain basis of lyrical improvisation in free-style rap (Liu et al., 2012). Twelve freestyle artists with at least 5 years of professional experience were sent a set of previously unknown lyrics to memorize in advance. These were to be recalled and performed in the "conventional" condition on an 8-bar instrumental track. In contrast, in the improvisation condition, the same 8-bar track was to be used to generate lyrics spontaneously. All artists were found to have verbal fluency scores above the 80th percentile for both phonological and semantic fluency tasks, which is evidence for enhanced linguistic processing capacity. Just as in the aforementioned poetry composition, improvisation relative to conventional lyric generation resulted in increased activation in some regions of the DMN (dorsal and ventral mPFC: BA 8, 9, 10), SCN and language network (inferior frontal gyrus: BA 44, 45, 47; superior temporal gyrus: BA 21, 22), and CEN (basal ganglia; cerebellum; supramarginal gyrus: BA 40). There was also decreased activity in other regions of the DMN (precuneus: BA 7), SCN (intraparietal sulcus), and CEN (frontal pole and dorsolateral PFC: BA 10, 9).

All in all, then, the pattern of findings in the creative writing studies, both prose and poetry/lyrics, shows consistency in that multiple brain networks are involved in idea generation in such contexts, and subcortical regions of the CEN, like the basal ganglia, are additionally recruited as a function of expertise.

9.5 Issues for Further Consideration

When considering what we can tell for sure from the neuroscience of verbal creativity, one might be tempted to assume that paradigms that are closer to "real world" literary creativity, such as those of story generation and creative writing, are de facto better than divergent thinking paradigms. They certainly have their unique advantages in possessing better ecological validity. However, notwithstanding the high degree of individual variability in responses as well as the severe technical shortcomings that are difficult to control and whose impact on brain activity patterns cannot be ruled out, a central limitation of in vivo creative writing paradigms is that the creativity condition is also more cognitively demanding than the control condition. In the absence of cognitively challenging control conditions, it is impossible to tell which aspects of brain activity are specifically relevant to creativity as opposed to general cognitive control (Abraham, 2013; see Chapter 7).

There is abundant literature on the association between mental illness, substance abuse, and creativity (especially literary creativity) that is of relevance to questions posed in the study of the neuroscience of literary creativity (see Box 9.3). Less common are reports of sudden surges in the expression of literary creativity following neurological insult. For instance, Wu et al. (2015) report the case of literary creativity in three neurological patients following primary progressive aphasia (PPA) or semantic dementia (SD), whose brain scans revealed relative sparing of some parts of the lateral temporal lobe within the superior and middle temporal gyri alongside severe atrophy of the temporal poles and medial temporal regions, such as the amygdala and parahippocampal gyri, as well as limbic regions like the insula. However, these forms of de novo creative emergence (see Box 4.2) are rare in the literary domain compared to visual artistic and musical domains.

The case that verbal and non-verbal domains are far apart in terms of their neural and information processing mechanisms also should not be overstated. In the drive to determine domain-general versus domain-specific dynamics (Palmiero, Nakatani, Raver, Belardinelli, & van Leeuwen, 2010), one can lose sight of cross-modal interactions that are real and vital to the creative process. For instance, improvements in creative writing, in terms of both originality and narrative construction, were found after training in visual literacy such as the PIE (Perception–Interpretation–Expression). Visual literacy approaches focus on deriving meaning from visual images and support the development of key skills such as identification, analysis, interpretation, categorization, and questioning that promote descriptive writing and the generation of ideas during creative writing (Barbot et al., 2013). Another example of cross-modal interactions comes from research on divergent creative thinking where creative performance on a verbal creative task was abetted by carrying out a spatial mental rotation task in the incubation period prior to problem solving, while creative performance on a spatial creative task was abetted by carrying out verbal anagram tasks in the incubation period (Gilhooly, Georgiou, & Devery, 2013).

There are several aspects of literary creativity that haven't even been broached from a neuroscientific perspective and are also rarely studied from the purview of psychology. The need to consider contexts of collaboration seem inevitable given that group-based ventures are increasingly the norm in several spheres of literary creativity, such as writers for television shows. Consideration of differences between premeditated and improvised literary composition and distinctions as a function of literary genre is also vital, as are comparisons across domains of creativity as evidence indicates that, while creativity in the visual domain is on the rise, the opposite is true of the verbal domain as the overall trend suggests a decline, both in terms of originality and technical proficiency (Weinstein, Clark, DiBartolomeo, & Davis, 2014).

Chapter Summary

- Literary creativity is derived from the human capacity for language, which is inherently generative.
- Individual factors like intrinsic motivation and domain-specific expertise are essential to proficiency in literary creativity.
- It is necessary to consider the stages of creative writing from inception of idea to delivery of final product to gain a systemic perspective of the interplay between individual, environmental, and cultural factors.
- The brain networks of relevance in understanding literary creativity include the language network, default mode network, central executive network, and semantic cognition network.
- Paradigms based on verbal divergent thinking tasks are not necessarily implemented in a meaningful manner to deliver insights about verbal creativity.
- Neuroscientific studies are increasingly implementing creative writing paradigms that have the advantage of bearing higher ecological validity but also the disadvantage of being less controlled than the alternatives.
- There is an association between literary creativity and mental illness, but the precise nature and extent of the association is yet to be determined.

Review Questions

1. What are the factors that render language and creativity inextricably linked?

2. Consider the role played by metaphors in literary creativity. How are they linked to wider aspects of semantic processing in language?
3. Can we understand the brain basis of literary creativity by focusing only on the language brain network?
4. Is verbal divergent thinking a true indicator of literary creativity?
5. Estimate the advantages and disadvantages of using creative writing paradigms in the neuroscience of literary creativity.

Further Reading

- Alexandrov, V. E. (2007). Literature, literariness, and the brain. *Comparative Literature*, *59*(2), 97–118.
- Boyd, B. (2017). The evolution of stories: From mimesis to language, from fact to fiction. *Cognitive Science*, *9*(1). doi: 10.1002/wcs.1444.
- Fedorenko, E., & Thompson-Schill, S. L. (2014). Reworking the language network. *Trends in Cognitive Sciences*, *18*(3), 120–126.
- Friederici, A. D. (2011). The brain basis of language processing: From structure to function. *Physiological Reviews*, *91*(4), 1357–1392.
- Shah, C., Erhard, K., Ortheil, H.-J., Kaza, E., Kessler, C., & Lotze, M. (2013). Neural correlates of creative writing: An fMRI study. *Human Brain Mapping*, *34*(5), 1088–1101.

CHAPTER TEN

Visual Artistic Creativity

"I invent nothing. I rediscover."

(Auguste Rodin)

Learning Objectives

- Differentiating bottom-up from top-down biases in artists' perception
- Identifying how artistic expertise influences visuospatial and motor capacities
- Evaluating the links between imagery, synesthesia, and creativity
- Understanding the paradigms and brain correlates of creating visual art
- Grasping insights about visual creativity from the disordered brain
- Recognizing the ties between perceiving, generating, and evaluating visual art

10.1 Visual Art and the Plastic Brain

The case of the polymath, Matthias Buchinger (1674–1739), defies the imagination. He was an artist and calligrapher who specialized in the technique of micrography, which requires extreme dexterity; a musician who played several instruments, including some of his own invention; a bowler; a marksman with a pistol; a magician; and much more. He was commissioned to draw portraits, coats of arms, and family trees, and his clientele included noblemen, kings, and emperors. These acclaimed feats are extraordinary in their own right. But they are even more astonishing when considering that they are the feats of a man who was born without feet or hands! A man who created art by using the stumps at the ends of his arms to wield drawing materials. He was highly acclaimed in his lifetime, and his work is still displayed in major museums across the world. The publicity accorded to him in his time even saw him billed him "The Greatest German Living" (Jay, 2016).

How are such remarkable feats made possible? Can our current knowledge from the psychological and neuroscientific literature on the capacity to create visual art explain the case of Matthias Buchinger? One postulation is that the manual dexterity afforded by his upper extremity stumps came about through cortical remapping between the hand and the forearm areas of the brain (Altschuler, 2016). This would then be a case of extreme neural plasticity, which refers to the capacity of the brain to continually reorganize itself as a function of experience by building new neural connections.

In the context of the creation of visual art, the sheer power of the plasticity of the brain is exemplified by cases of blind artists. The case of EW, who made raised-line drawings and invented her own symbolic devices to represent physical elements as she experienced and imagined them as well as emotions and thoughts, is one such example (Kennedy, 2009). The case of EA is also fascinating as he generates recognizable images of an object after exploring it through touch. His brain activity while drawing engages visual processing regions including the primary visual cortex (Amedi et al., 2008). Even training a congenitally blind person to draw has been shown to result in rapid cortical reorganization, as indicated by novel recruitment of the primary visual cortex (which prior to training displayed an undifferentiated response) for a non-visual task (Likova, 2012).

This chapter will explore what we know about the psychological and neural underpinnings of visual artistic creativity, and how these are further differentiated as a function of artistic expertise.

10.2 Information Processing in Visual Artistic Creativity

The idea that artists perceive the world differently as a result of their extensive experience in artistic media is one that resonates across many academic disciplines, including psychology, art, and art history (Seeley & Kozbelt, 2008). One prominent idea is that artists have better access to raw bottom-up information or stimulus features that are ordinarily not perceived because it is not necessary to do so, and this "clarified sense perception" allows them to better perceive the parts that make up the whole (Fry, 1909). Evidence supports this notion. One study, for instance, compared four matched groups – (a) an autistic, visual artistic savant group, (b) a non-autistic artistic group, (c) a non-artistic autistic group, and (d) a non-autistic and non-artistic control group – on a block design task, which required restructuring and bringing together patterned smaller blocks to form a predefined larger and more complex pattern as fast as possible. The findings revealed superior performance on the perceptual task as a function of artistic talent, as both the artistic groups (autistic savant and non-autistic) were much faster at the task than the other groups. Moreover, even the non-artistic autistic group outperformed the non-autistic non-artistic control group. This led to the conclusion that,

a facility for seeing wholes in terms of their parts, rather than as unified gestalts, may be characteristic not only of those with autism, but may even be more dominant in those individuals with an aptitude for drawing, independently of whether they are, or are not, autistic. (Pring, Hermelin, & Heavey, 1995, 1073)

Enhanced perceptual functioning is even held to be integral to the mechanisms that underlie savant capacities, including those specific to creative abilities (Mottron, Dawson, & Soulières, 2009), although these are believed to be different from those associated with autism (Drake & Winner, 2009).

The alternative view is that differences between artists and non-artists do not lie in automatic aspects of perception per se but in top-down factors in the methods employed to analyze the perceptual experience and create the desired perceptual effects (Gombrich, 1960). An example of evidence in favor of this idea is a case study of the artist Humphrey Ocean, whose brain activity and eye movement strategies were recorded while making art. The eye movement patterns of the artist indicated that the duration of his fixations while drawing or painting were twice as lengthy as when he was not drawing or painting (Miall & Tchalenko, 2001), which is indicative of the influence of context, experience, and intent on perception.

While few psychological theories have been directed at explaining the information processing mechanisms that underlie the emergence of visual artistic creativity as a whole, there are several frameworks about biases in different aspects of information processing that are relevant to visual art. For instance, Albert Rothenberg (1980, 2006) outlined three creative cognitive operations – articulation, janusian processing, and homospatial processing – the last of which was held to be especially relevant to visual forms of creativity. Articulation is the process of "concomitantly separating and connecting," such as when parts of an artwork are distinct and separate from one another yet integrated in a novel and valuable manner to form a whole. Janusian processing occurs when actively conceptualizing "multiple opposites or antitheses simultaneously," such that previously irreconcilable viewpoints are brought to a place of coexistence. Homospatial processing, in contrast, occurs when purposively "conceiving two or more discrete entities occupying the same space, a conception leading to the articulation of new identities," which allows for visual metaphors to be derived (Rothenberg, 2006, S9). Indeed, there is evidence to suggest that superimpositions of dissimilar visual images, which necessitate integration of content and thereby require homospatial thinking, are rated by artists to be higher in creativity than the mere combination of the same images in the form of a figure-and-ground relation, which only necessitates combinations in an additive manner (Rothenberg, 1986).

In relation to this, it is relevant to note that visual artists have also been shown to demonstrate high allusive or loosened associational thinking in semantic categorization (Tucker, Rothwell, Armstrong, & McConaghy, 1982) and heuristic rather than algorithmic thinking (Haller & Courvoisier, 2010). As such propensities are domain-general, it is reasonable to expect that this could translate to better creative performance on generic tasks of creativity. In fact, there is empirical work that supports this idea, as visual artists have been shown to outperform their non-visual artist counterparts in measures of creative divergent thinking (Ram-Vlasov, Tzischinsky, Green, & Shochat, 2016) (see Section 10.3.1).

The following subsections will explore the dominant factors that have been shown to be especially relevant to visual artistic creativity within the psychological domain.

10.2.1 Visuospatial Ability

Evidence in relation to purely perceptual differences among artists and non-artists is somewhat mixed. For instance, a comparison of professional artists, art students, and non-artists revealed that all three groups were entirely comparable in perceptual constancy for size, brightness, and shape (Perdreau & Cavanagh, 2011). Behavioral differences as a function of artistic expertise are more consistently found in the perception of ambiguous figures. Ambiguous figures in the Gestalt psychology tradition are those in which figure–ground reversals occur during the perceptual process despite the stimulus information remaining exactly the same. Examples of the same include the Necker cube illusion and the Jastrow duck-rabbit image. Greater ease in ambiguous figure reversal is associated with both self-rated creativity and ideational fluency in divergent thinking (Wiseman, Watt, Gilhooly, & Georgiou, 2011).

A comprehensive study examining differences between art students and non-art students on 4 perception tasks and 12 drawing tasks found superior performance for the trained artists across both categories of task (Kozbelt, 2001). The art students were better able to identify the subject in images (Out-of-Focus Pictures task), identify the subject in images with only partial information provided (Gestalt Completion task), find a simple form within a complex pattern (Embedded Figures task), and imagine rotating two figures to judge whether they match (Mental Rotation task). The drawing tasks mainly involved copying line drawings and the art students outperformed the untrained students on 10 of the 12 tasks. Moreover, the group differences between the artists and non-artists on the perception tasks were attributable to visual processes that were common to both the perception and drawing tasks (Kozbelt, 2001). So this constitutes evidence of enhanced visuospatial abilities as a function of artistic experience.

Enhanced visual abilities are also positively associated with visual forms of creative thinking. For instance, better performance on tasks of divergent creative thinking (fluency, flexibility, originality, elaboration) and creative imagery (originality) is linked to greater speed in visual restructuring of ambiguous figures (Palmiero et al., 2010).

Some researchers examine differences in relation to gaze frequency, which is the rate at which glances are made between a drawing and the stimulus to be drawn. High gaze frequencies are instantiated as relatively quick alternations between the drawing and the stimulus, and the opposite is the case with low gaze frequencies. In a comparison of trained artists and non-artists, not only was drawing accuracy higher in the expert group, but gaze frequency was also positively correlated with drawing accuracy such that the higher the gaze frequencies, the greater the drawing accuracy (Cohen, 2005).

More precise analyses of eye movement patterns are also a subject of major interest. In one study, such patterns were recorded while artists and artistically untrained participants viewed several pictures from several categories ranging from the depiction of ordinary scenes to abstraction. These were classified into three groups as either affording a viewing mode that was object-oriented (marked by a selection of recognizable objects), pictorial (marked by a selection of more structural features), or abstract (Vogt & Magnussen, 2007). Artists spent more time in the free-scanning session on structural and abstract features of the pictures whereas non-artists displayed a preference for viewing human features and objects. However, in the second memory session, in which they were instructed that they would later be tested on memory recall of the pictures they were about to see, the eye movement pattern of the artists switched toward objects and human features. Moreover, artists were better at recalling the pictorial features they saw and this was true across all picture types. This finding indicates that, under natural conditions (e.g., free scanning as opposed to memory instruction), the perceptual processing of visually trained artists "will sacrifice a functional mode of visual perception in favor of a purely pictorial one" (Vogt, 1999, 325).

10.2.2 Drawing and Hand–Eye Coordination

Greater efficiency in perceptual processing and motor output has been noted on the part of expert artists compared to novices, regardless of the level of familiarity with the images to be sketched (Glazek, 2012). Complex visuomotor transformations take place during the production of any visual art form. The strategies undertaken via eye movements and hand–eye interactions differ from context to context, such as copying directly or copying from memory. Conditions of direct copying are best explained by the *drawing hypothesis*, "where the drawing of shape is the result of visuomotor mapping that can be executed directly while perceiving the original and without vision of the drawing surface" (Tchalenko & Miall, 2009, 370).

An examination of strategies adopted during gaze shifts between the "original" object, model, or scene to be depicted and the "drawing" of the same on the medium of choice (e.g., paper, canvas, touchscreen) reveals that there are periods of "blind drawing," where drawing takes place while the gaze is maintained on the original (Tchalenko, Nam, Ladanga, & Miall, 2014). Blind drawing is seen as a method by which top-down influences can be overcome as there is a direct visuomotor transformation of the visual input into the drawing action, which thus does not necessitate visual encoding for later recall of memory. When comparing different types of line drawing task, blind drawing increases progressively between copying ("reproducing a preexisting well-defined line"), contouring ("delineating the boundary of a three-dimensional entity"), and generating a graded zone (rendering "a transition between light and shade with a discrete line") (ibid., 336). What is more, expertise-based comparisons reveal that this direct hand–eye strategy used in blind drawing is used to a greater degree by experts and enables more accurate drawings via segmentation of a whole image into simple segments that are rendered one after the other (Tchalenko, 2009).

Seeley and Kozbelt (2007) proposed a six-stage visuomotor model to explain artists' superior perceptual processing (Figure 10.1). The first stage involves coding sensory inputs in a "visual buffer" (primary visual regions). The second stage, "feature extraction" of basic structures, sees diagnostic image elements like color, orientation, and contour derived from the sensory inputs in the visual buffer by means of pattern recognition (secondary visual regions). The third stage, "object recognition,"

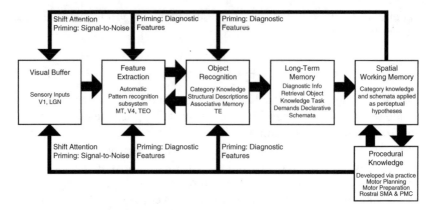

Figure 10.1 A model of visuomotor processing

The enhanced encoding of expected features and inhibition of distractors, which is brought about by declarative schemata and motor plans, is proposed to explain perceptual advantages in artists [LGN: lateral geniculate nucleus; MT: secondary visual area – motion processing; PMC: premotor cortex; SMA: supplementary motor area; TE and TEO: areas in the inferior temporal cortex; V1: primary visual cortex; V4: secondary visual area – color processing]. Reprinted from Kozbelt A & Seeley WP (2007). Integrating art historical, psychological, and neuroscientific explanations of artists' advantages in drawing and perception. *Psychology of Aesthetics, Creativity, and the Arts, 1*(2), 80–90.

seeks matching between these diagnostic image features and category-based general knowledge in artists' associative memory. The criterion of the best match is used to instantiate a "perceptual hypothesis" on the identity of the stimulus, and, if an adequate match is made, the processing cycle ends. The fourth and fifth stages occur when there are multiple matches. Then the closest match is used to generate a perceptual hypothesis regarding the form and identify of the stimulus. Additional category knowledge or declarative schemata about the potential object is retrieved from "long-term memory," which is used to redirect attention and prime the pattern-recognition mechanism to the expectation of specific stimulus features or object parts. By drawing attention to the appearance of hidden and subtle contours, attention-tuning mechanisms serve to confirm or disconfirm the perceptual hypothesis being maintained in "spatial working memory" about the identity of the object. The sixth stage occurs when the task involves dynamic interaction with the environment, such as during reaching, grasping, or drawing, and here motor plans are derived from procedural knowledge. Just as declarative schemata direct attention to object recognition, motor plans shift attention in preparation for action. The information processing advantages exhibited by artists are held to be at the level of both declarative schemata and motor plans that play complementary roles in the generation of visual art (Kozbelt & Seeley, 2007; Seeley & Kozbelt, 2008). Positive associations between drawing skill and artistic creativity across age groups, from children to young adults, constitute evidence that speaks in favor of this idea (Chan & Zhao, 2010).

10.2.3 Imagery

The link between visual creativity and visual imagery is an elusive one. Acts of the imagination are not necessarily creative, but creativity necessarily emanates from the imagination. "Imaginative perception … *seeing as* in both the literal and metaphorical senses of that expression, opens up the possibility of seeing things in new ways" (Thomas, 2014, 167), and it is against such a backdrop that ideational originality emerges.

But how crucial is visual imagery to visual creativity? The conjunction model proposes that vividness and originality in perceptual imagery and transformative imagery abilities allow for the emergence of the creative imagination (Figure 10.2) (Dziedziewicz & Karwowski, 2015). There is some evidence for complex interactions between these variables such that a greater ability to transform visual imagery is associated with greater "originality in creative imagery" whereas greater vividness in visual imagery is linked to greater usefulness or "practicality in creative imagery" (Palmiero et al., 2011, 2015). In fact, the results of a meta-analysis suggest that the relationship between self-reported imagery and divergent thinking in creativity is modest yet significant (LeBoutillier & Marks, 2003).

But how does artistic expertise influence this relationship? This question was explored by researchers who carried out a series of studies using a figure combination task (Finke, 1990), where three simple geometrical components (e.g., cube, cylinder, cone) are combined to form objects (Verstijnen, van Leeuwen, Goldschmidt, Hamel, & Hennessey, 1998). They distinguished between *combination*, as reflecting the degree of variety in the spatial configurations of the constructions (e.g., components aligned vertically, horizontally, or diagonally), and *restructuring*, as reflecting the degree of variety in the structure of the constructions (e.g., embedding, modification, or proportion of components). These were examined in expert and novice sketchers in relation to the effects of imagery only (imagining the constructions) and externalization (sketching of imagined constructions).

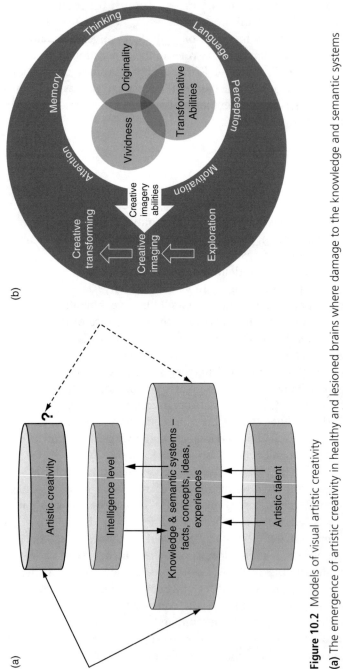

Figure 10.2 Models of visual artistic creativity

(a) The emergence of artistic creativity in healthy and lesioned brains where damage to the knowledge and semantic systems (dashed line) compromises artistic creativity. Reproduced with permission from Zaidel DW. (2014). Creativity, brain, and art: Biological and neurological considerations. *Frontiers in Human Neuroscience, 8,* 389. **(b)** The conjunction model of creative visual imagination in child development. Reprinted by permission of the publisher (Taylor & Francis Ltd) from Dziedziewicz D & Karwowski M. (2015). Development of children's creative visual imagination: A theoretical model and enhancement programmes. *Education 3–13, 43*(4), 382–392.

The results indicated that combination and restructuring are very separable processes. Combining is unaffected by expertise as it is performed equivalently by novices and experts. It is also undifferentiated by whether sketching is required (externalization) or not (imagery only) and outputs under both conditions are positively correlated with creativity. Restructuring, on the other hand, is affected by expertise and externalization such that it occurs significantly more often when expert sketchers are allowed to sketch than when they are not. Novices do not show this pattern in that their performance on restructuring is unaffected by sketching. Moreover, only restructuring under sketching conditions was positivity correlated with creativity, not sketching under imagery-only conditions. So imagery alone is insufficient for restructuring in figural tasks of generativity (ibid.).

10.2.4 Synesthesia

People with synesthesia, a rare condition, have highly unusual perceptual experiences that can be cross-modal or unimodal. In the cross-modal situation, perceptual experiences in one stimulus modality (e.g., auditory perception in the hearing of the sound of a church bell) triggers perceptual experience in another stimulus modality (e.g., visual perception in seeing colors). In the unimodal situation, perceptual experiences in one stimulus modality (e.g., visual perception when reading numbers) triggers an unrelated perceptual experience in the same stimulus modality (e.g., visual perception in seeing colors). These are conscious experiences that are automatically and consistently elicited (Hubbard & Ramachandran, 2005). A possible association between synesthesia and creativity has been touted because unusual cross-modal and unimodal associations are indicative of bridging across wide-ranging conceptual spaces within our knowledge or semantic networks. A bias toward forming associations between typically unrelated concepts should be advantageous for creativity (Ramachandran & Hubbard, 2003). This is a reasonable postulation given that originality in creative ideation is incumbent on forming novel associative links between unlinked concepts. However, the fact that the stability of the synesthetic experiences over time is high (e.g., always seeing the color pink when faced with the number 5) suggests that flexibility in the widening of associations is limited once formed.

Although the incidence of synesthesia is higher among artists than non-artists (Domino, 1989; Rothen & Meier, 2010), the evidence for enhanced creative abilities among synesthetes is mixed (Chun & Hupé, 2016; Domino, 1989; Ward, Thompson-Lake, Ely, & Kaminski, 2008). For instance, an examination of creative ability in relation to synesthesia found that synesthetes engaged more in the creative arts and have an advantage in relation to convergent creative thinking compared to non-synesthetes, but not divergent creative thinking. This was interpreted as evidence that synesthetes do indeed have more access to wider associative knowledge (explaining their superior performance in convergent creative thinking) but they are unable to use this information flexibly (explaining their lack of advantage in divergent creative thinking) (Ward et al., 2008).

10.3 Visual Artistic Creativity and the Healthy Brain

In specifying the relationship between seeing and generating visual art, Stephen Grossberg (Grossberg, 2008; Grossberg & Zajac, 2017) postulated that the brain's critical perceptual units are boundaries and surfaces. Moreover, far from the visual system being orchestrated by independent modules, each of which deals with one facet of the visual scene (e.g., depth, color, form, motion), the visual processing in actuality reflects "complementary computing" where pairs of processing streams exhibit mutually informative dynamics in handling complementary stimulus properties. When viewing any scene (in a painting or the real world), information extracted most quickly with a glance from boundaries and surfaces is the "gist," which enables rapid recognition of what one is viewing. The paintings of renowned visual artists indicate their keen awareness of perceptual principles such as invisible boundaries, how the gist can convey the identity of the scene as well as the painter, filling-in of feature contours, figure–ground separations, and so on.

To date, two meta-analyses have been undertaken to determine commonalities across studies of the brain basis of visual artistic creativity (Boccia et al., 2015; Pidgeon et al., 2016). This is despite the fact that relatively few neuroscientific studies have been carried out to examine this question (5 fMRI studies in the 2015 meta-analysis and 7 in the 2016 meta-analysis), and in the studies that do so, the paradigms used are vastly different from one another. The inconsistencies and contradictory findings in the EEG literature on visual artistic creativity have been especially highlighted, as has the general lack of appropriate control tasks to the visual creativity task (Pidgeon et al., 2016).

Some of the prominent neuroimaging studies that have examined the brain correlates of visual artistic creativity are detailed below in separate subsections that distinguish between the different constellations of empirical paradigms used in this domain. The dominant brain networks that will be referred to in the following subsections include the default mode network (DMN), the central executive network (CEN), and the semantic cognition network (SCN). These have been detailed in previous chapters (see Chapters 4 and 5).

10.3.1 Visual Divergent Thinking

Different approaches are used here, with some studies looking at visual creativity using figural forms of divergent thinking tasks in neuroscientific studies, others focusing on the roles played by single regions, and yet others considering the role played by whole brain networks.

Using images from the figural form of the Torrance Tests of Creative Thinking (TTCT), participants were presented with simple geometrical drawings composed of 1–2 lines and asked to expand upon and complete the image in their mind. Some drawings were to be completed in a creative manner (in 25 seconds), and others in an uncreative manner (in 15 seconds). These tasks were carried out in silence in the MRI scanner, and participants produced their drawings after the scanning session. The drawings produced under the instruction of creative generation were judged to be more original than those under the uncreative condition, and engaged lateral frontal lobe regions involved in cognitive control and semantic retrieval, including the inferior frontal gyrus (part of the SCN and CEN: BA 47, 45) and the middle frontal gyrus (part of the CEN: BA 46, 9, 6) (Huang et al., 2013).

Comparing the brain network correlates of the figural and verbal forms of the TTCT revealed that better performance on both visual and verbal creativity was associated with lower resting state activity in regions of the superior parietal cortex (part of the CEN). Another commonality associated with visual and verbal creativity was the positive connectivity between the DMN and CEN in relation to both forms. Higher visual creativity, in particular, was associated with lower functional connectivity in two regions – the posterior middle frontal gyrus (part of the CEN) and the precuneus (part of the DMN) – and the latter relationship was mediated by regions of the CEN. So the authors argue for the specific relevance of the middle frontal gyrus and the precuneus in visual creativity given the involvement of these structures in visuo-spatial information processing, mental rotation, mental imagery, and object representation (Zhu et al., 2017). Another study that examined resting state connectivity in relation to visual divergent creativity using the same creativity measures came to dissimilar conclusions. Specifically, the results indicated reduced connectivity within the DMN, and that increased connectivity within the CEN was associated with better performance (Li et al., 2016).

10.3.2 Creative Imagery and Drawing

Another focus is to examine creative imagery with or without drawing. For instance, upon being presented with Rorschach inkblot images and asked to report what they perceived in them, participants' responses were classified as unique, infrequent, or frequent depending on the commonness of the association. Brain activity in relation to perceptual experiences that were classified unique compared to those that were deemed frequent revealed the involvement of the anterior medial prefrontal cortex (BA 10), the temporal poles (BA 38), and the angular gyrus (BA 39), all of which are core regions of the DMN. The DMN is thus involved in unique perception (Asari et al., 2008).

A comparison of the brain response when engaging in a visual creativity task compared to a non-creative visual task demonstrated the involvement of left hemisphere brain regions within the dorsolateral prefrontal cortex (part of CEN: BA 8), dorsomedial prefrontal cortex (part of CEN and DMN: BA 8), ventrolateral (part of SCN and LAN: BA 47, 45, 44), posterior extent of the middle temporal gyrus (part of SCN: BA 22), as well as the premotor cortex and the supplementary motor area (BA 6) (Aziz-Zadeh et al., 2012). While the non-creative task involved mentally putting together three resected parts of simple geometrical shapes (e.g., rectangle) to form the original shape and verbalize the correct solution, the creative task involved giving participants 3 distinct shapes (e.g., an "8" shape, a "C" shape, a circle) to rearrange and make into a nameable composite image (e.g., a smiley face). While the name was given to this image from within the scanner, no check was made of the pattern of visual rearrangement of the stimuli within the scanning environment or outside. Also, the non-creative control task took on average about 12½ seconds to complete across 20 trials of the same, the visual creativity task took much longer, an average of 20 seconds.

Using MRI-compatible drawing tablets, it is possible to make sketches and draw in real time within a scanning environment. For instance, a comparison of Pictionary-style image creation, whereby participants are given a word to depict pictorially, with a simple drawing task, whereby they simply have to depict zigzags, leads to extensive activations across motor control regions, such as the cerebellum and premotor cortices, visual perception regions in the occipital lobe, and the thalamus, which is involved in both motor and visual processing (Saggar et al., 2015).

In aiming for more ecologically valid paradigms in the study of visual artistic creativity, Ellamil et al. (2012) also employed an MRI-compatible drawing tablet and examined brain engagement in art students while illustrating book cover designs based on a provided summary description of the book (Figure 10.3). They separated the generation phase (draw or write down book cover ideas for 30 seconds) and the evaluation phase (draw or write down evaluations of the ideas for 20 seconds) with control tracing tasks. It is questionable, however, whether it can be assumed that the generation and evaluation phases can be artificially clearly separated by instruction alone; also, the instruction to not evaluate in the generation phase (and to not generate in the evaluation phase) interferes with the spontaneity inherent in creative ideation. Nonetheless, the utility of the study lies in the innovative approach and the findings indicate that, among young artists, the generation of visual art compared to the evaluation of the same leads to bilateral activity in hippocampal, premotor, and superior parietal regions whereas the evaluation of visual art compared with the generation of the same is accompanied by bombastic activations across extensive regions of all networks in questions – the DMN, CEN, SCN, and visual cortices.

The opposite pattern was found in a study conducted by De Pisapia et al. (2016), who examined functional connectivity during creative performance in professional artists demonstrating significant creative achievement compared to non-artists. The creativity task involved mentally creating a novel image that would fit into the category of "landscape" and comparisons of the brain activity indicated stronger functional connectivity of regions along the medial parietal wall of the brain and the dorsolateral prefrontal cortex as well as several other non-DMN and non-CEN brain regions, such as the premotor cortex.

At present, the field is not at a stage where we can figure out how to reconcile such discrepant findings. Complex interactions between brain regions across different brain networks are indicated in the neuropsychological literature in terms of the dissociations between the impact of brain damage on the originality and relevance components of creative imagery. While lesions of the lateral prefrontal cortex (part of the CEN) selectively impaired the ability to generate original responses in relation to creative imagery, the ability to generate practical, functional, or relevant responses was compromised in all patient groups, regardless of lesion site in the frontal lobe, basal ganglia, and parieto-temporal region (part of CEN and SCN) (Abraham, Beudt, et al., 2012).

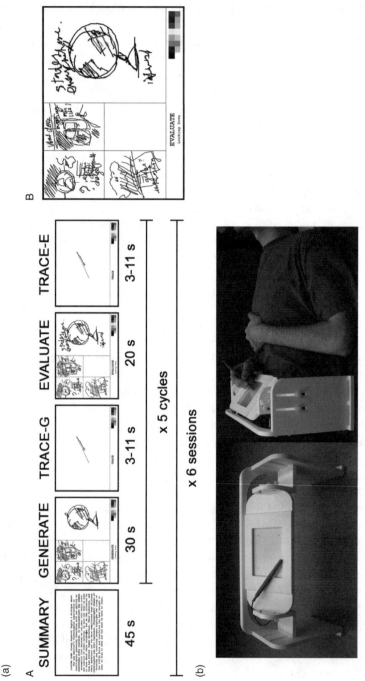

Figure 10.3 An example of a visual artistic creativity study in an fMRI environment

(a) Schematic diagram showing **A** the trial events with **B** the evaluation phase magnified. **(b)** The experimental testing set up. Reprinted from *NeuroImage, 59(2)*, Ellamil M, Dobson C, Beeman M, & Christoff K, Evaluative and generative modes of thought during the creative process, pages 1783–1794, Copyright 2012, © with permission from Elsevier.

10.3.3 Artistic Expertise and Training

The brain correlates of the very complex visual-motor skill of drawing have been examined for decades now (see Box 10.1), and as a natural next step, an increasing number of researchers are examining the brain correlates of drawing proficiency among artists. For instance, art students and non-art undergraduates were given photographs of a hand and of a tower made from blocks, and were required to make drawings of these images that were as accurate as possible. Drawings rendered by the artists were judged to be more accurate than those of non-artists, and this proficiency in drawing was significantly associated with greater gray matter density in the left anterior cerebellum (Chamberlain et al., 2014).

Box 10.1 Brain Correlates of Drawing

Drawing is a complex motor behavior and determining its brain basis is quite a challenge. Several brain regions are involved in the same and the nature of their interactions is determined by the subtleties of the drawing task and the conditions under which they are produced (Trojano, Grossi, & Flash, 2009). In one of the key studies published in the field, participants who were untrained in the visual arts were given simple cartoon faces to observe, retain, and then reproduce from memory (Miall, Gowen, & Tchalenko, 2009). Encoding of a cartoon face compared to a field of randomly placed dots was accompanied by activations in extrastriate visual areas in the occipital lobe and the fusiform face area (FFA). Drawing from memory (recalling a previously presented cartoon), drawing without memory (new cartoon currently being viewed), and drawing from both memory and vision (old cartoon currently being viewed) extensively activates the motor network, including sensory-motor cortical areas, the premotor cortex, supplementary motor area, parietal areas and cerebellum, implicating the involvement of dorsal stream areas that guide and control action as well as frontal areas that are involved in the planning of hand movement sequences. The key point was the contrast between the brain bases of drawing from vision and drawing from memory. Drawing from vision was found to engage visual regions of the occipital cortex and the FFA, whereas drawing from memory engages inferior parietal and premotor frontal regions. That the occipital regions were not engaged in a face-selective manner during the memory retention interval was taken as evidence of the conversion of the visual information into refined visuomotor or spatial signals that more suitably aid the drawing of faces in the absence of direct visual input.

An innovative longitudinal study examined two groups of participants at the start and end of a 3-month period in terms of behavioral and brain changes as a function of art training (Schlegel et al., 2015). The experimental group carried out a 3-month introductory course in either drawing or painting, whereas the matched control group did not undertake any course in visual art learning. These groups were examined with regard to changes in brain structure both in general and specifically in relation to their non-verbal divergent thinking (as measured by the figural form of the TTCT), perceptual abilities (as assessed by their judgments of luminance and length of visual illusions), and perception-to-action abilities (based on their 30-second gesture drawings of an observed human figure) (Figure 6.2).

General brain-based differences were found between the groups such that the structural integrity of white matter in the frontal lobe regions was reduced in the artistically trained group following the 3 months of visual art training, whereas the brains of the untrained group were not associated with significant changes in gross neuroanatomy over time. While the behavioral findings indicated that there were no differences as a function of training in perceptual abilities, enhanced performance was found in the artistic training group but not the untrained control group on gesture drawing ability and figural divergent thinking following training. So artistic training led to improvements in domain-specific perception-to-action skills (drawing) as well as in domain-general skills (creative cognition) in terms of the ability to generate original and flexible ideas, model narratives, and processes, as well as to depict rich, complex, and effective imagery. What is more, greater adeptness at gesture drawing was positively correlated with changes in a brain region that projects to the hand and arm area of the motor cortex, namely, the right anterior lobe of the cerebellum (ibid.). So, anterior regions in the cerebellum appear to play a key role, not just in facilitating drawing in general (see Box 10.1 for the brain correlates of drawing), but specifically in relation to visual art learning and artistic expertise in drawing.

10.4 Visual Artistic Creativity and the Disordered Brain

An intriguing paradox in the literature on creative cognition and brain function is that, while certain key brain structures, like the prefrontal cortex are clearly engaged during different types of creative ideation (Dietrich & Kanso, 2010), damage to the prefrontal cortex in some contexts leads to impoverished creative performance and in other contexts lead to enhanced creative performance (Abraham, Beudt, et al., 2012; Reverberi et al., 2005; Shamay-Tsoory et al., 2011). This paradox is also apparent in the specific context of visual artistic creativity and disordered brain function (de Souza et al., 2014), and some of the themes therein will be explored in the following sections (see Box 10.2 on the relation between dopamine and creativity).

Box 10.2 Dopamine and Creativity

- Parkinson's disease (PD) is a chronic movement disorder that comes about as a result of progressive depletion of dopamine production in the midbrain. Unlike other psychological functions, the artistic proficiency of artists with PD appears not to be adversely affected by the onset of the disease (Lakke, 1999). Taking dopamine antagonists following the onset of the disease can even enhance pre-existing artistic abilities (Walker, Warwick, & Cercy, 2006), and reduction of dopamine agonists is associated with a decrease in creativity (Lhommée et al., 2014). Such findings speak for the relevance of the role of dopamine in creative expression.

- The nature of this positive influence that mesolimbic dopamine exerts on creativity was held to be via its influence on novelty seeking, as dopamine does not exert a direct impact on creative ability as such but does so indirectly on motivational aspects of the creative drive (Flaherty, 2005).

- A contemporary framework differentiates between the influences of prefrontal and striatal dopamine, with the former facilitating persistent information processing and the latter mediating flexible information processing. Both forms of processing are held to be necessary components of creative cognition, as persistent processing is key for convergent creative thinking and flexible processing is inherent to divergent creative thinking (Boot et al., 2017).

10.4.1 Brain Injury in Artists

There are now innumerable case studies of artists who have endured altered brain function or experienced some form of brain damage (Finger, Zaidel, Boller, & Bogousslavsky, 2013; Rose, 2006). Prominent examples include the artists Louis Corinth (visuospatial neglect following a right hemisphere stroke), Vincent van Gogh (potential candidates: psychosis, substance abuse, epilepsy), and Willem de Kooning (Alzheimer's disease).

What is intriguing is that, while artists with brain insufficiencies tend to exhibit a range of psychological deficits, such as in memory retrieval and language production, they continue to produce art, seemingly unimpeded unless their motor functions are directly affected. Changes are usually resulting from techniques that need to be altered depending on the degree to which their movement capacity is compromised. While genres tend to stay relatively consistent in most patients, there is also much evidence of changes in style and content of expression (Chatterjee, 2004). This remarkable state of affairs has been taken as evidence of the damage-resistant capacity of the power of the human brain to communicate and express via art (Zaidel, 2013a).

A case of exquisite narrative symmetry was described in a neuropsychological study of Annie Adams, a Canadian artist who developed primary progressive aphasia (PPA), a neurodegenerative disorder marked by the deterioration of speech and language (also refer to Section 2.2.1). She was fascinated by the composer Maurice Ravel, who himself had PPA, and she rendered the musical elements of his work into visual forms in her own work (Seeley et al., 2008). Quite serendipitously, brain scans of this visual artist are available from the time she was pre-symptomatic up until the period when she was diagnosed with PPA. As she was an active artist who produced several works throughout this period, it is possible to match her artistic output with the appearance and intensification of her PPA symptoms and continued brain atrophy. A shift in style was seen in her case such that she moved from highly abstract to almost photographic realism over the span of 6 years. It is, however, not possible to say with full confidence that her change in artistic style is fully attributable to changes in brain structure and function, as many artists evolve their expressive styles over time. Another case study in fact reported the opposite trajectory pattern whereby the patient began painting following traumatic brain injury and his styles changed from realistic and representational to abstract and obscure (Midorikawa & Kawamura, 2015).

10.4.2 Dyslexia

The relation between dyslexia and heightened visual creativity mainly derives from case studies. These indicate that a high proportion of extremely gifted people, not only those who achieve eminence in their fields, like Thomas Edison and Lewis Carroll, but also less famous ones, are visual thinkers who may have had dyslexia or other learning difficulties (West, 1997). Indeed, dyslexia is over-represented in professions that necessitate visuo-spatial skills such as art, engineering, and architecture, and a comparison of students who attended extremely competitive art schools with non-art university students revealed a higher incidence of dyslexia in the former group (Wolff & Lundberg, 2002). However, somewhat counterintuitively, visual-spatial processing skills as tested in laboratory settings tend to be undifferentiated or even subpar in the case of dyslexia compared to typical populations (Winner et al., 2001). Differentiating between types of visual-spatial processing is revealing of specific advantages, though. For instance, dyslexia is associated with greater speed in recognizing impossible figures, which speaks for a specific advantage in global information processing (von Károlyi, Winner, Gray, & Sherman, 2003), which may be confined to males (Brunswick, Martin, & Marzano, 2010). This fits with the magnocellular theory of dyslexia whereby impoverished maturation of the visual magnocellular system results in the development of an enhanced visual parvocellular system, which biases the system toward holistic information processing (Stein, 2001).

10.4.3 De Novo Artistic Proficiency

Another fascinating occurrence is when artistic tendencies suddenly develop in non-artists following brain injury. This de novo generative capacity is most often manifested in the visual and musical arts (see Section 4.2.2). A wide range of conditions is associated with this phenomenon, including frontotemporal dementia (FTD), migraine, epilepsy, and traumatic brain injury (Schott, 2012). In the first paper of its kind, Miller et al. (1996) reported the case of three patients who went on to become accomplished painters following the onset of FTD. All three had the temporal-lobe variant of FTD, in which the frontal lobe is relatively intact but the temporal poles are dysfunctional. While the de novo emergence of artistic proficiency is a rare occurrence in relation to these conditions as it is a feature of only a minority of cases (e.g., 17% of the 69 FTD patients reported in Miller et al., 2000), there are consistencies across cases (e.g., compulsiveness of the need to paint) that afford meaningful analysis of this behavior. It is also very likely that the appearance of such features is underreported (Schott, 2012).

So how can this sudden manifestation of previously unknown skills in such individuals be explained? One compelling idea is that the need to communicate and express continues unabated and when brain damage has a deleterious effect on the ability to communicate in one's normal or accustomed capacity, the brain pushes other avenues for accommodating this drive. In putting forward this suggestion, Dahlia Zaidel (2014, 2) also makes a sage distinction between artistic expression and creative artistic expression in relation to the de novo emergence of artistic abilities: "In such neurological cases, the turning to art is itself innovative; the produced art, however, is not necessarily creative." Intact connectivity within semantic networks that house associative knowledge is vital, as originality in creativity involves not just generating open-ended responses but also going beyond the known (see Chapter 1). Mere generativity without heeding or having cognizance of the constraints will not lead to higher artistic creativity (Figure 10.2).

10.5 Issues for Further Consideration

Very complex interactions determine how we experience art. Variables that have yet to be explored in much detail include individual factors like personality and personal preference (see Box 10.3 on neuroaesthetics). The former has received far more focus than the latter in the psychological study of creativity. Historiometric investigations have indicated a higher prevalence of psychopathology among eminent visual artists and writers (Post, 1994). Much of the empirical work examining whether this association bears out when considering the personality traits of highly creative populations has largely confirmed the same. Compared to control groups, visual artists and poets demonstrated higher levels of schizotypal personality traits such as unusual experiences and impulsive nonconformity (Nettle, 2006). This relationship appears most significant in the case of visual artists. For example, a comparison of 53 visual artists and 54 non-visual artists indicated that schizotypal personality traits, such as unusual experiences, cognitive disorganization, and impulsive nonconformity, were significantly more characteristic of the visual artists, as were other personality traits such as openness to experience and neuroticism (Burch, Pavelis, Hemsley, & Corr, 2006). A comparison of two groups of artists (visual artists and musicians) and two groups of scientists (biological and physical) revealed similarities between the dispositional characteristics of the artist and scientist groups (Rawlings & Locarnini, 2008). Visual artists were similar to musicians in reporting more unusual experiences and having higher levels of hypomanic traits and they reported more idiosyncratic responses in a word association task relative to both scientist groups.

Box 10.3 Neuroaesthetics versus Neuroscience of Artistic Creativity

The term "neuroaesthetics" is often taken to reflect the neuroscience of art. But this is too vague a description and also a potentially misleading construal. Neuroaesthetics is the study of the brain basis of aesthetic experience (Zeki, 2002). In averring that visual art "obeys the laws of the visual brain, and thus reveals these laws to us," Zeki (2001, 52) outlined two laws that are of especial relevance to the perception of art, the law of constancy, and the law of abstraction. The first refers to the automatic propensity of the visual system when perceiving an object or a surface to be tuned to properties that are indicative of constancies in shape, size, color, and movement. The second refers to "the process by which the particular is subordinated to the general, so that what is represented is applicable to many particulars" (ibid., 52). Abstraction allows for the emergence of individual and collective experience when viewing a work of art: "individual" in relation to one's unique aesthetic experience when faced with a work of art, and "collective" in the emergent consensus about properties of the artwork across the aesthetic experience of many persons.

While the brain basis underlying the perception and appraisal of art has potential value in allowing us to understand why an artifact produced by an artist affects us in multitudinous ways, it is not directly informative in telling us *how* the artist was led to create and complete the piece. Different facets of imagination are at play here given that "the ability to appreciate things that are expressive or revelatory of the meaning of human life" is not the same as "the ability to create works of art that express something deep about the meaning of life" and, by the same token, "the sensuous component in the appreciation of works of art or objects of natural beauty" is distinct from "the ability to create works of art that encourage such sensuous appreciation" (Stevenson, 2003, 238). Indeed, the brain basis of creative forms of imagination is quite distinct from that of aesthetic appraisal (Abraham, 2016).

The factor of personal preference has received less attention in the context of creativity but is no less pertinent. For instance, when shown a set of portraits made by five different groups of artists (eminent, average-regular, average deviant, prisoners, serial killers), the paintings of the average deviant group were judged to be higher in creativity, warmth, and likeability than all other groups, even the eminent artists, suggesting complex effects of artistic background and participant background on aesthetic judgment (White, Kaufman, & Riggs, 2014). Some forms of art like abstract expressionism, which is non-representational and where meaning is conveyed through the use of color, brush strokes, and composition, are sometimes regarded as requiring little skill. However, evidence suggests that we can distinguish between intentionally produced abstract art and incidentally generated abstract art (by young children and animals; see Snapper, Oranç, Hawley-Dolan, Nissel, & Winner, 2015), and computer algorithms can predict the perceived intentionality behind real abstract paintings (Shamir, Nissel, & Winner, 2016).

Expertise also plays a role here as there are key differences between art history experts' and laypersons' aesthetic judgments and emotional ratings of paintings such that only in non-experts do these estimations progressively decrease (i.e., indicating less "good art" and less "positive emotion evoked") in relation to the progressive increase in image ambiguity from representational art to abstract art (Pihko et al., 2011). Art experts also estimate abstract and complex art to be more interesting and find it easier to understand (Silvia, 2006). So phenomenological experience in relation to abstraction is perceived differently as a function of artistic expertise. This also ties in well with neuroscientific evidence that the brain activity of artists compared to non-artists shows greater attentional engagement and early visual processing for all types of art (representational, abstract, indeterminate twentieth century art), with the strongest activity reflected when processing abstract art (Else, Ellis, & Orme, 2015). The influence of such factors on creative capacity invites further exploration because, as we have seen in detail in this chapter, how we perceive and appraise the world fundamentally affects how we create art.

Chapter Summary

- Differences in visual perceptual processing are held to underlie the genesis of visual artistic abilities.
- Artistic expertise is related to both quantitative and qualitative differences in visuospatial abilities and hand–eye coordination.
- Visuomotor models have been proposed to explain enhanced visual perception as a function of artistic proficiency.
- Contextual factors strongly modulate the dynamics of the neural response during drawing in terms of perceptual versus memory-based processing.
- An enhanced capacity for visual imagery and a propensity for cross-modal interactions in synesthetic perception are also candidate factors.

- The neural correlates of visual artistic creativity have been examined using a wide range of paradigms evaluating divergent thinking, imagery, and drawing.
- Critical insights have emerged from case studies of subjects with brain disorders, who feature sustained visual artistic capacities despite damage and sometimes even the sudden emergence of such capacities following neurological insult.

Review Questions

1. Can the perceptual skills of artists be best explained in terms of top-down or bottom-up information processing biases?
2. In what way are eye and hand movements during drawing different in artists compared to novices?
3. Is imagery the cornerstone of visual artistic creativity?
4. What is the big picture concerning the brain correlates of drawing compared to those underlying visual artistic creativity?
5. Under what conditions is the disordered brain more creative than the healthy brain?

Further Reading

- Finke, R. A. (1990). Creative imagery: Discoveries and inventions in visualization. Hillsdale, NJ: Lawrence Erlbaum.
- Schlegel, A., Alexander, P., Fogelson, S. V., Li, X., Lu, Z., Kohler, P. J., Riley, E., Tse, P. U., & Meng, M. (2015). The artist emerges: Visual art learning alters neural structure and function. *NeuroImage, 105*, 440–451.
- Rose, F. C. (Ed.). (2006). *The neurobiology of painting.* Amsterdam: Elsevier.
- Tchalenko, J. (2009). Segmentation and accuracy in copying and drawing: Experts and beginners. *Vision Research, 49*(8), 791–800.
- Trojano, L., Grossi, D., & Flash, T. (2009). Cognitive neuroscience of drawing: Contributions of neuropsychological, experimental and neurofunctional studies. *Cortex, 45*(3), 269–277.

CHAPTER ELEVEN

Kinesthetic Creativity

"I have spent many, many hours, countless hours, on the court working for my one moment in time, not knowing when it would come."

(Serena Williams)

Learning Objectives

- Determining the creative elements in body movement
- Identifying the outcomes of the association between perception and action
- Grasping the concept of flow and its relevance to kinesthetic creativity
- Recognizing the information processing mechanisms underlying dance
- Understanding the brain correlates of dance performance and observation
- Evaluating the factors of relevance for creativity in sports

11.1 Creativity in Body Movement: Is This a Real Thing?

Young gazelles occasionally demonstrate a curious and beautiful behavior pattern while being pursued by predators. When chased in a herd, a gazelle suddenly leaps gracefully into the air with all four limbs simultaneously off the ground, and this display typically also features its back arched and its head pointing toward the ground. The limbs are maintained in this taut position in the air for a fraction of a second before they touch the ground again and the gazelle continues to dash on the escape path. This "stotting" behavior is a costly one to engage in given that it adds further risk to survival in an exceedingly dangerous context. However, this seemingly "look what I can do!" display apparently signals to the predators that the stotting gazelle will be difficult to catch given its peak level of fitness (FitzGibbon & Fanshawe, 1988). Bodily movement in the service of expression and information transmission is seen in insects as well. Honeybees have a symbolic dance language that aids them in collaboration during foraging. The elaborate patterns of the honeybee waggle dance are informative in that they indicate the distance to and direction of food sources to their collective (Dyer, 2002).

Displays of physical prowess are greatly admired in our own species and we have developed a multitude of distinct physical activities and sports through which the limits of different aspects of human physicality can be pushed and celebrated. Our attentional system cannot but be captivated by complex movement-based behavior displays that are indicative of peak physical fitness and mastery. It has been proposed that proprioception, which is the sense we have of the position and movements of our own body and its parts through joints, muscles and so on, also serves as an aesthetic sense in the same manner as do vision and hearing (Montero, 2006). The proprioceptive sense allows us to experience aesthetic properties like beauty and grace through our own movement. This feature of the human body and mind is exapted for use during the aesthetic response to perceiving movements in others through the experience of kinesthetic empathy, sympathy, and contagion (Montero, 2006; Reason & Reynolds, 2010).

The most common means through which human beings engage in feats of body-based expression and problem solving in the physical world are dance and sports. Dance is a ubiquitous art form found in every known human culture and one that is inseparable from music (see Chapter 8) (Fitch, 2016; Laland, Wilkins, & Clayton, 2016). There are thousands of dance forms using varied formats across cultures and new forms are generated at an astounding pace. The intense physicality involved in many dance forms has even led to the proposal that dancers be considered "performing athletes" (Koutedakis & Jamurtas, 2004). In his influential theory of multiple intelligences, Howard Gardner made a case for *bodily-kinesthetic intelligence*, the characteristics of which include,

the ability to use one's body in highly differentiated and skilled ways, for expressive as well as goal-directed purposes … the capacity to work skillfully with objects, both those that involve the fine motor movements of one's fingers and hands and those that exploit gross motor movements of the body … I treat these two capacities – control of one's bodily motions and capacity to handle objects skillfully – as the cores of bodily intelligence … skill in the use of the body for functional or expressive purposes tends to go hand in hand with skill in the manipulation of objects. (1983, 206)

Some, however, question whether knowledge and control of one's body and the ability to skillfully manipulate objects necessarily belong in the same constellation of skills, particularly when considering the context of dance (Blumenfeld-Jones, 2009).

As the subject of this book is creativity, a question that arises in this context is whether sufficient grounds exist to consider movement-based or kinesthetic forms of creativity a distinct category. We need to be cognizant of the fact that, following the definition of creativity (Chapter 1), the components of "originality" and "relevance" must be present for a performance to be viewed as creative. This means that the mere act of physical performance in dance or sports in and of itself is not necessarily creative. This is also true of musical performance (Chapter 8). Having said that, the simple answer to the question at the start of this paragraph is "yes," and that is because these activities afford real forms of creativity that are distinct from other instantiations. For instance, unlike verbal or visuospatial forms of creativity, the kinesthetic forms of dance and sports involve sensations of whole body movement or "kinesthesia," which refers to the integration of information from the vestibular system (the sensory experience of balance and spatial orientation) and the proprioceptive system (the sensory experience from forces within the body – muscles, tendons, joints). Some accounts of kinesthesia include not only proprioception but also exteroception (the sensory experience – visual, auditory, tactile – from stimuli outside the body), making kinesthesia integral to multisensory and active perception (Reason & Reynolds, 2010).

The immense constraints imposed by the physical limitations of the body itself means that bona fide instantiations of creativity in performance may be few and far between. But the impact of those creative instants is momentous. In sports, it can make the difference between winning and losing a game, breaking records, and even achieving eminence. We see these moments in every sport. They are the ones we crave, enjoy, and remember best as spectators. In any sport, the best players are those who can be relied on to make optimal use of unpredicted opportunities or indeed create opportunities that lead to a successful shot. The word "creativity," in fact, features very often in the context of sports. Coaches routinely lament the lack of creativity in their teams upon failure and, conversely, praise the creativity of their players in times of success. So creativity in sports and other kinesthetic activities refers to the same set of operations (originality/novelty meets relevance/fit) as in the fine arts and sciences given that it involves discovering or creating novel actions or opportunities to optimal effect.

This chapter will explore factors that are relevant to kinesthetic forms of creativity. The focus will largely be limited to dance and sports, as other potentially relevant forms such as drama (Kemp, 2012) and hunting (Walls & Malafouris, 2016), are less well studied from neuroscientific and psychological perspectives.

11.2 Concepts Relevant to Psychology and Neuroscience

The single most influential idea in relation to the mechanisms under-lying kinesthetic performance is that one's own kinesthetic experience informs one's rich implicit knowledge of kinematics, and our kinematic repertoire directly informs our understanding of the kinematics and movement-based intentions of another person. This is most commonly referred to as the embodied cognition perspective but several other terms are commonly used in relation to this idea too, including common coding, the mirror neuron system, action simulation, and joint action. Each of these different concepts and the relations between them are teased apart briefly in the sections that follow. It must be noted, though, that these views are not unanimously accepted as explanations for the complex phenomena that they aim to cover (Davies, 2011). However, given that alternative theoretical frameworks receive substantially less focus (e.g., the behavioral dynamics perspective; Schmidt, Fitzpatrick, Caron, & Mergeche, 2011), and the bulk of the empirical work has been guided by the dominant framework of embodied cognition, the focus in the current chapter will necessarily be mostly limited to this perspective.

11.2.1 Common Coding, Mirror Neurons, and Embodied Cognition

Action–effect bindings that are derived from the functional rela-tionship between perception and action lie at the foundation of the common coding principle because actions, which are events caused by body movement, are represented in terms of their perceptual effects or consequences (Hommel, Müsseler, Aschersleben, & Prinz, 2001; Prinz, 1997). The discovery of mirror neurons in macaque monkeys in regions homologous to premotor and inferior parietal regions of the human brain was widely taken to be evidence of common codes given that their func-tional specialty lay in the fact that they fired not only when executing an action but also when observing someone else performing the same action (Gallese, Fadiga, Fogassi, & Rizzolatti, 1996). Following on from this, the function of the mirror system in humans was held not only to mediate goal-directed action but also to be the basis of action understanding (Rizzolatti, Cattaneo, Fabbri-Destro, & Rozzi, 2014), a claim which has been strongly challenged (Dinstein, Thomas, Behrmann, & Heeger, 2008; Hickok, 2009).

The rationale of the common coding and mirror neuron hypotheses has been extended to even more complex forms of psychological function in a social context, such as action simulation, action prediction, and joint action (Sebanz & Knoblich, 2009). Studies indicated not only that the execution of action and observation of actions leads to activity in the mirror neuron system, but also that merely imagining the action activates the same network of brain regions (Filimon, Nelson, Hagler, & Sereno, 2007). This fed the idea that our perception of the world is embodied in that it is tied in a congruent manner to the form of our own bodily experience (Wilson, 2002). So, for instance, there is evidence that sports experience influences language processing. Having expert ice-hockey players passively listen to sentences that described either hockey actions or everyday actions and examining their brain activity while they were doing so revealed activations in parts of the motor system when hearing the hockey sentences but not everyday actions. So there is an integration of input from brain areas involved in action selection and language comprehension (Beilock, Lyons, Mattarella-Micke, Nusbaum, & Small, 2008).

11.2.2 Joint Improvisation

Research on joint action proved to be very useful as it redirected the focus of research on goal-directed actions to consider the social context (Sebanz, Bekkering, & Knoblich, 2006). However, very few contexts in our world require two people to perform the same or complimentary goal-directed actions in unison. Most contexts of joint action involve two or more people performing actions that are different from one another in service of a common goal. In the context of team-based sports, social factors become exceedingly complex as they involve reading the actions and intentions of all players involved in each moment, and optimal interpersonal synchrony with one's own team to engage in movements that will be conducive to the team's goal of winning, in direct opposition to the goals and intentions of the opposing team.

Newer developments in this field have moved closer to evaluating joint action in more complex contexts. One example of the same is joint improvisation. The paradigm used to study this is a mirror task whereby two people face each other and are asked to move handles along parallel tracks. While for joint improvisation participants are instructed to "imitate each other, create synchronized and interesting motions, and enjoy playing together," the instructions can be modified to induce low to high levels of spontaneity in the improvised movement (Noy, Dekel, & Alon, 2011, 2015). The participants either involuntarily determine the directionality of their own dynamic interactions when improvising or are instructed to systematically switch leader and follower roles over the course of an experiment. The involuntary or spontaneous condition is associated with superior performance in producing synchronized motion. In a study examining associations between kinematic, physiological, and subjective indices of performance, achieving a sense of interpersonal synchrony, social connectedness, or "togetherness" while playing a joint improvisation game was associated with biomarkers such as higher cardiovascular activity in both players, increased positive correlations between the heart rates of the players, and high motion intensity (Noy, Levit-Binun, & Golland, 2015). Peak moments like these in joint improvisation are considered to reflect "group flow"' (Sawyer, 2003).

11.2.3 Flow: The Cornerstone of Kinesthetic Creativity?

The experience of flow is counterintuitive in some ways. It occurs when one's attention is fully absorbed in any activity in which one's skills are perfectly matched with the demands of the task at hand (Csikszentmihalyi, 1997, 2008). The phenomenological state that accompanies a flow experience includes a sense of expansiveness and distorted time perception, where fatigue and other negative emotions are not experienced in the effort exerted to maintain this optimal level of performance.

Nine components of flow have been identified across a range of activities (e.g., dance, sports, chess playing, arts, work): (a) *challenge–skill balance*, where individual skill is commensurate with the challenge at hand; (b) *action and awareness* merging to the point that one's actions feel spontaneous and virtually automatic; (c) *clear goals* in what one is doing; (d) *unambiguous feedback* about one's actions that is direct and immediate; (e) *concentration on the task at hand* and an intense focus on the present moment; (f) *sense of control* over the situation; (g) *loss of self-consciousness*; (h) *transformation of time* in one's perception of it; and (i) *autotelic experience* where engaging in the activity is intrinsically rewarding. The first three of these components are considered proximal conditions to the flow experience, with the remaining six components being part of the flow state itself, and this has been confirmed in investigations of self-reported flow experience in physical activity (Kawabata & Mallett, 2011).

Physical activities involving movements of the body, such as sports, exercise, and dance, are the contexts in which flow experience is most widely investigated and that is because flow experiences are more readily possible in these contexts (Jackson & Eklund, 2002). After all, optimal performances in such physical activities involve precision in timing, rhythm and synchrony in movements across the whole body, and the proximal conditions in these situations can be readily ascertained. Indeed, some research suggests that activities involving whole body movements are more conducive than most to flow experiences. For instance, on self-report measures both dancers and athletes report higher levels of dispositional flow compared to opera singers (Thomson & Jaque, 2016). Flow experience is also associated with superior actual performance. A study of almost 400 talented Dutch soccer players, in which the experience of flow during performance was reported following the match, found that the team-level experience of flow was greater during matches that resulted in a win or a draw compared to a loss. This constitutes evidence of a positive association between better sports performance and flow (Bakker, Oerlemans, Demerouti, Slot, & Ali, 2011). Athletes and performing artists recognize flow experiences as conducive to their performance and actively work "to get into the zone." The experience of being in the zone is, in fact, intertwined with the perception of performing well on a task (Kennedy, Miele, & Metcalfe, 2014). Christopher Bergland, a world-class endurance triathlete and ultrarunner who became famous for running almost 154 miles on a treadmill in 24 hours, came up with a related concept to flow, which he named "superfluidity." To him, superfluidity "is a state of performing with zero friction, zero viscosity, and superconductivity – it is a state of absolute harmony and endless energy" (Bergland, 2011).

With regard to the brain basis of the flow experience, the most dominant idea to date is that of "transient hypofrontality" (Dietrich, 2004a) (see Section 5.2.2). In this framework, the state of flow arises when the frontal lobes of the brain, which are the key hub of the explicit system of the brain that orchestrate cognitive control, flexible problem solving, analytical and meta-conscious operations, are temporarily suppressed. The explicit system "being offline" allows for the experiential and implicit system of the brain, which is facilitated by subcortical brain structures like the basal ganglia, to take over. The operations that evolved from the learning and implementation of highly practiced sensorimotor skills take over information processing in this context, and these are characterized by speed, efficiency, and automaticity as they have no interference from the explicit system. While the limitations of neuroscientific techniques make it difficult to gather empirical evidence to test this theory, there is some indirect support for it (see Box 11.3).

11.3 Dance

Multimodal experience across motor, proprioceptive, vestibular, auditory, and visual domains lies at the heart of this form of the performing arts. The core elements with reference to movements in a dance from the perspective of the dancer is that they reflect purposeful, intentionally rhythmical, and "culturally patterned sequences of nonverbal body movements" that have aesthetic value (as determined by appropriate reference groups) and are not "ordinary motor activities" (Hanna et al., 1979, 316) (Figure 11.1). All dance forms involve large-scale and small-scale bodily movements, which means gross and fine motor control is essential in order to coordinate the action of independent sets of muscles in the body. The auditory system also plays a key role through the perception of rhythm via beats and metrical structure as they temporally unfold in music (see Section 8.2.1).

In fact, interactions between auditory and motor systems have been proposed as musical meters that tend to correspond to generic body movement patterns. For instance, the meter for samba and reggae dance styles is 4/4, the same as that of simple bipedal walking (right – up – left – up) where 1 and 3 are downbeats where the foot touches the ground and 2 and 4 are upbeats where the foot is raised to the highest point (Fitch, 2016). The visual system is also vital as dancers rely on this capacity to perceive the dance movements of others in order to directly imitate the motor patterns to perfectly render the necessary postures. Visual information is essential in honing performance and it begins with observing the new steps of a choreography with an instructor and continues with self-observation through mirrors or videos (Laland et al., 2016). Dance therefore involves the multimodal integration of information from sensory and motor systems (Whitehead, 2010). It has in fact been described as an "integrated, crossmodal, projective kinesthetic perceptual capacity that engages embodied motoric, skeletomuscular, somatosensory, visual, and auditory processes" (Carroll & Seeley, 2013, 178).

Several other factors outside the individual need to be taken into consideration as dance often takes place in a collective context, such as during religious rituals and other cultural group practices. So dance often involves coordination between two or more individuals. Indeed, our information processing systems seem to have been developed to this end. Each individual's inherent ability, from birth onwards, to detect rhythm in isochronous pulses or evenly paced beats allows us to "entrain" or synchronize our movements with the rhythm because of the predictability of the temporal pattern. Such conditions allow for collective synchrony

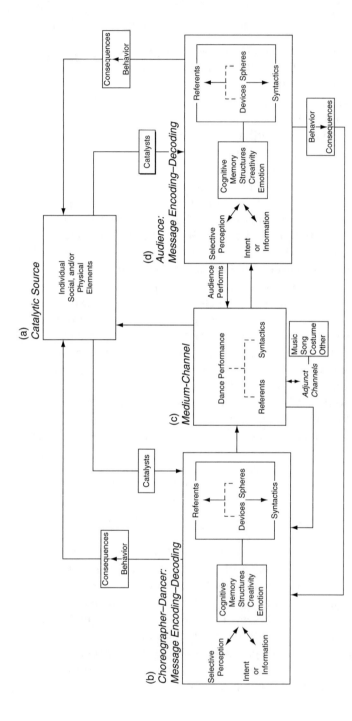

Figure 11.1 A processual model of dance semiotics

A dynamic communication model from the anthropology of dance. Republished with permission of The University of Chicago Press, from Movements toward understanding humans through the anthropological study of dance [and comments and reply], Hanna JL, Abrahams RD, Crumrine NR, Dirks R, Von Gizycki R, Heyer P, Shapiro A, Ikegami Y, Kaeppler AL, Kealiinohomoku JW, Kubik G, Lange R, Royce AP, Sweet JD & Wild SA, *Current Anthropology*, 20(2), 313–339, © 1979; permission conveyed through Copyright Clearance Center, Inc.

to emerge between people and enables rhythmic singing and dancing (Merker, Madison, & Eckerdal, 2009).

11.3.1 Information Processing in Dance

Central to expertise in dance are "kinesis" (motion) and "aesthesis" (awareness of sensation) in the form of a tacit understanding of one's own movement or "personal knowing" of one's own motion in a manner that is integrative (Blumenfeld-Jones, 2009). The term "integrative" here means that the dancer is aware of their whole body at once when making any motion. In addition, because the expressive intentions are embedded in the motion and the dancer experiences these intentions simultaneously with the motion, the dancer fully inhabits the performative moment. This astute awareness and knowledge of one's body and its motion or "personal knowing" is implicit for the dancer, and is not overtly visible to others. It is also not a capacity that lends itself to verbalization, as the dancer often cannot describe it with words. Dancers also inherently understand how to precisely direct attention in order to fulfill a particular intent both in spectacle and non-spectacle moments. So, in addition to the "internal knowing of one's motion," other facets of bodily-kinesthetic intelligence in dance include "facility at reproducing motion, ability to display one's attention linked to intention, a knowing precision of motion, and the ability to perform particularly difficult motion with relative ease" (ibid., 66).

As dancing most often takes place in a collective context, any theory of dance performance needs to be able to account for those influences as well. Indeed, some accounts argue for kinesthetic brainstorming or "bodystorming" during collaborative dance improvisation where cognitive events are distributed across dancers (Stevens & Leach, 2015). Similar proposals have been made in the context of theater improvisation (Sawyer & DeZutter, 2009). Extending the Geneplore model (see Section 3.3.2) to the context of dance performance sees the processes in dance creation play out over a lengthy period of time. The generation of preinventive structures follows through from information provided by the choreographer. These structures are explored and interpreted by the dancer, and these are either focused or expanded in line with the choreographer's intention. The movement sequences that form the dance are put together and then rehearsed until the point of the performance (Stevens, Malloch, McKechnie, & Steven, 2003) (Figure 11.2).

The intent to communicate using body language in dance was central to a prescient early systemic model of dance performance (Figure 11.1). The "communication model" highlighted the interaction between determinant factors that were individual (human endowment), sociocultural, and ecological, in addition to factors about the dance itself and elements that are assigned to it (Hanna et al., 1979). Dance commences with a catalyst (A) that determines "who dances, why, where, and how" as a function of "cultural values, society, polity, economy, and religion" (319). The dancer (B) makes intentional movements to communicate information based on the selective perception of the situation via a specific channel or communication medium (C). To communicate, the core dance elements of body movement, space, rhythm, and dynamics are employed via a range of "devices" (e.g., metaphor, icon, stylization) operating in one or more "spheres" (e.g., the pattern of the whole performance). Appropriate contexts for the audience (D) are also generated by the catalytic information, and members use their own selective perception and intentional systems to follow and evaluate the performance. Depending on the context, the interactions between audience and performers may take place at the level of individuals or groups, and the audience may have a recognized, an unrecognized, or no effect on the performance. Interactions and feedback systems are in place at every level within this model. This communication model can also be construed as a "dance semiotics" model as it is clearly influenced by language theory. It highlights how body language and communication is facilitated by syntactics (how signs may be combined), semantics (relation of signs to what they mean), and pragmatics (relation of signs to interpreters, both performers and audience) (Hanna et al., 1979).

There is, in fact, evidence to suggest that systemic views are necessary to attain a representative understanding of dance performance. For instance, Daprati, Iosa, and Haggard (2009), in a study that used photographs and video material to track changes in the body posture of dancers in a leading ballet company over a 60-year period, found systematic posture differences over time in the form of increasingly vertical positions (e.g., angle of leg elevation in the *arabesque penchée*). Moreover, the aesthetic choices of present-day observers indicated a preference for the more vertical later postures over the less vertical earlier postures. Such findings evidence the dynamic interactions between the artistic tradition, the environmental context of the time, and the individual dancer's artistry and skillset.

11.3.2 Neural Processing in Dance

To date, there have been no brain-based investigations that specifically look at creativity in dance, not in terms of choreography, observation, or performance (for an fMRI study of a single subject, see May et al., 2011). Indeed, it would be difficult to devise a workable experimental paradigm for performance given the limitations of neuroscientific techniques that prevent extensive movement or testing over lengthy periods of time (see Chapter 7). And this is why the neural basis of dance is largely based on brain activity in relation to observations of dance performance (Karpati, Giacosa, Foster, Penhune, & Hyde, 2015). Given this state of affairs, though, there is a sizeable gap in the literature given that the brain correlates of observation (and recognition) of creativity in dance performance have also not been studied, although it is certainly possible to systematically investigate the same.

One study examined dance imagery by contrasting the brain activity patterns of professional and novice dancers who imagined undertaking a novel dance improvisation (high creative demand dance condition), a waltz (low creative demand dance condition), and the alternate uses task (creative non-dance condition) (Fink, Graif, & Neubauer, 2009). The researchers found that professional dancers exhibited more right hemisphere alpha synchronization than the novice dancers during the dance improvisation imagination condition; however, there were no differences between the groups in terms of brain activity related to imagining the waltz performance. Interestingly, the highest level of alpha synchronization over parietal regions was seen in professional dancers during the alternate uses task, a non-dance creativity measure, on which they also demonstrated higher ideational fluency. This is indicative of evidence in favor of improved domain-general creativity skills as a function of dance expertise.

A few studies have examined the brain correlates of actual dance performance. The first neuroimaging study to do so examined bipedal dance movements of amateur dancers while they underwent PET (Brown, Martinez, & Parsons, 2006). A comparison of the brain activity generated during the *metric condition*, where they made patterned leg movements to a tango musical beat, relative to both a *motor condition*, where they made similar but self-paced movements, and a *listening condition*, where they passively listened to music, revealed that synchrony of leg movement to an auditory rhythm was accompanied by activations in the anterior cerebellar vermis. This suggests a specific role for this brain area in entrainment of movement to an external timing stimulus. Comparisons were also made of brain engagement during the metric condition compared to a non-metric condition, where the dancers made patterned leg movements to highly unpredictable and irregular rhythms. Increased activity in the basal ganglia was seen in the former context of predictable and regular movement, fitting with the role of this region in rhythm perception, whereas the thalamus was involved in the latter context of unpredictable and irregular patterns, and this fits with the role of this region in orchestrating motor control operations (Brown et al., 2006).

Another study that examined the brain basis of dance performance employed an innovative EEG and motion capture paradigm, albeit with very few participants, to examine expressive body movement in dancers (Cruz-Garza, Hernandez, Nepaul, Bradley, & Contreras-Vidal, 2014). The dancers were experts in analysis and performance of Laban movement analysis (Box 11.1) and, alongside their brain activity recordings, their movement kinematics were captured using wireless magnetic, angular rate and gravity (MARG) sensors. They performed three action types. The "neutral" condition involved making functional movements with no specific expressive qualities, the "think" condition also involved making non-expressive functional movements but also involved the imagination of a specific movement quality that the dancers were instructed to think about, and the "do" condition involved enacting the previously imagined expressive movement from the "think" condition. Machine learning algorithms were used to classify the thought and performed expressions. The brain regions that were implicated in the same included core regions of the action observation network, such as the premotor, motor, and dorsal parietal areas (Cruz-Garza et al., 2014).

Alternative systems, like the Observational System of Motor Skills (OSMOS), have been used when investigating collaborative dance forms like *contact improvisation*, which involves physical contact, improvisation, and motor creativity between multiple dance improvisers (Torrents, Castañer, Dinošová, & Anguera, 2010).

The vast majority of neuroscientific studies investigating the neural basis of dance are observation-based. The most consistent finding across studies is the increased involvement of the action observation and action simulation brain networks during dance performance, which are heightened as a function of expertise. A comparison of the brain activity of two groups of dancers, ballet and capoeira, and an untrained group when watching video clips of ballet and capoeira actions showed an expertise-specific effect (Calvo-Merino, Glaser, Grèzes, Passingham, & Haggard, 2005). Expert dancers showed stronger engagement of the action observation brain network (premotor cortex, intraparietal sulcus, posterior superior temporal sulcus) when watching clips of their own dance style compared to the style in which they had no training.

Box 11.1 Assessing Creativity in Movement

Extending the work of Rudolph Laban, choreographer and movement theorist, who proposed a system of "effort actions" to characterize how actions are used to expressive ends in a variety of contexts, David Petersen proposed kinematic principles for the structured observation of creative movement. Efforts are "mental precursors to action" and can be categorized into four types: space, time, weight, and flow (Petersen, 2008). These can be used to appraise expressive tendencies and stylistic differences between individuals:

- *Space effort and kinematics*: Identifying elements of space in presentation through features of imaginary lines as traced by the limbs across personal space (movement traces, reach spaces, shapes in space).
- *Time effort and kinematics*: Assessing the elements of time in presentation via changes in position across a movement trace (duration, tempo, rhythm).
- *Weight effort and kinematics*: Estimating the elements of weight or force in presentation through the grounded elements of time and space (tempo changes, muscle tone, interaction with gravity).
- *Flow effort and kinematics*: As indicated by smoothness/abruptness perceived in the movement or "jerk," which is determined through repeated derivation of position information via space (continuity, phrasing, control).

This was taken as evidence that dancers use their own motor repertoire when understanding the actions of others by motor simulation. Further confirmation of the same came from another comparison of dance observations made by male and female ballet dancers who were deeply familiar with ballet moves of both genders from experience, but possessed only a deep sensorimotor repertoire of their own gender-specific ballet moves. Enhanced activity of the action observation network (premotor cortex, intraparietal sulcus, cerebellum) was found when viewing video clips of dance moves made by dancers of their own gender.

A longitudinal study of expert dancers learning new dance sequences for 5 hours a day over the course of 5 weeks were evaluated in terms of behavioral and brain function at the end of each week (Cross, Hamilton, & Grafton, 2006). The action simulation brain circuit, which is engaged when imagining a movement sequence without overt movement, includes the premotor cortex, inferior parietal lobule, superior temporal sulcus, primary motor cortex, and supplementary motor area. These overlap partially with the aforementioned action observation network, with the ventral aspects of the premotor cortex being particularly implicated in action simulation. Not only did dancers' observation and simulation of dance moves lead to higher activity in both the action simulation and action observation brain networks for learned dance sequences compared to unlearned dance sequences, but their ratings of their own ability to perform the new dance sequences modulated activity in the ventral premotor cortex and the inferior parietal lobule. Similar training-related brain activity changes were also found in naïve participants with no formal training in dance or experience in playing dance video games (Cross, Kraemer, Hamilton, Kelley, & Grafton, 2009). However, somewhat counterintuitively, structural neuroimaging studies show reduced gray matter volume in the premotor cortex among professional ballet dancers compared to nondancers (Hänggi, Koeneke, Bezzola, & Jäncke, 2010). Such structural neuroimaging findings are difficult to integrate with those of functional neuroimaging.

In summary, the neuroscientific literature on dance perception and performance leans very heavily on embodied cognition-based explanations, although several concerns have been raised about the extent to which the increasingly elaborate functions extended to this framework are empirically grounded. Dancers demonstrate excellent motor control with reference to posture, balance and stabilization; their ability to synchronize is influenced by their level of motor experience; they show an enhanced capacity for sequence learning and sequence memory; they make strategic use of visuomotor imagery; and their perception of dance is modulated by their action repertoire (Bläsing et al., 2012). However, creativity in dance remains an unstudied topic from an empirical standpoint (but see Box 11.2).

Box 11.2 Neurofeedback and Biofeedback in the Performing Arts

As in the case of music performance (Box 8.2), the effects of neurofeedback and biofeedback during performance have been investigated in dance and acting to evaluate whether they lead to improvements in performance (Gruzelier, 2014).

- The objective in alpha/theta (A/T) training is to increase the EEG alpha/theta wave ratio to the level typical of a hypnagogic state that is held to abet creativity given that it is conducive to lucid, dreamlike, and unusual associative thought. The aim in heart rate variability (HRV) training is to increase HRV as it is related to increased flexibility of emotional/affective regulation. Sensory-motor rhythm (SMR) training involves elevating SMR with the objective of attaining relaxation as well as efficiency in sustained attention.
- A comparison of A/T and HRV training compared to no training of competitive ballroom dancers and Latin dancers revealed that both forms of feedback training improved overall execution compared to receiving no training. Timing improvements were associated with A/T neurofeedback training and technique improvements were associated with HRV biofeedback training (Raymond, Sajid, Parkinson, & Gruzelier, 2005). However, these findings were not replicated in another study on contemporary dance conservatoire students, although HRV training led to reductions in anxiety. Reduced anxiety was in turn associated with improvements in artistry and technique (Gruzelier, Thompson, Redding, Brandt, & Steffert, 2014).
- One study in relation to drama found that SMR neurofeedback training improved acting performance overall as well as creative aspects such as imaginative expression and characterization (Gruzelier, Inoue, Smart, Steed, & Steffert, 2010).

11.3.3 Creativity in Dance: What about Theoretical Viewpoints?

One theoretical idea takes an "autopoetic" view of creativity in dance where the dynamics are those of physical systems like cells, which display autopoesis in that they have the capacity to maintain and reproduce themselves (Bishop & al-Rifaie, 2017). An autopoietic dancer is situated in a "dance-field," which is comprised of "meaning-distinctions" that emanate from their field of movement across sensory spaces (sight, sound, touch) and personal memories via choreographic interactions with the environment. Creative processes in dance commence upon attending to specific meaning-distinctions and the dancer chooses to interpret elements of these over successive instances. These reinterpretations give rise to new meanings that become embedded in the ever-evolving dance-field, and which in turn can themselves be subject to novel reinterpretations (Figure 11.2). The result of these dynamics is that "the autopoietic dancer can never be fully satisfied with her work, but continually re-engages a

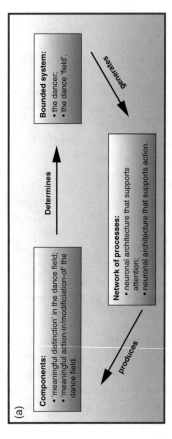
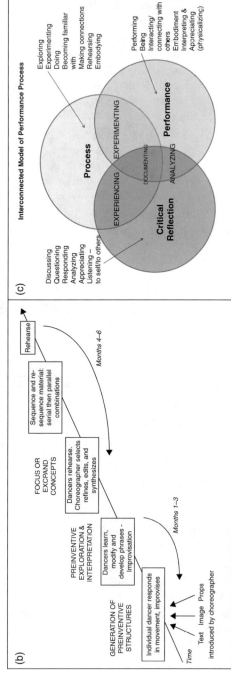

Figure 11.2 Models of creativity in dance performance

(a) Autopoiesis in dance and creativity whereby individuals interacting within a dance-field generate and transform meaning. Reprinted by permission of the publisher (Taylor & Francis Ltd) from Bishop JM & al-Rifaie MM. (2017). Autopoiesis, creativity and dance. *Connection Science*, 29(1), 21–35. **(b)** The major components of the Geneplore model (see Figure 3.4) extended to dance performance. Reprinted with permission of the John Benjamins Publishing Company (www.benjamins.com/catalog/pc) from Stevens C, Malloch S, McKechnie S & Steven N (2003). Choreographic cognition: The time-course and phenomenology of creating a dance. *Pragmatics & Cognition, 11*(2), 297–326. **(c)** The interconnected model of performance which highlights the interactive, collaborative and integrated nature of the creative process. Reprinted by permission of the publisher (Taylor & Francis Ltd) from Brooks P. (2014). Performers, creators and audience: Co-participants in an interconnected model of performance and creative process. *Research in Dance Education, 15*(2), 120–137.

complex process of 'attention' (on her current movement context) and 'reconstitution' (of her body), as she creatively reflects and enacts her world" (Bishop & al-Rifaie, 2017, 23). As this bounded conceptualization of creativity in dance has been proposed to explain generativity in the individual, how it can be extended to the context of group dance is unclear. There is evidence from the perspective of an individual dancer that speaks for the evolving nature of the "dance-field" as one's direct sensorimotor experience with a novel dance routine reshapes one's aesthetic experiences. This is indirectly indicated by increased enjoyment when viewing actions following direct sensorimotor experience of the same when compared to mere exposure to those actions through sensory channels only (Kirsch, Urgesi, & Cross, 2016).

Another systemic model that emphasizes the intertwined relations between process and performance, but is readily applicable to the context of group dance, is the interconnected model of performance and creative process (Brooks, 2014). Performance of a dance is seen as comprising three phases: proto performance (training and rehearsal of the choreography), the performance itself, and the aftermath (critical responses and memories). Through these stages, the performance and creative process involves creators, performers, and the audience within the parallel and intersecting components of process (e.g., experimenting and familiarizing), performance (e.g., embodying, interpreting, and appreciating), and critical reflection (e.g., questioning and analyzing self and others) (Figure 11.2).

11.4 Sports

Explaining the sporting brain has been highlighted as potentially one of the greatest challenges in neuroscience (Walsh, 2014) owing to the extreme demands placed on the brain in elite sports performance and the limitations of current neuroscientific techniques (see Chapter 7) in terms of delivering direct results in relation to the same. So the challenge in being able to empirically assess creativity within the context of exceptional sporting performance is even more immense.

There is extensive data pointing to the critical role of both nature (heritable factors) and nurture (environmental factors) in the development of athletic talent. Studies of Olympians have revealed 6 precursors and prerequisites of exceptional athletic talent: (a) appropriate body status and flexibility that fits the demands of the target sport, (b) high ability to learn novel technical and cognitive skills, (c) high improvement rate in performance, (d) exceptional attitude to training as characterized by discipline, initiative, and performing at the highest level of quality, (e) conducive personality traits such as intrinsic motivation, perseverance, and creativity, and (f) early acquisition of psychological skills that aid focus, emotional regulation, stability, and mental toughness The theory of 10,000 hours of practice being necessary for mastery and the 10-year rule for achieving excellence (Ericsson, Krampe, & Tesch-Römer, 1993) are applicable to highly coordinative aesthetic sports (e.g., gymnastics) but less so to team, combat, or endurance sports (Issurin, 2017).

Long-term motor training results in cortical reorganization that affects motor task performance. A meta-analysis of studies that have examined brain activity in relation to motor task performance (prediction and execution) in motor experts (athletes, musicians, and dancers) relative to novices revealed higher engagement of the inferior parietal lobule, whereas motor observation tasks led to stronger engagement of the premotor cortex (Yang, 2015).

11.4.1 Neural and Information Processing in Sports

Expert proficiency in sports is associated with numerous information processing advantages across perceptual, cognitive, and motor domains of psychological function (see Box 11.3). There are also a growing number of investigations that seek to determine behavioral and neural differences as a function of expertise in sport. For instance, a comparison of high division and low division soccer players and a standardized norm group on executive functions of cognitive flexibility, response inhibition, and attentional control revealed superior executive functions in the high division group relative to the other two groups, and better performance in the low division group relative to the norm group (Vestberg, Gustafson, Maurex, Ingvar, & Petrovic, 2012). There was also evidence of a positive correlation such that better executive function skills were associated with superior performance in soccer games in the form of more goals and assists two years later. With regard to brain-based differences, a structural neuroimaging study of short-track speed skaters compared to a matched control group showed greater right cerebellar volume in the skaters, and this was attributed to reflect neural changes that come about from honing highly specialized whole body skills in balance and coordination (Park et al., 2012).

Box 11.3 The Effects of Physical Exercise on Creativity

- Engaging in simple forms of physical exercise induces significant changes in mental states, and is associated with several positive outcomes, including improved wellbeing and mood (Dietrich & McDaniel, 2004). Neuroscientific investigations have demonstrated that running, for instance, is associated with neurogenesis, neural plasticity, and memory enhancement (Schulkin, 2016).
- The evidence that such advantages extend to creativity is mixed. For example, increases in positive mood as well as ideational flexibility in divergent creative thinking were reported following a brief aerobic workout (Steinberg et al., 1997). However, factors like athletic expertise, intensity of exercise, and type of creativity measure also need to be taken into consideration. One study showed that non-athletes exhibit poorer convergent creativity under conditions of intense exercise compared to conditions of moderate exercise or rest, whereas the performance of athletes was not significantly differentiable across the three conditions. Moreover, divergent creative thinking was not affected by level of athleticism and ideational flexibility was superior under conditions of rest than under intense exercise across all participants (Colzato, Szapora, Pannekoek, & Hommel, 2013). The benefits of a simple physical activity like walking were found to vary depending on the creativity measure. It improved performance on originality in divergent creative thinking in 81% of participants but only in 23% of participants for convergent creative thinking (Oppezzo & Schwartz, 2014).
- Exercise is related to the experience of flow and a comparison of the mental states of marathon runners over a period of 6 hours of running showed elevated flow and physical relaxation, which peaked after 1 hour of running and then subsided over the next 5 hours. There was also a corresponding decrease in frontal beta EEG brain activity after 1 hour of running, and this pattern remained stable thereafter for the remaining 5 hours (Wollseiffen et al., 2016). As beta waves index focused attention and alertness, a reduction of the same following exercise was held to constitute supportive evidence of the transient hypofrontality hypothesis of flow (Dietrich, 2004a).

The topic that has received most attention in this regard is that the perceptual advantages among athletes and explanations for the same largely derive from the literature on the action observation brain network and the motor control network. A comparison of world class and non-expert badminton players, for instance, indicated that the experts showed superior attunement in detecting kinematic constraints of the movement pattern of play (Abernethy, Zawi, & Jackson, 2008). Similar findings were reported in a study on pro-volleyball players, expert watchers of the game, and novices evaluating their accuracy in predicting the fate of a volleyball from its initial trajectory. Players who had both visual and motor experience performed better than watchers and novices, and expert watchers who had visual experience outperformed novices (Urgesi, Savonitto, Fabbro, & Aglioti, 2012). Similar behavioral findings in relation to perceptual advantages as a function of context-specific visuomotor experience in extracting kinematic information in service of predicting movement-based outcomes were found in relation to soccer and basketball.

A comparison of expert kickers, goalkeepers, and novices in predicting kick direction based on initial body movements of a soccer playing model found superior performance in the former two groups, who boasted greater visuomotor expertise. But the goalkeepers and novices demonstrated a specific advantage relative to expert kickers as they were less fooled by incongruent actions, and this was taken to be indicative of the importance of visual experience over motor experience in this specific context (Tomeo, Cesari, Aglioti, & Urgesi, 2013). Direct evidence of the action observation brain network facilitating such perceptual abilities comes from a study using TMS, a technique that allows for the temporary disruption of neural processing by means of magnetic pulses to the brain delivered via the scalp. Disrupting activity in the superior temporal sulcus was found to impair performance in both expert and novice groups, and this was especially so in goalkeepers, who have greater visual expertise than the other groups. Disrupting activity in the dorsal premotor cortex, however, was found to impair performance in the outfield players and goalkeepers more than in novices. And this was linked to the extensive visuomotor experience that is common to both the expert groups (Makris & Urgesi, 2015).

Superior action anticipation in predicting the success of free throws was also found in elite basketball players, who boast exceedingly high levels of visuomotor expertise in the game, as compared to coaches and sports journalists, who have comparable levels of visual expertise as basketball players but not direct motor experience in the same, like novices. Stimulus information was processed differently by the groups too: elite players gleaned information from body kinematics whereas the other groups relied on ball trajectory information. While psychophysiological data showed increased corticospinal excitability via motor evoked potentials for all expert groups upon observation of the throws, only the players showed time-locked motor activation that discriminated erroneous from accurate throws. This evidence suggests that elite basketball players have enhanced motor resonance neural mechanisms that give them superior action prediction capacities, which come about through embodied mapping of actions (Aglioti, Cesari, Romani, & Urgesi, 2008).

However, findings that do not fit as well with the embodied narrative also exist. For instance, expertise-specific effects were not found in one neuroimaging study of hockey and non-hockey players and both groups showed comparable brain activity in inferior parietal regions when viewing brief video clips of scenes from hockey games compared to badminton games (Wimshurst, Sowden, & Wright, 2016). Nonetheless, the dominant view is that embodied perspectives are central to the information processing mechanisms in sports as the "sharing of cognitive and neural codes between perception and action may be crucial for achieving the sensorimotor excellence required by elite athletes" (Aglioti et al., 2008, 1115). How creativity in sports arises from within this neurocognitive circuitry is still unknown.

11.4.2 Creativity in Sports

Just as in the case of dance, no neuroscientific studies have as yet specifically investigated creativity in sports. There are a variety of behavioral investigations of creativity in sport, in a variety of forms, including case studies (e.g., on Steve Nash, the basketball player; Martin & Cox, 2016). The objective across studies is to uncover the factors (dispositional, training-based, etc.) that are conducive to creativity in sports performance. For instance, both deliberate practice and unstructured play activities in the formative years of one's training are important determinants of later creativity. This finding was reported in relation to professional players of team ball sports (basketball, soccer, field hockey, handball), who were asked to detail the quality and quantity of the activities they were engaged in between the ages of 5–14, thus providing a thorough picture of their involvement and investment in sport. The players were rated by their trainers in terms of their level of creativity (Memmert, Baker, & Bertsch, 2010). The importance of both deliberate practice and play lies at the heart of the Creativity Developmental Framework (Santos, Memmert, Sampaio, & Leite, 2016), which elucidates how creativity emerges in team sports across differing levels of proficiency (Figure 11.3).

One particular focus in sports creativity has been on the influence of attention. Daniel Memmert, who is possibly the most prolific researcher investigating creativity in sports from the purview of psychology, has made a special case for inattentional blindness, which is a failure to

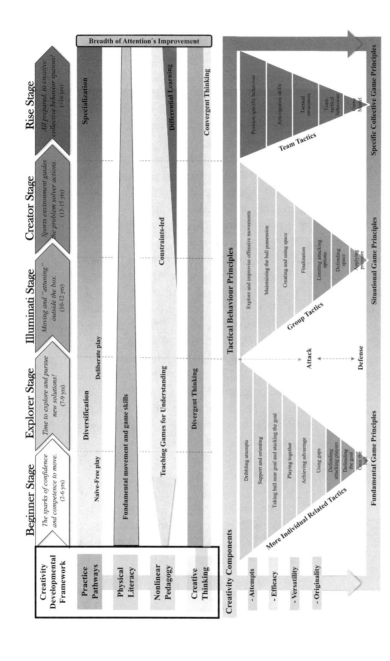

Figure 11.3 A model of creative behavior in team sports

The creativity development framework (CDF) structure. Reprinted with permission from Santos SDL, Memmert D, Sampaio J & Leite N. (2016). The spawns of creative behavior in team sports: A creativity developmental framework. *Frontiers in Psychology, 7*, 1282. A black and white version of this figure will appear in some formats. For the color version, please refer to the plate section.

notice an unexpected stimulus that happens to be in plain view. Less inattentional blindness is held to reflect wider breadth in the focus of attention that would allow for the better detection of unexpected possibilities in dynamic spaces and, as a result, more divergent tactical creativity. While "convergent tactical thinking" is concerned with reaching the best solution, "divergent tactical thinking" reflects the "surprising, original and flexible production of tactical response patterns" (Memmert, 2009, 132). A significant factor to consider in relation to coaching of dynamic team ball sports is that detailed tactical instructions are associated with an increase in inattentional blindness (that is, they are less conductive to divergent tactical creativity) whereas fewer tactical instructions are accompanied by broadened attentional focus (and are thus advantageous for divergent tactical creativity) (Memmert & Furley, 2007). By the same token, attention-broadening training leads to improved creative performance on complex sport-related tasks (Memmert, 2007).

The only neuroscientific theory that specifically provides a focus on forms of creativity that are akin to kinesthetic creativity is a multiple-factor model that adopts an evolutionary predictive perspective (Dietrich, 2015) (detailed in Section 4.3.2). Expanding from the aforementioned transient hypofrontality hypothesis, performance-based creativity is held to be orchestrated by the implicit system as it is motor skill-based and the operations involved are neither consciously accessible nor verbalizable by the performer. While the theory as it currently stands does not specify the workings of mechanisms that detail how truly creative responses come about in such contexts, it is clear that trust and confidence in being able to exert exquisite control over one's bodily movement is a key element. Roger Federer said it best when he shared the following insight: "My game is a lot about footwork. If I move well, I play well."

Chapter Summary

- Dance and sport are kinesthetic forms of creativity that rely on proprioceptive, vestibular, and exteroceptive systems in the human body.
- The common coding principle holds that action and perception derive from the same representation or common codes.
- Mirror neuron theory is the basis of the dominant conceptualizations regarding embodied cognition, action simulation, and joint action.
- The experience of flow is especially relevant in relation to kinesthetic forms of creativity.
- Neuroimaging studies of dance have indicated the involvement of the action observation network.

- Perceptual advantages as a function of visuomotor expertise have been reported across a variety of sports.
- The challenges in uncovering the neural basis of kinesthetic creativity are mainly due to the limitations of current neuroscientific techniques with regard to movement and duration of testing.

Review Questions

1. What makes kinesthetic creativity distinct from other forms of creativity?
2. Describe embodied cognition in terms of its antecedents and consequences.
3. Contrast the models of creativity in dance performance.
4. How are attention and creativity in sport related?
5. Describe the impact of physical exercise on creativity.

Further Reading

- Carroll, N., & Seeley, W. P. (2013). Kinesthetic understanding and appreciation in dance. *Journal of Aesthetics and Art Criticism*, *71*(2), 177–186
- Dietrich, A. (2015). How creativity happens in the brain. New York: Palgrave Macmillan.
- Karpati, F. J., Giacosa, C., Foster, N. E. V., Penhune, V. B., & Hyde, K. L. (2015). Dance and the brain: A review. *Annals of the New York Academy of Sciences*, *1337*, 140–146.
- Santos, S. D. L., Memmert, D., Sampaio, J., & Leite, N. (2016). The spawns of creative behavior in team sports: A creativity developmental framework. *Frontiers in Psychology*, *7*, 1282.
- Yang, J. (2015). The influence of motor expertise on the brain activity of motor task performance: A meta-analysis of functional magnetic resonance imaging studies. *Cognitive, Affective, & Behavioral Neuroscience*, *15*(2), 381–394.

CHAPTER TWELVE

Scientific Creativity

"I am among those who think that science has great beauty. A scientist in his laboratory is not only a technician: he is also a child placed before natural phenomena which impress him like a fairy tale."

(Marie Curie)

Learning Objectives

- Identifying the grounds that explain why scientific creativity is understudied
- Distinguishing between different types of reasoning in scientific creativity
- Recognizing the brain basis of reasoning and the key structures therein
- Grasping how depth and breadth of knowledge impact creative ideation
- Understanding the factors that promote scientific creativity in the real world
- Considering the differences in the theoretical frameworks of scientific creativity

12.1 Scientific Creativity is Understudied

In the pursuit of understanding the nature of creativity, most researchers and theorists in psychology and neuroscience have largely devoted their energy to understanding domain-general creativity (common to all forms of creativity) or domain-specific creativity in the arts (verbal, music, visual artistic, or kinesthetic forms of creativity). Scientific creativity is a comparatively ignored domain. This is paradoxical when considering the fact that researchers have ready access at the workplace, conferences, and so on to populations that can be recruited for this purpose – scientists!

It is worth considering what the reasons for this glaring oversight might be. One possibility is that there are few tests of scientific creativity in use. However, this situation is also true of domain-specific creativity in the arts. Another reason could be that the dominant method used to evaluate the products/outputs of domain-specific creativity, the consensual assessment technique (CAT; see Section 2.4), can be less easily applied to scientific creativity. After all, a high level of relevant background expertise is required on the part of the raters to be able to make sound judgments concerning levels of scientific creativity that are displayed. This is because extensive academic training in a particular field (e.g., consciousness) within a specific discipline (e.g., psychology) is necessary in order to be in a position where one can make any judgments about the degree of creativity associated with new developments in that field (e.g., a new theory) (see Section 1.4.2).

A further issue to mull over is the reluctance of many (including scientists) to regard science as a domain that evidences human creativity, or, if it does, certainly not to the extent that the arts do. The notion that logical reasoning is antithetical to creative ideation is a grave misconception, as different forms of logical reasoning – deductive, inductive, abductive, and analogical – are utilized in service of creative ideation (Morris, 1992). Scientific creativity is mostly discussed in relation to eminence or scientific genius where the focus is on revolutionary theories in the natural, life, or social sciences that have great explanatory power or exert substantial influence on our understanding of the world (e.g., Darwin, Einstein, Cajal, Freud, Foucault, Marx). But creativity in science happens at other scales as well. For instance, ideas in science not only have the potential to be pioneering when they are theoretical, but can also be groundbreaking when they involve the creation of novel paradigms that help us understand phenomena in ways that were not possible before (Bohm, 2004). The Stroop task in experimental psychology is a case in point. A seminal contribution to the scientific understanding of attentional control was made with the creation of the Stroop task, and it remains widely used more than 80 years on (Washburn, 2016).

If "true" creativity in science is regarded as being showcased only by a "radical rethinking of the epistemological (knowledge-knowing) bases of humanity" (Pope, 2005, 59), then the bar is set very high indeed. It is no wonder then that there are few investigations of the same apart from those following the historiometry approach, the analysis of retrospective data to evaluate factors that influence creative eminence (Simonton, 2004).

The high bar of the criterion applied to the recognition of scientific creativity largely stems from Thomas Kuhn's influential ideas on intellectual developments in science as outlined in his book, *The Structure of Scientific Revolutions* (1970). He differentiated between "normal science," which builds cumulatively from existing ideas, and "a revolution in science," which is a non-cumulative development. As the latter is incompatible with the prevailing paradigm or orthodoxy, it affords a shift from the same.

Kuhn's central thesis, that scientific revolutions occur via paradigm shifts, has not gone unchallenged. In his book, *Outline of an Anarchistic Theory of Knowledge* (1974), Paul Feyerabend contends that the concept of a single paradigm-based "normal science" is illusory as multiple paradigms and worldviews are contending for supremacy at any given time. This view is rooted in epistemological anarchism and holds that there are always ideological revolutions being undertaken in any given moment but we are not necessarily always aware of them. By mainly limiting explorations of scientific creativity to extraordinary and well-known cases, we forfeit the opportunity to cultivate an understanding of it to the same extent as and in relation to other types of creativity (see Box 12.1). In fact, the view that creative ideas emerge from "ordinary thinking" through purposive and goal-directed operations is one that is espoused by eminent creativity theorists in the field of psychology (Weisberg, 2006).

Box 12.1 Science and the Pursuit of Beauty

In his eloquent treatise *On Creativity*, the physicist David Bohm (2004) introspects on what the potential driving factors behind scientific creativity may be. He overrules several single explanations, such as the utility of the work, the pleasure derived from solving puzzles, and wanting to predict natural phenomena and participate in the natural process in order to be able to produce the desired results. He makes a case that the best explanation is that scientific pursuits are fuelled by the creative drive to discover something novel, something that was previously unknown. What a creative scientist

is really seeking is to learn something new that has a fundamental kind of significance: i.e. a hitherto unknown lawfulness in the order of nature, which exhibits *unity* in a *broad range* of phenomena. Thus, he wishes to find in the reality in which he lives a certain oneness and totality, or wholeness, constituting a kind of *harmony* that is felt to be beautiful. In this respect, the scientist is perhaps not basically different from the artist, the architect, the musical composer, etc., who all want to *create* this sort of thing in their work ... in order to discover oneness and totality, the scientist has to create the new overall structure of ideas, which are needed to express the harmony and the beauty that can be found in nature. Likewise, he has to create the sensitive instruments which aid perception and thus make possible both the testing of new ideas for their truth or falsity, and the disclosure of new and unexpected kinds of facts ... the artist, the musical composer, the architect, the scientist all feel a fundamental need to discover and create something new that is whole and total, harmonious and beautiful. Few ever get the chance to try and do this, and even fewer actually manage to do it. (Bohm, 1968, 138)

12.2 Mental Operations Relevant to Scientific Creativity

Hypothesis generation (problem finding), hypothesis testing (problem solving), and logical inference generation lie at the heart of scientific reasoning. Of these, problem solving has been most widely studied in the context of creativity (Section 12.2.3), and among logical reasoning strategies, inference by analogy has received abundant attention (Section 12.2.2). What must be kept in mind, though, is that investigations of such operations in direct relation to scientific creativity are entirely lacking. This is because the studies are largely limited to domain-general problem solving and reasoning as opposed to domain-specific scientific problem solving and reasoning.

12.2.1 Deductive, Inductive, and Abductive Reasoning

The types of logical inference that have been understudied in relation to creativity as a whole are deductive, inductive, and abductive, which are the three key kinds of inference identified by the logician, Charles Sanders Peirce (Morris, 1992). As the conclusions drawn during *deductive reasoning* necessarily follow from premises that are taken to be true (if p, then q: The weekly basketball game runs either on Thursday or Friday. The game is not on Thursday this week. Therefore, the game must be on Friday.), deductive reasoning is not often regarded as a context in which creative thinking can occur. However, from a field of study like mathematical deduction, it is clear that deductive reasoning is not merely an identification of the obvious, but is often transformative as "the goal is to see if one can make different things the same, or the same things different" (ibid., 93). So deductive reasoning also potentially allows for the creation of novel insights depending on the context. *Inductive reasoning*, on the other hand, involves reaching conclusions on the basis of premises that are likely to be true (as opposed to definitively true). The likelihood of the premises can be weak or strong and this in turn influences the degree of probability associated with the derived conclusion (e.g., All basketball players in my school are tall, so all basketball players must be tall.). Inductive reasoning therefore more readily allows for creative idea generation to take place compared to deductive reasoning as "the reasoner is going beyond what is strictly known, to arrive at a new supposition" (ibid.).

This is even more the case in *abductive reasoning* given that conclusions following inductive reasoning proceed from what is "probable" whereas conclusions following abductive reasoning proceed from what is "possible." Thus, "[a]bduction is a creative enterprise" as it is a "logical activity that goes well beyond the given" (Morris, 1992, 95). It starts from the position of incomplete observations from which one makes an educated guess of the best possible or most likely explanation for the pattern of observations. Different forms of abduction that are considered especially relevant to scientific creativity (given that they involve the generation of novel hypotheses) are "element-creative abduction," where an as yet unknown factor is predicted to explain the observations, and "rule-creative abduction," where a new law is hypothesized that best summarizes the observations (Prendinger & Ishizuka, 2005).

Scientific advances across theoretical and applied contexts use all these forms of inference generation via logical reasoning across the fields of science, math, medicine, and engineering. Deductive reasoning is the most widely studied and abductive reasoning is the least well studied of these. Meta-analyses and reviews of brain engagement during reasoning tasks consistently indicate the involvement of extensive regions within the CEN, such as the ventrolateral and dorsolateral prefrontal cortex, posterior parietal cortex, and basal ganglia (Goel, 2007; Prado, Chadha, & Booth, 2011; Turner, Marinsek, Ryhal, & Miller, 2015; Van Overwalle, 2011). It is worth nothing that these frontoparietal regions overlap considerably with those implicated in general intelligence (Colom, Karama, Jung, & Haier, 2010; Jung & Haier, 2007). The parieto-temporal integration (P-FIT) theory of intelligence proposes that the frontal areas are involved in hypothesis testing (stage 3: BA 6, 9, 10, 45, 47, 46) and response selection (stage 4: BA 32), while the parietal regions are involved in integration and abstraction of sensory information (stage 2: BA 7, 39, 40), and both dynamically interact during problem solving, evaluation, and hypothesis testing (Figure 12.1). While there is some evidence of better performance in inductive reasoning tasks being associated with better performance on creativity measures (Silvia & Beaty, 2012; Vartanian, Martindale, & Kwiatkowski, 2003), there have been no brain-related investigations in relation to the same.

A final issue to take note of in the context of reasoning is the dual systems models of reasoning and higher-order cognition. The general principle is that reasoning processes are conceived of as reflecting type 1 operations, which are intuitive, fast, automatic, associative, autonomous, and implicit. This is in contrast to type 2 operations, which are reflective, slow, controlled, rule-based, explicit, and require working memory (Evans & Stanovich, 2013) (Figure 12.2). Following this model, reasoning-based operations that are used for hypothesis testing and hypothetical reasoning would be undertaken by the type 2 system. However, what

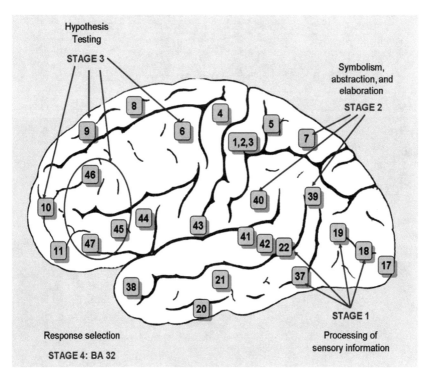

Figure 12.1 Information processing stages in the P-FIT model of intelligence

Reprinted from *Dialogues in Clinical Neuroscience* with the permission of the publisher (Les Laboratoires Servier, Suresnes, France): Colom R, Karama S, Jung RE, Haier RJ. Human intelligence and brain networks. *Dialogues Clin Neurosci.* 2010;*12*(4):489–501. © LLS. A black and white version of this figure will appear in some formats. For the color version, please refer to the plate section.

these tidy divisions do not take into account is the influence of expertise on the automaticity of the reasoning process.

Across applied contexts that require complex problem solving, there is evidence to suggest that novices use explicit reasoning processes whereas experts use implicit reasoning processes. For instance, in a longitudinal study of pathologists over the course of 4 years of medical residency, their examination of breast biopsies using eye-tracking technology revealed a significant yearly reduction in the amount of time fixations per slide and the viewing of non-diagnostic regions (Krupinski, Graham, & Weinstein, 2013). This enhanced ability in visual search and pattern recognition as a function of expertise is reported in complex problem-solving domains,

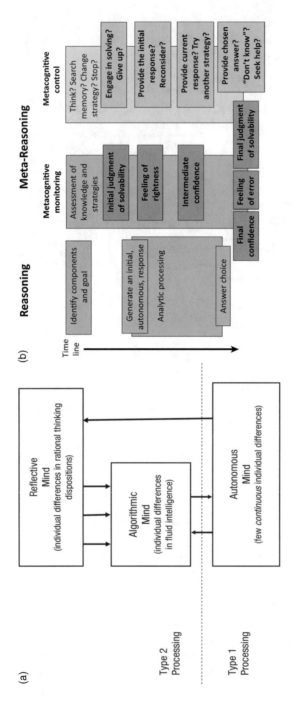

Figure 12.2 Models of reasoning

(a) The tripartite model of the mind based on dual systems theories of reasoning. Reprinted from Evans JSBT & Stanovich KE (2013). Dual-process theories of higher cognition: Advancing the debate. *Perspectives on Psychological Science: A Journal of the Association for Psychological Science, 8*(3), 223–241. (b) The purported time course for reasoning and metareasoning operations. Reprinted from *Trends in Cognitive Sciences, 21*(8), Ackerman R & Thompson VA, Meta-reasoning: Monitoring and control of thinking and reasoning, pages 607–617, © 2017, with permission from Elsevier. A black and white version of this figure will appear in some formats. For the color version, please refer to the plate section.

such as medicine and chess, and is regarded as evidence of implicit processing and tacit knowledge that is not consciously accessible (Reingold & Sheridan, 2011) (see Box 12.2 on mathematical creativity). Such findings indicate that discussion in relation to scientific creativity, which necessitates domain-specific expertise, needs to consider the relevance of both type 1 (intuitive) and type 2 (reflective) operations to arrive at an accurate picture of its mechanisms.

Box 12.2 Mathematical Creativity

Of all the scientific disciplines, mathematics is customarily allotted pedestal position given that it represents the pinnacle of abstraction in reasoning. As mathematical reasoning is associated with criteria like elegance, aesthetics, pattern making, representations, creativity, discovery, and invention, many have drawn attention to the parallels between mathematics and art (Emmer, 1994; Miller, 1995).

With regard to the brain areas involved in mathematical reasoning, arguments have been made for the relevance of the regions in the intraparietal sulcus for numerosity and elementary arithmetic (Dehaene, 2009). The neural circuitry underlying advanced mathematical reasoning includes these intraparietal areas alongside regions of the bilateral prefrontal and inferior temporal regions, which are distinct from the brain networks that underly linguistic processing (Amalric & Dehaene, 2016). Evidence in favor of the bilateral engagement of wide brain networks in relation to mathematical precocity have also been widely noted (Desco et al., 2011; Navas-Sánchez et al., 2014; O'Boyle et al., 2005).

There is evidence linking heightened mathematical abilities and creative achievement. For instance, exceptional mathematical talent at the age of 13 (top 1% of mathematical reasoning ability) was associated with significantly higher creative accomplishments in later life using a range of metrics such as number of book publications and secured patents (Lubinski, Benbow, & Kell, 2014).

12.2.2 Analogical and Relational Reasoning

Significant scientific breakthroughs have resulted from the application of knowledge from one domain to another in an analogical manner such that the structure of conceptual relations in two disparate realms is found to be analogous in form despite being non-analogous in content. A famous example is Rutherford's metaphorical connection between the structure of the solar system and the structure of the atom (Miller, 1996). In contemporary times, neuroscience-inspired algorithms for use in artificial intelligence have been gaining momentum (Cox & Dean, 2014; Hassabis, Kumaran, Summerfield, & Botvinick, 2017). The most famous recent outcome of such a confluence was the creation of the AlphaGo program by the company DeepMind, which beat the Go Champion, Fan Hui (Silver et al., 2016).

Analogical reasoning is held to be central to fluid intelligence, and visuo-spatial analogy tasks are used to evaluate fluid reasoning (Geake & Hansen, 2005). The intimate association between analogical reasoning and creativity has long been noted (Hofstadter & Fluid Analogies Research Group, 1996), and psychological and neuroscientific studies that have examined analogical thinking make a case for the relevance of analogical distance in creativity. This refers to the level of semantic distance between the domains across which connections are being mapped in deriving analogies (see Sections 3.4.2 and 5.3.2). In fact, the very act of generating solutions to semantically distant verbal analogies induces a relational thinking mindset that promotes analogical transfer in an unrelated task (Vendetti, Wu, & Holyoak, 2014). Both divergent and convergent creative thinking have been found to be predictors of the generation and selection of verbal analogies (Jones & Estes, 2015). Across visuospatial and verbal analogy tasks, the brain region that is consistently engaged during analogical reasoning is the left frontal pole (BA 10) (Hobeika, Diard-Detoeuf, Garcin, Levy, & Volle, 2016).

The frontal lobe has long been postulated to play a key role in creative innovation as it exerts dynamic control over other brain regions in line with contextual demands (Heilman, Nadeau, & Beversdorf, 2003). The prefrontal cortex in particular is consistently shown to be involved in complex reasoning, with posterior regions engaged during more concrete operations and anterior regions processing more abstract operations (Badre, 2008; Krawczyk, McClelland, & Donovan, 2011). The frontal pole is considered the apex in representing the most abstract and complex aspects of relational reasoning as its role has been attributed to the integration of output of two or more different cognitive operations (Ramnani & Owen, 2004). For instance, a comparison of the brain engagement during deductive reasoning relative to mathematical calculation showed that the frontal pole was recruited during deductive reasoning only when the problem necessitated searching for counterexamples to conclusions, that is, during a context that called for a higher order of relational reasoning (Kroger, Nystrom, Cohen, & Johnson-Laird, 2008). The integration of interrelated rules during complex problem solving is referred to as relational integration and the frontal pole is regarded as the neural hub for its workings (Krawczyk, 2012; Parkin et al., 2015). One structural neuroimaging study, in fact, reported a positive correlation between the frontal pole and scientific creativity such that higher gray matter volume in this brain region was associated with higher creative achievement in scientific domains (Shi, Cao, Chen, Zhuang, & Qiu, 2017).

It is worth noting, though, that analogical reasoning is typically examined in a generic manner within psychology and neuroscience, as the contexts are not specific to scientific problem solving (but see Box 12.3). However, there is evidence from the applied scientific domain of engineering that the use of distant or far analogies leads to the generation of highly novel concepts (Chan & Schunn, 2015). It must be noted, however, that analogy in creative problem solving is construed more widely in engineering. It is not necessarily limited to the notion of semantic distance, given that

analogy, as customarily understood, stands at one end of a creative continuum that ranges from purely syntactic transformations that can be studied synchronically, to extremely complex instances spread over time and external structures.... To understand how analogy functions in creative problem solving in science, cognitive theories need to take into account such model-constructive, imagistic, and simulative processes. (Nersessian & Chandrasekharan, 2009, 187)

Box 12.3 Real-World Scientific Creativity: Three Favorable Factors

Most investigations of creativity are laboratory-based, where the tasks used to measure creativity often have little resemblance to creativity in the real world. The psychologist Kevin Dunbar (1997, 1999, 2001) recognized that this was a particular problem in the case of scientific creativity, where research in many fields involves collaboration between several individuals who work toward congruent objectives. So he abandoned orthodoxy and did something radically different instead. Dunbar investigated creativity in real-world contexts by shadowing 21 scientists in 4 molecular biology laboratories at universities over the course of a year and amassed observations for a total of 19 projects. The goal of the project was to identify the points at which creative scientific thinking took place during the day-to-day events of the laboratories. He stayed in the laboratories over the day, became familiar with the scientists, interviewed them, attended their laboratory meetings and read their research papers and draft proposals. The take-home message from Dunbar's research was that the central point of creative idea generation within scientific environments is during the regular laboratory meetings, where researchers present their work. This is a context in which spontaneous discussions occur and openness in reasoning is possible. The senior scientist of the laboratory and the researchers' colleagues give informed feedback to the presenter, often proposing key modifications, making suggestions for new experiments, and providing deeper insights about interpretations. Within this context, Dunbar highlights three sources of creative cognition that abet conceptual change in science:

- *Analogical reasoning*: Analogies are often used as a scaffold during scientific problem solving. Scientists mainly make near analogical connections from related domains when generating hypotheses and explaining unexpected findings. Far analogical connections from distant domains are mainly relied on when explaining the findings to other laboratory members or a more general audience.
- *Distributed reasoning*: The reasoning process that leads to the generation of new ideas is typically distributed across many individuals who contribute in a unique manner to the discussion (e.g., inductive versus deductive). A key point is the composition of the group, as people from differing backgrounds allow for the provision of multiple perspectives compared to the findings of a group comprised of individuals with a similar background.
- *Focusing on the unexpected*: Not only does this approach avoid the tendency toward confirmation biases in science but, as a result of trying to understand why an unexpected finding occurred (as opposed to ignoring it), it also leads to a deeper understanding of the phenomenon in question as it uncovers new directions that need to be considered.

12.2.3 Problem Solving and Insight

We apply our multifaceted capacity for reasoning in the service of problem solving. Although problem solving is integral to creative thinking across all domains, the relevance of operations specific to problem solving and problem finding have been particularly emphasized in the context of scientific creativity (Hoover & Feldhusen, 1994). Problems are defined as situations for which there is no obvious immediate solution. The problem-solving process comprises an initial state (the problem), a goal state (the solution), and the operations state (the path from the initial state to the goal state). Problems that can be solved via a series of logical steps are categorized as incremental or non-insight problems that involve "analysis" alone whereas problems requiring a perspective shift or restructuring of the problem elements and are accompanied by a suddenness in the arrival of the solution are categorized as non-incremental or "insight" problems (see Section 3.4.1). Insight problems are held to be more relevant to creativity than purely analytical problem solving, and a range of problems – riddles, mathematical, geometrical, and manipulative – has been devised to evaluate insight problem solving (Weisberg, 1995) (for an example, see Section 2.3.1).

While insight and purely analytic problem solving have long been held to be quite separable and qualitatively distinct from one another, the evidence does not entirely speak to this notion. Insight in problem solving cannot transpire without the capacity of analytical thought, which means that it is erroneous to regard them as mutually exclusive. In fact, a recent proposal calls for an integrated approach to understanding problem solving in which insight builds on different levels of analytical operations (Weisberg, 2018). In this model, analytical operations are consecutively applied across three stages. In Stage 1, problem solving occurs by means of the transfer of problem-specific knowledge from an old problem, which is applied to solve the new problem. When Stage 1 operations are unsuccessful and no new information is brought to light, Stage 2 comes to pass. It involves the application of rules of thumb or heuristics to the problem. When the problem solving process continues to be unsuccessful or brings no new information to light, an impasse is reached and Stage 3 is invoked. This involves the deliberate and conscious restructuring of the problem so as to be able to reach the solution through analytic thought. Impasses can lead to the inhibition or the initial incorrect interpretation of the problem state and necessitate a redistribution of activation to alternate interpretations. When this restructuring leads to a solution, it is experienced as insight (Figure 12.3).

Only a few studies have explored the neural basis of insight versus incremental problem solving using analytical problems. Patients with lesions of the basal ganglia showed impaired performance compared to that of healthy matched controls on an incremental problem-solving task but not an insight problem-solving task in one study (Abraham, Beudt, et al., 2012), and, in another study (Reverberi et al., 2005), patients with lesions of the lateral PFC displayed superior performance on insight problem-solving tasks but not incremental problem-solving tasks compared to a healthy matched control group. This indicates that disruptions to core regions of the CEN, which, as detailed earlier, is involved in logical reasoning, does *not* impair insight problem solving, and might even

STAGE 1 – MATCHING PROBLEM WITH KNOWLEDGE

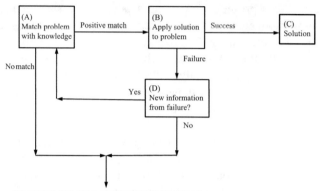

GO ON TO STAGE 2: HEURISTIC METHODS

STAGE 2 – APPLYING HEURISTICS TO PROBLEM

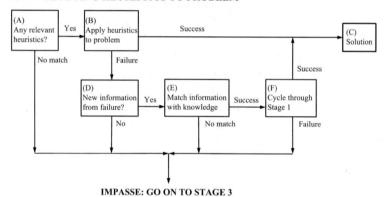

IMPASSE: GO ON TO STAGE 3

STAGE 3 – RESTRUCTURING HEURISTICS IN RESPONSE TO IMPASSE

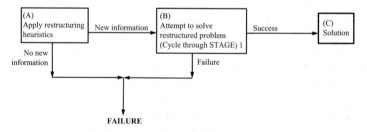

FAILURE

Figure 12.3 The stages of problem solving in the integrated theory of insight

Reprinted with permission from Weisberg, R. W. (2018). Reflections on a personal journey studying the psychology of creativity. In R. J. Sternberg & J. C. Kaufman (Eds.), *The nature of human creativity*. New York: Cambridge University Press.

exert a facilitative effect on the same under certain conditions. This fits with evidence that insight is separable from executive processes, as factors such as working memory, verbal intelligence, divergent thinking, and the ability to overcome functional fixedness independently predict insight problem solving performance (DeYoung, Flanders, & Peterson, 2008). Studies involving children aged 5–8 have shown that differences in innovative problem solving are not predicted by divergent thinking, working memory, or other aspects of executive function (Beck, Williams, Cutting, Apperly, & Chappell, 2016).

12.2.4 Breadth of Knowledge

The importance of domain-specific knowledge in creativity has received a great deal of attention (see Box 3.2) and, although there are differing views on the extent of this relationship, it is clear that domain expertise is indispensible for creative achievement (Weisberg, 1999). In fact, there is even evidence of domain-specific disposition, as personality-based studies have indicated that "intellect," a trait that reflects the propensity to engage with abstract and semantic information through reasoning and other forms of complex cognition, is predictive of creative achievement in the sciences (Kaufman et al., 2016). In fact, scientific creativity is associated with a range of intellect-based traits, such as a preference for intellectual challenges, keen observation, "discontent with the obvious," and the use of "wide" as opposed to "narrow" categories for the compilation of information (Boxenbaum, 1991, 480). What has received less focus is breadth of knowledge in relation to scientific creativity. Eminent creative scientists are known to have wide interests and to engage in great depth with information outside their own fields of expertise (Root-Bernstein et al., 2008; Simonton, 2004). Creative scientists are known for the "network of enterprises" they create over many years as a result of engaging in different projects not necessarily connected with each other (Gruber, 1989). In fact, highly successful scientists are associated with well-integrated networks of enterprise and multiple avocations (Root-Bernstein, Bernstein, & Garnier, 1995). A study that used peer nominations to classify 65 physical scientists as falling in 1 of 3 groups – creative and productive, productive but not creative, and non-creative and non-productive – found that creative scientists were distinguished by their sourcing of information from multiple disciplines, emphasizing the importance of breadth of knowledge (Kasperson, 1978). Indeed, even removing the scientist from the picture and examining the impact of the published ideas reveals that "search scope, search depth, and atypical connections between different research domains significantly increase a paper's impact (Schilling & Green, 2011, 1321).

One further factor to bear in mind is that breadth of knowledge is utilized differently depending on context. Some evidence indicates that, when faced with a problem to be solved, the type of cognitive search strategies employed during problem solving depend on the distance of the knowledge domain from the individual's own expertise. Examining cognitive search strategies used in solutions that were generated in a science competition revealed that, when their expertise was close to the knowledge domain, individuals were more creative when using high cognitive search variation strategies across several different knowledge domains. However, when their expertise was far from the knowledge domain being tested, individuals were more creative with low cognitive search variations in a focused knowledge domain (Acar & van den Ende, 2016).

12.3 Theoretical Views of Scientific Creativity

Few theoretical frameworks have been proposed to explain scientific creativity. One early formulation adopted a systemic approach to distinguishing between scientific and artistic creativity and identified several factors that bear consideration, such as subjective testing in the arts versus objective testing in science (Pearlman, 1983). Another model postulates a hierarchy of scientific disciplines ranging from the physical "hard" sciences to the "soft" social sciences based on the domain-specific impact of scientific output, which is far higher in the former than in the latter (Simonton, 2009). The need to consider the influence of demographic factors, personality, motivation, and working style on scientific eminence were highlighted in a structural model (Feist, 1993). Three conceptualizations that are discussed in contemporary research in the context of scientific creativity are: (a) the 4-stage model of the creative process, (b) scientific creativity as constrained stochastic behavior, and (c) the chance configuration theory of scientific creativity.

While this theoretical formulation is not limited to explaining creativity in the context of science, Graham Wallas's (1926) 4-stage theory of the creative process was based strongly on introspective reflections of the eminent mathematician, Henri Poincaré (Ghiselin, 1985) (see Section 3.3.1). The problem-solving stages during creative ideation begin with the *preparation* stage, where the problem is thoroughly examined. This is followed by the *incubation* stage, which is a period of rest and disengagement from the problem to be solved. The sudden arrival of a solution is a mark of the *illumination* stage, where the fully-formed solution pops into one's mind in a flash of insight. The final stage, *verification*, involves conscious deliberation whereby the details of the solution are worked out. The importance of both conscious and unconscious forces in scientific discovery was emphasized in this model.

Dean Keith Simonton is a leading expert on creativity in general and scientific creativity in particular, and has championed the historiometric approach in studying eminence in creative achievement (Simonton, 2004). In integrating insights from multiple approaches in the study of creativity – person, place, and process – he argues that genuine instantiations of scientific creativity cannot be entirely explained unless one incorporates randomly determined or stochastic elements as an integral part of the discovery process (Simonton, 2003). Many scientific discoveries and trajectories of success occur due to serendipitous events. Let us take the example of development of neuroimaging technology in the spirit of the theme of this book. The first research scientists to have access to neuroimaging facilities conducted the earliest neuroimaging studies in cognitive neuroscience and their papers, which related psychological variables to brain function, became the most influential and cited in their respective academic fields. Simonton (2003) emphasized other chance elements such as the low reliability of the peer review process and the random distribution of good ideational combinations across and within the careers of the many scientists working in a domain. This is random because ideational combinations are generated blindly as they cannot be predictably evoked with a prompt. Also noted in this context are discipline-based differences, as some disciplines have more "overlapping ideational samples" that dominate in their pool of scientists than in others. As stochastic principles operate at the multiple levels of person, process, and place, any conceptualization of scientific creativity would be incomplete if it did not take the element of chance into account.

Yet another key idea forwarded by Simonton builds on the Blind-Variation–Selective-Retention (BVSR) model of creative thought (Campbell, 1960). The essence of this theory is that creativity occurs via "blind-variation" in the generation of idea variants followed by "selective-retention," where viable idea variants are chosen in order to be preserved and reproduced (for other theories derived from evolutionary principles, see Section 4.3). In emphasizing that the idea variant-generation process is probabilistic rather than random in the chance configuration theory (Simonton, 1989a), mental elements (e.g., facts, relations, images) are combined with one another by means of "chance permutations" of the elements. The chance permutations vary in stability as a function of the chance confluence of multiple determinants and the permutations range from transitory and unstable "aggregates" to stable and patterned "configurations." Once a configuration is deemed to have utility and is successful in that it leads to cognitive restructuring, the discovery needs to be transmitted to others and succeed via acceptance by scientific colleagues within the relevant discipline. Contemporary theoretical models in cognitive science merge evolutionary principles and Bayesian inferences by conceiving of stochastic search algorithms as including both the generation and selection elements of BVSR. Creativity is held to emerge from stochastic searches within semantic networks (Suchow, Bourgin, & Griffiths, 2017).

12.4 Issues for Further Consideration

In terms of building an understanding of the psychology and neuroscience of scientific creativity much work remains to be done. For one, it would be useful to have some foundational behavioral evidence indicating whether information processing biases in scientific reasoning abilities, including problem finding, problem solving, and inference generation, vary as a function of scientific expertise, talent, and/or domain. The sparse evidence on hand indicates that some of the abilities measured in the laboratory (e.g., insight problem solving) and discussed throughout this book do not predict creative achievement (Beaty, Nusbaum, & Silvia, 2014). On the other hand, studies of gifted individuals certainly speak for the positive link between scientifically relevant cognitive abilities in youth and later creative achievement in science (Heller, 2007; Kell, Lubinski, & Benbow, 2013; Lubinski, Webb, Morelock, & Benbow, 2001; Park, Lubinski, & Benbow, 2008).

In addition, it seems critical to consider factors beyond simple problem solving and reasoning processes and take into account complex problem solving and other variables in scientific creativity. These include consideration of relational knowledge and its dynamics with reference to working memory, semantic cognition, and reasoning processes (Halford, Wilson, & Phillips, 2010), probabilities in relation to reasoning (Johnson-Laird, Khemlani, & Goodwin, 2015; Oaksford, 2015), conceptual simulation in scientific reasoning (Trickett & Trafton, 2007), and meta-reasoning via metacognitive monitoring and metacognitive control (Ackerman & Thompson, 2017; Fletcher & Carruthers, 2012) (Figure 12.2). Other factors that beg consideration are differences in the information processing biases associated with different scientific domains (e.g., Trickett, Trafton, & Schunn, 2009) and the influence of environmental factors on the capacity to innovate in science.

Indeed, comparisons of scientists who obtained similar funding but whose funding bodies had different expectations revealed that high-impact articles are produced by investigators who have great freedom to experiment, where there is tolerance of early failure, and where the incentives are incumbent on long-term success (Azoulay, Zivin, & Manso, 2011). Only following a great deal of groundwork can the final frontier be approached; namely, identifying the commonalities and differences between scientific and artistic forms of creativity as few theoretical formulations have been put forward to explain how such different instantiations emanate from our creative minds (Guillemin, 2010; Lionnais, 1969; Pearlman, 1983).

Intellectual developments in science contribute greatly to the building of our knowledge, and often enable us to apply novel perspectives to viewing the world. We need to adapt our lenses to view science for what it is: an enormously creative endeavor that is associated with wonder, curiosity, and a sense of adventure that leads to novel discoveries. This chapter began with a quote from Marie Curie that captured this very spirit of scientific enquiry. Let it end with the sentence that followed directly after:

We should not allow it to be believed that all scientific progress can be reduced to mechanisms, machines, gearings, even though such machinery also has its beauty. Neither do I believe that the spirit of adventure runs any risk of disappearing in our world. If I see anything vital around me, it is precisely that spirit of adventure, which seems indestructible and is akin to curiosity. (Marie Curie, quoted in Curie, 1937, 341)

Chapter Summary

- Scientific creativity is the least well-studied domain of creativity and this may be due to misconceptions regarding what constitutes creativity in this sphere.
- The logical processes of deductive, inductive, and abductive reasoning are considered especially relevant to scientific creativity.
- The frontal and parietal regions of the central executive network are consistently implicated during logical reasoning.
- Analogical and relational reasoning are regarded as key operations of relevance in creative problem solving and involve the frontal pole.
- Insight problem solving is not tied to the workings of the central executive network in the same manner as reasoning or generic problem solving.

- Breadth of knowledge is a key variable that influences success in scientific domains.
- In vivo research on real-world creativity emphasizes the dynamics between members of a shared collective in relation to the emergence of creative ideas.

Review Questions

1. Why is scientific creativity understudied in psychology and neuroscience?
2. How do reasoning processes contribute to the generation of novel ideas?
3. In what manner does insight problem solving differ from non-insight problem solving?
4. What is known about the interactions of knowledge and scientific output?
5. Describe how the unique insights that emerge from studying scientific creativity in the real world can inform laboratory-based studies of scientific creativity.

Further Reading

- Ackerman, R., & Thompson, V. A. (2017). Meta-reasoning: Monitoring and control of thinking and reasoning. *Trends in Cognitive Sciences*, *21*(8), 607–617.
- Dunbar, K. N. (1999). Scientific creativity. In M. A. Runco & S. R. Pritzker (Eds.), *Encyclopedia of creativity*, Vol. 1 (pp. 1379–1384). New York: Academic Press.
- Morris, H. C. (1992). Logical creativity. *Theory & Psychology*, *2*(1), 89–107.
- Simonton, D. K. (2004). *Creativity in science: Chance, logic, genius, and Zeitgeist*. New York: Cambridge University Press.
- Weisberg, R. W. (2015). Toward an integrated theory of insight in problem solving. *Thinking & Reasoning*, *21*(1), 5–39.

Afterword – From Cave Art to Latte Art

"My DNA not for imitation."

(Kendrick Lamar)

There can be no question about it. As a species, human beings are indefatigably creative. We use any means available to express ourselves in order to communicate with others and with ourselves. We want to be understood, and we want to understand. And in expressing ourselves in order to communicate, we create. And we leave an impression with what we create; an impression that is unique and individual, yet recognizable and fulfilling. And the more unique and original the trace, the more the individual stands out as a creative entity.

From prehistoric cave dwellers who left us their impressions of the world through depictional art that still endures from 17,000 to 27,000 years ago on the interior walls of the Lascaux and Cosquer caves, to local baristas who make their transitory impressions on foamy lattes, the evidence is unmistakable. Our inherent drive to communicate makes us alert to our ever-unfolding possibility space, and so we cannot help but zone in on the myriad ways therein to express ourselves and make our impressions. Any and every available avenue is a potential channel that can be used in order to create. And create we do. For create we must.

As yet, we know little about this fundamental human drive and spirit to create, the conditions that promote optimal creative experiences, or the real consequences of having this drive thwarted. This book provides an overview of our current understanding of the creative mind from the neuroscientific perspective, and it has highlighted many of the crucial questions that still beg exploration. Through each of the preceding 12 chapters, what has been highlighted is how unusually difficult it is to study creativity in comparison to other complex aspects of human psychological function that lend themselves more easily to objective scientific inquiry. Creativity as a phenomenon is fundamentally multifaceted;

it can manifest in a multitude of different forms; and it is enormously difficult to pin down.

Undertaking the tantalizing enterprise of applying our creative minds in order to understand our creative minds is therefore exceedingly challenging. And I hope the reflective reader will be motivated to engage in this enterprise using the many means available to each of us in our lives, formal or informal, professional or personal. The more creative minds there are at work individually and collaboratively unraveling the puzzle from a variety of perspectives, the more efficient and energetic the progress.

The polymath Rabindranath Tagore once stated, "everything comes to us that belongs to us if we create the capacity to receive it." In order to inch ever closer toward attaining a truer understanding of our dynamic creative minds, each of us needs to do just that on our paths of discovery: create our own capacity to receive.

References

Aarts, E., van Holstein, M., & Cools, R. (2011). Striatal dopamine and the interface between motivation and cognition. *Frontiers in Psychology*, *2*, 163.

Abernethy, B., Zawi, K., & Jackson, R. C. (2008). Expertise and attunement to kinematic constraints. *Perception*, *37*(6), 931–948.

Abraham, A. (2013). The promises and perils of the neuroscience of creativity. *Frontiers in Human Neuroscience*, *7*, 246.

(2014a). Creative thinking as orchestrated by semantic processing vs. cognitive control brain networks. *Frontiers in Human Neuroscience*, *8*, 95.

(2014b). Is there an inverted-U relationship between creativity and psychopathology? *Frontiers in Psychology*, *5*, 750.

(2014c). Neurocognitive mechanisms underlying creative thinking: Indications from studies of mental illness. In J. C. Kaufman (Ed.), *Creativity and mental illness*. Cambridge: Cambridge University Press.

(Ed.). (2015). *Madness and creativity: Yes, no or maybe?* Lausanne: Frontiers Media SA.

(2016). The imaginative mind. *Human Brain Mapping*, *37*(11), 4197–4211.

(2018). The forest versus the trees: Creativity, cognition and imagination. In R. E. Jung & O. Vartanian (Eds.), *The Cambridge handbook of the neuroscience of creativity* (pp. 195–210). New York: Cambridge University Press.

Abraham, A., & Windmann, S. (2007). Creative cognition: The diverse operations and the prospect of applying a cognitive neuroscience perspective. *Methods*, *42*(1), 38–48.

Abraham, A., Beudt, S., Ott, D. V. M., & von Cramon, D. Y. (2012). Creative cognition and the brain: Dissociations between frontal, parietal-temporal and basal ganglia groups. *Brain Research*, *1482*, 55–70.

Abraham, A., Pieritz, K., Thybusch, K., Rutter, B., Kröger, S., Schweckendiek, J., … Hermann, C. (2012). Creativity and the brain: Uncovering the neural signature of conceptual expansion. *Neuropsychologia*, *50*(8), 1906–1917.

Abraham, A., Schubotz, R. I., & von Cramon, D. Y. (2008). Thinking about the future versus the past in personal and non-personal contexts. *Brain Research*, *1233*, 106–119.

Abraham, A., Windmann, S., Daum, I., & Güntürkün, O. (2005). Conceptual expansion and creative imagery as a function of psychoticism. *Consciousness and Cognition*, *14*(3), 520–534.

Abraham, A., Windmann, S., McKenna, P., & Güntürkün, O. (2007). Creative thinking in schizophrenia: The role of executive dysfunction and symptom severity. *Cognitive Neuropsychiatry, 12*(3), 235–258.

Abraham, A., Windmann, S., Siefen, R., Daum, I., & Güntürkün, O. (2006). Creative thinking in adolescents with attention deficit hyperactivity disorder (ADHD). *Child Neuropsychology: A Journal on Normal and Abnormal Development in Childhood and Adolescence, 12*(2), 111–123.

Acar, O. A., & van den Ende, J. (2016). Knowledge distance, cognitive-search processes, and creativity: The making of winning solutions in science contests. *Psychological Science, 27*(5), 692–699.

Ackerman, R., & Thompson, V. A. (2017). Meta-reasoning: Monitoring and control of thinking and reasoning. *Trends in Cognitive Sciences, 21*(8), 607–617.

Addessi, A. R. (2014). Developing a theoretical foundation for the reflexive interaction paradigm with implications for training music skill and creativity. *Psychomusicology: Music, Mind, and Brain, 24*(3), 214–230.

Adhikari, B. M., Norgaard, M., Quinn, K. M., Ampudia, J., Squirek, J., & Dhamala, M. (2016). The brain network underpinning novel melody creation. *Brain Connectivity, 6*(10), 772–785.

Adorno, T. W., & Gillespie, S. (1993). Music, language, and composition. *Musical Quarterly, 77*(3), 401–414.

Aglioti, S. M., Cesari, P., Romani, M., & Urgesi, C. (2008). Action anticipation and motor resonance in elite basketball players. *Nature Neuroscience, 11*(9), 1109–1116.

Albert, Á., & Kormos, J. (2011). Creativity and narrative task performance: An exploratory study. *Language Learning, 61*, 73–99.

Aleman, A., Nieuwenstein, M. R., Böcker, K. B., & de Haan, E. H. (2000). Music training and mental imagery ability. *Neuropsychologia, 38*(12), 1664–1668.

Alexandrov, V. E. (2007). Literature, literariness, and the brain. *Comparative Literature, 59*(2), 97–118.

Allan, K. (2016). Pragmatics in language change and lexical creativity. *SpringerPlus, 5*, 342.

Alossa, N., & Castelli, L. (2009). Amusia and musical functioning. *European Neurology, 61*(5), 269–277.

Altenmüller, E., & Schlaug, G. (2015). Apollo's gift: New aspects of neurologic music therapy. *Progress in Brain Research, 217*, 237–252.

Altenmüller, E., Finger, S., & Boller, F. (Eds.). (2015). *Music, neurology, and neuroscience: Historical connections and perspectives.* Amsterdam: Elsevier.

Altschuler, E. (2016). Did cortical remapping lend artist a hand? *Current Biology, 26*(6), R228.

Amabile, T. M. (1982). Social psychology of creativity: A consensual assessment technique. *Journal of Personality and Social Psychology, 43*(5), 997–1013.

(1983). The social psychology of creativity: A componential conceptualization. *Journal of Personality and Social Psychology, 45*(2), 357–376.

(1985). Motivation and creativity: Effects of motivational orientation on creative writers. *Journal of Personality and Social Psychology, 48*(2), 393–399.

(1996). *Creativity in context*. Boulder, CO: Westview Press.

(1998). How to kill creativity. *Harvard Business Review, 76*(5), 76–87, 186.

(2014). Big C, Little C, Howard, and me: Approaches to understanding creativity. In H. Gardner, M. L. Kornhaber, & E. Winner (Eds.), *Mind, work, and life: A festschrift on the occasion of Howard Gardner's 70th birthday*, Vol. 1 (pp. 5–25). Cambridge, MA: CreateSpace Independent Publishing Platform.

Amabile, T. M., & Pillemer, J. (2012). Perspectives on the social psychology of creativity. *Journal of Creative Behavior, 46*(1), 3–15.

Amalric, M., & Dehaene, S. (2016). Origins of the brain networks for advanced mathematics in expert mathematicians. *Proceedings of the National Academy of Sciences of the United States of America, 113*(18), 4909–4917.

Amaro, E. Jr, & Barker, G. J. (2006). Study design in fMRI: Basic principles. *Brain and Cognition, 60*(3), 220–232.

Amedi, A., Merabet, L. B., Camprodon, J., Bermpohl, F., Fox, S., Ronen, I., … Pascual-Leone, A. (2008). Neural and behavioral correlates of drawing in an early blind painter: A case study. *Brain Research, 1242*, 252–262.

American Psychiatric Association. (2013). *Diagnostic and statistical manual of mental disorders: DSM-5*. Washington, DC: American Psychiatric Association.

Anderson, C. C. (1964). The psychology of the metaphor. *Journal of Genetic Psychology, 105*(1), 53–73.

Andreasen, N. C. (1987). Creativity and mental illness: Prevalence rates in writers and their first-degree relatives. *American Journal of Psychiatry, 144*(10), 1288–1292.

(2006). *The creative brain: The science of genius*. New York: London: Plume.

(2012). Creativity in art and science: Are there two cultures? *Dialogues in Clinical Neuroscience, 14*(1), 49–54.

Andreasen, N. C., & Powers, P. S. (1975). Creativity and psychosis. An examination of conceptual style. *Archives of General Psychiatry, 32*(1), 70–73.

Andreasen, N. C., O'Leary, D. S., Cizadlo, T., Arndt, S., Rezai, K., Watkins, G. L., … & Hichwa, R. D. (1995). Remembering the past: Two facets of episodic memory explored with positron emission tomography. *American Journal of Psychiatry, 152*(11), 1576–1585.

Andrews-Hanna, J. R., Reidler, J. S., Huang, C., & Buckner, R. L. (2010). Evidence for the default network's role in spontaneous cognition. *Journal of Neurophysiology, 104*(1), 322–335.

Andrews-Hanna, J. R., Smallwood, J., & Spreng, R. N. (2014). The default network and self-generated thought: Component processes, dynamic control, and clinical relevance. *Annals of the New York Academy of Sciences, 1316*, 29–52.

Ansburg, P. I., & Hill, K. (2003). Creative and analytic thinkers differ in their use of attentional resources. *Personality and Individual Differences, 34*(7), 1141–1152.

Antal, A., Ambrus, G. G., & Chaieb, L. (2014). The impact of electrical stimulation techniques on behavior. *Cognitive Science, 5*(6), 649–659.

Arden, R., Chavez, R. S., Grazioplene, R., & Jung, R. E. (2010). Neuroimaging creativity: A psychometric view. *Behavioural Brain Research, 214*(2), 143–156.

Aron, A. R. (2007). The neural basis of inhibition in cognitive control. *Neuroscientist: A Review Journal Bringing Neurobiology, Neurology and Psychiatry, 13*(3), 214–228.

(2011). From reactive to proactive and selective control: Developing a richer model for stopping inappropriate responses. *Biological Psychiatry, 69*(12), e55–e68.

Asari, T., Konishi, S., Jimura, K., Chikazoe, J., Nakamura, N., & Miyashita, Y. (2008). Right temporopolar activation associated with unique perception. *NeuroImage, 41*(1), 145–152.

Ashby, W. R., & Bassett, M. (1949). The effect of leucotomy on creative ability. *British Journal of Psychiatry, 95*(399), 418–430.

Atchley, R. A., Keeney, M., & Burgess, C. (1999). Cerebral hemispheric mechanisms linking ambiguous word meaning retrieval and creativity. *Brain and Cognition, 40*(3), 479–499.

Averill, J. R., Chon, K. K., & Hahn, D. W. (2001). Emotions and creativity, East and West. *Asian Journal of Social Psychology, 4*(3), 165–183.

Awh, E., Belopolsky, A. V., & Theeuwes, J. (2012). Top-down versus bottom-up attentional control: A failed theoretical dichotomy. *Trends in Cognitive Sciences, 16*(8), 437–443.

Aziz-Zadeh, L., Kaplan, J. T., & Iacoboni, M. (2009). "Aha!": The neural correlates of verbal insight solutions. *Human Brain Mapping, 30*(3), 908–916.

Aziz-Zadeh, L., Liew, S.-L., & Dandekar, F. (2012). Exploring the neural correlates of visual creativity. *Social Cognitive and Affective Neuroscience, 8*(4), 475–480.

Azoulay, P., Zivin, J. S. G., & Manso, G. (2011). Incentives and creativity: Evidence from the academic life sciences. *RAND Journal of Economics*, *42*(3), 527–554.

Badre, D. (2008). Cognitive control, hierarchy, and the rostro-caudal organization of the frontal lobes. *Trends in Cognitive Sciences*, *12*(5), 193–200.

Badre, D., & Wagner, A. D. (2007). Left ventrolateral prefrontal cortex and the cognitive control of memory. *Neuropsychologia*, *45*(13), 2883–2901.

Baer, J. (2011). How divergent thinking tests mislead us: Are the Torrance Tests still relevant in the 21st century? The Division 10 debate. *Psychology of Aesthetics, Creativity, and the Arts*, *5*(4), 309–313.

Baer, J., & McKool, S. S. (2009). Assessing creativity using the consensual assessment technique. In C. S. Schreiner (Ed.), *Handbook of research on assessment technologies, methods, and applications in higher education* (pp. 1–13). IGI Global.

Baer, J., Kaufman, J. C., & Gentile, C. A. (2004). Extension of the consensual assessment technique to nonparallel creative products. *Creativity Research Journal*, *16*(1), 113–117.

Baetens, K. L. M. R., Ma, N., & Overwalle, F. V. (2017). The dorsal medial prefrontal cortex is recruited by high construal of non-social stimuli. *Frontiers in Behavioral Neuroscience*, *11*, 44.

Baker, F. A., & MacDonald, R. A. R. (2013). Flow, identity, achievement, satisfaction and ownership during therapeutic songwriting experiences with university students and retirees. *Musicae Scientiae*, *17*(2), 131–146.

Bakker, A. B., Oerlemans, W., Demerouti, E., Slot, B. B., & Ali, D. K. (2011). Flow and performance: A study among talented Dutch soccer players. *Psychology of Sport and Exercise*, *12*(4), 442–450.

Ballan, H., & Abraham, A. (2016). Multimodal imagery in music: Active ingredients and mechanisms underlying musical engagement. *Music & Medicine*, *8*(4), 170–179.

Banfield, J., & Burgess, M. (2013). A phenomenology of artistic doing: Flow as embodied knowing in 2D and 3D professional artists. *Journal of Phenomenological Psychology*, *44*(1), 60–91.

Bar, M. (2007). The proactive brain: Using analogies and associations to generate predictions. *Trends in Cognitive Sciences*, *11*(7), 280–289.

Barbot, B., Randi, J., Tan, M., Levenson, C., Friedlaender, L., & Grigorenko, E. L. (2013). From perception to creative writing: A multi-method pilot study of a visual literacy instructional approach. *Learning and Individual Differences*, *28*, 167–176.

Barbot, B., Tan, M., Randi, J., Santa-Donato, G., & Grigorenko, E. L. (2012). Essential skills for creative writing: Integrating multiple domain-specific perspectives. *Thinking Skills and Creativity*, *7*(3), 209–223.

Baror, S., & Bar, M. (2016). Associative activation and its relation to exploration and exploitation in the brain. *Psychological Science, 26*(7), 776–689.

Barrett, K. C., Ashley, R., Strait, D. L., & Kraus, N. (2013). Art and science: How musical training shapes the brain. *Frontiers in Psychology, 4,* 713.

Barrett, L. F. (2009). The future of psychology: Connecting mind to brain. *Perspectives on Psychological Science: A Journal of the Association for Psychological Science, 4*(4), 326–339.

Barrett, L. F., & Satpute, A. B. (2013). Large-scale brain networks in affective and social neuroscience: Towards an integrative functional architecture of the brain. *Current Opinion in Neurobiology, 4,* 713.

Barron, F. (1955). The disposition toward originality. *Journal of Abnormal and Social Psychology, 51*(3), 478–485.

Barron, F., & Harrington, D. M. (1981). Creativity, intelligence, and personality. *Annual Review of Psychology, 32*(1), 439–476.

Başar, E. (2012). A review of alpha activity in integrative brain function: Fundamental physiology, sensory coding, cognition and pathology. *International Journal of Psychophysiology, 86*(1), 1–24.

Bashwiner, D. M., Wertz, C. J., Flores, R. A., & Jung, R. E. (2016). Musical creativity "revealed" in brain structure: Interplay between motor, default mode, and limbic networks. *Scientific Reports, 6,* 73–102.

Batey, M., & Furnham, A. (2006). Creativity, intelligence, and personality: A critical review of the scattered literature. *Genetic, Social, and General Psychology Monographs, 132*(4), 355–429.

Bazanova, O. M., & Vernon, D. (2014). Interpreting EEG alpha activity. *Neuroscience and Biobehavioral Reviews, 44,* 94–110.

Beaty, R. E. (2015). The neuroscience of musical improvisation. *Neuroscience and Biobehavioral Reviews, 51,* 108–117.

Beaty, R. E., & Silvia, P. J. (2013). Metaphorically speaking: Cognitive abilities and the production of figurative language. *Memory & Cognition, 41*(2), 255–267.

Beaty, R. E., Benedek, M., Kaufman, S. B., & Silvia, P. J. (2015). Default and executive network coupling supports creative idea production. *Scientific Reports, 5,* 10964.

Beaty, R. E., Benedek, M., Silvia, P. J., & Schacter, D. L. (2016). Creative cognition and brain network dynamics. *Trends in Cognitive Sciences, 20*(2), 87–95.

Beaty, R. E., Benedek, M., Wilkins, R. W., Jauk, E., Fink, A., Silvia, P. J., ... Neubauer, A. C. (2014). Creativity and the default network: A functional connectivity analysis of the creative brain at rest. *Neuropsychologia, 64,* 92–98.

Beaty, R. E., Kenett, Y. N., Christensen, A. P., Rosenberg, M. D., Benedek, M., Chen, Q., ... Silvia, P. J. (2018). Robust prediction of individual creative ability from brain functional connectivity. *Proceedings of the National Academy of Sciences, 115*(5), 1087–1092.

Beaty, R. E., Nusbaum, E. C., & Silvia, P. J. (2014). Does insight problem solving predict real-world creativity? *Psychology of Aesthetics, Creativity, and the Arts, 8*(3), 287–292.

Beaty, R. E., Silvia, P. J., & Benedek, M. (2017). Brain networks underlying novel metaphor production. *Brain and Cognition, 111*, 163–170.

Beaty, R. E., Silvia, P. J., Nusbaum, E. C., Jauk, E., & Benedek, M. (2014). The roles of associative and executive processes in creative cognition. *Memory & Cognition, 42*(7), 1186–1197.

Beaty, R. E., Smeekens, B. A., Silvia, P. J., Hodges, D. A., & Kane, M. J. (2013). A first look at the role of domain-general cognitive and creative abilities in jazz improvisation. *Psychomusicology: Music, Mind, and Brain, 23*(4), 262–268.

Bechtereva, N. P., Korotkov, A. D., Pakhomov, S. V., Roudas, M. S., Starchenko, M. G., & Medvedev, S. V. (2004). PET study of brain maintenance of verbal creative activity. *International Journal of Psychophysiology: Official Journal of the International Organization of Psychophysiology, 53*(1), 11–20.

Beck, S. R., Williams, C., Cutting, N., Apperly, I. A., & Chappell, J. (2016). Individual differences in children's innovative problem-solving are not predicted by divergent thinking or executive functions. *Philosophical Transactins of the Royal Society B, 19*, 371.

Beeman, M. J., & Bowden, E. M. (2000). The right hemisphere maintains solution-related activation for yet-to-be-solved problems. *Memory & Cognition, 28*(7), 1231–1241.

Beghetto, R. A., & Kaufman, J. C. (2007). Toward a broader conception of creativity: A case for "mini-c" creativity. *Psychology of Aesthetics, Creativity, and the Arts, 1*(2), 73–79.

Beilock, S. L., Lyons, I. M., Mattarella-Micke, A., Nusbaum, H. C., & Small, S. L. (2008). Sports experience changes the neural processing of action language. *Proceedings of the National Academy of Sciences, 105*(36), 13269–13273.

Beisteiner, R., Altenmuller, E., Lang, W., Lindinger, G., & Deecke, L. (1994). Musicians processing music: Measurement of brain potentials with EEG. *European Journal of Cognitive Psychology, 6*(3), 311–327.

Benedek, M., & Neubauer, A. C. (2013). Revisiting Mednick's model on creativity-related differences in associative hierarchies: Evidence for a common path to uncommon thought. *Journal of Creative Behavior, 47*(4), 273–289.

Benedek, M., Beaty, R., Jauk, E., Koschutnig, K., Fink, A., Silvia, P. J., ... Neubauer, A. C. (2014). Creating metaphors: The neural basis of figurative language production. *NeuroImage, 90*, 99–106.

Benedek, M., Borovnjak, B., Neubauer, A. C., & Kruse-Weber, S. (2014). Creativity and personality in classical, jazz and folk musicians. *Personality and Individual Differences*, *63*(100), 117–121.

Benedek, M., Franz, F., Heene, M., & Neubauer, A. C. (2012). Differential effects of cognitive inhibition and intelligence on creativity. *Personality and Individual Differences*, *53*(4), 480–485.

Benedek, M., Könen, T., & Neubauer, A. C. (2012). Associative abilities underlying creativity. *Psychology of Aesthetics, Creativity, and the Arts*, *6*(3), 273–281.

Benedek, M., Schickel, R. J., Jauk, E., Fink, A., & Neubauer, A. C. (2014). Alpha power increases in right parietal cortex reflect focused internal attention. *Neuropsychologia*, *56*, 393–400.

Bengtsson, S. L., Csíkszentmihályi, M., & Ullén, F. (2007). Cortical regions involved in the generation of musical structures during improvisation in pianists. *Journal of Cognitive Neuroscience*, *19*(5), 830–842.

Bennett, M. R., & Hacker, P. M. S. (2003). *Philosophical foundations of neuroscience*. Malden, MA: Blackwell.

Bergland, C. (2011). Superfluidity: Peak performance beyond a state of "flow." Retrieved from www.psychologytoday.com/blog/the-athletes-way/201110/superfluidity-peak-performance-beyond-state-flow

Berkowitz, A. L., & Ansari, D. (2008). Generation of novel motor sequences: The neural correlates of musical improvisation. *NeuroImage*, *41*(2), 535–543.

(2010). Expertise-related deactivation of the right temporoparietal junction during musical improvisation. *NeuroImage*, *49*(1), 712–719.

Bernays, M., & Traube, C. (2014). Investigating pianists' individuality in the performance of five timbral nuances through patterns of articulation, touch, dynamics, and pedaling. *Frontiers in Psychology*, *5*, 157.

Biasutti, M. (2015). Pedagogical applications of cognitive research on musical improvisation. *Frontiers in Psychology*, *6*, 614.

Biasutti, M., & Frezza, L. (2009). Dimensions of music improvisation. *Creativity Research Journal*, *21*(2–3), 232–242.

Bidelman, G. M., & Krishnan, A. (2011). Brainstem correlates of behavioral and compositional preferences of musical harmony. *NeuroReport: For Rapid Communication of Neuroscience Research*, *22*(5), 212–216.

Bigand, E. (2003). More about the musical expertise of musically untrained listeners. *Annals of the New York Academy of Sciences*, *999*, 304–312.

Bigand, E., & Poulin-Charronnat, B. (2006). Are we "experienced listeners"? A review of the musical capacities that do not depend on formal musical training. *Cognition*, *100*(1), 100–130.

Bilalić, M., McLeod, P., & Gobet, F. (2008). Why good thoughts block better ones: The mechanism of the pernicious Einstellung (set) effect. *Cognition*, *108*(3), 652–661.

Binder, J. R., & Desai, R. H. (2011). The neurobiology of semantic memory. *Trends in Cognitive Sciences*, *15*(11), 527–536.

Binder, J. R., Desai, R. H., Graves, W. W., & Conant, L. L. (2009). Where is the semantic system? A critical review and meta-analysis of 120 functional neuroimaging studies. *Cerebral Cortex*, *19*(12), 2767–2796.

Birn, R. M., Bandettini, P. A., Cox, R. W., Jesmanowicz, A., & Shaker, R. (1998). Magnetic field changes in the human brain due to swallowing or speaking. *Magnetic Resonance in Medicine*, *40*(1), 55–60.

Birn, R. M., Bandettini, P. A., Cox, R. W., & Shaker, R. (1999). Event-related fMRI of tasks involving brief motion. *Human Brain Mapping*, *7*(2), 106–114.

Birn, R. M., Cox, R. W., & Bandettini, P. A. (2004). Experimental designs and processing strategies for fMRI studies involving overt verbal responses. *NeuroImage*, *23*(3), 1046–1058.

Bishop, J. M., & al-Rifaie, M. M. (2017). Autopoiesis, creativity and dance. *Connection Science*, *29*(1), 21–35.

Blanchette, I., & Dunbar, K. (2002). Representational change and analogy: How analogical inferences alter target representations. *Journal of Experimental Psychology: Learning, Memory, and Cognition*, *28*(4), 672–685.

Blasi, G., Goldberg, T. E., Weickert, T., Das, S., Kohn, P., Zoltick, B., ... Mattay, V. S. (2006). Brain regions underlying response inhibition and interference monitoring and suppression. *European Journal of Neuroscience*, *23*(6), 1658–1664.

Bläsing, B., Calvo-Merino, B., Cross, E. S., Jola, C., Honisch, J., & Stevens, C. J. (2012). Neurocognitive control in dance perception and performance. *Acta Psychologica*, *139*(2), 300–308.

Blumenfeld-Jones, D. (2009). Bodily-kinesthetic intelligence and dance education: Critique, revision, and potentials for the democratic ideal. *Journal of Aesthetic Education*, *43*(1), 59–76.

Boccia, M., Piccardi, L., Palermo, L., Nori, R., & Palmiero, M. (2015). Where do bright ideas occur in our brain? Meta-analytic evidence from neuroimaging studies of domain-specific creativity. *Frontiers in Psychology*, *6*, 1195.

Boden, M. (2004). *The creative mind: Myths and mechanisms* (2nd edn.). London: Routledge.

(2012). *Creativity and art: Three roads to surprise*. Oxford: Oxford University Press.

Bogen, J. E., & Bogen, G. M. (1969). The other side of the brain. 3. The corpus callosum and creativity. *Bulletin of the Los Angeles Neurological Societies*, *34*(4), 191–220.

Bohm, D. (1968). On creativity. *Leonardo*, *1*(2), 137–149.

(2004). *On creativity* (2nd edn.). Abingdon: Routledge.

Boisgueheneuc, F. du, Levy, R., Volle, E., Seassau, M., Duffau, H., Kinkingnehun, S., ... Dubois, B. (2006). Functions of the left superior frontal gyrus in humans: A lesion study. *Brain: A Journal of Neurology*, *129*(12), 3315–3328.

Bookheimer, S. (2002). Functional MRI of language: New approaches to understanding the cortical organization of semantic processing. *Annual Review of Neuroscience*, *25*, 151–188.

Boot, N., Baas, M., van Gaal, S., Cools, R., & De Dreu, C. K. W. (2017). Creative cognition and dopaminergic modulation of fronto-striatal networks: Integrative review and research agenda. *Neuroscience and Biobehavioral Reviews*, *78*, 13–23.

Bourgeois-Bougrine, S., Glaveanu, V., Botella, M., Guillou, K., De Biasi, P. M., & Lubart, T. (2014). The creativity maze: Exploring creativity in screenplay writing. *Psychology of Aesthetics, Creativity, and the Arts*, *8*(4), 384–399.

Bowden, E. M., & Jung-Beeman, M. (2003). Normative data for 144 compound remote associate problems. *Behavior Research Methods, Instruments, & Computers: A Journal of the Psychonomic Society*, *35*(4), 634–639.

Bowden, E. M., Jung-Beeman, M., Fleck, J., & Kounios, J. (2005). New approaches to demystifying insight. *Trends in Cognitive Sciences*, *9*(7), 322–328.

Boxenbaum, H. (1991). Scientific creativity: A review. *Drug Metabolism Reviews*, *23*(5–6), 473–492.

Boyd, B. (2010). *On the origin of stories: Evolution, cognition, and fiction.* Cambridge, MA: Belknap Press of Harvard University Press.

    (2017). The evolution of stories: From mimesis to language, from fact to fiction. *Cognitive Science*, *9*(1).

Brattico, E., & Tervaniemi, M. (2006). Musical creativity and the human brain. In I. Deliège & G. A. Wiggins (Eds.), *Musical creativity: Multidisciplinary research in theory and practice* (pp. 290–321). Hove: Psychology Press.

Bressler, S. L., & Menon, V. (2010). Large-scale brain networks in cognition: Emerging methods and principles. *Trends in Cognitive Sciences*, *14*(6), 277–290.

Brooks, P. (2014). Performers, creators and audience: Co-participants in an interconnected model of performance and creative process. *Research in Dance Education*, *15*(2), 120–137.

Brophy, D. R. (2001). Comparing the attributes, activities, and performance of divergent, convergent, and combination thinkers. *Creativity Research Journal*, *13*(3–4), 439–455.

Brouwer, H., Fitz, H., & Hoeks, J. (2012). Getting real about semantic illusions: Rethinking the functional role of the P600 in language comprehension. *Brain Research*, *1446*, 127–143.

Brown, A. S. (1973). An empirical verification of Mednick's associative theory of creativity. *Bulletin of the Psychonomic Society*, *2*(6), 429–430.

Brown, R. M., Zatorre, R. J., & Penhune, V. B. (2015). Expert music performance: Cognitive, neural, and developmental bases. *Progress in Brain Research*, *217*, 57–86.

Brown, S., Martinez, M. J., & Parsons, L. M. (2006). The neural basis of human dance. *Cerebral Cortex*, *16*(8), 1157–1167.

Brunn, S. D., & Dodge, M. (Eds.). (2017). *Mapping across academia*. Dordrecht: Springer Netherlands.

Brunswick, N., Martin, G. N., & Marzano, L. (2010). Visuospatial superiority in developmental dyslexia: Myth or reality? *Learning and Individual Differences*, *20*(5), 421–426.

Bubić, A., & Abraham, A. (2014). Neurocognitive bases of future oriented cognition. *Review of Psychology*, *21*(1), 3–15.

Bubić, A., von Cramon, D. Y., & Schubotz, R. I. (2010). Prediction, cognition and the brain. *Frontiers in Human Neuroscience*, *4*, 25.

Buckner, R. L., Andrews-Hanna, J. R., & Schacter, D. L. (2008). The brain's default network: Anatomy, function, and relevance to disease. *Annals of the New York Academy of Sciences*, *1124*, 1–38.

Bungay, H., & Vella-Burrows, T. (2013). The effects of participating in creative activities on the health and well-being of children and young people: A rapid review of the literature. *Perspectives in Public Health*, *133*(1), 44–52.

Bunge, S. A., Wendelken, C., Badre, D., & Wagner, A. D. (2005). Analogical reasoning and prefrontal cortex: Evidence for separable retrieval and integration mechanisms. *Cerebral Cortex*, *15*(3), 239–249.

Burch, G. S. J., Hemsley, D. R., Pavelis, C., & Corr, P. J. (2006). Personality, creativity and latent inhibition. *European Journal of Personality*, *20*(2), 107–122.

Burch, G. S. J., Pavelis, C., Hemsley, D. R., & Corr, P. J. (2006). Schizotypy and creativity in visual artists. *British Journal of Psychology*, *97*(2), 177–190.

Burnard, P. (1999). Bodily intention in children's improvisation and composition. *Psychology of Music*, *27*(2), 159–174.

  (2012). *Musical creativities in practice*. Oxford: Oxford University Press.

Burnard, P., & Younker, B. A. (2004). Problem-solving and creativity: Insights from students' individual composing pathways. *International Journal of Music Education*, *22*(1), 59–76.

Burton, L. J., & Fogarty, G. J. (2003). The factor structure of visual imagery and spatial abilities. *Intelligence*, *31*(3), 289–318.

Byrne, C., MacDonald, R., & Carlton, L. (2003). Assessing creativity in musical compositions: Flow as an assessment tool. *British Journal of Music Education*, *20*(3), 277–290.

Cabeza, R., & St Jacques, P. (2007). Functional neuroimaging of autobiographical memory. *Trends in Cognitive Sciences, 11*(5), 219–227.

Calvo-Merino, B., Glaser, D. E., Grèzes, J., Passingham, R. E., & Haggard, P. (2005). Action observation and acquired motor skills: An fMRI study with expert dancers. *Cerebral Cortex, 15*(8), 1243–1249.

Calvo-Merino, B., Grèzes, J., Glaser, D. E., Passingham, R. E., & Haggard, P. (2006). Seeing or doing? Influence of visual and motor familiarity in action observation. *Current Biology, 16*(19), 1905–1910.

Campbell, D. T. (1960). Blind variation and selective retention in creative thought as in other knowledge processes. *Psychological Review, 67,* 380–400.

Campbell, D. W., Wallace, M. G., Modirrousta, M., Polimeni, J. O., McKeen, N. A., & Reiss, J. P. (2015). The neural basis of humour comprehension and humour appreciation: The roles of the temporoparietal junction and superior frontal gyrus. *Neuropsychologia, 79,* 10–20.

Canonne, C., & Aucouturier, J.-J. (2016). Play together, think alike: Shared mental models in expert music improvisers. *Psychology of Music, 44*(3), 544–558.

Carlsson, I., Wendt, P. E., & Risberg, J. (2000). On the neurobiology of creativity: Differences in frontal activity between high and low creative subjects. *Neuropsychologia, 38*(6), 873–885.

Carrithers, M. (1990). Why humans have cultures. *Man, 25*(2), 189–206.

Carroll, N., & Seeley, W. P. (2013). Kinesthetic understanding and appreciation in dance. *Journal of Aesthetics and Art Criticism, 71*(2), 177–186.

Carruthers, P. (2002). Human creativity: Its cognitive basis, its evolution, and its connections with childhood pretence. *British Journal for the Philosophy of Science, 53*(2), 225–249.

Carson, S. H. (2011). Creativity and psychopathology: A shared vulnerability model. *Canadian Journal of Psychiatry, 56*(3), 144–153.

Carson, S. H., Peterson, J. B., & Higgins, D. M. (2003). Decreased latent inhibition is associated with increased creative achievement in high-functioning individuals. *Journal of Personality and Social Psychology, 85*(3), 499–506.

Carson, S. H., Peterson, J. B., & Higgins, D. M. (2005). Reliability, validity, and factor structure of the Creative Achievement Questionnaire. *Creativity Research Journal, 17*(1), 37–50.

Cavanna, A. E., & Trimble, M. R. (2006). The precuneus: A review of its functional anatomy and behavioural correlates. *Brain: A Journal of Neurology, 129,* 564–583.

Chamberlain, R., McManus, I. C., Brunswick, N., Rankin, Q., Riley, H., & Kanai, R. (2014). Drawing on the right side of the brain: A voxel-based morphometry analysis of observational drawing. *NeuroImage, 96,* 167–173.

Chan, D. W., & Zhao, Y. (2010). The relationship between drawing skill and artistic creativity: Do age and artistic involvement make a difference? *Creativity Research Journal, 22*(1), 27–36.

Chan, J., & Schunn, C. (2015). The impact of analogies on creative concept generation: Lessons from an in vivo study in engineering design. *Cognitive Science, 39*(1), 126–155.

Chan, Y.-C., Chou, T.-L., Chen, H.-C., Yeh, Y.-C., Lavallee, J. P., Liang, K.-C., & Chang, K.-E. (2013). Towards a neural circuit model of verbal humor processing: An fMRI study of the neural substrates of incongruity detection and resolution. *NeuroImage, 66*, 169–176.

Chand, G., & Dhamala, M. (2015). Interactions among the brain default-mode, salience and central-executive networks during perceptual decision-making of moving dots. *Brain Connectivity, 6*(3), 249–254.

Chang, A., Livingstone, S. R., Bosnyak, D. J., & Trainor, L. J. (2017). Body sway reflects leadership in joint music performance. *Proceedings of the National Academy of Sciences of the United States of America, 114*(21), 4134–4141.

Chatterjee, A. (2004). The neuropsychology of visual artistic production. *Neuropsychologia, 42*(11), 1568–1583.

Chavez, R. A. (2016). Imagery as a core process in the creativity of successful and awarded artists and scientists and its neurobiological correlates. *Frontiers in Psychology, 7*, 351.

Chávez-Eakle, R. A., Graff-Guerrero, A., García-Reyna, J.-C., Vaugier, V., & Cruz-Fuentes, C. (2007). Cerebral blood flow associated with creative performance: A comparative study. *NeuroImage, 38*(3), 519–528.

Chemi, T. (2016). The experience of flow in artistic creation. In L. Harmat, F. Ø. Andersen, F. Ullén, J. Wright, & G. Sadlo (Eds.), *Flow experience: Emperical research and applications* (pp. 37–50). Berlin: Springer International.

Chen, A. C., Oathes, D. J., Chang, C., Bradley, T., Zhou, Z.-W., Williams, L. M., … Etkin, A. (2013). Causal interactions between fronto-parietal central executive and default-mode networks in humans. *Proceedings of the National Academy of Sciences of the United States of America, 110*(49), 19944–19949.

Chen, Q.-L., Xu, T., Yang, W.-J., Li, Y.-D., Sun, J.-Z., Wang, K.-C., … Qiu, J. (2015). Individual differences in verbal creative thinking are reflected in the precuneus. *Neuropsychologia, 75*, 441–449.

Chermahini, S. A., & Hommel, B. (2011). Creative mood swings: Divergent and convergent thinking affect mood in opposite ways. *Psychological Research, 76*(5), 634–640.

Chi, R. P., & Snyder, A. W. (2011). Facilitate insight by non-invasive brain stimulation. *PloS One, 6*(2), e16655.

Chomsky, N. (2006). *Language and mind* (3rd edn.). New York: Cambridge University Press.

Chouinard, B., Boliek, C., & Cummine, J. (2016). How to interpret and critique neuroimaging research: A tutorial on use of functional magnetic resonance imaging in clinical populations. *American Journal of Speech-Language Pathology, 25*(3), 269–289.

Christoff, K., Prabhakaran, V., Dorfman, J., Zhao, Z., Kroger, J. K., Holyoak, K. J., & Gabrieli, J. D. (2001). Rostrolateral prefrontal cortex involvement in relational integration during reasoning. *NeuroImage, 14*(5), 1136–1149.

Chrysikou, E. G., & Thompson-Schill, S. L. (2011). Dissociable brain states linked to common and creative object use. *Human Brain Mapping, 32*(4), 665–675.

Chrysikou, E. G., & Weisberg, R. W. (2005). Following the wrong footsteps: Fixation effects of pictorial examples in a design problem-solving task. *Journal of Experimental Psychology: Learning, Memory, and Cognition, 31*(5), 1134–1148.

Chrysikou, E. G., Novick, J. M., Trueswell, J. C., & Thompson-Schill, S. L. (2011). The other side of cognitive control: Can a lack of cognitive control benefit language and cognition? *Topics in Cognitive Science, 3*(2), 253.

Chrysikou, E. G., Weber, M. J., & Thompson-Schill, S. L. (2014). A matched filter hypothesis for cognitive control. *Neuropsychologia, 62*, 341–355.

Chun, C. A., & Hupé, J. (2016). Are synesthetes exceptional beyond their synesthetic associations? A systematic comparison of creativity, personality, cognition, and mental imagery in synesthetes and controls. *British Journal of Psychology, 107*(3), 397–418.

Code, C. (Ed.). (2003). *Classic cases in neuropsychology*, Vol. 2. Hove: Psychology Press.

Cohen, D. J. (2005). Look little, look often: The influence of gaze frequency on drawing accuracy. *Perception & Psychophysics, 67*(6), 997–1009.

Cole, M. W., & Schneider, W. (2007). The cognitive control network: Integrated cortical regions with dissociable functions. *NeuroImage, 37*(1), 343–360.

Collins, A. M., & Loftus, E. F. (1975). A spreading-activation theory of semantic processing. *Psychological Review, 82*(6), 407–428.

Collins, A. M., & Quillian, M. R. (1969). Retrieval time from semantic memory. *Journal of Verbal Learning and Verbal Behavior, 8*(2), 240–247.

Colom, R., Karama, S., Jung, R. E., & Haier, R. J. (2010). Human intelligence and brain networks. *Dialogues in Clinical Neuroscience, 12*(4), 489–501.

Coltheart, M. (2013). How can functional neuroimaging inform cognitive theories? *Perspectives on Psychological Science: A Journal of the Association for Psychological Science, 8*(1), 98–103.

Colzato, L., Szapora, A., Pannekoek, J. N., & Hommel, B. (2013). The impact of physical exercise on convergent and divergent thinking. *Frontiers in Human Neuroscience, 7*, 824.

Corbett, F., Jefferies, E., & Ralph, M. A. L. (2009). Exploring multimodal semantic control impairments in semantic aphasia: Evidence from naturalistic object use. *Neuropsychologia, 47*(13), 2721–2731.

Corbett, F., Jefferies, E., & Ralph, M. A. L. (2011). Deregulated semantic cognition follows prefrontal and temporo-parietal damage: Evidence from the impact of task constraint on nonverbal object use. *Journal of Cognitive Neuroscience, 23*(5), 1125–1135.

Cox, D. D., & Dean, T. (2014). Neural networks and neuroscience-inspired computer vision. *Current Biology, 24*(18), R921–R929.

Craig, J., & Baron-Cohen, S. (1999). Creativity and imagination in autism and Asperger syndrome. *Journal of Autism and Developmental Disorders, 29*(4), 319–326.

Cramond, B., Matthews-Morgan, J., Bandalos, D., & Zuo, L. (2005). A report on the 40-year follow-up of the Torrance Tests of Creative Thinking: Alive and well in the new millennium. *Gifted Child Quarterly, 49*(4), 283–291.

Cropley, A. J. (2000). Defining and measuring creativity: Are creativity tests worth using? *Roeper Review, 23*(2), 72–79.

(2006). In praise of convergent thinking. *Creativity Research Journal, 18*(3), 391–404.

Cross, E. S., Hamilton, A. F. de C., & Grafton, S. T. (2006). Building a motor simulation de novo: Observation of dance by dancers. *NeuroImage, 31*(3), 1257–1267.

Cross, E. S., Kraemer, D. J. M., Hamilton, A. F. de C., Kelley, W. M., & Grafton, S. T. (2009). Sensitivity of the action observation network to physical and observational learning. *Cerebral Cortex, 19*(2), 315–326.

Cross, I. (2001). Music, cognition, culture, and evolution. *Annals of the New York Academy of Sciences, 930*, 28–42.

Crowther, P. (2003). Literary metaphor and philosophical insight: The significance of archilochus. In G. R. Boys-Stones (Ed.), *Metaphor, allegory, and the classical tradition: Ancient thought and modern revisions* (pp. 83–100). New York: Oxford University Press.

Cruz-Garza, J. G., Hernandez, Z. R., Nepaul, S., Bradley, K. K., & Contreras-Vidal, J. L. (2014). Neural decoding of expressive human movement from scalp electroencephalography (EEG). *Frontiers in Human Neuroscience, 8*, 188.

Cseh, G. M. (2016). Flow in creativity: A review of potential theoretical conflict. In L. Harmat, F. Ørsted Andersen, F. Ullén, & G. Sadlo (Eds.), *Flow experience: Empirical research and applications*. Berlin: Springer International.

Cseh, G. M., Phillips, L. H., & Pearson, D. G. (2015). Flow, affect and visual creativity. *Cognition & Emotion, 29*(2), 281–291.

Cseh, G. M., Phillips, L. H., & Pearson, D. G. (2016). Mental and perceptual feedback in the development of creative flow. *Consciousness and Cognition, 42*, 150–161.

Csikszentmihalyi, M. (1988). Society, culture, and person: A systems view of creativity. In R. J. Sternberg (Ed.), *The nature of creativity: Contemporary psychological perspectives* (pp. 325–340). Cambridge: Cambridge University Press.

(1997). *Creativity: Flow and the psychology of discovery and invention.* London: Harper & Row.

(1999). Implications of a systems perspective for the study of creativity. In R. J. Sternberg (Ed.), *Handbook of creativity* (pp. 313–335). Cambridge: Cambridge University Press.

(2008). *Flow: The psychology of optimal experience.* New York: Harper Perennial.

Csikszentmihalyi, M., & Csikszentmihalyi, I. S. (1993). Family influences on the development of giftedness. *Ciba Foundation Symposium, 178*, 187–200.

Csikszentmihalyi, M., & Sawyer, K. (1995). Creative insight: The social dimension of a solitary moment. In R. J. Sternberg & J. E. Davidson (Eds.), *The nature of insight* (pp. 329–363). Cambridge, MA: MIT Press.

Curie, E. (1937). *Madame Curie: A biography.* Literary Guild of America.

Custers, R., & Aarts, H. (2010). The unconscious will: How the pursuit of goals operates outside of conscious awareness. *Science, 329*(5987), 47–50.

Cuypers, K., Krokstad, S., Holmen, T. L., Skjei Knudtsen, M., Bygren, L. O., & Holmen, J. (2012). Patterns of receptive and creative cultural activities and their association with perceived health, anxiety, depression and satisfaction with life among adults: The HUNT study, Norway. *Journal of Epidemiology and Community Health, 66*(8), 698–703.

Dacey, J. S., & Madaus, G. F. (1969). Creativity: Definitions, explanations and facilitation. *Irish Journal of Education/Iris Eireannach an Oideachais, 3*(1), 55–69.

Daprati, E., Iosa, M., & Haggard, P. (2009). A dance to the music of time: Aesthetically-relevant changes in body posture in performing art. *PloS One, 4*(3), e5023.

D'Ausilio, A., Novembre, G., Fadiga, L., & Keller, P. E. (2015). What can music tell us about social interaction? *Trends in Cognitive Sciences, 19*(3), 111–114.

Davelaar, E. J. (2015). Semantic search in the remote associates test. *Topics in Cognitive Science, 7*(3), 494–512.

Davies, D. (2011). "I'll Be Your Mirror"? Embodied agency, dance, and neuroscience. In E. Schellekens & P. Goldie (Eds.), *The aesthetic mind: Philosophy and psychology* (pp. 346–356). Oxford: Oxford University Press.

De Deyne, S., Navarro, D. J., Perfors, A., & Storms, G. (2016). Structure at every scale: A semantic network account of the similarities between unrelated concepts. *Journal of Experimental Psychology. General*, *145*(9), 1228–1254.

De Pisapia, N., Bacci, F., Parrott, D., & Melcher, D. (2016). Brain networks for visual creativity: A functional connectivity study of planning a visual artwork. *Scientific Reports*, *6*, 39185.

De Poli, G. (2003). Analysis and modeling of expressive intentions in music performance. *Annals of the New York Academy of Sciences*, *999*, 118–123.

Dean, R. T., & Bailes, F. (2015). Using time series analysis to evaluate skin conductance during movement in piano improvisation. *Psychology of Music*, *43*(1), 3–23.

Defelipe, J. (2011). The evolution of the brain, the human nature of cortical circuits, and intellectual creativity. *Frontiers in Neuroanatomy*, *5*, 29.

Dehaene, S. (2009). Origins of mathematical intuitions: The case of arithmetic. *Annals of the New York Academy of Sciences*, *1156*(1), 232–259.

Desco, M., Navas-Sanchez, F. J., Sanchez-González, J., Reig, S., Robles, O., Franco, C., … Arango, C. (2011). Mathematically gifted adolescents use more extensive and more bilateral areas of the fronto-parietal network than controls during executive functioning and fluid reasoning tasks. *NeuroImage*, *57*(1), 281–292.

Desmond, J. E., & Glover, G. H. (2002). Estimating sample size in functional MRI (fMRI) neuroimaging studies: Statistical power analyses. *Journal of Neuroscience Methods*, *118*(2), 115–128.

DeYoung, C. G., Flanders, J. L., & Peterson, J. B. (2008). Cognitive abilities involved in insight problem solving: An individual differences model. *Creativity Research Journal*, *20*(3), 278–290.

Diamond, J. M. (1982). Evolution of bowerbirds' bowers: Animal origins of the aesthetic sense. *Nature*, *297*(5862), 99–102.

Diedrichsen, J., & Shadmehr, R. (2005). Detecting and adjusting for artifacts in fMRI time series data. *NeuroImage*, *27*(3), 624–634.

Dietrich, A. (2004a). Neurocognitive mechanisms underlying the experience of flow. *Consciousness and Cognition*, *13*(4), 746–761.

(2004b). The cognitive neuroscience of creativity. *Psychonomic Bulletin & Review*, *11*(6), 1011–1026.

(2007a). The wavicle of creativity. *Methods*, *42*(1), 1–2.

(2007b). Who's afraid of a cognitive neuroscience of creativity? *Methods*, *42*(1), 22–27.

(2014). The mythconception of the mad genius. *Frontiers in Psychology*, *5*, 79.

(2015). *How creativity happens in the brain*. Basingstoke: Palgrave Macmillan.

Dietrich, A., & Haider, H. (2015). Human creativity, evolutionary algorithms, and predictive representations: The mechanics of thought trials. *Psychonomic Bulletin & Review*, *22*(4), 897–915.

Dietrich, A., & Kanso, R. (2010). A review of EEG, ERP, and neuroimaging studies of creativity and insight. *Psychological Bulletin*, *136*(5), 822–848.

Dietrich, A., & McDaniel, W. (2004). Endocannabinoids and exercise. *British Journal of Sports Medicine*, *38*(5), 536.

Dijksterhuis, A., & Aarts, H. (2010). Goals, attention, and (un)consciousness. *Annual Review of Psychology*, *61*, 467–490.

Dijksterhuis, A., & Meurs, T. (2006). Where creativity resides: The generative power of unconscious thought. *Consciousness and Cognition*, *15*(1), 135–146.

Dinstein, I., Thomas, C., Behrmann, M., & Heeger, D. J. (2008). A mirror up to nature. *Current Biology*, *18*(1), R13–R18.

Dixon, M. L., Fox, K. C. R., & Christoff, K. (2014). A framework for understanding the relationship between externally and internally directed cognition. *Neuropsychologia*, *62*, 321–330.

Dollinger, S. J. (2003). Need for uniqueness, need for cognition, and creativity. *Journal of Creative Behavior*, *37*(2), 99–116.

Domino, G. (1989). Synesthesia and creativity in fine arts students: An empirical look. *Creativity Research Journal*, *2*(1–2), 17–29.

Donoso, M., Collins, A. G. E., & Koechlin, E. (2014). Foundations of human reasoning in the prefrontal cortex. *Science*, *344*(6191), 1481–1486.

Dorfman, L., Martindale, C., Gassimova, V., & Vartanian, O. (2008). Creativity and speed of information processing: A double dissociation involving elementary versus inhibitory cognitive tasks. *Personality and Individual Differences*, *44*(6), 1382–1390.

Doyle, C. L. (1998). The writer tells: The creative process in the writing of literary fiction. *Creativity Research Journal*, *11*(1), 29–37.

Drake, J. E., & Winner, E. (2009). Precocious realists: Perceptual and cognitive characteristics associated with drawing talent in non-autistic children. *Philosophical Transactions of the Royal Society B: Biological Sciences*, *364*(1522), 1449–1458.

Duff, M. C., Kurczek, J., Rubin, R., Cohen, N. J., & Tranel, D. (2013). Hippocampal amnesia disrupts creative thinking. *Hippocampus*, *23*(12), 1143–1149.

Dunbar, K. N. (1997). How scientists think: On-line creativity and conceptual change in science. In T. B. Ward, S. M. Smith, & J. Viad (Eds.), *Creative thought: An investigation of conceptual structures and processes* (pp. 461–493). Washington, DC: American Psychological Association.

    (1999). Scientific creativity. In M. A. Runco & S. R. Pritzker (Eds.), *Encyclopedia of Creativity* (Vol. 1, pp. 1379–1384). New York: Academic Press.

    (2001). What scientific thinking reveals about the nature of cognition. In K. Crowley, C. D. Schunn, & T. Okada (Eds.), *Designing for science: Implications from everyday classroom and professional settings* (pp. 115–140). Mahwah, NJ: Lawrence Erlbaum.

Duncker, K. (1945). On problem solving. *Psychological Monographs*, *58*(5), 1–113.

Durante, D., & Dunson, D. B. (2016). Bayesian inference and testing of group differences in brain networks. *Bayesian Analysis*, 13(1), 29–58.

Dutta, S. (Ed.). (2012). *The global innovation index 2012: Stronger innovation linkages for global growth*. New Delhi: INSEAD, World Intellectual Property Organization.

Dyer, F. C. (2002). The biology of the dance language. *Annual Review of Entomology*, *47*, 917–949.

Dykes, M., & McGhie, A. (1976). A comparative study of attentional strategies of schizophrenic and highly creative normal subjects. *British Journal of Psychiatry: The Journal of Mental Science*, *128*, 50–56.

Dziedziewicz, D., & Karwowski, M. (2015). Development of children's creative visual imagination: A theoretical model and enhancement programmes. *Education*, 43(4), 382–392.

Early, G. L. (2001). The art of the muscle: Miles Davis as American knight and American knave. In G. L. Early (Ed.), *Miles Davis and American culture* (pp. 2–23). St. Louis, MO: Missouri Historical Society Press.

Edelman, G. M. (1989). *The remembered present: A biological theory of consciousness*. New York: Basic Books.

Edwards, B. (1982). *Drawing on the right side of the brain*. Glasgow: Fontana.

Ellamil, M., Dobson, C., Beeman, M., & Christoff, K. (2012). Evaluative and generative modes of thought during the creative process. *NeuroImage*, *59*(2), 1783–1794.

Ellis, A. W., & Young, A. W. (2000). *Human cognitive neuropsychology: A textbook with readings*. Hove: Psychology Press.

Else, J. E., Ellis, J., & Orme, E. (2015). Art expertise modulates the emotional response to modern art, especially abstract: An ERP investigation. *Frontiers in Human Neuroscience*, *9*, 525.

Emmer, M. (1994). Art and visual mathematics. *Leonardo*, *27*(3), 237–240.

Endler, J. A. (2012). Bowerbirds, art and aesthetics. *Communicative & Integrative Biology, 5*(3), 281–283.

Engel, A., & Keller, P. E. (2011). The perception of musical spontaneity in improvised and imitated jazz performances. *Frontiers in Psychology, 2*, 83.

Erhard, K., Kessler, F., Neumann, N., Ortheil, H.-J., & Lotze, M. (2014a). Professional training in creative writing is associated with enhanced fronto-striatal activity in a literary text continuation task. *NeuroImage, 100*, 15–23.

Ericsson, K. A., Krampe, R. T., & Tesch-Römer, C. (1993). The role of deliberate practice in the acquisition of expert performance. *Psychological Review, 100*(3), 363–406.

Eriksson, J., Vogel, E. K., Lansner, A., Bergström, F., & Nyberg, L. (2015). Neurocognitive architecture of working memory. *Neuron, 88*(1), 33–46.

Evans, J. S. B. T. (2008). Dual-processing accounts of reasoning, judgment, and social cognition. *Annual Review of Psychology, 59*, 255–278.

Evans, J. S. B. T., & Stanovich, K. E. (2013). Dual-process theories of higher cognition: Advancing the debate. *Perspectives on Psychological Science: A Journal of the Association for Psychological Science, 8*(3), 223–241.

Eysenck, H. J. (1994). The measurement of creativity. In M. Boden (Ed.), *Dimensions of creativity* (pp. 199–242). Cambridge, MA: MIT Press.

   (1995). *Genius: The natural history of creativity.* Cambridge: Cambridge University Press.

Faust, M., & Kenett, Y. N. (2014). Rigidity, chaos and integration: Hemispheric interaction and individual differences in metaphor comprehension. *Frontiers in Human Neuroscience, 8*, 511.

Fedorenko, E., & Thompson-Schill, S. L. (2014). Reworking the language network. *Trends in Cognitive Sciences, 18*(3), 120–126.

Fedorenko, E., Duncan, J., & Kanwisher, N. (2012). Language-selective and domain-general regions lie side by side within Broca's area. *Current Biology, 22*(21), 2059–2062.

Feist, G. J. (1993). A structural model of scientific eminence. *Psychological Science, 4*(6), 366–371.

   (1998). A meta-analysis of personality in scientific and artistic creativity. *Personality and Social Psychology Review, 2*(4), 290–309.

Ferstl, E. C., & von Cramon, D. Y. (2001). The role of coherence and cohesion in text comprehension: An event-related fMRI study. *Cognitive Brain Research, 11*(3), 325–340.

Ferstl, E. C., & von Cramon, D. Y. (2002). What does the frontomedian cortex contribute to language processing: Coherence or theory of mind? *NeuroImage, 17*(3), 1599–1612.

Feyerabend, P. (1974). *Against method: Outline of an anarchistic theory of knowledge.* Atlantic Highlands, NJ: Humanities Press.

Field, D. T., & Inman, L. A. (2014). Weighing brain activity with the balance: A contemporary replication of Angelo Mosso's historical experiment. *Brain, 137*(2), 634–639.

Filimon, F., Nelson, J. D., Hagler, D. J., & Sereno, M. I. (2007). Human cortical representations for reaching: Mirror neurons for execution, observation, and imagery. *NeuroImage, 37*(4), 1315–1328.

Finger, S., Zaidel, D. W., Boller, F., & Bogousslavsky, J. (Eds.). (2013). *The fine arts, neurology, and neuroscience: New discoveries and changing landscapes.* Amsterdam: Elsevier.

Fink, A., & Benedek, M. (2014). EEG alpha power and creative ideation. *Neuroscience and Biobehavioral Reviews, 44,* 111–123.

Fink, A., Benedek, M., Koschutnig, K., Pirker, E., Berger, E., Meister, S., … Weiss, E. M. (2015). Training of verbal creativity modulates brain activity in regions associated with language- and memory-related demands. *Human Brain Mapping, 36*(10), 4104–4115.

Fink, A., Grabner, R. H., Benedek, M., Reishofer, G., Hauswirth, V., Fally, M., … Neubauer, A. C. (2009). The creative brain: Investigation of brain activity during creative problem solving by means of EEG and fMRI. *Human Brain Mapping, 30*(3), 734–748.

Fink, A., Grabner, R. H., Gebauer, D., Reishofer, G., Koschutnig, K., & Ebner, F. (2010). Enhancing creativity by means of cognitive stimulation: Evidence from an fMRI study. *NeuroImage, 52*(4), 1687–1695.

Fink, A., Graif, B., & Neubauer, A. C. (2009). Brain correlates underlying creative thinking: EEG alpha activity in professional vs. novice dancers. *NeuroImage, 46*(3), 854–862.

Fink, A., Koschutnig, K., Benedek, M., Reishofer, G., Ischebeck, A., Weiss, E. M., & Ebner, F. (2012). Stimulating creativity via the exposure to other people's ideas. *Human Brain Mapping, 33*(11), 2603–2610.

Fink, A., Koschutnig, K., Hutterer, L., Steiner, E., Benedek, M., Weber, B., … Weiss, E. M. (2014). Gray matter density in relation to different facets of verbal creativity. *Brain Structure & Function, 219*(4), 1263–1269.

Fink, A., Weber, B., Koschutnig, K., Benedek, M., Reishofer, G., Ebner, F., … Weiss, E. M. (2013). Creativity and schizotypy from the neuroscience perspective. *Cognitive, Affective, & Behavioral Neuroscience, 14*(1), 1–10.

Finke, R. A. (1990). *Creative imagery: Discoveries and inventions in visualization.* Hillsdale, NJ: Lawrence Erlbaum.

(1996). Imagery, creativity, and emergent structure. *Consciousness and Cognition, 5*(3), 381–393.

Finke, R. A., & Slayton, K. (1988). Explorations of creative visual synthesis in mental imagery. *Memory & Cognition, 16*(3), 252–257.

Finke, R. A., Ward, T. B., & Smith, S. M. (1996). *Creative cognition: Theory, research, and applications*. Cambridge, MA: MIT Press.

Fitch, W. T. (2016). Dance, music, meter and groove: A forgotten partnership. *Frontiers in Human Neuroscience, 10*, 64.

FitzGibbon, C. D., & Fanshawe, J. H. (1988). Stotting in Thomson's gazelles: An honest signal of condition. *Behavioral Ecology and Sociobiology, 23*(2), 69–74.

Fitzpatrick, R. (2011, August 18). Red Hot Chili Peppers: The band that couldn't be stopped. *The Guardian*. Retrieved from www.theguardian.com/music/2011/aug/18/red-hot-chili-peppers-interview

Flaherty, A. W. (2005). Frontotemporal and dopaminergic control of idea generation and creative drive. *Journal of Comparative Neurology, 493*(1), 147–153.

Fletcher, L., & Carruthers, P. (2012). Metacognition and reasoning. *Philosophical Transactions of the Royal Society B: Biological Sciences, 367*(1594), 1366–1378.

Fletcher, P. D., Downey, L. E., Witoonpanich, P., & Warren, J. D. (2013). The brain basis of musicophilia: Evidence from frontotemporal lobar degeneration. *Frontiers in Psychology, 4*, 347.

Fogarty, L., Creanza, N., & Feldman, M. W. (2015). Cultural evolutionary perspectives on creativity and human innovation. *Trends in Ecology & Evolution, 30*(12), 736–754.

Folley, B. S., & Park, S. (2005). Verbal creativity and schizotypal personality in relation to prefrontal hemispheric laterality: A behavioral and near-infrared optical imaging study. *Schizophrenia Research, 80*(2–3), 271–282.

Forgeard, M. J. C., & Eichner, K. V. (2014). Creativity as a target and tool for positive interventions. In A. C. Parks & S. M. Schueller (Eds.), *The Wiley Blackwell handbook of positive psychological interventions* (pp. 135–154). Chichester: Wiley.

Fothergill, A., & Linfield, M. (Directors) (2012). *Chimpanzee* [Motion picture]. USA: Walt Disney Studios Motion Pictures.

Fox, K. C. R., Spreng, R. N., Ellamil, M., Andrews-Hanna, J. R., & Christoff, K. (2015). The wandering brain: Meta-analysis of functional neuroimaging studies of mind-wandering and related spontaneous thought processes. *NeuroImage, 111*, 611–621.

Fox, M. D., Snyder, A. Z., Vincent, J. L., Corbetta, M., Van Essen, D. C., & Raichle, M. E. (2005). The human brain is intrinsically organized into dynamic, anticorrelated functional networks. *Proceedings of the National Academy of Sciences of the United States of America, 102*(27), 9673–9678.

Fox, M. D., Zhang, D., Snyder, A. Z., & Raichle, M. E. (2009). The global signal and observed anticorrelated resting state brain networks. *Journal of Neurophysiology, 101*(6), 3270–3283.

Freed, J., & Parsons, L. (1998). *Right-brained children in a left-brained world: Unlocking the potential of your ADD child*. New York: Simon & Schuster.

Friederici, A. D. (2011). The brain basis of language processing: From structure to function. *Physiological Reviews*, *91*(4), 1357–1392.

(2015). White-matter pathways for speech and language processing. *Handbook of Clinical Neurology*, *129*, 177–186.

Fry, R. (1909). An essay in aesthetics. In J. B. Bullen (Ed.), *Vision and design* (pp. 12–27). Mineola, NY: Dover.

Fuchs-Beauchamp, K. D., Karnes, M. B., & Johnson, L. J. (1993). Creativity and intelligence in preschoolers. *Gifted Child Quarterly*, *37*(3), 113–117.

Gallese, V., Fadiga, L., Fogassi, L., & Rizzolatti, G. (1996). Action recognition in the premotor cortex. *Brain*, *119*(2), 593–609.

Gardner, H. E. (1983). *Frames of mind: The theory of multiple intelligences*. New York: Basic Books.

(1994). The creators' patterns. In M. Boden (Ed.), *Dimensions of creativity* (pp. 143–158). Cambridge, MA: MIT Press.

(2011). *Creating minds: An anatomy of creativity seen through the lives of Freud, Einstein, Picasso, Stravinsky, Eliot, Graham, and Ghandi*. New York: Basic Books.

Gazzaniga, M. S. (1967). The split brain in man. *Scientific American*, *217*(2), 24–29.

(2000). Cerebral specialization and interhemispheric communication: Does the corpus callosum enable the human condition? *Brain*, *123*(7), 1293–1326.

Geake, J. G., & Hansen, P. C. (2005). Neural correlates of intelligence as revealed by fMRI of fluid analogies. *NeuroImage*, *26*(2), 555–564.

Geretsegger, M., Elefant, C., Mössler, K. A., & Gold, C. (2014). Music therapy for people with autism spectrum disorder. *Cochrane Database of Systematic Reviews*, *6*, CD004381.

Getzels, J. W., & Jackson, P. W. (1962). *Creativity and intelligence: Explorations with gifted students*. New York: Wiley.

Ghiselin, B. (Ed.). (1985). *The creative process: A symposium*. Berkeley, CA: University of California Press.

Gibson, C., Folley, B. S., & Park, S. (2009). Enhanced divergent thinking and creativity in musicians: A behavioral and near-infrared spectroscopy study. *Brain and Cognition*, *69*(1), 162–169.

Gilhooly, K. J. (2016). Incubation and intuition in creative problem solving. *Cognitive Science*, *117*(3), 994–1024.

Gilhooly, K. J., Ball, L. J., & Macchi, L. (2015). Insight and creative thinking processes: Routine and special. *Thinking & Reasoning*, *21*(1), 1–4.

Gilhooly, K. J., Georgiou, G., & Devery, U. (2013). Incubation and creativity: Do something different. *Thinking & Reasoning*, *19*(2), 137–149.

Glăveanu, V. P. (2013). Rewriting the language of creativity: The Five A's framework. *Review of General Psychology, 17*(1), 69–81.

Glazek, K. (2012). Visual and motor processing in visual artists: Implications for cognitive and neural mechanisms. *Psychology of Aesthetics, Creativity, and the Arts, 6*(2), 155–167.

Glowinski, D., Mancini, M., Cowie, R., Camurri, A., Chiorri, C., & Doherty, C. (2013). The movements made by performers in a skilled quartet: A distinctive pattern, and the function that it serves. *Frontiers in Psychology, 4*, 841.

Goel, V. (2007). Anatomy of deductive reasoning. *Trends in Cognitive Sciences, 11*(10), 435–441.

(2014). Creative brains: Designing in the real world. *Frontiers in Human Neuroscience, 8*, 241.

Gold, R., Faust, M., & Ben-Artzi, E. (2012). Metaphors and verbal creativity: The role of the right hemisphere. *Laterality, 17*(5), 602–614.

Golden, C. J. (1975). The measurement of creativity by the Stroop Color and Word Test. *Journal of Personality Assessment, 39*(5), 502–506.

Gombrich, E. H. (1960). *Art and illusion: A study in the psychology of pictorial representation.* New York: Pantheon Books.

(2011). *The story of art.* London: Phaidon Press.

Gonen-Yaacovi, G., de Souza, L. C., Levy, R., Urbanski, M., Josse, G., & Volle, E. (2013). Rostral and caudal prefrontal contribution to creativity: A meta-analysis of functional imaging data. *Frontiers in Human Neuroscience, 7*, 465.

Gosselin, N., Paquette, S., & Peretz, I. (2015). Sensitivity to musical emotions in congenital amusia. *Cortex; a Journal Devoted to the Study of the Nervous System and Behavior, 71*, 171–182.

Gotts, S. J., Jo, H. J., Wallace, G. L., Saad, Z. S., Cox, R. W., & Martin, A. (2013). Two distinct forms of functional lateralization in the human brain. *Proceedings of the National Academy of Sciences of the United States of America, 110*(36), E3435.

Gough, H. G. (1979). A creative personality scale for the Adjective Check List. *Journal of Personality and Social Psychology, 37*(8), 1398–1405.

Goulden, N., Khusnulina, A., Davis, N. J., Bracewell, R. M., Bokde, A. L., McNulty, J. P., & Mullins, P. G. (2014). The salience network is responsible for switching between the default mode network and the central executive network: Replication from DCM. *NeuroImage, 99*, 180–190.

Gracco, V. L., Tremblay, P., & Pike, B. (2005). Imaging speech production using fMRI. *NeuroImage, 26*(1), 294–301.

Green, A. E. (2016). Creativity, within reason semantic distance and dynamic state creativity in relational thinking and reasoning. *Current Directions in Psychological Science, 25*(1), 28–35.

Green, A. E., Kraemer, D. J. M., Fugelsang, J. A., Gray, J. R., & Dunbar, K. N. (2010). Connecting long distance: Semantic distance in analogical reasoning modulates frontopolar cortex activity. *Cerebral Cortex*, *20*(1), 70–76.

Green, A. E., Kraemer, D. J. M., Fugelsang, J. A., Gray, J. R., & Dunbar, K. N. (2012). Neural correlates of creativity in analogical reasoning. *Journal of Experimental Psychology: Learning, Memory, and Cognition*, *38*(2), 264–272.

Green, A. E., Spiegel, K. A., Giangrande, E. J., Weinberger, A. B., Gallagher, N. M., & Turkeltaub, P. E. (2016). Thinking cap plus thinking zap: tDCS of frontopolar cortex improves creative analogical reasoning and facilitates conscious augmentation of state creativity in verb generation. *Cerebral Cortex*, 27(4), 2628–2639.

Green, D. M., & Swets, J. A. (1966). *Signal detection theory and psychophysics.* New York: Wiley.

Greve, D. N. (2011). An absolute beginner's guide to surface- and voxel-based morphometric analysis. *Proceedings of the International Society for Magnetic Resonance in Medicine*, 19, 7–13.

Griffiths, T. L., Steyvers, M., & Tenenbaum, J. B. (2007). Topics in semantic representation. *Psychological Review*, *114*(2), 211–244.

Grimm, O., Pohlack, S., Cacciaglia, R., Winkelmann, T., Plichta, M. M., Demirakca, T., & Flor, H. (2015). Amygdalar and hippocampal volume: A comparison between manual segmentation, Freesurfer and VBM. *Journal of Neuroscience Methods*, *253*, 254–261.

Groborz, M., & Nęcka, E. (2003). Creativity and cognitive control: Explorations of generation and evaluation skills. *Creativity Research Journal*, *15*(2–3), 183–197.

Grossberg, S. (2008). The art of seeing and painting. *Spatial Vision*, *21*(3–5), 463–486.

Grossberg, S., & Zajac, L. (2017). How humans consciously see paintings and paintings illuminate how humans see. *Art & Perception*, *5*(1), 1–95.

Gruber, H. E. (1989). Networks of enterprise in creative scientific work. In B. Gholson, W. R. Shadish Jr, R. A. Neimeyer, & A. C. Houts (Eds.), *Psychology of science: Contributions to metascience* (pp. 246–265). Cambridge: Cambridge University Press.

Gruzelier, J. H. (2014). EEG-neurofeedback for optimising performance. II: Creativity, the performing arts and ecological validity. *Neuroscience and Biobehavioral Reviews*, *44*, 142–158.

Gruzelier, J. H., Inoue, A., Smart, R., Steed, A., & Steffert, T. (2010). Acting performance and flow state enhanced with sensory-motor rhythm neurofeedback comparing ecologically valid immersive VR and training screen scenarios. *Neuroscience Letters*, *480*(2), 112–116.

Gruzelier, J. H., Thompson, T., Redding, E., Brandt, R., & Steffert, T. (2014). Application of alpha/theta neurofeedback and heart rate variability training to young contemporary dancers: State anxiety and creativity. *International Journal of Psychophysiology, 93*(1), 105–111.

Guilford, J. P. (1950). Creativity. *American Psychologist, 5*(9), 444–454.

(1957). Creative abilities in the arts. *Psychological Review, 64*(2), 110–118.

(1959). Three faces of intellect. *American Psychologist, 14*(8), 469–479.

(1967). *The nature of human intelligence.* New York: McGraw-Hill.

(1970). Creativity: Retrospect and prospect. *Journal of Creative Behavior, 4*(3), 149–168.

(1975). Creativity: A quarter century of progress. In I. A. Taylor & J. W. Getzels (Eds.), *Perspectives in creativity* (pp. 37–59). Chicago, IL: Aldine.

(1988). Some changes in the structure-of-intellect model. *Educational and Psychological Measurement, 48*(1), 1–4.

Guilford, J. P., Christensen, P. R., Merrifield, P. R., & Wilson, R. C. (1960). *Alternate Uses manual.* Menlo Park, CA: Mind Garden.

Guillemin, R. (2010). Similarities and contrasts in the creative processes of the sciences and the arts. *Leonardo, 43*(1), 59–62.

Gupta, N., Jang, Y., Mednick, S. C., & Huber, D. E. (2012). The road not taken: Creative solutions require avoidance of high-frequency responses. *Psychological Science, 23*(3), 288–294.

Gurd, J. M. (Ed.). (2012). *Handbook of clinical neuropsychology* (2nd edn.). Oxford: Oxford University Press.

Gusnard, D. A., Raichle, M. E., & Raichle, M. E. (2001). Searching for a baseline: Functional imaging and the resting human brain. *Nature Reviews Neuroscience, 2*(10), 685–694.

Hackman, D. A., Farah, M. J., & Meaney, M. J. (2010). Socioeconomic status and the brain: Mechanistic insights from human and animal research. *Nature Reviews Neuroscience, 11*(9), 651–659.

Hagoort, P. (2014). Nodes and networks in the neural architecture for language: Broca's region and beyond. *Current Opinion in Neurobiology, 28*, 136–141.

Hald, S. V., Baker, F. A., & Ridder, H. M. (2017). A preliminary evaluation of the interpersonal music-communication competence scales. *Nordic Journal of Music Therapy, 26*(1), 40–61.

Halford, G. S., Wilson, W. H., & Phillips, S. (2010). Relational knowledge: The foundation of higher cognition. *Trends in Cognitive Sciences, 14*(11), 497–505.

Haller, C. S., & Courvoisier, D. S. (2010). Personality and thinking style in different creative domains. *Psychology of Aesthetics, Creativity, and the Arts, 4*(3), 149–160.

Hänggi, J., Koeneke, S., Bezzola, L., & Jäncke, L. (2010). Structural neuroplasticity in the sensorimotor network of professional female ballet dancers. *Human Brain Mapping, 31*(8), 1196–1206.

Hanna, J. L., Abrahams, R. D., Crumrine, N. R., Dirks, R., Von Gizycki, R., Heyer, P., … Wild, S. A. (1979). Movements toward understanding humans through the anthropological study of dance (and comments and reply). *Current Anthropology*, *20*(2), 313–339.

Hargreaves, D. J. (2012). Musical imagination: Perception and production, beauty and creativity. *Psychology of Music*, *40*(5), 539–557.

Hargreaves, D. J., Miell, D., & MacDonald, R. A. R. (Eds.). (2012). *Musical imaginations: Multidisciplinary perspectives on creativity, performance, and perception*. Oxford: Oxford University Press.

Harnad, S. (2006). Creativity: Method or magic? *Hungarian Studies*, *20*(1), 163–177.

Harp, J. P., & High, W. M. (2017). The brain and its maps: An illustrative history. In S. D. Brunn & M. Dodge (Eds.), *Mapping across academia* (pp. 123–144). Amsterdam: Springer.

Harrington, D. M. (1990). The ecology of human creativity: A psychological perspective. In M. A. Runco & R. S. Albert (Eds.), *Theories of creativity* (pp. 143–169). Thousand Oaks, CA: Sage.

Hart, E., & Di Blasi, Z. (2015). Combined flow in musical jam sessions: A pilot qualitative study. *Psychology of Music*, *43*(2), 275–290.

Hass, R. W., & Weisberg, R. W. (2009). Career development in two seminal American songwriters: A test of the equal odds rule. *Creativity Research Journal*, *21*(2–3), 183–190.

Hassabis, D., Kumaran, D., Summerfield, C., & Botvinick, M. (2017). Neuroscience-inspired artificial intelligence. *Neuron*, *95*(2), 245–258.

Haueis, P. (2014). Meeting the brain on its own terms. *Frontiers in Human Neuroscience*, *8*, 815.

Haught-Tromp, C. (2017). The Green Eggs and Ham hypothesis: How constraints facilitate creativity. *Psychology of Aesthetics, Creativity, and the Arts*, *11*(1), 10–17.

Haxby, J. V., Connolly, A. C., & Guntupalli, J. S. (2014). Decoding neural representational spaces using multivariate pattern analysis. *Annual Review of Neuroscience*, *37*, 435–456.

Heilman, K. M., & Valenstein, E. (Eds.). (2012). *Clinical neuropsychology* (5th edn.). Oxford: Oxford University Press.

Heilman, K. M., Nadeau, S. E., & Beversdorf, D. O. (2003). Creative innovation: Possible brain mechanisms. *Neurocase*, *9*(5), 369–379.

Heller, K. A. (2007). Scientific ability and creativity. *High Ability Studies*, *18*(2), 209–234.

Heller, K., Bullerjahn, C., & von Georgi, R. (2015). The relationship between personality traits, flow-experience, and different aspects of practice behavior of amateur vocal students. *Frontiers in Psychology*, *6*, 1901.

Helson, R., & Pals, J. L. (2000). Creative potential, creative achievement, and personal growth. *Journal of Personality*, *68*(1), 1–27.

Hemsley, D. R. (2005). The schizophrenic experience: Taken out of context? *Schizophrenia Bulletin, 31*(1), 43–53.

Hennessey, B. A., & Amabile, T. M. (1988). The conditions of creativity. In R. J. Sternberg (Ed.), *The nature of creativity: Contemporary psychological perspectives* (pp. 11–43). Cambridge: Cambridge University Press.

Hennessey, B. A., & Amabile, T. M. (2010). Creativity. *Annual Review of Psychology, 61*, 569–598.

Herholz, S. C., Lappe, C., Knief, A., & Pantev, C. (2009). Imagery mismatch negativity in musicians. *Annals of the New York Academy of Sciences, 1169*, 173–177.

Hermann, I., Haser, V., van Elst, L. T., Ebert, D., Müller-Feldmeth, D., Riedel, A., & Konieczny, L. (2013). Automatic metaphor processing in adults with Asperger syndrome: A metaphor interference effect task. *European Archives of Psychiatry and Clinical Neuroscience, 263*(Suppl. 2), S177–S187.

Hickok, G. (2009). Eight problems for the mirror neuron theory of action understanding in monkeys and humans. *Journal of Cognitive Neuroscience, 21*(7), 1229–1243.

(2012). Computational neuroanatomy of speech production. *Nature Reviews Neuroscience, 13*(2), 135–145.

Hickok, G., & Poeppel, D. (2007). The cortical organization of speech processing. *Nature Reviews Neuroscience, 8*(5), 393–402.

(2015). Neural basis of speech perception. *Handbook of Clinical Neurology, 129*, 149–160.

Hikosaka, O., & Isoda, M. (2010). Switching from automatic to controlled behavior: Cortico-basal ganglia mechanisms. *Trends in Cognitive Sciences, 14*(4), 154–161.

Hobeika, L., Diard-Detoeuf, C., Garcin, B., Levy, R., & Volle, E. (2016). General and specialized brain correlates for analogical reasoning: A meta-analysis of functional imaging studies. *Human Brain Mapping, 37*(5), 1953–1969.

Hofstadter, D. R. (2001). Analogy as the core of cognition. In D. Gentner, K. J. Holyoak, & B. N. Kokinov (Eds.), *The analogical mind: Perspectives from cognitive science* (pp. 499–538). Cambridge, MA: MIT Press.

Hofstadter, D. R., & Fluid Analogies Research Group. (1996). *Fluid concepts and creative analogies: Computer models of the fundamental mechanisms of thought.* New York: Basic Books.

Holyoak, K. J., & Thagard, P. (1995). *Mental leaps: Analogy in creative thought.* Cambridge, MA: MIT Press.

Hommel, B., Müsseler, J., Aschersleben, G., & Prinz, W. (2001). The Theory of Event Coding (TEC): A framework for perception and action planning. *Behavioral and Brain Sciences, 24*(5), 849–878.

Honing, H., ten Cate, C., Peretz, I., & Trehub, S. E. (2015). Without it no music: Cognition, biology and evolution of musicality. *Philosophical Transactions of the Royal Society B: Biological Sciences, 370*(1664).

Hoover, S. M., & Feldhusen, J. F. (1994). Scientific problem solving and problem finding: A theoretical model. In M. A. Runco (Ed.), *Problem finding, problem solving, and creativity* (pp. 201–219). Norwood, NJ: Ablex Publishing.

Hoppe, K. D. (1988). Hemispheric specialization and creativity. *Psychiatric Clinics of North America, 11*(3), 303–315.

Horvath, J. C., Carter, O., & Forte, J. D. (2014). Transcranial direct current stimulation: Five important issues we aren't discussing (but probably should be). *Frontiers in Systems Neuroscience, 8*, 2.

Horvath, J. C., Forte, J. D., & Carter, O. (2015). Evidence that transcranial direct current stimulation (tDCS) generates little-to-no reliable neurophysiologic effect beyond MEP amplitude modulation in healthy human subjects: A systematic review. *Neuropsychologia, 66*, 213–236.

Howard-Jones, P. A., Blakemore, S.-J., Samuel, E. A., Summers, I. R., & Claxton, G. (2005). Semantic divergence and creative story generation: An fMRI investigation. *Cognitive Brain Research, 25*(1), 240–250.

Huang, F., Fan, J., & Luo, J. (2015). The neural basis of novelty and appropriateness in processing of creative chunk decomposition. *NeuroImage, 113*, 122–132.

Huang, J., Francis, A. P., & Carr, T. H. (2008). Studying overt word reading and speech production with event-related fMRI: A method for detecting, assessing, and correcting articulation-induced signal changes and for measuring onset time and duration of articulation. *Brain and Language, 104*(1), 10–23.

Huang, P., Qiu, L., Shen, L., Zhang, Y., Song, Z., Qi, Z., … Xie, P. (2013). Evidence for a left-over-right inhibitory mechanism during figural creative thinking in healthy nonartists. *Human Brain Mapping, 34*(10), 2724–2732.

Hubbard, E. M., & Ramachandran, V. S. (2005). Neurocognitive mechanisms of synesthesia. *Neuron, 48*(3), 509–520.

Huettel, S. A., & McCarthy, G. (2001). The effects of single-trial averaging upon the spatial extent of fMRI activation. *Neuroreport, 12*(11), 2411–2416.

Huettel, S. A., Song, A. W., & McCarthy, G. (2014). *Functional magnetic resonance imaging* (3rd edn.). Sunderland, MA: Sinauer Associates.

Hull, R., Tosun, S., & Vaid, J. (2017). What's so funny? Modelling incongruity in humour production. *Cognition & Emotion, 31*(3), 484–499.

Hulme, C., & Snowling, M. J. (2014). The interface between spoken and written language: Developmental disorders. *Philosophical Transactions of the Royal Society B: Biological Sciences, 369*(1634).

Huron, D. B. (2006). *Sweet anticipation: Music and the psychology of expectation*. Cambridge, MA: MIT Press.

(2015). Affect induction through musical sounds: An ethological perspective. *Philosophical Transactions of the Royal Society B: Biological Sciences, 370*(1664).

Hutton, E. L., & Bassett, M. (1948). The effect of leucotomy on creative personality. *Journal of Mental Science, 94*(395), 332–350.

Hyde, L. (2012). *The gift: How the creative spirit transforms the world*. Edinburgh: Canongate.

Ioannides, A. A. (2007). Dynamic functional connectivity. *Current Opinion in Neurobiology, 17*(2), 161–170.

Issurin, V. B. (2017). Evidence-based prerequisites and precursors of athletic talent: A review. *Sports Medicine, 47*(10), 1993–2010.

Jackendoff, R., & Lerdahl, F. (2006). The capacity for music: What is it, and what's special about it? *Cognition, 100*(1), 33–72.

Jackson, S. A., & Eklund, R. C. (2002). Assessing flow in physical activity: The Flow State Scale–2 and Dispositional Flow Scale–2. *Journal of Sport and Exercise Psychology, 24*(2), 133–150.

Jakobson, R. (1960). Linguistics and poetics. In T. A. Sebeok (Ed.), *Style in language* (pp. 350–377). Cambridge, MA: MIT Press.

James, W. (1891). *The principles of psychology*, Vol. 1. New York: Holt, Rinehart, & Winston.

Jamison, K. R. (1989). Mood disorders and patterns of creativity in British writers and artists. *Psychiatry, 52*(2), 125–134.

Janata, P. (2015). Neural basis of music perception. *Handbook of Clinical Neurology, 129*, 187–205.

Jankowska, D. M., & Karwowski, M. (2015). Measuring creative imagery abilities. *Frontiers in Psychology, 6*, 1591.

Jauk, E., Benedek, M., Dunst, B., & Neubauer, A. C. (2013). The relationship between intelligence and creativity: New support for the threshold hypothesis by means of empirical breakpoint detection. *Intelligence, 41*(4), 212–221.

Jauk, E., Neubauer, A. C., Dunst, B., Fink, A., & Benedek, M. (2015). Gray matter correlates of creative potential: A latent variable voxel-based morphometry study. *NeuroImage, 111*, 312–320.

Jay, R. (2016). *Matthias Buchinger: "The greatest German living."* Los Angeles, CA: Siglio.

Jebb, A. T., & Pfordresher, P. Q. (2016). Exploring perception–action relations in music production: The asymmetric effect of tonal class. *Journal of Experimental Psychology: Human Perception and Performance, 42*(5), 658–670.

Jefferies, E. (2013). The neural basis of semantic cognition: Converging evidence from neuropsychology, neuroimaging and TMS. *Cortex;*

a Journal Devoted to the Study of the Nervous System and Behavior, *49*(3), 611–625.

Jeon, H.-A., & Friederici, A. D. (2015). Degree of automaticity and the prefrontal cortex. *Trends in Cognitive Sciences*, *19*(5), 244–250.

Johansen-Berg, H., & Behrens, T. E. J. (Eds.). (2014). *Diffusion MRI: From quantitative measurement to in-vivo neuroanatomy* (2nd edn.). Waltham, MA: Elsevier/Academic Press.

Johnson, R. A. (1979). Creative imagery in blind and sighted adolescents. *Journal of Mental Imagery*, *3*(1–2), 23–30.

Johnson-Laird, P. N. (2002). How jazz musicians improvise. *Music Perception: An Interdisciplinary Journal*, *19*(3), 415–442.

Johnson-Laird, P. N., Khemlani, S. S., & Goodwin, G. P. (2015). Logic, probability, and human reasoning. *Trends in Cognitive Sciences*, *19*(4), 201–214.

Johnstone, B. (2000). The individual voice in language. *Annual Review of Anthropology*, *29*, 405–424.

Jones, L. L., & Estes, Z. (2015). Convergent and divergent thinking in verbal analogy. *Thinking & Reasoning*, *21*(4), 473–500.

Jung, R. E., & Haier, R. J. (2007). The Parieto-Frontal Integration Theory (P-FIT) of intelligence: Converging neuroimaging evidence. *Behavioral and Brain Sciences*, *30*(2), 135–154.

Jung, R. E., & Vartanian, O. (Eds.). (2018). *The Cambridge handbook of the neuroscience of creativity*. New York: Cambridge University Press.

Jung, R. E., Mead, B. S., Carrasco, J., & Flores, R. A. (2013). The structure of creative cognition in the human brain. *Frontiers in Human Neuroscience*, *7*, 330.

Jung, R. E., Segall, J. M., Jeremy Bockholt, H., Flores, R. A., Smith, S. M., Chavez, R. S., & Haier, R. J. (2010). Neuroanatomy of creativity. *Human Brain Mapping*, *31*(3), 398–409.

Jung, R. E., Wertz, C. J., Meadows, C. A., Ryman, S. G., Vakhtin, A. A., & Flores, R. A. (2015). Quantity yields quality when it comes to creativity: A brain and behavioral test of the equal-odds rule. *Frontiers in Psychology*, *6*, 864.

Jung-Beeman, M. (2005). Bilateral brain processes for comprehending natural language. *Trends in Cognitive Sciences*, *9*(11), 512–518.

Jung-Beeman, M., Bowden, E. M., Haberman, J., Frymiare, J. L., Arambel-Liu, S., Greenblatt, R., ... Kounios, J. (2004). Neural activity when people solve verbal problems with insight. *PLoS Biology*, *2*(4), e97.

Kadosh, R. C. (Ed.). (2014). *The stimulated brain: Cognitive enhancement using non-invasive brain stimulation*. San Diego, CA: Elsevier/Academic Press.

Kandel, E. R. (2012). *The age of insight: The quest to understand the unconscious in art, mind, and brain: From Vienna 1900 to the present*. New York: Random House.

Kandler, C., Riemann, R., Angleitner, A., Spinath, F. M., Borkenau, P., & Penke, L. (2016). The nature of creativity: The roles of genetic factors, personality traits, cognitive abilities, and environmental sources. *Journal of Personality and Social Psychology*, 111(2), 230–249.

Kapur, N. (1996). Paradoxical functional facilitation in brain-behaviour research: A critical review. *Brain: A Journal of Neurology, 119*(5), 1775–1790.

Károlyi, C. von, Winner, E., Gray, W., & Sherman, G. F. (2003). Dyslexia linked to talent: Global visual-spatial ability. *Brain and Language, 85*(3), 427–431.

Karpati, F. J., Giacosa, C., Foster, N. E. V., Penhune, V. B., & Hyde, K. L. (2015). Dance and the brain: A review. *Annals of the New York Academy of Sciences, 1337*, 140–146.

Kasirer, A., & Mashal, N. (2014). Verbal creativity in autism: Comprehension and generation of metaphoric language in high-functioning autism spectrum disorder and typical development. *Frontiers in Human Neuroscience*, 8, 615.

(2016a). Comprehension and generation of metaphoric language in children, adolescents, and adults with dyslexia. *Dyslexia: An International Journal of Research and Practice*, 23(2), 99–118.

(2016b). Comprehension and generation of metaphors by children with autism spectrum disorder. *Research in Autism Spectrum Disorders, 32*, 53–63.

Kasperson, C. J. (1978). Psychology of the scientist: XXXVII. Scientific creativity: A relationship with information channels. *Psychological Reports, 42*(3), 691–694.

Kastner, S., & Ungerleider, L. G. (2000). Mechanisms of visual attention in the human cortex. *Annual Review of Neuroscience, 23*, 315–341.

Kaufman, J. C. (2002). Dissecting the golden goose: Components of studying creative writers. *Creativity Research Journal, 14*(1), 27–40.

Kaufman, J. C. (Ed.). (2014). *Creativity and mental illness*. Cambridge: Cambridge University Press.

Kaufman, J. C., & Beghetto, R. A. (2009). Beyond big and little: The four C model of creativity. *Review of General Psychology, 13*(1), 1–12.

Kaufman, J. C., & Kaufman, A. B. (2004). Applying a creativity framework to animal cognition. *New Ideas in Psychology, 22*(2), 143–155.

Kaufman, A. B., Kaufman, J. C. (2015). *Animal creativity and innovation*. San Diego, CA: Academic Press.

Kaufman, J. C., & Plucker, J. A. (2010). Intelligence and creativity. In J. C. Kaufman & R. J. Sternberg (Eds.), *The Cambridge handbook of creativity* (pp. 771–783). New York: Cambridge University Press.

Kaufman, J. C., & Skidmore, L. E. (2010). Taking the propulsion model of creative contributions into the 21st century. *Psychologie in Österreich, 5*, 387–381.

Kaufman, J. C., Baer, J., Cole, J. C., & Sexton, J. D. (2008). A comparison of expert and nonexpert raters using the consensual assessment technique. *Creativity Research Journal, 20*(2), 171–178.

Kaufman, J. C., Waterstreet, M. A., Ailabouni, H. S., Whitcomb, H. J., Roe, A. K., & Riggs, M. (2010). Personality and self-perceptions of creativity across domains. *Imagination, Cognition and Personality, 29*(3), 193–209.

Kaufman, S. B., Quilty, L. C., Grazioplene, R. G., Hirsh, J. B., Gray, J. R., Peterson, J. B., & DeYoung, C. G. (2016). Openness to experience and intellect differentially predict creative achievement in the arts and sciences. *Journal of Personality, 84*(2), 248–258.

Kawabata, M., & Mallett, C. J. (2011). Flow experience in physical activity: Examination of the internal structure of flow from a process-related perspective. *Motivation and Emotion, 35*(4), 393–402.

Keefer, L. A., & Landau, M. J. (2016). Metaphor and analogy in everyday problem solving. *Cognitive Science, 7*(6), 394–405.

Kell, H. J., Lubinski, D., & Benbow, C. P. (2013). Who rises to the top? Early indicators. *Psychological Science, 24*(5), 648–659.

Keller, P. E. (2012). Mental imagery in music performance: Underlying mechanisms and potential benefits. *Annals of the New York Academy of Sciences, 1252*, 206–213.

Kemp, R. (2012). *Embodied acting: What neuroscience tells us about performance.* New York: Routledge.

Kenett, Y. N., Anaki, D., & Faust, M. (2014). Investigating the structure of semantic networks in low and high creative persons. *Frontiers in Human Neuroscience, 8*, 407.

Kenett, Y. N., Levy, O., Kenett, D. Y., Stanley, H. E., Faust, M., & Havlin, S. (2018). Flexibility of thought in high creative individuals represented by percolation analysis. *Proceedings of the National Academy of Sciences, 115*(5), 867–872.

Kennedy, J. M. (2009). Outline, mental states, and drawings by a blind woman. *Perception, 38*(10), 1481–1496.

Kennedy, P., Miele, D. B., & Metcalfe, J. (2014). The cognitive antecedents and motivational consequences of the feeling of being in the zone. *Consciousness and Cognition, 30*, 48–61.

Kim, K. H. (2006a). Can we trust creativity tests? A review of the Torrance Tests of Creative Thinking (TTCT). *Creativity Research Journal, 18*(1), 3–14.

(2006b). Is creativity unidimensional or multidimensional? Analyses of the Torrance Tests of Creative Thinking. *Creativity Research Journal, 18*(3), 251–259.

(2008). Meta-analyses of the relationship of creative achievement to both IQ and divergent thinking test scores. *Journal of Creative Behavior, 42*(2), 106–130.

King, M. J. (1997). Apollo 13 creativity: In-the-box innovation. *Journal of Creative Behavior, 31*(4), 299–308.

Kirsch, L. P., Urgesi, C., & Cross, E. S. (2016). Shaping and reshaping the aesthetic brain: Emerging perspectives on the neurobiology of embodied aesthetics. *Neuroscience and Biobehavioral Reviews, 62*, 56–68.

Kishiyama, M. M., Boyce, W. T., Jimenez, A. M., Perry, L. M., & Knight, R. T. (2009). Socioeconomic disparities affect prefrontal function in children. *Journal of Cognitive Neuroscience, 21*(6), 1106–1115.

Kleinmintz, O. M., Goldstein, P., Mayseless, N., Abecasis, D., & Shamay-Tsoory, S. G. (2014). Expertise in musical improvisation and creativity: The mediation of idea evaluation. *PloS One, 9*(7), e101568.

Klimesch, W. (1999). EEG alpha and theta oscillations reflect cognitive and memory performance: A review and analysis. *Brain Research Reviews, 29*(2–3), 169–195.

Koechlin, E. (2015). Prefrontal executive function and adaptive behavior in complex environments. *Current Opinion in Neurobiology, 37*, 1–6.

Koelsch, S., & Friederici, A. D. (2003). Toward the neural basis of processing structure in music: Comparative results of different neurophysiological investigation methods. *Annals of the New York Academy of Sciences, 999*, 15–28.

Koelsch, S., Gunter, T., Friederici, A. D., & Schröger, E. (2000). Brain indices of music processing: "Nonmusicians" are musical. *Journal of Cognitive Neuroscience, 12*(3), 520–541.

Koestler, A. (1969). *The act of creation.* London: Hutchinson.

Köhler, W. (1926). *The mentality of apes.* New York: Harcourt Brace.

Kounios, J., & Beeman, M. (2014). The cognitive neuroscience of insight. *Annual Review of Psychology, 65*, 71–93.

Koutedakis, Y., & Jamurtas, A. (2004). The dancer as a performing athlete: Physiological considerations. *Sports Medicine, 34*(10), 651–661.

Koutsoupidou, T., & Hargreaves, D. J. (2009). An experimental study of the effects of improvisation on the development of children's creative thinking in music. *Psychology of Music, 37*(3), 251–278.

Kozbelt, A. (2001). Artists as experts in visual cognition. *Visual Cognition, 8*(6), 705–723.

Kozbelt, A., & Durmysheva, Y. (2007). Understanding creativity judgments of invented alien creatures: The roles of invariants and other predictors. *Journal of Creative Behavior, 41*(4), 223–248.

Kozbelt, A., & Seeley, W. P. (2007). Integrating art historical, psychological, and neuroscientific explanations of artists' advantages in drawing and perception. *Psychology of Aesthetics, Creativity, and the Arts, 1*(2), 80–90.

Kozbelt, A., Beghetto, R. A., & Runco, M. A. (2010). Theories of creativity. In J. C. Kaufman & R. J. Sternberg (Eds.), *The Cambridge handbook of creativity* (pp. 20–47). Cambridge: Cambridge University Press.

Krawczyk, D. C. (2012). The cognition and neuroscience of relational reasoning. *Brain Research, 1428*, 13–23.

Krawczyk, D. C., McClelland, M. M., & Donovan, C. M. (2011). A hierarchy for relational reasoning in the prefrontal cortex. *Cortex; a Journal Devoted to the Study of the Nervous System and Behavior, 47*(5), 588–597.

Kris, E. (1952). *Psychoanalytic explorations in art.* New York: International Universities Press.

Kroger, J. K., Nystrom, L. E., Cohen, J. D., & Johnson-Laird, P. N. (2008). Distinct neural substrates for deductive and mathematical processing. *Brain Research, 1243*, 86–103.

Kröger, S., Rutter, B., Hill, H., Windmann, S., Hermann, C., & Abraham, A. (2013). An ERP study of passive creative conceptual expansion using a modified alternate uses task. *Brain Research, 1527*, 189–198.

Kröger, S., Rutter, B., Stark, R., Windmann, S., Hermann, C., & Abraham, A. (2012). Using a shoe as a plant pot: Neural correlates of passive conceptual expansion. *Brain Research, 1430*, 52–61.

Krop, H. D., Alegre, C. E., & Williams, C. D. (1969). Effect of induced stress on convergent and divergent thinking. *Psychological Reports, 24*(3), 895–898.

Krupinski, E. A., Graham, A. R., & Weinstein, R. S. (2013). Characterizing the development of visual search expertise in pathology residents viewing whole slide images. *Human Pathology, 44*(3), 357–364.

Kuhn, T. S. (1970). *The structure of scientific revolutions* (2nd edn.). Chicago, IL: University of Chicago Press.

Kumar, J. S., & Bhuvaneswari, P. (2012). Analysis of electroencephalography (EEG) signals and its categorization: A study. *Procedia Engineering, 38*, 2525–2536.

Kutas, M., & Federmeier, K. D. (2011). Thirty years and counting: Finding meaning in the N400 component of the event-related brain potential (ERP). *Annual Review of Psychology, 62*, 621–647.

Kuypers, K. P. C., Riba, J., de la Fuente Revenga, M., Barker, S., Theunissen, E. L., & Ramaekers, J. G. (2016). Ayahuasca enhances creative divergent thinking while decreasing conventional convergent thinking. *Psychopharmacology, 233*(18), 3395–3403.

Kwiatkowski, J., Vartanian, O., & Martindale, C. (1999). Creativity and speed of mental processing. *Empirical Studies of the Arts, 17*(2), 187–196.

Kyaga, S., Landén, M., Boman, M., Hultman, C. M., Långström, N., & Lichtenstein, P. (2013). Mental illness, suicide and creativity: 40-year prospective total population study. *Journal of Psychiatric Research, 47*(1), 83–90.

Kyaga, S., Lichtenstein, P., Boman, M., Hultman, C., Långström, N., & Landén, M. (2011). Creativity and mental disorder: Family study of 300,000 people with severe mental disorder. *British Journal of Psychiatry: The Journal of Mental Science, 199*(5), 373–379.

Laeng, B., Eidet, L. M., Sulutvedt, U., & Panksepp, J. (2016). Music chills: The eye pupil as a mirror to music's soul. *Consciousness and Cognition, 44,* 161–178.

Lakke, J. P. (1999). Art and Parkinson's disease. *Advances in Neurology, 80,* 471–479.

Lakoff, G. (2014). Mapping the brain's metaphor circuitry: Metaphorical thought in everyday reason. *Frontiers in Human Neuroscience, 8,* 958.

Lakoff, G., & Johnson, M. (2003). *Metaphors we live by.* Chicago, IL: University of Chicago Press.

Laland, K., Wilkins, C., & Clayton, N. (2016). The evolution of dance. *Current Biology, 26*(1), R5–R9.

Lau, E. F., Phillips, C., & Poeppel, D. (2008). A cortical network for semantics: (De)constructing the N400. *Nature Reviews Neuroscience, 9*(12), 920–933.

Lauronen, E., Veijola, J., Isohanni, I., Jones, P. B., Nieminen, P., & Isohanni, M. (2004). Links between creativity and mental disorder. *Psychiatry, 67*(1), 81–98.

LeBoutillier, N., & Marks, D. F. (2003). Mental imagery and creativity: A meta-analytic review study. *British Journal of Psychology, 94*(1), 29–44.

Legrenzi, P., & Umilta, C. (2011). *Neuromania: On the limits of brain science* (F. Anderson, Trans.). Oxford: Oxford University Press.

Lengfelder, A., & Gollwitzer, P. M. (2001). Reflective and reflexive action control in patients with frontal brain lesions. *Neuropsychology, 15*(1), 80–100.

Lerdahl, F. (2001). Cognitive constraints on compositional systems. In J. Sloboda (Ed.), *Generative processes in music: The psychology of performance, improvisation, and composition.* Oxford: Oxford University Press.

Leung, A. K. Y., Kim, S., Polman, E., Ong, L. S., Qiu, L., Goncalo, J. A., & Sanchez-Burks, J. (2012). Embodied metaphors and creative "acts." *Psychological Science, 23*(5), 502–509.

Levens, S. M., Larsen, J. T., Bruss, J., Tranel, D., Bechara, A., & Mellers, B. A. (2014). What might have been? The role of the ventromedial prefrontal cortex and lateral orbitofrontal cortex in counterfactual emotions and choice. *Neuropsychologia, 54,* 77–86.

Lewis, P. M., Thomson, R. H., Rosenfeld, J. V., & Fitzgerald, P. B. (2016). Brain neuromodulation techniques: A review. *The Neuroscientist: A Review Journal Bringing Neurobiology, Neurology and Psychiatry, 22*(4), 406–421.

Lhommée, E., Batir, A., Quesada, J.-L., Ardouin, C., Fraix, V., Seigneuret, E., … Krack, P. (2014). Dopamine and the biology of creativity: Lessons from Parkinson's disease. *Frontiers in Neurology*, *5*, 55.

Li, W., Li, X., Huang, L., Kong, X., Yang, W., Wei, D., … Liu, J. (2015). Brain structure links trait creativity to openness to experience. *Social Cognitive and Affective Neuroscience*, *10*(2), 191–198.

Li, W., Yang, J., Zhang, Q., Li, G., & Qiu, J. (2016). The association between resting functional connectivity and visual creativity. *Scientific Reports*, *6*, 25395.

Lieven, E., Behrens, H., Speares, J., & Tomasello, M. (2003). Early syntactic creativity: A usage-based approach. *Journal of Child Language*, *30*(2), 333–367.

Light, G. A., Williams, L. E., Minow, F., Sprock, J., Rissling, A., Sharp, R., … Braff, D. L. (2010). Electroencephalography (EEG) and event-related potentials (ERPs) with human participants. *Current Protocols in Neuroscience*. doi.org/10.1002/0471142301.ns0625s52

Likert, R. (1932). A technique for the measurement of attitudes. *Archives of Psychology*, *22*(140), 55.

Likova, L. T. (2012). Drawing enhances cross-modal memory plasticity in the human brain: A case study in a totally blind adult. *Frontiers in Human Neuroscience*, *6*, 44.

Limb, C. J., & Braun, A. R. (2008). Neural substrates of spontaneous musical performance: An fMRI study of jazz improvisation. *PloS One*, *3*(2), e1679.

Lindell, A. K. (2011). Lateral thinkers are not so laterally minded: Hemispheric asymmetry, interaction, and creativity. *Laterality*, *16*(4), 479–498.

Lionnais, F. L. (1969). Science is an art. *Leonardo*, *2*(1), 73–78.

Liu, A., Werner, K., Roy, S., Trojanowski, J. Q., Morgan-Kane, U., Miller, B. L., & Rankin, K. P. (2009). A case study of an emerging visual artist with frontotemporal lobar degeneration and amyotrophic lateral sclerosis. *Neurocase*, *15*(3), 235–247.

Liu, S., Chow, H. M., Xu, Y., Erkkinen, M. G., Swett, K. E., Eagle, M. W., … Braun, A. R. (2012). Neural correlates of lyrical improvisation: An fMRI study of freestyle rap. *Scientific Reports*, *2*, 834.

Liu, S., Erkkinen, M. G., Healey, M. L., Xu, Y., Swett, K. E., Chow, H. M., & Braun, A. R. (2015). Brain activity and connectivity during poetry composition: Toward a multidimensional model of the creative process. *Human Brain Mapping*, *36*(9), 3351–3372.

Liu, T. T., Frank, L. R., Wong, E. C., & Buxton, R. B. (2001). Detection power, estimation efficiency, and predictability in event-related fMRI. *NeuroImage*, *13*(4), 759–773.

Logothetis, N. K., Pauls, J., Augath, M., Trinath, T., & Oeltermann, A. (2001). Neurophysiological investigation of the basis of the fMRI signal. *Nature, 412*(6843), 150–157.

Lopata, J. A., Nowicki, E. A., & Joanisse, M. F. (2017). Creativity as a distinct trainable mental state: An EEG study of musical improvisation. *Neuropsychologia, 99*, 246–258.

Lotze, M., Erhard, K., Neumann, N., Eickhoff, S. B., & Langner, R. (2014). Neural correlates of verbal creativity: Differences in resting-state functional connectivity associated with expertise in creative writing. *Frontiers in Human Neuroscience, 8*, 516.

Lu, J., Yang, H., Zhang, X., He, H., Luo, C., & Yao, D. (2015). The brain functional state of music creation: An fMRI study of composers. *Scientific Reports, 5*, 12277.

Lubart, T. I. (2001). Models of the creative process: Past, present and future. *Creativity Research Journal, 13*(3–4), 295–308.

Lubinski, D., Benbow, C. P., & Kell, H. J. (2014). Life paths and accomplishments of mathematically precocious males and females four decades later. *Psychological Science, 25*(12), 2217–2232.

Lubinski, D., Webb, R. M., Morelock, M. J., & Benbow, C. P. (2001). Top 1 in 10,000: A 10-year follow-up of the profoundly gifted. *Journal of Applied Psychology, 86*(4), 718–729.

Luck, S. J. (2014). *An introduction to the event-related potential technique* (2nd edn.). Cambridge, MA: MIT Press.

Ludwig, A. M. (1992). Creative achievement and psychopathology: Comparison among professions. *American Journal of Psychotherapy, 46*(3), 330–356.

(1994). Mental illness and creative activity in female writers. *American Journal of Psychiatry, 151*(11), 1650–1656.

(1995). *The price of greatness: Resolving the creativity and madness controversy.* New York: Guilford Press.

Lund, N. L., & Kranz, P. L. (1994). Notes on emotional components of musical creativity and performance. *Journal of Psychology, 128*(6), 635–640.

Lustenberger, C., Boyle, M. R., Foulser, A. A., Mellin, J. M., & Fröhlich, F. (2015). Functional role of frontal alpha oscillations in creativity. *Cortex; a Journal Devoted to the Study of the Nervous System and Behavior, 67*, 74–82.

MacDonald, R., Byrne, C., & Carlton, L. (2006). Creativity and flow in musical composition: An empirical investigation. *Psychology of Music, 34*(3), 292–306.

MacKenzie, I. (2000). Improvisation, creativity, and formulaic language. *Journal of Aesthetics and Art Criticism, 58*(2), 173–179.

Mackinnon, D. W. (1965). Personality and the realization of creative potential. *American Psychologist, 20*(4), 273–281.

(1970). Creativity: A multifaceted phenomenon. In J. D. Roslansky (Ed.), *Creativity* (pp. 17–32). London: North-Holland.

(1978). *In search of human effectiveness*. Buffalo, NY: Creative Education Foundation.

Maidhof, C., Vavatzanidis, N., Prinz, W., Rieger, M., & Koelsch, S. (2010). Processing expectancy violations during music performance and perception: An ERP study. *Journal of Cognitive Neuroscience, 22*(10), 2401–2413.

Makris, S., & Urgesi, C. (2015). Neural underpinnings of superior action prediction abilities in soccer players. *Social Cognitive and Affective Neuroscience, 10*(3), 342–351.

Malloch, S., & Trevarthen, C. (Eds.). (2009). *Communicative musicality: Exploring the basis of human companionship*. Oxford: Oxford University Press.

Manzano, O. de, Theorell, T., Harmat, L., & Ullén, F. (2010). The psychophysiology of flow during piano playing. *Emotion, 10*(3), 301–311.

Marin, M. M., & Bhattacharya, J. (2013). Getting into the musical zone: Trait emotional intelligence and amount of practice predict flow in pianists. *Frontiers in Psychology, 4*, 853.

Marinkovic, K., Baldwin, S., Courtney, M. G., Witzel, T., Dale, A. M., & Halgren, E. (2011). Right hemisphere has the last laugh: Neural dynamics of joke appreciation. *Cognitive, Affective & Behavioral Neuroscience, 11*(1), 113–130.

Marsh, R. L., Landau, J. D., & Hicks, J. L. (1996). How examples may (and may not) constrain creativity. *Memory & Cognition, 24*(5), 669–680.

Marshall, P. J., & Kenney, J. W. (2009). Biological perspectives on the effects of early psychosocial experience. *Developmental Review, 29*(2), 96–119.

Martin, J., & Cox, D. (2016). Positioning Steve Nash: A theory-driven, social psychological, and biographical case study of creativity in sport. *Sport Psychologist, 30*(4), 388–398.

Martindale, C. (1999). Biological bases of creativity. In R. J. Sternberg (Ed.), *Handbook of creativity* (pp. 137–152). Cambridge: Cambridge University Press.

(2007). Creativity, primordial cognition, and personality. *Personality and Individual Differences, 43*(7), 1777–1785.

Martindale, C., & Hasenfus, N. (1978). EEG differences as a function of creativity, stage of the creative process, and effort to be original. *Biological Psychology, 6*(3), 157–167.

Martindale, C., & Hines, D. (1975). Creativity and cortical activation during creative, intellectual and EEG feedback tasks. *Biological Psychology*, *3*(2), 91–100.

Mashal, N., Faust, M., Hendler, T., & Jung-Beeman, M. (2007). An fMRI investigation of the neural correlates underlying the processing of novel metaphoric expressions. *Brain and Language*, *100*(2), 115–126.

Maslej, M. M., Oatley, K., & Mar, R. A. (2017). Creating fictional characters: The role of experience, personality, and social processes. *Psychology of Aesthetics, Creativity, and the Arts*, 11(4), 487–499.

Maslow, A. H. (1943). A theory of human motivation. *Psychological Review*, *50*(4), 370–396.

May, J., Calvo-Merino, B., deLahunta, S., McGregor, W., Cusack, R., Owen, A. M., … Barnard, P. (2011). Points in mental space: An interdisciplinary study of imagery in movement creation. *Dance Research*, *29*(Suppl.), 404–432.

Mayseless, N., & Shamay-Tsoory, S. G. (2015). Enhancing verbal creativity: Modulating creativity by altering the balance between right and left inferior frontal gyrus with tDCS. *Neuroscience*, *291C*, 167–176.

Mayseless, N., Aharon-Peretz, J., & Shamay-Tsoory, S. (2014). Unleashing creativity: The role of left temporoparietal regions in evaluating and inhibiting the generation of creative ideas. *Neuropsychologia*, *64C*, 157–168.

McGlone, M. S. (2007). What is the explanatory value of a conceptual metaphor? *Language & Communication*, *27*(2), 109–126.

McPherson, M. J., & Limb, C. J. (2013). Difficulties in the neuroscience of creativity: Jazz improvisation and the scientific method. *Annals of the New York Academy of Sciences*, *1303*, 80–83.

Medaglia, J. D., Lynall, M.-E., & Bassett, D. S. (2015). Cognitive network neuroscience. *Journal of Cognitive Neuroscience*, *27*(8), 1471–1491.

Mednick, S. A. (1962). The associative basis of the creative process. *Psychological Review*, *69*, 220–232.

Meehan, T. P., & Bressler, S. L. (2012). Neurocognitive networks: Findings, models, and theory. *Neuroscience & Biobehavioral Reviews*, 36(10), 2232–2234.

Melogno, S., Pinto, M. A., & Orsolini, M. (2016). Novel metaphors comprehension in a child with high-functioning autism spectrum disorder: A study on assessment and treatment. *Frontiers in Psychology*, *7*, 2004.

Memmert, D. (2007). Can creativity be improved by an attention-broadening training program? An exploratory study focusing on team sports. *Creativity Research Journal*, *19*(2–3), 281–291.

    (2009). Pay attention! A review of visual attentional expertise in sport. *International Review of Sport and Exercise Psychology*, *2*(2), 119–138.

Memmert, D., & Furley, P. (2007). "I spy with my little eye!": Breadth of attention, inattentional blindness, and tactical decision making in team sports. *Journal of Sport & Exercise Psychology*, 29(3), 365–381.

Memmert, D., Baker, J., & Bertsch, C. (2010). Play and practice in the development of sport-specific creativity in team ball sports. *High Ability Studies*, 21(1), 3–18.

Mendelsohn, G. A. (1974). Associative and attentional processes in creative performance. *Journal of Personality*, 44, 341–369.

Mendelsohn, G. A., & Griswold, B. B. (1964). Differential use of incidental stimuli in problem solving as a function of creativity. *Journal of Abnormal and Social Psychology*, 68(4), 431–436.

Menon, V., & Uddin, L. Q. (2010). Saliency, switching, attention and control: A network model of insula function. *Brain Structure & Function*, 214(5–6), 655–667.

Merker, B. H. (2006). Layered constraints on the multiple creativities of music. In I. Deliège & G. A. Wiggins (Eds.), *Musical creativity: Multidisciplinary research in theory and practice* (pp. 25–41). Hove: Psychology Press.

Merker, B. H., Madison, G. S., & Eckerdal, P. (2009). On the role and origin of isochrony in human rhythmic entrainment. *Cortex; a Journal Devoted to the Study of the Nervous System and Behavior*, 45(1), 4–17.

Merleau-Ponty, M. (1993). Cézanne's doubt. In G. A. Johnson (Ed.), *The Merleau-Ponty aesthetics reader: Philosophy and painting* (pp. 59–75). Evanston, IL: Northwestern University Press.

Metcalfe, J., & Wiebe, D. (1987). Intuition in insight and noninsight problem solving. *Memory & Cognition*, 15(3), 238–246.

Miall, R. C., & Tchalenko, J. (2001). A painter's eye movements: A study of eye and hand movement during portrait drawing. *Leonardo*, 34(1), 35–40.

Miall, R. C., Gowen, E., & Tchalenko, J. (2009). Drawing cartoon faces – a functional imaging study of the cognitive neuroscience of drawing. *Cortex*, 45(3), 394–406.

Midorikawa, A., & Kawamura, M. (2015). The emergence of artistic ability following traumatic brain injury. *Neurocase*, 21(1), 90–94.

Mihov, K. M., Denzler, M., & Förster, J. (2010). Hemispheric specialization and creative thinking: A meta-analytic review of lateralization of creativity. *Brain and Cognition*, 72(3), 442–448.

Miller, A. I. (1995). Aesthetics, representation and creativity in art and science. *Leonardo*, 28(3), 185–192.

(1996). Metaphors in creative scientific thought. *Creativity Research Journal*, 9(2–3), 113–130.

Miller, B. L., Boone, K., Cummings, J. L., Read, S. L., & Mishkin, F. (2000). Functional correlates of musical and visual ability in frontotemporal dementia. *British Journal of Psychiatry: The Journal of Mental Science*, *176*, 458–463.

Miller, B. L., Ponton, M., Benson, D. F., Cummings, J. L., & Mena, I. (1996). Enhanced artistic creativity with temporal lobe degeneration. *Lancet*, *348*(9043), 1744–1745.

Miniussi, C., & Ruzzoli, M. (2013). Transcranial stimulation and cognition. *Handbook of Clinical Neurology*, *116*, 739–750.

Miran, M., & Miran, E. (1984). Cerebral asymmetries: Neuropsychological measurement and theoretical issues. *Biological Psychology*, *19*(3–4), 295–304.

Mithen, S. (2014). *Creativity in human evolution and prehistory*. London: Routledge.

Miyapuram, K. P., & Pammi, V. S. C. (2013). Understanding decision neuroscience: A multidisciplinary perspective and neural substrates. *Progress in Brain Research*, *202*, 239–266.

Mode, E. B. (1962). The two most original creations of the human spirit. *Mathematics Magazine*, *35*(1), 13–20.

Mohr, C., Graves, R. E., Gianotti, L. R., Pizzagalli, D., & Brugger, P. (2001). Loose but normal: A semantic association study. *Journal of Psycholinguistic Research*, *30*(5), 475–483.

Mölle, M., Marshall, L., Lutzenberger, W., Pietrowsky, R., Fehm, H. L., & Born, J. (1996). Enhanced dynamic complexity in the human EEG during creative thinking. *Neuroscience Letters*, *208*(1), 61–64.

Molnar-Szakacs, I., & Heaton, P. (2012). Music: A unique window into the world of autism. *Annals of the New York Academy of Sciences*, *1252*, 318–324.

Montero, B. (2006). Proprioception as an aesthetic sense. *Journal of Aesthetics and Art Criticism*, *64*(2), 231–242.

Moran, N., Hadley, L. V., Bader, M., & Keller, P. E. (2015). Perception of 'back-channeling' nonverbal feedback in musical duo improvisation. *PLoS One*, *10*(6), e0130070.

Morris, H. C. (1992). Logical creativity. *Theory & Psychology*, *2*(1), 89–107.

Mottron, L., Dawson, M., & Soulières, I. (2009). Enhanced perception in savant syndrome: Patterns, structure and creativity. *Philosophical Transactions of the Royal Society B: Biological Sciences*, *364*(1522), 1385–1391.

Moulton, S. T., & Kosslyn, S. M. (2009). Imagining predictions: Mental imagery as mental emulation. *Philosophical Transactions of the Royal Society B: Biological Sciences*, *364*(1521), 1273–1280.

Mullally, S. L., & Maguire, E. A. (2013). Memory, imagination, and predicting the future: A common brain mechanism? *The Neuroscientist: A Review Journal Bringing Neurobiology, Neurology and Psychiatry*, *20*(3), 220–234.

Munakata, Y., Herd, S. A., Chatham, C. H., Depue, B. E., Banich, M. T., & O'Reilly, R. C. (2011). A unified framework for inhibitory control. *Trends in Cognitive Sciences*, *15*(10), 453–459.

Nabokov, V. V., & Bowers, F. (1980). *Lectures on literature*. New York: Harcourt Brace Jovanovich.

Navas-Sánchez, F. J., Alemán-Gómez, Y., Sánchez-Gonzalez, J., Guzmán-De-Villoria, J. A., Franco, C., Robles, O., … Desco, M. (2014). White matter microstructure correlates of mathematical giftedness and intelligence quotient. *Human Brain Mapping*, *35*(6), 2619–2631.

Nee, D. E., & D'Esposito, M. (2016). The hierarchical organization of the lateral prefrontal cortex. *eLife*, *5*.

Nersessian, N. J., & Chandrasekharan, S. (2009). Hybrid analogies in conceptual innovation in science. *Cognitive Systems Research*, *10*(3), 178–188.

Nettle, D. (2001). *Strong imagination: Madness, creativity and human nature*. Oxford: Oxford University Press.

(2006). Schizotypy and mental health amongst poets, visual artists, and mathematicians. *Journal of Research in Personality*, *40*(6), 876–890.

Nettle, D., & Clegg, H. (2006). Schizotypy, creativity and mating success in humans. *Proceedings of the Royal Society B: Biological Sciences*, *273*(1586), 611–615.

Nidal, K., & Malik, A. S. (Eds.). (2014). *EEG/ERP analysis: Methods and applications*. Boca Raton, FL: CRC Press.

Niendam, T. A., Laird, A. R., Ray, K. L., Dean, Y. M., Glahn, D. C., & Carter, C. S. (2012). Meta-analytic evidence for a superordinate cognitive control network subserving diverse executive functions. *Cognitive, Affective & Behavioral Neuroscience*, *12*(2), 241–268.

Nijs, L., Lesaffre, M., & Leman, M. (2013). The musical instrument as a natural extension of the musician. In M. Castellengo & H. Genevois (Eds.), *Music and its instruments* (pp. 467–484). Sampzon, France: Editions Delatour.

Nijstad, B. A., Dreu, C. K. W. D., Rietzschel, E. F., & Baas, M. (2010). The dual pathway to creativity model: Creative ideation as a function of flexibility and persistence. *European Review of Social Psychology*, *21*(1), 34–77.

Nitsche, M. A., Cohen, L. G., Wassermann, E. M., Priori, A., Lang, N., Antal, A., … Pascual-Leone, A. (2008). Transcranial direct current stimulation: State of the art 2008. *Brain Stimulation*, *1*(3), 206–223.

Novembre, G., & Keller, P. E. (2014). A conceptual review on action-perception coupling in the musician's brain: What is it good for? *Frontiers in Human Neuroscience*, *8*, 603.

Noy, L., Dekel, E., & Alon, U. (2011). The mirror game as a paradigm for studying the dynamics of two people improvising motion together.

Proceedings of the National Academy of Sciences of the United States of America, 108(52), 20947–20952.

Noy, L., Levit-Binun, N., & Golland, Y. (2015). Being in the zone: Physiological markers of togetherness in joint improvisation. *Frontiers in Human Neuroscience, 9,* 187.

Nunez, P. L., & Srinivasan, R. (2006). *Electric fields of the brain: The neurophysics of EEG* (2nd edn.). Oxford: Oxford University Press.

Nusbaum, E. C., Silvia, P. J., & Beaty, R. E. (2017). Ha ha? Assessing individual differences in humor production ability. *Psychology of Aesthetics, Creativity, and the Arts, 11*(2), 231–241.

Oaksford, M. (2015). Imaging deductive reasoning and the new paradigm. *Frontiers in Human Neuroscience, 9,* 101.

O'Boyle, M. W., Cunnington, R., Silk, T. J., Vaughan, D., Jackson, G., Syngeniotis, A., & Egan, G. F. (2005). Mathematically gifted male adolescents activate a unique brain network during mental rotation. *Cognitive Brain Research, 25*(2), 583–587.

Ohlsson, S. (1984). Restructuring revisited. *Scandinavian Journal of Psychology, 25*(2), 117–129.

Oller, D. K., & Griebel, U. (Eds.). (2008). *Evolution of communicative flexibility: Complexity, creativity, and adaptability in human and animal communication.* Cambridge, MA: MIT Press.

Oppezzo, M., & Schwartz, D. L. (2014). Give your ideas some legs: The positive effect of walking on creative thinking. *Journal of Experimental Psychology: Learning, Memory, and Cognition, 40*(4), 1142–1152.

Orme-Johnson, D. W., & Haynes, C. T. (1981). EEG phase coherence, pure consciousness, creativity, and TM – Sidhi experiences. *International Journal of Neuroscience, 13*(4), 211–217.

Otte, A., & Halsband, U. (2006). Brain imaging tools in neurosciences. *Journal of Physiology-Paris, 99*(4–6), 281–292.

Page, M. P. A. (2006). What can't functional neuroimaging tell the cognitive psychologist? *Cortex; a Journal Devoted to the Study of the Nervous System and Behavior, 42*(3), 428–443.

Palmer, C. (2005). Time course of retrieval and movement preparation in music performance. *Annals of the New York Academy of Sciences, 1060,* 360–367.

Palmiero, M., Cardi, V., & Belardinelli, M. O. (2011). The role of vividness of visual mental imagery on different dimensions of creativity. *Creativity Research Journal, 23*(4), 372–375.

Palmiero, M., Nakatani, C., Raver, D., Belardinelli, M. O., & van Leeuwen, C. (2010). Abilities within and across visual and verbal domains: How specific is their influence on creativity? *Creativity Research Journal, 22*(4), 369–377.

Palmiero, M., Nori, R., Aloisi, V., Ferrara, M., & Piccardi, L. (2015). Domain-specificity of creativity: A study on the relationship between visual creativity and visual mental imagery. *Frontiers in Psychology*, *6*, 1870.

Pantev, C., Ross, B., Fujioka, T., Trainor, L. J., Schulte, M., & Schulz, M. (2003). Music and learning-induced cortical plasticity. *Annals of the New York Academy of Sciences*, *999*, 438–450.

Park, G., Lubinski, D., & Benbow, C. P. (2008). Ability differences among people who have commensurate degrees matter for scientific creativity. *Psychological Science*, *19*(10), 957–961.

Park, H. R. P., Kirk, I. J., & Waldie, K. E. (2015). Neural correlates of creative thinking and schizotypy. *Neuropsychologia*, *73*, 94–107.

Park, I. S., Lee, N. J., Kim, T.-Y., Park, J.-H., Won, Y.-M., Jung, Y.-J., ... Rhyu, I. J. (2012). Volumetric analysis of cerebellum in short-track speed skating players. *The Cerebellum*, *11*(4), 925–930.

Park, S., Lee, J., Folley, B., & Kim, J. (2003). Schizophrenia: Putting context in context. *Behavioral and Brain Sciences*, *26*(01), 98–99.

Parkin, B. L., Hellyer, P. J., Leech, R., & Hampshire, A. (2015). Dynamic network mechanisms of relational integration. *Journal of Neuroscience: The Official Journal of the Society for Neuroscience*, *35*(20), 7660–7673.

Pearlman, C. (1983). A theoretical model for creativity. *Education*, *103*(3), 294–304.

Pearsall, E. (1999). Mind and music: On intentionality, music theory, and analysis. *Journal of Music Theory*, *43*(2), 231–255.

Pearson, J., & Kosslyn, S. M. (2015). The heterogeneity of mental representation: Ending the imagery debate. *Proceedings of the National Academy of Sciences of the United States of America*, 112(33), 10089–10092.

Perdreau, F., & Cavanagh, P. (2011). Do artists see their retinas? *Frontiers in Human Neuroscience*, *5*, 171.

Peretz, I. (2006). The nature of music from a biological perspective. *Cognition*, *100*(1), 1–32.

Peretz, I., & Coltheart, M. (2003). Modularity of music processing. *Nature Neuroscience*, *6*(7), 688.

Peretz, I., & Zatorre, R. J. (Eds.). (2003). *The cognitive neuroscience of music*. New York: Oxford University Press.

Perky, C. W. (1910). An experimental study of imagination. *American Journal of Psychology*, *21*(3), 422–452.

Perlovsky, L. I., & Levine, D. S. (2012). The drive for creativity and the escape from creativity: Neurocognitive mechanisms. *Cognitive Computation*, *4*(3), 292–305.

Pesce, C., Masci, I., Marchetti, R., Vazou, S., Sääkslahti, A., & Tomporowski, P. D. (2016). Deliberate play and preparation jointly benefit motor and cognitive development: Mediated and moderated effects. *Frontiers in Psychology, 7,* 349.

Petersen, D. (2008). Space, time, weight, and flow: Suggestions for enhancing assessment of creative movement. *Physical Education & Sport Pedagogy, 13*(2), 191–198.

Petersen, S. E., & Sporns, O. (2015). Brain networks and cognitive architectures. *Neuron, 88*(1), 207–219.

Petersen, S. E., Fox, P. T., Posner, M. I., Mintun, M., & Raichle, M. E. (1988). Positron emission tomographic studies of the cortical anatomy of single-word processing. *Nature, 331*(6157), 585–589.

Petrides, M. (2005). Lateral prefrontal cortex: Architectonic and functional organization. *Philosophical Transactions of the Royal Society B: Biological Sciences, 360*(1456), 781–795.

Petsche, H. (1996). Approaches to verbal, visual and musical creativity by EEG coherence analysis. *International Journal of Psychophysiology: Official Journal of the International Organization of Psychophysiology, 24*(1–2), 145–159.

Pfordresher, P. Q. (2012). Musical training and the role of auditory feedback during performance. *Annals of the New York Academy of Sciences, 1252,* 171–178.

Pfurtscheller, G., Stancák, A., & Neuper, C. (1996). Event-related synchronization (ERS) in the alpha band – an electrophysiological correlate of cortical idling: A review. *International Journal of Psychophysiology, 24*(1–2), 39–46.

Pidgeon, L. M., Grealy, M., Duffy, A. H. B., Hay, L., McTeague, C., Vuletic, T., … Gilbert, S. J. (2016). Functional neuroimaging of visual creativity: A systematic review and meta-analysis. *Brain and Behavior, 6*(10), e00540.

Pihko, E., Virtanen, A., Saarinen, V.-M., Pannasch, S., Hirvenkari, L., Tossavainen, T., … Hari, R. (2011). Experiencing art: The influence of expertise and painting abstraction level. *Frontiers in Human Neuroscience, 5,* 94.

Pinho, A. L., Manzano, Ö. de, Fransson, P., Eriksson, H., & Ullén, F. (2014). Connecting to create: Expertise in musical improvisation is associated with increased functional connectivity between premotor and prefrontal areas. *Journal of Neuroscience, 34*(18), 6156–6163.

Pinho, A. L., Ullén, F., Castelo-Branco, M., Fransson, P., & de Manzano, Ö. (2015). Addressing a paradox: Dual strategies for creative performance in introspective and extrospective networks. *Cerebral Cortex, 26*(7), 3052–3063.

Plucker, J. A., & Renzulli, J. S. (1999). Psychometric approaches to the study of human creativity. In R. J. Sternberg (Ed.), *Handbook of creativity* (pp. 35–61). New York: Cambridge University Press.

Plucker, J. A., Qian, M., & Wang, S. (2011). Is originality in the eye of the beholder? Comparison of scoring techniques in the assessment of divergent thinking. *Journal of Creative Behavior*, *45*(1), 1–22.

Poldrack, R. A. (2012). The future of fMRI in cognitive neuroscience. *NeuroImage*, *62*(2), 1216–1220.

Pope, R. (2005). *Creativity: Theory, history, practice*. New York: Routledge.

Post, F. (1994). Creativity and psychopathology: A study of 291 world-famous men. *British Journal of Psychiatry: The Journal of Mental Science*, *165*(2), 22–34.

(1996). Verbal creativity, depression and alcoholism. An investigation of one hundred American and British writers. *British Journal of Psychiatry: The Journal of Mental Science*, *168*(5), 545–555.

Power, J. D., Cohen, A. L., Nelson, S. M., Wig, G. S., Barnes, K. A., Church, J. A., … Petersen, S. E. (2011). Functional network organization of the human brain. *Neuron*, *72*(4), 665–678.

Power, R. A., Steinberg, S., Bjornsdottir, G., Rietveld, C. A., Abdellaoui, A., Nivard, M. M., … Stefansson, K. (2015). Polygenic risk scores for schizophrenia and bipolar disorder predict creativity. *Nature Neuroscience*, *18*(7), 953–955.

Prado, J., Chadha, A., & Booth, J. R. (2011). The brain network for deductive reasoning: A quantitative meta-analysis of 28 neuroimaging studies. *Journal of Cognitive Neuroscience*, *23*(11), 3483–3497.

Prendinger, H., & Ishizuka, M. (2005). A creative abduction approach to scientific and knowledge discovery. *Knowledge-Based Systems*, *18*(7), 321–326.

Pressing, J. (2001). Improvisation: Methods and models. In J. Sloboda (Ed.), *Generative processes in music: The psychology of performance, improvisation, and composition*. Oxford: Oxford University Press.

Pretz, J. E. (2008). Intuition versus analysis: Strategy and experience in complex everyday problem solving. *Memory & Cognition*, *36*(3), 554–566.

Priest, T. (2001). Using creativity assessment experience to nurture and predict compositional creativity. *Journal of Research in Music Education*, *49*(3), 245–257.

(2006). Self-evaluation, creativity, and musical achievement. *Psychology of Music*, *34*(1), 47–61.

Pring, L., Hermelin, B., & Heavey, L. (1995). Savants, segments, art and autism. *Journal of Child Psychology and Psychiatry, and Allied Disciplines*, *36*(6), 1065–1076.

Pring, L., Ryder, N., Crane, L., & Hermelin, B. (2012). Creativity in savant artists with autism. *Autism: The International Journal of Research and Practice*, *16*(1), 45–57.

Prinz, W. (1997). Perception and action planning. *European Journal of Cognitive Psychology, 9*(2), 129–154.

Putkinen, V., Tervaniemi, M., Saarikivi, K., Ojala, P., & Huotilainen, M. (2014). Enhanced development of auditory change detection in musically trained school-aged children: A longitudinal event-related potential study. *Developmental Science, 17*(2), 282–297.

Radel, R., Davranche, K., Fournier, M., & Dietrich, A. (2015). The role of (dis)inhibition in creativity: Decreased inhibition improves idea generation. *Cognition, 134*, 110–120.

Raichle, M. E. (2009). A brief history of human brain mapping. *Trends in Neurosciences, 32*(2), 118–126.

(2015). The brain's default mode network. *Annual Review of Neuroscience, 38*, 433–447.

Rajagopalan, V., & Pioro, E. P. (2015). Disparate voxel based morphometry (VBM) results between SPM and FSL softwares in ALS patients with frontotemporal dementia: Which VBM results to consider? *BMC Neurology, 15*, 32.

Ramachandran, V. S., & Hirstein, W. (1999). The science of art: A neurological theory of aesthetic experience. *Journal of Consciousness Studies, 6*(6–7), 15–41.

Ramachandran, V. S., & Hubbard, E. M. (2003). Hearing colors, tasting shapes. *Scientific American, 288*(5), 52–59.

Ramnani, N., & Owen, A. M. (2004). Anterior prefrontal cortex: Insights into function from anatomy and neuroimaging. *Nature Reviews Neuroscience, 5*(3), 184–194.

Ramsey, G., Bastian, M. L., & van Schaik, C. (2007). Animal innovation defined and operationalized. *Behavioral and Brain Sciences, 30*(4), 393–407.

Ram-Vlasov, N., Tzischinsky, O., Green, A., & Shochat, T. (2016). Creativity and habitual sleep patterns among art and social sciences undergraduate students. *Psychology of Aesthetics, Creativity, and the Arts, 10*(3), 270–277.

Rapp, A. M., Leube, D. T., Erb, M., Grodd, W., & Kircher, T. T. J. (2004). Neural correlates of metaphor processing. *Cognitive Brain Research, 20*(3), 395–402.

Rawlings, D., & Locarnini, A. (2008). Dimensional schizotypy, autism, and unusual word associations in artists and scientists. *Journal of Research in Personality, 42*(2), 465–471.

Raymond, J., Sajid, I., Parkinson, L. A., & Gruzelier, J. H. (2005). Biofeedback and dance performance: A preliminary investigation. *Applied Psychophysiology and Biofeedback, 30*(1), 65–73.

Reason, M., & Reynolds, D. (2010). Kinesthesia, empathy, and related pleasures: An inquiry into audience experiences of watching dance. *Dance Research Journal, 42*(2), 49–75.

Reingold, E. M., & Sheridan, H. (2011). Eye movements and visual expertise in chess and medicine. In S. P. Liversedge, I. D. Gilchrist, & S. Everling (Eds.), *Oxford handbook on eye movements* (pp. 528–550). Oxford: Oxford University Press.

Reinhart, R. M. G., Cosman, J. D., Fukuda, K., & Woodman, G. F. (2017). Using transcranial direct-current stimulation (tDCS) to understand cognitive processing. *Attention, Perception & Psychophysics*, *79*(1), 3–23.

Reitman, F. (1947). The creative spell of schizophrenics after leucotomy. *Journal of Mental Science*, *93*(390), 55–61.

Reti, I. (Ed.). (2015). *Brain stimulation: Methodologies and interventions*. Hoboken, NJ: Wiley Blackwell.

Reverberi, C., Laiacona, M., & Capitani, E. (2006). Qualitative features of semantic fluency performance in mesial and lateral frontal patients. *Neuropsychologia*, *44*(3), 469–478.

Reverberi, C., Toraldo, A., D'Agostini, S., & Skrap, M. (2005). Better without (lateral) frontal cortex? Insight problems solved by frontal patients. *Brain: A Journal of Neurology*, *128*(12), 2882–2890.

Rhodes, M. (1961). An analysis of creativity. *Phi Delta Kappan*, *42*(7), 305–310.

Richards, R. L. (1981). Relationships between creativity and psychopathology: An evaluation and interpretation of the evidence. *Genetic Psychology Monographs*, *103*, 261–324.

  (1993). Everyday creativity, eminent creativity, and psychopathology. *Psychological Inquiry*, *4*(3), 212–217.

Ridley, M. (2015). *The evolution of everything: How new ideas emerge*. London: Harper Collins.

Rinck, P. A. (2017). *Magnetic Resonance in Medicine: The basic textbook of the European Magnetic Resonance Forum* (10th edn.). E-version 10.1 beta.

Riquelme, H. (2002). Can people creative in imagery interpret ambiguous figures faster than people less creative in imagery? *Journal of Creative Behavior*, *36*(2), 105–116.

Rizzolatti, G., Cattaneo, L., Fabbri-Destro, M., & Rozzi, S. (2014). Cortical mechanisms underlying the organization of goal-directed actions and mirror neuron-based action understanding. *Physiological Reviews*, *94*(2), 655–706.

Robbins, T. W., Gillan, C. M., Smith, D. G., de Wit, S., & Ersche, K. D. (2012). Neurocognitive endophenotypes of impulsivity and compulsivity: Towards dimensional psychiatry. *Trends in Cognitive Sciences*, *16*(1), 81–91.

Roels, H. (2016). Comparing the main compositional activities in a study of eight composers. *Musicae Scientiae*, *20*(3), 413–435.

Root-Bernstein, R., Allen, L., Beach, L., Bhadula, R., Fast, J., Hosey, C., … Weinlander, S. (2008). Arts foster scientific success: Avocations of

Nobel, National Academy, Royal Society, and Sigma Xi members. *Journal of Psychology of Science and Technology, 1*(2), 51–63.

Root-Bernstein, R., Bernstein, M., & Garnier, H. (1995). Correlations between avocations, scientific style, work habits, and professional impact of scientists. *Creativity Research Journal, 8,* 115–137.

Rose, F. C. (Ed.). (2006). *The neurobiology of painting.* Amsterdam: Elsevier.

Rosen, D. S., Erickson, B., Kim, Y. E., Mirman, D., Hamilton, R. H., & Kounios, J. (2016). Anodal tDCS to right dorsolateral prefrontal cortex facilitates performance for novice jazz improvisers but hinders experts. *Frontiers in Human Neuroscience, 10,* 579.

Rossmann, E., & Fink, A. (2010). Do creative people use shorter associative pathways? *Personality and Individual Differences, 49*(8), 891–895.

Rothen, N., & Meier, B. (2010). Higher prevalence of synaesthesia in art students. *Perception, 39*(5), 718–720.

Rothenberg, A. (1980). Visual art: Homospatial thinking in the creative process. *Leonardo, 13*(1), 17–27.

(1986). Artistic creation as stimulated by superimposed versus combined-composite visual images. *Journal of Personality and Social Psychology, 50*(2), 370–381.

(2006). Creativity – the healthy muse. *The Lancet, 368,* S8–S9.

Rothmaler, K., Nigbur, R., & Ivanova, G. (2017). New insights into insight: Neurophysiological correlates of the difference between the intrinsic "aha" and the extrinsic "oh yes" moment. *Neuropsychologia, 95,* 204–214.

Rubin, R. D., Watson, P. D., Duff, M. C., & Cohen, N. J. (2014). The role of the hippocampus in flexible cognition and social behavior. *Frontiers in Human Neuroscience, 8,* 742.

Runco, M. A. (2004). Creativity. *Annual Review of Psychology, 55,* 657–687.

(2007a). A hierarchical framework for the study of creativity. *New Horizons in Education, 55*(3), 1–9.

(2007b). *Creativity: Theories and themes: research, development, and practice.* Boston, MA: Elsevier Academic Press.

Runco, M. A., & Acar, S. (2012). Divergent thinking as an indicator of creative potential. *Creativity Research Journal, 24*(1), 66–75.

Runco, M. A., & Albert, R. S. (1986). The threshold theory regarding creativity and intelligence: An empirical test with gifted and nongifted children. *Creative Child and Adult Quarterly, 11*(4), 212–218.

Runco, M. A., & Jaeger, G. J. (2012). The standard definition of creativity. *Creativity Research Journal, 24*(1), 92–96.

Runco, M. A., Millar, G., Acar, S., & Cramond, B. (2010). Torrance Tests of Creative Thinking as predictors of personal and public achievement: A fifty-year follow-up. *Creativity Research Journal, 22*(4), 361–368.

Runco, M. A., Okuda, S. M., & Thurston, B. J. (1987). The psychometric properties of four systems for scoring divergent thinking tests. *Journal of Psychoeducational Assessment*, *5*(2), 149–156.

Rundblad, G., & Annaz, D. (2010a). Development of metaphor and metonymy comprehension: Receptive vocabulary and conceptual knowledge. *British Journal of Developmental Psychology*, *28*(3), 547–563.

(2010b). The atypical development of metaphor and metonymy comprehension in children with autism. *Autism: The International Journal of Research and Practice*, *14*(1), 29–46.

Rushdie, S. (1981). *The Moor's last sigh*. London: Jonathan Cape.

(1995). *Midnight's children*. London: Vintage.

Rusou, Z., Zakay, D., & Usher, M. (2013). Pitting intuitive and analytical thinking against each other: The case of transitivity. *Psychonomic Bulletin & Review*, *20*(3), 608–614.

Rutter, B., Kröger, S., Hill, H., Windmann, S., Hermann, C., & Abraham, A. (2012). Can clouds dance? Part 2: An ERP investigation of passive conceptual expansion. *Brain and Cognition*, *80*(3), 301–310.

Rutter, B., Kröger, S., Stark, R., Schweckendiek, J., Windmann, S., Hermann, C., & Abraham, A. (2012). Can clouds dance? Neural correlates of passive conceptual expansion using a metaphor processing task: Implications for creative cognition. *Brain and Cognition*, *78*(2), 114–122.

Rydell, R. J., & McConnell, A. R. (2006). Understanding implicit and explicit attitude change: A systems of reasoning analysis. *Journal of Personality and Social Psychology*, *91*(6), 995–1008.

Sacks, O. (2008). *Musicophilia: Tales of music and the brain*. New York: Vintage.

(2015). *On the move: A life*. New York: Alfred A. Knopf.

Sadler-Smith, E. (2015). Wallas' four-stage model of the creative process: More than meets the eye? *Creativity Research Journal*, *27*(4), 342–352.

Saggar, M., Quintin, E.-M., Kienitz, E., Bott, N. T., Sun, Z., Hong, W.-C., … Reiss, A. L. (2015). Pictionary-based fMRI paradigm to study the neural correlates of spontaneous improvisation and figural creativity. *Scientific Reports*, *5*, 10894.

Sági, M., & Vitányi. (2001). Experimental research into musical generative ability. In J. Sloboda (Ed.), *Generative processes in music: The psychology of performance, improvisation, and composition*. Oxford: Oxford University Press.

Salimpoor, V. N., Benovoy, M., Larcher, K., Dagher, A., & Zatorre, R. J. (2011). Anatomically distinct dopamine release during anticipation and experience of peak emotion to music. *Nature Neuroscience*, *14*(2), 257–262.

Salvi, C., Bricolo, E., Franconeri, S. L., Kounios, J., & Beeman, M. (2015). Sudden insight is associated with shutting out visual inputs. *Psychonomic Bulletin & Review*, *22*(6), 1814–1819.

Sandbank, S. (1989). *After Kafka: The influence of Kafka's fiction.* Athens, GA: University of Georgia Press.

Sandrone, S., Bacigaluppi, M., Galloni, M. R., Cappa, S. F., Moro, A., Catani, M., ... Martino, G. (2014). Weighing brain activity with the balance: Angelo Mosso's original manuscripts come to light. *Brain, 137*(2), 621–633.

Santos, S. D. L., Memmert, D., Sampaio, J., & Leite, N. (2016). The spawns of creative behavior in team sports: A creativity developmental framework. *Frontiers in Psychology, 7*, 1282.

Sarath, E. (1996). A new look at improvisation. *Journal of Music Theory, 40*(1), 1–38.

Särkämö, T., & Soto, D. (2012). Music listening after stroke: Beneficial effects and potential neural mechanisms. *Annals of the New York Academy of Sciences, 1252*, 266–281.

Satpute, A. B., & Lieberman, M. D. (2006). Integrating automatic and controlled processes into neurocognitive models of social cognition. *Brain Research, 1079*(1), 86–97.

Savoy, R. L. (2001). History and future directions of human brain mapping and functional neuroimaging. *Acta Psychologica, 107*(1–3), 9–42.

Sawyer, K. (2011). The cognitive neuroscience of creativity: A critical review. *Creativity Research Journal, 23*(2), 137–154.

Sawyer, R. K. (2003). *Group creativity: Music, theater, collaboration.* Mahwah, NJ: Lawrence Erlbaum.

    (2006). Group creativity: Musical performance and collaboration. *Psychology of Music, 34*(2), 148–165.

    (2014). How to transform schools to foster creativity. *Teachers College Record, 118*(4).

Sawyer, R. K., & DeZutter, S. (2009). Distributed creativity: How collective creations emerge from collaboration. *Psychology of Aesthetics, Creativity, and the Arts, 3*(2), 81–92.

Schacter, D. L., Addis, D. R., Hassabis, D., Martin, V. C., Spreng, R. N., & Szpunar, K. K. (2012). The future of memory: Remembering, imagining, and the brain. *Neuron, 76*(4), 677–694.

Schaefer, R. S. (2014). Auditory rhythmic cueing in movement rehabilitation: Findings and possible mechanisms. *Philosophical Transactions of the Royal Society B: Biological Sciences, 369*(1658), 20130402.

Schilling, M. A., & Green, E. (2011). Recombinant search and breakthrough idea generation: An analysis of high impact papers in the social sciences. *Research Policy, 40*(10), 1321–1331.

Schlaug, G. (2001). The brain of musicians. A model for functional and structural adaptation. *Annals of the New York Academy of Sciences, 930*, 281–299.

(2015). Musicians and music making as a model for the study of brain plasticity. *Progress in Brain Research*, 217, 37–55.

Schlegel, A., Alexander, P., Fogelson, S. V., Li, X., Lu, Z., Kohler, P. J., … Meng, M. (2015). The artist emerges: Visual art learning alters neural structure and function. *NeuroImage*, 105, 440–451.

Schlesinger, J. (2009). Creative mythconceptions: A closer look at the evidence for the "mad genius" hypothesis. *Psychology of Aesthetics, Creativity, and the Arts*, 3(2), 62–72.

Schmidt, R. C., Fitzpatrick, P., Caron, R., & Mergeche, J. (2011). Understanding social motor coordination. *Human Movement Science*, 30(5), 834–845.

Schneider, W., & Shiffrin, R. M. (1977). Controlled and automatic human information processing: I. Detection, search, and attention. *Psychological Review*, 84(1), 1–66.

Schober, M. F., & Spiro, N. (2016). Listeners' and performers' shared understanding of jazz improvisations. *Frontiers in Psychology*, 7, 1629.

Schooler, J. W., Ohlsson, S., & Brooks, K. (1993). Thoughts beyond words: When language overshadows insight. *Journal of Experimental Psychology: General*, 122(2), 166.

Schott, G. D. (2012). Pictures as a neurological tool: Lessons from enhanced and emergent artistry in brain disease. *Brain: A Journal of Neurology*, 135(6), 1947–1963.

Schubert, E. (2011). Spreading activation and dissociation: A cognitive mechanism for creative processing in music. In D. Hargreaves, D. Miell, & R. MacDonald (Eds.), *Musical imaginations: Multidisciplinary perspectives on creativity, performance and perception*. Oxford: Oxford University Press.

Schulkin, J. (2016). Evolutionary basis of human running and its impact on neural function. *Frontiers in Systems Neuroscience*, 10, 59.

Schwab, D., Benedek, M., Papousek, I., Weiss, E. M., & Fink, A. (2014). The time-course of EEG alpha power changes in creative ideation. *Frontiers in Human Neuroscience*, 8, 310.

Schwartz, M. F., & Dell, G. S. (2010). Case series investigations in cognitive neuropsychology. *Cognitive Neuropsychology*, 27(6), 477–494.

Schwartze, M., Keller, P. E., Patel, A. D., & Kotz, S. A. (2011). The impact of basal ganglia lesions on sensorimotor synchronization, spontaneous motor tempo, and the detection of tempo changes. *Behavioural Brain Research*, 216(2), 685–691.

Sebanz, N., & Knoblich, G. (2009). Prediction in joint action: What, when, and where. *Topics in Cognitive Science*, 1(2), 353–367.

Sebanz, N., Bekkering, H., & Knoblich, G. (2006). Joint action: Bodies and minds moving together. *Trends in Cognitive Sciences*, 10(2), 70–76.

Seeley, W. P., & Kozbelt, A. (2008). Art, artists, and perception: A model for premotor contributions to perceptual analysis and form recognition. *Philosophical Psychology, 21*(2), 149–171.

Seeley, W. W., Crawford, R. K., Zhou, J., Miller, B. L., & Greicius, M. D. (2009). Neurodegenerative diseases target large-scale human brain networks. *Neuron, 62*(1), 42.

Seeley, W. W., Matthews, B. R., Crawford, R. K., Gorno-Tempini, M. L., Foti, D., Mackenzie, I. R., & Miller, B. L. (2008). Unravelling Boléro: Progressive aphasia, transmodal creativity and the right posterior neocortex. *Brain: A Journal of Neurology, 131*(1), 39–49.

Seeley, W. W., Menon, V., Schatzberg, A. F., Keller, J., Glover, G. H., Kenna, H., ... Greicius, M. D. (2007). Dissociable intrinsic connectivity networks for salience processing and executive control. *Journal of Neuroscience: The Official Journal of the Society for Neuroscience, 27*(9), 2349–2356.

Segal, E. (2004). Incubation in insight problem solving. *Creativity Research Journal, 16*(1), 141–148.

Seghier, M. L. (2013). The angular gyrus: Multiple functions and multiple subdivisions. *The Neuroscientist: A Review Journal Bringing Neurobiology, Neurology and Psychiatry, 19*(1), 43–61.

Seli, P., Risko, E. F., Smilek, D., & Schacter, D. L. (2016). Mind-wandering with and without intention. *Trends in Cognitive Sciences, 20*(8), 605–617.

Sepulcre, J., Sabuncu, M. R., & Johnson, K. A. (2012). Network assemblies in the functional brain. *Current Opinion in Neurology, 25*(4), 384–391.

Shah, C., Erhard, K., Ortheil, H.-J., Kaza, E., Kessler, C., & Lotze, M. (2013). Neural correlates of creative writing: An fMRI study. *Human Brain Mapping, 34*(5), 1088–1101.

Shallice, T. (2003). Functional imaging and neuropsychology findings: How can they be linked? *NeuroImage, 20*(Suppl. 1), S146–S154.

Shamay-Tsoory, S. G., Adler, N., Aharon-Peretz, J., Perry, D., & Mayseless, N. (2011). The origins of originality: The neural bases of creative thinking and originality. *Neuropsychologia, 49*(2), 178–185.

Shamir, L., Nissel, J., & Winner, E. (2016). Distinguishing between abstract art by artists vs. children and animals: Comparison between human and machine perception. *ACM Transactions on Applied Perception, 13*(3), 1–17.

Shi, B., Cao, X., Chen, Q., Zhuang, K., & Qiu, J. (2017). Different brain structures associated with artistic and scientific creativity: A voxel-based morphometry study. *Scientific Reports, 7*, 42911.

Shibasaki, H. (2008). Human brain mapping: Hemodynamic response and electrophysiology. *Clinical Neurophysiology, 119*(4), 731–743.

Siebörger, F. T., Ferstl, E. C., & von Cramon, D. Y. (2007). Making sense of nonsense: An fMRI study of task induced inference processes during discourse comprehension. *Brain Research, 1166*, 77–91.

Silver, D., Huang, A., Maddison, C. J., Guez, A., Sifre, L., van den Driessche, G., ... Hassabis, D. (2016). Mastering the game of Go with deep neural networks and tree search. *Nature, 529*(7587), 484–489.

Silvia, P. J. (2006). Artistic training and interest in visual art: Applying the appraisal model of aesthetic emotions. *Empirical Studies of the Arts, 24*(2), 139–161.

Silvia, P. J., & Beaty, R. E. (2012). Making creative metaphors: The importance of fluid intelligence for creative thought. *Intelligence, 40*(4), 343–351.

Silvia, P. J., Beaty, R. E., Nusbaum, E. C., Eddington, K. M., & Kwapil, T. R. (2014). Creative motivation: Creative achievement predicts cardiac autonomic markers of effort during divergent thinking. *Biological Psychology, 102*, 30–37.

Silvia, P. J., Wigert, B., Reiter-Palmon, R., & Kaufman, J. C. (2012). Assessing creativity with self-report scales: A review and empirical evaluation. *Psychology of Aesthetics, Creativity, and the Arts, 6*(1), 19–34.

Silvia, P. J., Winterstein, B. P., Willse, J. T., Barona, C. M., Cram, J. T., Hess, K. I., ... Richard, C. A. (2008). Assessing creativity with divergent thinking tasks: Exploring the reliability and validity of new subjective scoring methods. *Psychology of Aesthetics, Creativity, and the Arts, 2*(2), 68–85.

Simonton, D. K. (1989a). Chance-configuration theory of scientific creativity. In B. Gholson, W. R. Shadish Jr, R. A. Neimeyer, & A. C. Houts (Eds.), *Psychology of science* (pp. 170–213). Cambridge: Cambridge University Press.

(1989b). The swan-song phenomenon: Last-works effects for 172 classical composers. *Psychology and Aging, 4*(1), 42–47.

(1990). History, chemistry, psychology, and genius: An intellectual autobiography of historiometry. In M. A. Runco & R. S. Albert (Eds.), *Theories of creativity* (pp. 61–91). Newbury Park, CA: Sage.

(1999). Creativity as blind variation and selective retention: Is the creative process Darwinian? *Psychological Inquiry, 10*(4), 309–328.

(2000). Creativity: Cognitive, personal, developmental, and social aspects. *American Psychologist, 55*(1), 151–158.

(2003). Scientific creativity as constrained stochastic behavior: The integration of product, person, and process perspectives. *Psychological Bulletin, 129*(4), 475–494.

(2004). *Creativity in science: Chance, logic, genius, and Zeitgeist.* New York: Cambridge University Press.

(2009). Varieties of (scientific) creativity: A hierarchical model of domain-specific disposition, development, and achievement. *Perspectives on Psychological Science, 4*(5), 441–452.

(2010). Creative thought as blind-variation and selective-retention: Combinatorial models of exceptional creativity. *Physics of Life Reviews, 7*(2), 190–194.

(2012a). Quantifying creativity: Can measures span the spectrum? *Dialogues in Clinical Neuroscience, 14*(1), 100–104.

(2012b). Taking the U.S. Patent Office criteria seriously: A quantitative three-criterion creativity definition and its implications. *Creativity Research Journal, 24*(2–3), 97–106.

(2014). Can creative productivity be both positively and negatively correlated with psychopathology? Yes! *Frontiers in Psychology, 5*, 455.

Simonton, D. K., & Ting, S.-S. (2010). Creativity in Eastern and Western civilizations: The lessons of historiometry. *Management and Organization Review, 6*(3), 329–350.

Sio, U. N., & Ormerod, T. C. (2009). Does incubation enhance problem solving? A meta-analytic review. *Psychological Bulletin, 135*(1), 94–120.

Skup, M. (2010). Longitudinal fMRI analysis: A review of methods. *Statistics and Its Interface, 3*(2), 235–252.

Slater, J., Azem, A., Nicol, T., Swedenborg, B., & Kraus, N. (2017). Variations on the theme of musical expertise: Cognitive and sensory processing in percussionists, vocalists and non-musicians. *European Journal of Neuroscience, 45*(7), 952–963.

Sloboda, J. A. (Ed.). (2000). *Generative processes in music: The psychology of performance, improvisation, and composition.* Oxford: Oxford University Press.

Smith, I. (2015). Psychostimulants and artistic, musical, and literary creativity. *International Review of Neurobiology, 120*, 301–326.

Smith, R., & Lane, R. D. (2015). The neural basis of one's own conscious and unconscious emotional states. *Neuroscience and Biobehavioral Reviews, 57*, 1–29.

Smith, S. M. (2012). The future of fMRI connectivity. *NeuroImage, 62*(2), 1257–1266.

Smith, S. M., Ward, T. B., & Schumacher, J. S. (1993). Constraining effects of examples in a creative generation task. *Memory & Cognition, 21*(6), 837–845.

Snapper, L., Oranç, C., Hawley-Dolan, A., Nissel, J., & Winner, E. (2015). Your kid could not have done that: Even untutored observers can discern intentionality and structure in abstract expressionist art. *Cognition, 137*, 154–165.

Snyder, A. W. (2009). Explaining and inducing savant skills: Privileged access to lower level, less-processed information. *Philosophical Transactions of the Royal Society B: Biological Sciences, 364*(1522), 1399–1405.

Snyder, A. W., Mulcahy, E., Taylor, J. L., Mitchell, D. J., Sachdev, P., & Gandevia, S. C. (2003). Savant-like skills exposed in normal people by suppressing the left fronto-temporal lobe. *Journal of Integrative Neuroscience, 2*(2), 149–158.

Soeiro-de-Souza, M. G., Dias, V. V., Bio, D. S., Post, R. M., & Moreno, R. A. (2011). Creativity and executive function across manic, mixed and depressive episodes in bipolar I disorder. *Journal of Affective Disorders, 135*(1–3), 292–297.

Souza, L. C. de, Guimarães, H. C., Teixeira, A. L., Caramelli, P., Levy, R., Dubois, B., & Volle, E. (2014). Frontal lobe neurology and the creative mind. *Frontiers in Psychology, 5*, 761.

Souza, L. C. de, Volle, E., Bertoux, M., Czernecki, V., Funkiewiez, A., Allali, G., … Levy, R. (2010). Poor creativity in frontotemporal dementia: A window into the neural bases of the creative mind. *Neuropsychologia, 48*(13), 3733–3742.

Sovansky, E. E., Wieth, M. B., Francis, A. P., & McIlhagga, S. D. (2016). Not all musicians are creative: Creativity requires more than simply playing music. *Psychology of Music, 44*(1), 25–36.

Sowden, P. T., Pringle, A., & Gabora, L. (2015). The shifting sands of creative thinking: Connections to dual-process theory. *Thinking & Reasoning, 21*(1), 40–60.

Speed, A. (2010). Abstract relational categories, graded persistence, and prefrontal cortical representation. *Cognitive Neuroscience, 1*(2), 126–137.

Sperry, R. W. (1961). Cerebral organization and behavior. *Science, 133*(3466), 1749–1757.

Spreng, R. N., Mar, R. A., & Kim, A. S. N. (2009). The common neural basis of autobiographical memory, prospection, navigation, theory of mind, and the default mode: A quantitative meta-analysis. *Journal of Cognitive Neuroscience, 21*(3), 489–510.

Spreng, R. N., Sepulcre, J., Turner, G. R., Stevens, W. D., & Schacter, D. L. (2013). Intrinsic architecture underlying the relations among the default, dorsal attention, and frontoparietal control networks of the human brain. *Journal of Cognitive Neuroscience, 25*(1), 74–86.

Squire, L. R. (1992). Declarative and nondeclarative memory: Multiple brain systems supporting learning and memory. *Journal of Cognitive Neuroscience, 4*(3), 232–243.

Sridharan, D., Levitin, D. J., & Menon, V. (2008). A critical role for the right fronto-insular cortex in switching between central-executive and default-mode networks. *Proceedings of the National Academy of Sciences of the United States of America, 105*(34), 12569–12574.

Srinivasan, N. (2007). Cognitive neuroscience of creativity: EEG based approaches. *Methods, 42*(1), 109–116.

Stanislaw, H., & Todorov, N. (1999). Calculation of signal detection theory measures. *Behavior Research Methods, Instruments, & Computers: A Journal of the Psychonomic Society, 31*(1), 137–149.

Stark, C. E. L., & Squire, L. R. (2001). When zero is not zero: The problem of ambiguous baseline conditions in fMRI. *Proceedings of the National Academy of Sciences, 98*(22), 12760–12766.

Stavridou, A., & Furnham, A. (1996). The relationship between psychoticism, trait-creativity and the attentional mechanism of cognitive inhibition. *Personality and Individual Differences, 21*(1), 143–153.

Stein, J. (2001). The magnocellular theory of developmental dyslexia. *Dyslexia, 7*(1), 12–36.

Stein, M. I. (1953). Creativity and culture. *Journal of Psychology, 36*(2), 311–322.

Steinberg, H., Sykes, E. A., Moss, T., Lowery, S., LeBoutillier, N., & Dewey, A. (1997). Exercise enhances creativity independently of mood. *British Journal of Sports Medicine, 31*(3), 240–245.

Sternberg, R. J. (1999). A propulsion model of types of creative contributions. *Review of General Psychology, 3*(2), 83–100.

Sternberg, R. J., & O'Hara, L. A. (1999). Creativity and intelligence. In R. J. Sternberg (Ed.), *Handbook of creativity*. Cambridge: Cambridge University Press.

Sternberg, R. J., Grigorenko, E. L., & Singer, J. L. (Eds.). (2004). *Creativity: From potential to realization*. Washington, DC: American Psychological Association.

Sternberg, R. J., Kaufman, J. C., & Pretz, J. E. (2001). The propulsion model of creative contributions applied to the arts and letters. *Journal of Creative Behavior, 35*(2), 75–101.

Stevens, C., & Leach, J. (2015). Bodystorming: Effects of collaboration and familiarity on improvising contemporary dance. *Cognitive Processing, 16*(Suppl. 1), 403–407.

Stevens, C., Malloch, S., McKechnie, S., & Steven, N. (2003). Choreographic cognition: The time-course and phenomenology of creating a dance. *Pragmatics & Cognition, 11*(2), 297–326.

Stevenson, L. (2003). Twelve conceptions of imagination. *British Journal of Aesthetics, 43*(3), 238–259.

Stewart, L., von Kriegstein, K., Warren, J. D., & Griffiths, T. D. (2006). Music and the brain: Disorders of musical listening. *Brain: A Journal of Neurology, 129*(10), 2533–2553.

Stringaris, A. K., Medford, N. C., Giampietro, V., Brammer, M. J., & David, A. S. (2007). Deriving meaning: Distinct neural mechanisms for metaphoric, literal, and non-meaningful sentences. *Brain and Language, 100*(2), 150–162.

Stuss, D. T. (2011). Functions of the frontal lobes: Relation to executive functions. *Journal of the International Neuropsychological Society, 17*(5), 759–765.

Suchow, J. W., Bourgin, D. D., & Griffiths, T. L. (2017). Evolution in mind: Evolutionary dynamics, cognitive processes, and Bayesian inference. *Trends in Cognitive Sciences, 21*(7), 522–530.

Sun, J., Chen, Q., Zhang, Q., Li, Y., Li, H., Wei, D., … Qiu, J. (2016). Training your brain to be more creative: Brain functional and structural changes induced by divergent thinking training. *Human Brain Mapping, 37*(10), 3375–3387.

Svoboda, E., McKinnon, M. C., & Levine, B. (2006). The functional neuroanatomy of autobiographical memory: A meta-analysis. *Neuropsychologia, 44*(12), 2189–2208.

Swartz, J. D. (1988). Torrance Tests of Creative Thinking. In D. J. Keyser & R. C. Sweetland (Eds.), *Test critique*, Vol. 7 (pp. 619–622). Kansas, MS: Test Corporation of America.

Taft, R., & Rossiter, J. R. (1966). The Remote Associates Test: Divergent or convergent thinking? *Psychological Reports, 19*(3), 1313–1314.

Takeuchi, H., Taki, Y., Hashizume, H., Sassa, Y., Nagase, T., Nouchi, R., & Kawashima, R. (2011). Cerebral blood flow during rest associates with general intelligence and creativity. *PloS One, 6*(9), e25532.

(2012). The association between resting functional connectivity and creativity. *Cerebral Cortex, 22*(12), 2921–2929.

Takeuchi, H., Taki, Y., Sassa, Y., Hashizume, H., Sekiguchi, A., Fukushima, A., & Kawashima, R. (2010a). Regional gray matter volume of dopaminergic system associated with creativity: Evidence from voxel-based morphometry. *NeuroImage, 51*(2), 578–585.

(2010b). White matter structures associated with creativity: Evidence from diffusion tensor imaging. *NeuroImage, 51*(1), 11–18.

Takeuchi, H., Taki, Y., Sekiguchi, A., Hashizume, H., Nouchi, R., Sassa, Y., … Kawashima, R. (2015). Mean diffusivity of globus pallidus associated with verbal creativity measured by divergent thinking and creativity-related temperaments in young healthy adults. *Human Brain Mapping, 36*(5), 1808–1827.

Taki, Y., Thyreau, B., Kinomura, S., Sato, K., Goto, R., Wu, K., … Fukuda, H. (2013). A longitudinal study of the relationship between personality traits and the annual rate of volume changes in regional gray matter in healthy adults. *Human Brain Mapping, 34*(12), 3347–3353.

Tan, M., & Grigorenko, E. L. (2013). All in the family: Is creative writing familial and heritable? *Learning and Individual Differences, 28*, 177–180.

Taylor, P. (1989). Insight and metaphor. *Analysis*, 49(2), 71–77.

Tchalenko, J. (2009). Segmentation and accuracy in copying and drawing: Experts and beginners. *Vision Research, 49*(8), 791–800.

Tchalenko, J., & Miall, R. C. (2009). Eye–hand strategies in copying complex lines. *Cortex, 45*(3), 368–376.

Tchalenko, J., Nam, S.-H., Ladanga, M., & Miall, R. C. (2014). The gaze-shift strategy in drawing. *Psychology of Aesthetics, Creativity, and the Arts, 8*(3), 330–339.

Teng, C.-I. (2011). Who are likely to experience flow? Impact of temperament and character on flow. *Personality and Individual Differences, 50*(6), 863–868.

Terai, A., Nakagawa, M., Kusumi, T., Koike, Y., & Jimura, K. (2015). Enhancement of visual attention precedes the emergence of novel metaphor interpretations. *Frontiers in Psychology, 6*, 892.

Terman, L. M., & Oden, M. (1940). The significance of deviates. III. Correlates of adult achievement in the California gifted group. *Yearbook of the National Society for the Study of Education, 39*(I), 74–89.

Tervaniemi, M. (2001). Musical sound processing in the human brain: Evidence from electric and magnetic recordings. *Annals of the New York Academy of Sciences, 930*, 259–272.

(2009). Musicians: Same or different? *Annals of the New York Academy of Sciences, 1169*, 151–156.

Tervaniemi, M., Janhunen, L., Kruck, S., Putkinen, V., & Huotilainen, M. (2015). Auditory profiles of classical, jazz, and rock musicians: Genre-specific–sensitivity to musical sound features. *Frontiers in Psychology, 6*, 1900.

Thaut, M. H. (2015). The discovery of human auditory–motor entrainment and its role in the development of neurologic music therapy. *Progress in Brain Research, 217*, 253–266.

Thomas, L. E., & Lleras, A. (2009). Covert shifts of attention function as an implicit aid to insight. *Cognition, 111*(2), 168–174.

Thomas, N. (2014). The multidimensional spectrum of imagination: Images, dreams, hallucinations, and active, imaginative perception. *Humanities, 3*(2), 132–184.

Thompson-Schill, S. L. (2003). Neuroimaging studies of semantic memory: Inferring "how" from "where." *Neuropsychologia, 41*(3), 280–292.

Thomson, P., & Jaque, S. V. (2016). Overexcitability and optimal flow in talented dancers, singers, and athletes. *Roeper Review: A Journal on Gifted Education, 38*(1), 32–39.

Thrash, T. M., Maruskin, L. A., Moldovan, E. G., Oleynick, V. C., & Belzak, W. C. (2016). Writer–reader contagion of inspiration and related states: Conditional process analyses within a cross-classified writer × reader framework. *Journal of Personality and Social Psychology*, 113(3), 466–491.

Tin, T. B. (2011). Language creativity and co-emergence of form and meaning in creative writing tasks. *Applied Linguistics*, 32(2), 215–235.

Tingen, P. (2001). *Miles beyond: The electric explorations of Miles Davis, 1967–1991*. New York: Billboard Books.

Tomalski, P., & Johnson, M. H. (2010). The effects of early adversity on the adult and developing brain. *Current Opinion in Psychiatry*, 23(3), 233–238.

Tomeo, E., Cesari, P., Aglioti, S. M., & Urgesi, C. (2013). Fooling the kickers but not the goalkeepers: Behavioral and neurophysiological correlates of fake action detection in soccer. *Cerebral Cortex*, 23(11), 2765–2778.

Torrance, E. P. (1974). *The Torrance Tests of Creative Thinking – norms; Technical Manual Research Edition – verbal tests, forms A and B – figural tests, forms A and B*. Princeton, NJ: Personnel Press.

Torrance, E. P., & Haensly, P. A. (2003). Assessment of creativity in children and adolescents. In C. R. Reynolds & R. W. Kamphaus (Eds.), *Handbook of psychological and educational assessment of children: Intelligence, aptitude, and achievement*, Vol. 1 (2nd edn., pp. 584–607). New York: Guilford Press.

Torrents, C., Castañer, M., Dinošová, M., & Anguera, M. T. (2010). Discovering new ways of moving: Observational analysis of motor creativity while dancing contact improvisation and the influence of the partner. *Journal of Creative Behavior*, 44(1), 45–61.

Trainor, L. J., & Cirelli, L. (2015). Rhythm and interpersonal synchrony in early social development. *Annals of the New York Academy of Sciences*, 1337, 45–52.

Treffert, D. A. (2009). The savant syndrome: An extraordinary condition. A synopsis: past, present, future. *Philosophical Transactions of the Royal Society B: Biological Sciences*, 364(1522), 1351–1357.

(2010). *Islands of genius: The bountiful mind of the autistic, acquired, and sudden savant*. London: Jessica Kingsley.

(2014). Savant syndrome: Realities, myths and misconceptions. *Journal of Autism and Developmental Disorders*, 44(3), 564–571.

Treffert, D. A., & Rebedew, D. L. (2015). The savant syndrome registry: A preliminary report. *WMJ: Official Publication of the State Medical Society of Wisconsin*, 114(4), 158–162.

Trickett, S. B., & Trafton, J. G. (2007). "What if…": The use of conceptual simulations in scientific reasoning. *Cognitive Science*, 31(5), 843–875.

Trickett, S. B., Trafton, J. G., & Schunn, C. D. (2009). How do scientists respond to anomalies? Different strategies used in basic and applied science. *Topics in Cognitive Science, 1*(4), 711–729.

Trojano, L., Grossi, D., & Flash, T. (2009). Cognitive neuroscience of drawing: Contributions of neuropsychological, experimental and neurofunctional studies. *Cortex, 45*(3), 269–277.

Tucker, P. K., Rothwell, S. J., Armstrong, M. S., & McConaghy, N. (1982). Creativity, divergent and allusive thinking in students and visual artists. *Psychological Medicine, 12*(4), 835.

Turner, B. O., Marinsek, N., Ryhal, E., & Miller, M. B. (2015). Hemispheric lateralization in reasoning. *Annals of the New York Academy of Sciences, 1359*(1), 47–64.

Turner, M., & Fauconnier, G. (1999). A mechanism of creativity. *Poetics Today, 20*(3), 397–418.

Uddin, L. Q. (2015). Salience processing and insular cortical function and dysfunction. *Nature Reviews Neuroscience, 16*(1), 55–61.

Ullén, F., de Manzano, Ö., Almeida, R., Magnusson, P. K. E., Pedersen, N. L., Nakamura, J., ... Madison, G. (2012). Proneness for psychological flow in everyday life: Associations with personality and intelligence. *Personality and Individual Differences, 52*(2), 167–172.

Ullsperger, M., & Debener, S. (2010). *Simultaneous EEG and fMRI: Recording, analysis, and application.* New York: Oxford University Press.

Urbanski, M., Bréchemier, M.-L., Garcin, B., Bendetowicz, D., Thiebaut de Schotten, M., Foulon, C., ... Volle, E. (2016). Reasoning by analogy requires the left frontal pole: Lesion-deficit mapping and clinical implications. *Brain: A Journal of Neurology, 139*(6), 1783–1799.

Urgesi, C., Savonitto, M. M., Fabbro, F., & Aglioti, S. M. (2012). Long- and short-term plastic modeling of action prediction abilities in volleyball. *Psychological Research, 76*(4), 542–560.

Utevsky, A. V., Smith, D. V., & Huettel, S. A. (2014). Precuneus is a functional core of the default-mode network. *Journal of Neuroscience: The Official Journal of the Society for Neuroscience, 34*(3), 932–940.

Van Overwalle, F. (2011). A dissociation between social mentalizing and general reasoning. *NeuroImage, 54*(2), 1589–1599.

Vartanian, O. (2012). Dissociable neural systems for analogy and metaphor: Implications for the neuroscience of creativity. *British Journal of Psychology, 103*(3), 302–316.

Vartanian, O., Bristol, A. S., & Kaufman, J. C. (2013). *Neuroscience of creativity.* Cambridge, MA: MIT Press.

Vartanian, O., Martindale, C., & Kwiatkowski, J. (2003). Creativity and inductive reasoning: The relationship between divergent thinking and performance on Wason's 2–4–6 task. *Quarterly Journal of Experimental*

Psychology Section. A: Human Experimental Psychology, 56(4), 641–655.

(2007). Creative potential, attention, and speed of information processing. *Personality and Individual Differences*, 43(6), 1470–1480.

Vendetti, M. S., Wu, A., & Holyoak, K. J. (2014). Far-out thinking: Generating solutions to distant analogies promotes relational thinking. *Psychological Science*, 25(4), 928–933.

Vendetti, M. S., Wu, A., Rowshanshad, E., Knowlton, B. J., & Holyoak, K. J. (2014). When reasoning modifies memory: Schematic assimilation triggered by analogical mapping. *Journal of Experimental Psychology: Learning, Memory, and Cognition*, 40(4), 1172–1180.

Verstijnen, I. M., van Leeuwen, C., Goldschmidt, G., Hamel, R., & Hennessey, J. M. (1998). Creative discovery in imagery and perception: Combining is relatively easy, restructuring takes a sketch. *Acta Psychologica*, 99(2), 177–200.

Vestberg, T., Gustafson, R., Maurex, L., Ingvar, M., & Petrovic, P. (2012). Executive functions predict the success of top-soccer players. *PloS One*, 7(4), e34731.

Vogt, S. (1999). Looking at paintings: Patterns of eye movements in artistically naïve and sophisticated subjects. *Leonardo*, 32(4), 325–325.

Vogt, S., & Magnussen, S. (2007). Expertise in pictorial perception: Eye-movement patterns and visual memory in artists and laymen. *Perception*, 36(1), 91–100.

Volpe, G., D'Ausilio, A., Badino, L., Camurri, A., & Fadiga, L. (2016). Measuring social interaction in music ensembles. *Philosophical Transactions of the Royal Society B: Biological Sciences*, 371(1693), 20150377.

Vuust, P., Brattico, E., Seppänen, M., Näätänen, R., & Tervaniemi, M. (2012). Practiced musical style shapes auditory skills. *Annals of the New York Academy of Sciences*, 1252, 139–146.

Wager, T. D., & Smith, E. E. (2003). Neuroimaging studies of working memory: A meta-analysis. *Cognitive, Affective & Behavioral Neuroscience*, 3(4), 255–274.

Walker, G. M., & Hickok, G. (2016). Bridging computational approaches to speech production: The semantic–lexical–auditory–motor model (SLAM). *Psychonomic Bulletin & Review*, 23(2), 339–352.

Walker, R. H., Warwick, R., & Cercy, S. P. (2006). Augmentation of artistic productivity in Parkinson's disease. *Movement Disorders: Official Journal of the Movement Disorder Society*, 21(2), 285–286.

Wallach, J. (1998). *Chanel: Her style and her life*. New York: N. Talese.

Wallach, M. A., & Kogan, N. (1965). *Modes of thinking in young children: A study of the creativity–intelligence distinction*. New York: Holt, Rinehart & Winston.

Wallas, G. (1926). *Art of thought*. Tunbridge Wells: Solis Press.

Walls, M., & Malafouris, L. (2016). Creativity as a developmental ecology. In V. P. Glăveanu (Ed.), *The Palgrave handbook of creativity and culture research* (pp. 623–638). London: Palgrave Macmillan.

Walsh, V. (2014). Is sport the brain's biggest challenge? *Current Biology, 24*(18), R859–R860.

Walton, A. E., Richardson, M. J., Langland-Hassan, P., & Chemero, A. (2015). Improvisation and the self-organization of multiple musical bodies. *Frontiers in Psychology, 6*, 313.

Ward, J., Thompson-Lake, D., Ely, R., & Kaminski, F. (2008). Synaesthesia, creativity and art: What is the link? *British Journal of Psychology, 99*(1), 127–141.

Ward, T. B. (1994). Structured imagination: The role of category structure in exemplar generation. *Cognitive Psychology, 27*, 1–40.

Ward, T. B., Finke, R. A., & Smith, S. M. (1995). *Creativity and the mind: Discovering the genius within*. Cambridge, MA: Perseus Books.

Ward, T. B., Patterson, M. J., & Sifonis, C. M. (2004). The role of specificity and abstraction in creative idea generation. *Creativity Research Journal, 16*(1), 1–9.

Ward, T. B., Patterson, M. J., Sifonis, C. M., Dodds, R. A., & Saunders, K. N. (2002). The role of graded category structure in imaginative thought. *Memory & Cognition, 30*(2), 199–216.

Ward, T. B., Smith, S. M., & Vaid, J. (1997). *Creative thought: An investigation of conceptual structures and processes*. Washington, DC: American Psychological Association.

Warren, D. E., Kurczek, J., & Duff, M. C. (2016). What relates newspaper, definite, and clothing? An article describing deficits in convergent problem solving and creativity following hippocampal damage. *Hippocampus, 26*(7), 835–840.

Washburn, D. A. (2016). The Stroop effect at 80: The competition between stimulus control and cognitive control. *Journal of the Experimental Analysis of Behavior, 105*(1), 3–13.

Wasserman, E., Epstein, C. M., & Ziemann, U. (Eds.). (2008). *The Oxford handbook of transcranial stimulation*. New York: Oxford University Press.

Webster, P. R. (1987). Refinement of a measure of creative thinking in music. In C. K. Madsen & C. A. Prickett (Eds.), *Applications of research in music behaviour* (pp. 257–271). Tuscaloosa, AL: University of Alabama Press.

(1994). *Measure of creative thinking in music (MCTM-II) administrative guidelines*. Evanston, IL: Northwestern University Press.

(2003). "What do you mean, make my music different?" Encouraging revision and extensions in children's music composition. In M. Hickey

(Ed.), *Why and how to teach music composition: A new horizon for music education* (pp. 55–69). Reston, VA: MENC.

(2016). Creative thinking in music, twenty-five years on. *Music Educators Journal, 102*(3), 26–32.

Weinberger, A. B., Green, A. E., & Chrysikou, E. G. (2017). Using transcranial direct current stimulation to enhance creative cognition: Interactions between task, polarity, and stimulation site. *Frontiers in Human Neuroscience, 11*, 246.

Weinstein, E. C., Clark, Z., DiBartolomeo, D. J., & Davis, K. (2014). A decline in creativity? It depends on the domain. *Creativity Research Journal, 26*(2), 174–184.

Weir, A. A. S., & Kacelnik, A. (2006). A New Caledonian crow (*Corvus moneduloides*) creatively re-designs tools by bending or unbending aluminium strips. *Animal Cognition, 9*(4), 317–334.

(1995). Prolegomena to theories of insight in problem solving: A taxonomy of problems. In R. J. Sternberg & J. E. Davidson (Eds.), *The nature of insight* (pp. 157–196). Cambridge, MA: MIT Press.

(1999). Creativity and knowledge: A challenge to theories. In R. J. Sternberg (Ed.), *Handbook of creativity* (pp. 226–250). New York: Cambridge University Press.

(2006). *Creativity: Understanding innovation in problem solving, science, invention, and the arts.* Hoboken, NJ: Wiley.

(2015). On the usefulness of "value" in the definition of creativity. *Creativity Research Journal, 27*(2), 111–124.

Weisberg, R. W. (2018). Reflections on a personal journey studying the psychology of creativity (pp. 351–373). In R. J. Sternberg & J. C. Kaufman (Eds.), *The nature of human creativity.* New York: Cambridge University Press.

Weiskrantz, L. (1985). Introduction: Categorization, cleverness and consciousness. *Philosophical Transactions of the Royal Society B: Biological Sciences, 308*(1135), 3–19.

Wendelken, C., Nakhabenko, D., Donohue, S. E., Carter, C. S., & Bunge, S. A. (2008). Brain is to thought as stomach is to ??: Investigating the role of rostrolateral prefrontal cortex in relational reasoning. *Journal of Cognitive Neuroscience, 20*(4), 682–693.

West, T. G. (1997). *In the mind's eye: Visual thinkers, gifted people with dyslexia and other learning difficulties, computer images, and the ironies of creativity.* Amherst, NY: Prometheus Books.

White, A. E., Kaufman, J. C., & Riggs, M. (2014). How "outsider" do we like our art? Influence of artist background on perceptions of warmth, creativity, and likeability. *Psychology of Aesthetics, Creativity, and the Arts, 8*(2), 144–151.

Whitehead, C. (2010). The culture ready brain. *Social Cognitive and Affective Neuroscience, 5*(2–3), 168–179.

Wiggins, G. A., Tyack, P., Scharff, C., & Rohrmeier, M. (2015). The evolutionary roots of creativity: Mechanisms and motivations. *Philosophical Transactions of the Royal Society B: Biological Sciences, 370*(1664).

Wiley, J. (1998). Expertise as mental set: The effects of domain knowledge in creative problem solving. *Memory & Cognition, 26*(4), 716–730.

Wilson, D. (1989). The role of patterning in music. *Leonardo, 22*(1), 101–106.

Wilson, E. B. Jr (1991). *An introduction to scientific research.* New York: Dover Publications.

Wilson, M. (2002). Six views of embodied cognition. *Psychonomic Bulletin & Review, 9*(4), 625–636.

Wilson, R. C., Guilford, J. P., & Christensen, P. R. (1953). The measurement of individual differences in originality. *Psychological Bulletin, 50*(5), 362–370.

Wilson, R. C., Guilford, J. P., Christensen, P. R., & Lewis, D. J. (1954). A factor-analytic study of creative-thinking abilities. *Psychometrika, 19*(4), 297–311.

Wimshurst, Z. L., Sowden, P. T., & Wright, M. (2016). Expert–novice differences in brain function of field hockey players. *Neuroscience, 315*, 31–44.

Winkler, I., Háden, G. P., Ladinig, O., Sziller, I., & Honing, H. (2009). Newborn infants detect the beat in music. *Proceedings of the National Academy of Sciences, 106*(7), 2468–2471.

Winner, E., von Karolyi, C., Malinsky, D., French, L., Seliger, C., Ross, E., & Weber, C. (2001). Dyslexia and visual-spatial talents: Compensation vs deficit model. *Brain and Language, 76*(2), 81–110.

Wiseman, R., Watt, C., Gilhooly, K. J., & Georgiou, G. (2011). Creativity and ease of ambiguous figural reversal. *British Journal of Psychology, 102*(3), 615–622.

Wolff, U., & Lundberg, I. (2002). The prevalence of dyslexia among art students. *Dyslexia, 8*(1), 34–42.

Wöllner, C. (2013). How to quantify individuality in music performance? Studying artistic expression with averaging procedures. *Frontiers in Psychology, 4*, 361.

Wollseiffen, P., Schneider, S., Martin, L. A., Kerhervé, H. A., Klein, T., & Solomon, C. (2016). The effect of 6 h of running on brain activity, mood, and cognitive performance. *Experimental Brain Research, 234*(7), 1829–1836.

Wolpert, D. M., Ghahramani, Z., & Jordan, M. I. (1995). An internal model for sensorimotor integration. *Science, 269*(5232), 1880–1882.

Wong, S. S. H., & Lim, S. W. H. (2017). Mental imagery boosts music compositional creativity. *PLoS One*, *12*(3), e0174009.

Woodman, G. F. (2010). A brief introduction to the use of event-related potentials in studies of perception and attention. *Attention, Perception & Psychophysics*, *72*(8), 2031–2046.

Wu, T. Q., Miller, Z. A., Adhimoolam, B., Zackey, D. D., Khan, B. K., Ketelle, R., ... Miller, B. L. (2015). Verbal creativity in semantic variant primary progressive aphasia. *Neurocase*, *21*(1), 73–78.

Yang, J. (2015). The influence of motor expertise on the brain activity of motor task performance: A meta-analysis of functional magnetic resonance imaging studies. *Cognitive, Affective & Behavioral Neuroscience*, *15*(2), 381–394.

Young, G., Bancroft, J., & Sanderson, M. (1993). Musi-tecture: Seeking useful correlations between music and architecture. *Leonardo Music Journal*, *3*, 39–43.

Yuan, Y., & Shen, W. (2016). Commentary: Incubation and intuition in creative problem solving. *Frontiers in Psychology*, *7*, 1807.

Zabelina, D. L., & Robinson, M. D. (2010). Creativity as flexible cognitive control. *Psychology of Aesthetics, Creativity, and the Arts*, *4*(3), 136–143.

Zabelina, D. L., O'Leary, D., Pornpattananangkul, N., Nusslock, R., & Beeman, M. (2015). Creativity and sensory gating indexed by the P50: Selective versus leaky sensory gating in divergent thinkers and creative achievers. *Neuropsychologia*, *69*, 77–84.

Zaidel, D. W. (2010). Art and brain: Insights from neuropsychology, biology and evolution. *Journal of Anatomy*, *216*(2), 177–183.

(2013a). Cognition and art: The current interdisciplinary approach. *Cognitive Science*, *4*(4), 431–439.

(2013b). Split-brain, the right hemisphere, and art: Fact and fiction. *Progress in Brain Research*, *204*, 3–17.

(2014). Creativity, brain, and art: Biological and neurological considerations. *Frontiers in Human Neuroscience*, *8*, 389.

Zander, T., Öllinger, M., & Volz, K. G. (2016). Intuition and insight: Two processes that build on each other or fundamentally differ? *Frontiers in Psychology*, *7*, 1395.

Zatorre, R. J. (2015). Musical pleasure and reward: Mechanisms and dysfunction. *Annals of the New York Academy of Sciences*, *1337*, 202–211.

Zatorre, R. J., & Halpern, A. R. (2005). Mental concerts: Musical imagery and auditory cortex. *Neuron*, *47*(1), 9–12.

Zatorre, R. J., & Salimpoor, V. N. (2013). From perception to pleasure: Music and its neural substrates. *Proceedings of the National Academy of Sciences of the United States of America*, *110*(Suppl. 2), 10430–10437.

Zatorre, R. J., Chen, J. L., & Penhune, V. B. (2007). When the brain plays music: Auditory–motor interactions in music perception and production. *Nature Reviews Neuroscience, 8*(7), 547.

Zatorre, R. J., Fields, R. D., & Johansen-Berg, H. (2012). Plasticity in gray and white: Neuroimaging changes in brain structure during learning. *Nature Neuroscience, 15*(4), 528–536.

Zeki, S. (2001). Artistic creativity and the brain. *Science, 293*(5527), 51–52.

(2002). Neural concept formation and art: Dante, Michelangelo, Wagner. *Journal of Consciousness Studies, 9*(3), 53–76.

Zhang, Z., Lei, Y., & Li, H. (2016). Approaching the distinction between intuition and insight. *Frontiers in Psychology, 7*, 1195.

Zhu, F., Zhang, Q., & Qiu, J. (2013). Relating inter-individual differences in verbal creative thinking to cerebral structures: An optimal voxel-based morphometry study. *PloS One, 8*(11), e79272.

Zhu, W., Chen, Q., Xia, L., Beaty, R. E., Yang, W., Tian, F., … Qiu, J. (2017). Common and distinct brain networks underlying verbal and visual creativity. *Human Brain Mapping, 38*(4), 2094–2111.

Ziemann, U. (2017). Thirty years of transcranial magnetic stimulation: Where do we stand? *Experimental Brain Research, 235*(4), 973–984.

Index